A CONCISE HISTORY OF THE AZTECS

Susan Kellogg's history of the Aztecs offers a concise yet comprehensive assessment of Aztec history and civilization, emphasizing how material life and the economy functioned in relation to politics, religion, and intellectual and artistic developments. Appreciating the vast number of sources available but also their limitations, Kellogg focuses on three concepts throughout – value, transformation, and balance. Aztecs created *value*, material, and symbolic worth. Value was created through *transformations* of bodies, things, and ideas. The overall goal of value creation and transformation was to keep the Aztec world – the cosmos, the earth, its inhabitants – in *balance*, a balance often threatened by spiritual and other forms of chaos. The book highlights the ethnicities that constituted Aztec peoples and sheds light on religion, political and economic organization, gender, sexuality and family life, intellectual achievements, and survival. Seeking to correct common misperceptions, Kellogg stresses the humanity of the Aztec women and men and problematizes the use of the terms "human sacrifice," "myth," and "conquest."

SUSAN KELLOGG is Professor Emerita at the University of Houston. An expert on Aztec history and culture, she is the author of *Law and the Transformation of Aztec Culture, 1500–1700* (University of Oklahoma Press, 1995) and *Weaving the Past: A History of Latin America's Indigenous Women from the Prehispanic Period to the Present* (Oxford University Press, 2005). In 2022, she received a lifetime achievement award from the American Society for Ethnohistory.

CAMBRIDGE CONCISE HISTORIES

Cambridge Concise Histories offer general introductions to a wide range of subjects. A series of authoritative overviews written by expert authors, these books make the histories of countries, events and topics accessible to both students and general readers.

A full list of titles in the series can be found at:
www.cambridge.org/concisehistories

A CONCISE HISTORY OF THE AZTECS

SUSAN KELLOGG
University of Houston

CAMBRIDGE
UNIVERSITY PRESS

CAMBRIDGE
UNIVERSITY PRESS

Shaftesbury Road, Cambridge CB2 8EA, United Kingdom

One Liberty Plaza, 20th Floor, New York, NY 10006, USA

477 Williamstown Road, Port Melbourne, VIC 3207, Australia

314–321, 3rd Floor, Plot 3, Splendor Forum, Jasola District Centre,
New Delhi – 110025, India

103 Penang Road, #05–06/07, Visioncrest Commercial, Singapore 238467

Cambridge University Press is part of Cambridge University Press &
Assessment, a department of the University of Cambridge.

We share the University's mission to contribute to society through the pursuit
of education, learning and research at the highest international
levels of excellence.

www.cambridge.org
Information on this title: www.cambridge.org/9781108498999

DOI: 10.1017/9781108614542

© Susan Kellogg 2024

This publication is in copyright. Subject to statutory exception and to the
provisions of relevant collective licensing agreements, no reproduction of any
part may take place without the written permission of Cambridge University
Press & Assessment.

First published 2024

A catalogue record for this publication is available from the British Library

*A Cataloging-in-Publication data record for this book is available from the Library
of Congress.*

ISBN 978-1-108-49899-9 Hardback
ISBN 978-1-108-71294-1 Paperback

Cambridge University Press & Assessment has no responsibility for the
persistence or accuracy of URLs for external or third-party internet websites
referred to in this publication and does not guarantee that any content on such
websites is, or will remain, accurate or appropriate.

To Caleb – with much love

CONTENTS

List of Figures   *page* viii
List of Maps   x
List of Tables   xi
Preface   xiii
Key Periods and Dates   xxv

1 Introduction   1

2 Living in the Aztecs' Cosmos   38

3 Communities, Kingdoms, "Empires"   81

4 Creating Value: Producing, Exchanging, Consuming   121

5 Sex and the Altepetl: Gender, Sexuality, and Aztec Family Values   158

6 Resilience: Part One: Aztec Intellectual Life   202

7 Resilience: Part Two: Trauma, Transformation, Tenacity   246

Glossary   285
Bibliographic Essay   294
Index   352

FIGURES

2.1	Schematic drawing of the Templo Mayor	*page* 50
2.2	Classifications of major deities and translations of their names	61
3.1	Abbreviated genealogy and approximate dates of rule of Mexica tlatoque of Tenochtitlan	87
3.2	Moteuczoma Xocoyotl's palace with council meeting and courtrooms	93
3.3	Coyolxauhqui relief image	115
4.1	Major categories of Aztec clothing	138
4.2	Women selling goods in a marketplace	153
5.1	Image of Itzpapalotl (Obsidian Butterfly)	162
5.2	Piercing children's ears by age four	165
5.3	Parents training and disciplining children	167
5.4	A woman tlacuilo (painter/writer)	169
5.5	Wedding scene	174
5.6	Commoner housing	180
5.7	What a tlatoani and his palace might have looked like	181
6.1	Ilancueitl's name written in the Aztec writing system	211
6.2	Phoneticism in Aztec writing	213
6.3	Drawing of Coatlicue statue	231
6.4	The Calendar Stone and its images of time and space	232

List of Figures

6.5	The Venus of Tetzcoco	240
6.6	Aztec tripod plate	243
7.1	Tlaxcalteca leader meets Cortés in the *Lienzo de Tlaxcala*	251
7.2	Malintzin translating	252

TABLES

2.1 The twenty day signs and thirteen numbers of the Aztec tonalpohualli   *page* 44
2.2 The eighteen months of the solar year   45
4.1 Some price equivalencies in the sixteenth century   151

MAPS

1.1 Basin of Mexico with important
    Postclassic altepeme   *page* 2
1.2 The five lakes in the Basin of Mexico,
    major altepeme near them, and chinampa
    areas   24
3.1 Map of the extent of the empire at the height
    of Moteuczoma Xocoyotl's reign   111

PREFACE

The Aztecs respected their elders and saw themselves reflected in them. That idea is meaningful to me as I reflect on the past that brought me to this book. I have always felt fortunate for the way I came to the field of Aztec ethnohistory. I first learned about the Aztecs as an undergraduate in the 1970s at SUNY Buffalo in a class on Mesoamerican archaeology taught by Warren Barbour. Prof. Barbour invited Edward Calnek from the University of Rochester to speak to our class. That day I began to learn what ethnohistorians could do with documents, the way they might employ theories and concepts from cultural anthropology and archaeology to analyze historical documents. I wish I could say that I was so persuaded of ethnohistory's appeal that I immediately decided to pursue its study at the graduate level, but I still intended to pursue the study of archaeology, preferably with René Millon at the University of Rochester, where Ed also taught, a big plus in my eyes.

Happily, I was accepted there and began to study both archaeology and what the non-archaeologically, non-ethnohistorically inclined members of that department called social anthropology. Those folks were idiosyncratic but also very rigorous thinkers. From them, I learned a lot about the British and American roots of anthropology and its deeply colonial origins as well. Naively, in those days I understood little about that aspect of what I was learning, something that in time I would come to think much more about in relation to the past and present. But the social anthropologists imparted a lot of information about anthropological theories of their time, along with ethnographic methods. The social and other anthropologists did not get along, to say the least. Despite a tense atmosphere, I was entranced by everything I was learning, not least by René Millon who was brilliant, funny, charming, an intimidating presence, yet such an excellent teacher.

I thought I wanted to study the archaeology of Teotihuacan, which I planned to do until I realized in the summer of 1977 that dirt and I were not meant for each other. That same summer I stopped by the Archivo General de la Nación (AGN) in Mexico City to look at a few documents for Ed who had convinced me, rightly so, that learning paleography was essential if at some point I wanted to do ethnohistorical research. In the archive, I gazed at and handled sixteenth-century documents in wonder and remembered that libraries had been my favorite places since I was a young child; I realized that I loved the archive. Ed, a more informal teacher than René, with an exceptional mind and an encyclopedic knowledge about what was then the canon of Mesoamerican written sources, Aztec and Maya, became my dissertation supervisor. Ed was one of several scholars pioneering a turn in Mesoamerican ethnohistory, taking research out of the libraries with published sources and into archives with different kinds of documentation that anthropologists could fruitfully analyze. He had moved on to legal documents concerning property to reconstruct more about the physical layout and economy of the Aztec capital city Tenochtitlan and its sister island city Tlatelolco. He was examining how that layout affected the environment, food supplies, population, and household structure of those cities. I picked up on the demographic and social aspects of Ed's research and decided to examine household arrangements, family organization, and kinship structures in greater detail.

That is how I ended up at the AGN later in 1977 and 1978 studying sixteenth-century documents. But after moving away from archaeology, there would be another big swerve, influenced by what surprised me in the documents, four people I met in Mexico City, and emerging intellectual trends. What surprised me, first, in the legal cases I was reading was how present women were as litigants, witnesses, testators, and actors in the family histories before and after the Spanish invaded. Their visibility helped explain how people came to own properties over which lawsuits were occurring. Second, I was not prepared for how many documents in Nahuatl would be part of sixteenth-century litigation. How fortuitous it was that I was able to study the language with Thelma Sullivan – brilliant linguist and translator, warm and wonderful woman – who died too soon. I've never stopped missing her. Around the same time as I began studying with Thelma, I got to know Luis Reyes and Teresa Rojas Rabiela and appreciate their deep knowledge of the Nahuatl language, sources, and archives. Both shared information and advice so generously. In the archive, I met Jim Lockhart. A larger-than-life figure with so much intellectual energy, Jim's knowledge of Nahuatl and ability to find voluminous amounts of Nahuatl-language documentation was an impressive sight. That he would build on the work of Mexican scholars such as Angel María Garibay and Miguel León-Portilla and lead the way to the turn in Mesoamerican and Aztec ethnohistory toward the New Philology, an Indigenous language-centered approach that focuses on what native peoples had and have to say about their own histories and societies, came as no surprise. This sharp move away from highlighting Spanish voices was crucial to the way the ethnohistory of Mesoamerican peoples has developed since the late 1970s.

As the New Philology defined itself, there were two other scholarly trends that would influence my thinking: one was Women's Studies. Finally, the time had come to give much more attention to the half of the world's population whose contributions to societies all over the world had yet to be fully rendered. The other was social history, which included many different approaches and methods for looking at people – women, people of color, working classes, and Indigenous language speakers – to whom historians had not paid nearly enough attention. I knew then as I know now that history is made as much from below as it is made from above. Insofar as we can grasp how people understand their worlds and how those understandings shape their actions and how actions can influence perceptions and the narratives through which we make sense of the world, we can gain a much fuller understanding of the past as it was actually lived.

While staying true to those ideas, all intellectual trends shift and change, and there are recent trends that have also been influential. This book represents a return to my initial interest in the Indigenous population of Mesoamerica before Europeans arrived, as much of my research and writing after my dissertation became focused on the impact of colonialism on native peoples, especially Aztecs. The intense discussions over types of colonialism that have taken place in recent years raised the question of whether the Spanish invasion was the precursor to extractive colonialism or settler colonialism, and how that early, violent, and exploitative period led to postcolonial colonialism (also known as neocolonialism) and helped me think more about both Aztec and Spanish imperial projects, both of which involved colonizing efforts and impacts, even if colonialism itself is not a focus of this book.

Another recent trend focuses on the archaeology of the everyday. This approach moves beyond household archaeology to look at the use of space within houses, the material residue of rituals performed at the household level, and how the life cycle might influence the nature of remains and be used to better differentiate among imperial, local, and household practices. All these themes helped deepen my understanding of the economic, religious, and social interactions within and beyond Aztec households and moved me to appreciate more the differences between life as experienced in the larger urban centers and life in smaller places and rural communities. An archaeology focused on the everyday can be seen as tied to another recent archaeological trend, one influencing ethnohistorians as well, and that is known as materiality studies. These involve examining how humans, things, and places interact, especially in the realm of ritual. Materiality offers a way to bring together older and newer scholarship, synthesizing material and cultural approaches.

An outgrowth of the New Philology, a further trend is one in which scholars seek to learn more about the intricate construction of colonial Indigenous-language texts. The intense focus on the production of these writings has not only enabled ethnohistorians to translate many new sources, either previously unknown or greatly underused, but also led to a much fuller grasp of the complex nature, polyvocality, even chronology of many texts. More is known now about who the authors of many primary sources were and the several or sometimes many voices to be found in writings long assumed to have a single author. Understanding the complicated authorships and chronologies allows scholars to trace the cross-influences among a variety of sources.

While this book synthesizes many secondary sources – the articles and monographs produced by brilliant scholars of the Aztecs across a number of generational cohorts – I have also relied heavily on a wide variety of primary sources. The bibliographic essay at the end of this book provides references for these sources. The New Philologists, and here I use the term as broadly as possible to refer to scholars on both sides of the border and beyond, brought great attention to the beauty and complexity of the Nahuatl language. In hopes that students and instructors will find it helpful to know about the texts and objects important to the various topics taken up in this book, these are discussed in the introductory chapter as well as in the opening section of each chapter's entry in the bibliographic essay. What I want to emphasize here is that Indigenous-language sources have offered a world of insights that Spanish-language texts, useful as they still are (I rely on some in this book), cannot. Where appropriate,

I use Nahuatl-language terms to identify and explore Aztec ideas, means of perceiving, and categorizing their world to introduce readers in a small way to some of the words and concepts through which they understood that world.

This point brings up two issues for those using Nahuatl terms, to be precise, the Classical Nahuatl spoken and written by Aztecs during the sixteenth century. One issue is spelling. While specialists will be sensitive to issues of vowel length (long or short), glottal stops (a consonant little used in English made by quickly closing the vocal cords), and spelling differences in the way Nahuatl sounds and words were rendered in sixteenth-century alphabetic writing, as an introduction to Aztec history and lifeways, I largely make use of conventional spellings that students and instructors not versed in current renditions of Classical Nahuatl would find across a variety of sources and many scholarly writings. I do follow two contemporary usages. I spell the word for lord (which can also be a part of deity names), *teuctli*, in this more accurate way, instead of *tecutli* or *tecuhtli* as was common in both early alphabetic texts in Nahuatl and in colonial and modern descriptive writings. Second, I dispense with accent marks often found with Nahuatl-language terms. These tend to indicate a pronunciation more appropriate to Spanish than Nahuatl. In the latter language, the emphasis is always on the penultimate syllable; therefore, an accent mark provides no useful information and represents a practice irrelevant to the period before Europeans arrived in Mesoamerica. One last style note: virtually all dates, whether I am describing periods before the arrival of Europeans or even after, are approximate. Archaeologists generally provide dates that offer ranges of time, not specific beginning and ending years, and Aztec calendars can only be approximately correlated with dates in the Gregorian calendar.

In thinking about languages, there is another aspect of the linguistic that should be explained. There are three words associated with the Aztecs whose usage is near constant and that reinforce their highly negative, even barbaric, popular image, an issue taken up further in the first chapter. Those terms are "myth" (a word widely associated with native peoples), "sacrifice," and "conquest." Storytelling, knowledge-creating, and worldview-explaining are human activities that occur across all societies. Myth and history relate to all three activities and are not opposed forms of knowledge. Both relate to the world as it was or is, and all people subscribe to myths to explain how their world came to be as it is. As religious studies scholar Kay Read explains, myths "describe the actual world in terms that we are not used to, using unusual analogies to model what is true – fantastic creatures doing strange things to impart true messages, or ordinary people acting in extraordinary ways." While I use the word "myth" in places, I do not subscribe to the idea that "they," Indigenous people, explain the world through myths, whereas "we," westerners, explain the world through history and science. Indigenous knowledges cut across all domains of life; the use of Indigenous-language texts represents an effort to explore those forms of knowledge in their cultural and historical contexts. To further highlight Aztec history and chronologies, a listing of key events and dates follows at the end of this preface.

Another term, "sacrifice," occurs frequently in descriptions and explanations of Aztec history and ways of life.

Preface

The word is almost always used in the form of "human sacrifice," a topic covered in Chapters 2 and 3. For the Aztecs, sacrifice was about providing precious offerings to nature and to deities. Foods, animals, blood from bloodletting, all could be offered and made up the majority of sacrificial offerings. Nevertheless, violent killing rituals have come to be so closely associated with the Aztecs, even though ritual killing long predated their civilization, that the association has become almost definitional.

The idea that the Aztecs were a conquered, defeated people whose largest city had been destroyed and much of its population perished is similarly ubiquitous still. But "conquest," too, is a loaded term. It implies a definitive end to a sovereignty in which the ruler Moteuczoma collaborated. But the story of this conquest is much more complicated than often assumed. Just as Aztec societies warred with and defeated other Aztec societies, so the Spanish defeated the Mexica, one among many Aztec peoples. Both Aztecs and Spaniards learned that their wars, violent and trauma-inducing, led to tenuous subjugation that required reinforcing efforts, not always successful, and that traumas could be survived through the tenacity of people who have endured waves of change over the centuries. Yet Aztec ways of thinking, forms of expression in spoken and written language, and means of organizing daily life have persisted, not in a pristine, timeless fashion, but nonetheless there has been survival.

I considered using scare quotes each time the words myth, sacrifice, or conquest occur but ultimately decided such a usage would greatly interrupt the flow of the text that follows. I do use such quotation marks in a few places to highlight a stereotypical usage that reinforces misperceptions and misinformation. And about translations: translations from the Nahuatl are mine; from Spanish-language texts, if an accessible English translation exists I have made use of it, otherwise the translations are mine.

My scholarly debts are many; I have already mentioned the earliest ones about people who taught and inspired me and whose work remains part of scholarly conversations, even when particular points have been rebutted as viewpoints shift and knowledge accumulates. There are many others whose names appear throughout the bibliographic essay to whom I am so very grateful, some I know, and others I do not. Aztec scholarship is highly multidisciplinary. I identify the fields of many scholars mentioned in the pages that follow to demonstrate that point. I have tried to read widely and deeply and to render ideas faithfully though filtered, of course, through my own long-term thinking about Aztec ways of living.

I also have personal debts. My husband, Bill Walker, offered staunch support and insights throughout the years I have worked on this book, even though his fields of expertise are far from my own. My two longest-lasting friends, Susan Deeds and Robin Vogel (Robin and I met in fifth grade), have listened to me about many things Aztec and other over the years as have my sons and daughter-in-law – Seth, Sean, and Lisa Mintz. A profound thanks as well to an anonymous reader who brought me up short by reminding me that for all my efforts to be careful in my use of both language and concepts, at times I uncritically employed terminology that can promote colonialist ideas and harmful stereotypes. Thinking about those comments made me realize that we are, to some degree, captive to the generations of scholars who trained us and to those we came into academic life with, but that we must strive to understand, contemplate critically, and make space in our thinking for new facts, ideas, and interpretations. Finally, I am very grateful for the editorial insights of Cecilia Cancellaro, her assistant Victoria Phillips, and Natasha Whelan, content manager at Cambridge University Press, who helped with matters large and small in the editing and production of this book. Fiona Cole, exceedingly talented copy editor, must also be mentioned as must F. Franklin Mathews Jebaraj for overseeing production and Donald Howes for his work on the index.

After I retired, it had been my hope to travel to many more libraries and attend more conferences than I had been able to while still teaching. Then Covid intervened. The internet has served me well but so have particular libraries, mostly online, sometimes in person. At the University of Houston and its Special Collections, their unfailingly helpful librarians and eclectic holdings were essential. The majority of my years in academia were spent at that university. I remain appreciative of the History Department, my undergraduate and graduate students, the College of Liberal Arts and Social Sciences, and the university as a whole for the opportunity it afforded me to teach, research, and write about that which interested me most. My students proved receptive, which suggests how ancient and early modern periods of history indeed have meaning for people seeking to understand the global issues that confront us today. The University of New Mexico's Zimmerman Library, which is exceptionally generous in its lending policies to residents of the state and those area scholars not affiliated with the university, houses the Center for Southwest Research and Special Collections. The library and the center have rich collections of materials on Latin America, especially Mexico. These were vital for this project. Finally, the Benson Latin American Collection at the University of Texas, Austin, perhaps because I lived in Texas for so long, with a collection now over a hundred years old, remains a library with particular meaning for me. Its staff has excelled in giving advice over the years and has been making more and more of their manuscripts, maps, photographs, and other materials widely available through digitization. May all these libraries and their rich holdings continue to be available for the next hundred years and beyond.

KEY PERIODS AND DATES

Note: Please bear in mind that dates before the arrival of Europeans are approximations by archaeologists and historians. Archaeologists use a variety of scientific methods to categorize periods of time. But these do not indicate exact years. While written sources used by historians may provide dates (in either the Aztec or European systems, depending on when they were written and by whom), dates remain approximations because correlating Aztec calendars with later European calendars cannot be exact. Aztec calendars varied by region or community, and sources not infrequently provide varying dates.

Formative Period 1800 BCE–150 CE (all dates after this refer to the Common Era, so CE is not repeated)
Classic Period 150–650
Epiclassic Period 650–900
Postclassic Period 900–1519
Teotihuacan 1–650
Xochicalco 650–900
Tollan 900–1200
Migration period 1100–1325
Mexica reached Chapultepec 1300
Mexica settled and built Tenochtitlan 1325 on
Founding of Tlatelolco, late 1550s
Acamapichtli became first dynastic ruler of Tenochtitlan 1372, ruled to 1391

Key Periods and Dates

Huitzilihuitl, ruled 1391–1415
Chimalpopoca, ruled 1415–1426
Nezahualcoyotl, Tetzcoco, ruled 1429–1472
Itzcoatl, ruled 1426–1440
Mexica and Tetzcoca defeated the Tepaneca 1428
Moteuczoma Ilhuicamina, ruled 1440–1468
Axayacatl, ruled 1468–1481
Nezahualpilli, Tetzcoco, ruled 1472–1515
Defeat of Moquihuix and Tlatelolco, 1473
Tizoc, ruled 1481–1486
Ahuitzotl, ruled 1486–1502
Moteuczoma Xocoyotl, ruled 1502–1520
Last New Fire ceremony before Spanish invasion, 1507
Hernández de Córdoba and Grijalva expeditions, 1517–1518
Cortés expedition arrived and began invasion, 1519
Death of Moteuczoma, Cuitlahua ruled briefly followed by Cuauhtemoc, 1520
Cuauhtemoc captured, Mexica defeated, August 13, 1521

I

Introduction

∼

We never think of the great city of Tenochtitlán, the capital of the Aztec Empire, which five centuries ago was bigger than London at that time. We never imagine sullen teenagers in some pre-Columbian Zona Rosa dive in that fabled Aztec metropolis, bad-mouthing the wretched war economy and the ridiculous human sacrifices that drove their empire.

Aztec culture provides a gateway to Mesoamerican studies because it represents the connecting point between the prehispanic past and the globalized present.

This book presents a concise overview of Aztec *civilization*. The use of the term "civilization" is not without controversy given its connection to outmoded ideas of cultural evolution and unwarranted implications of cultural superiority. It appears here not to imply that superiority or that a single pathway toward civilization has ever existed. Instead, the term acknowledges the complex, class-based, and culturally diverse practices encompassed by the Nahuatl-speaking peoples of the Basin of Mexico region and its surrounding areas (see Map 1.1). Before explaining more about the Basin of Mexico, Aztec ethnicities, and the Nahuatl language, there is a question to answer: Why write such a book when a number of overviews exist?

How I wish I could find out what those sullen Aztec teenagers mentioned above thought about their world. While I cannot approach that granular, micro-level of information, there is still a lot to be learned about how

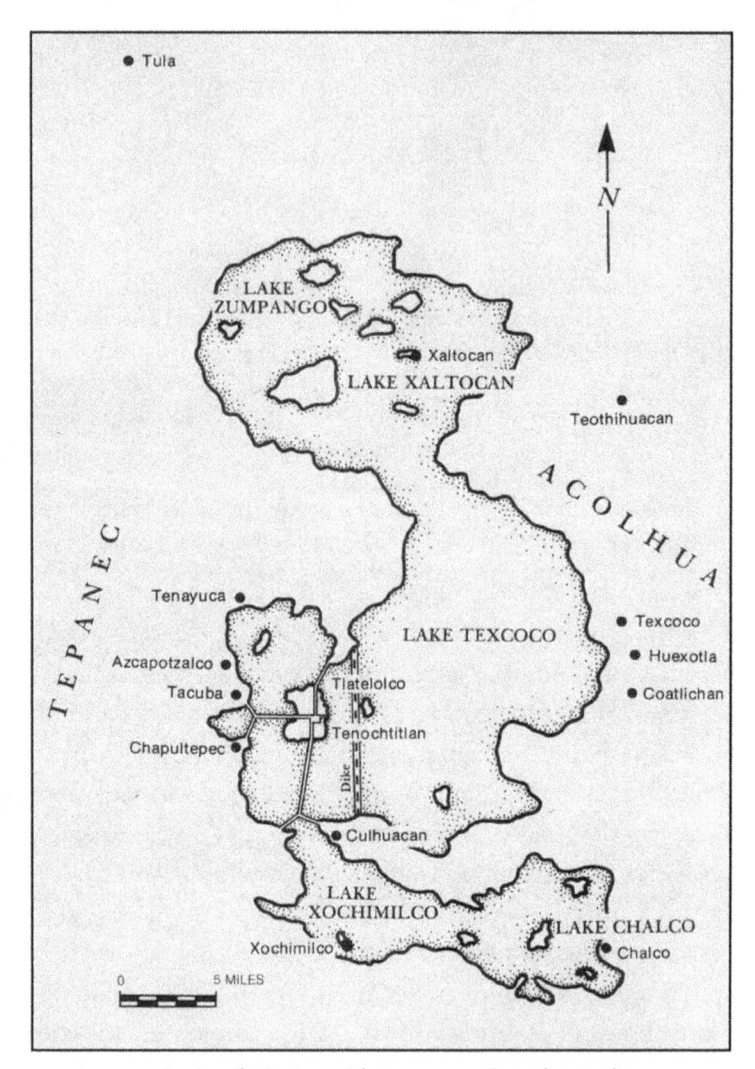

MAP 1.1 Basin of Mexico with important Postclassic altepeme
From Geoffrey W. Conrad and Arthur A. Demarest, *Religion and Empire: The Dynamics of Aztec and Inca Expansionism*, 1984, p.12, Cambridge University Press; by permission of Cambridge University Press. Reproduced with permission of the Licensor through PLSClear

they lived, thought, and represented their world to themselves and others. Beyond the micro-level of analysis, their macro-level importance to world history as the "connecting point" between the prehispanic Americas and an early modern Europe that would birth our "globalized present" should be more widely recognized. We know a great deal about the Aztecs. Nonetheless, conveying who they were, how they lived their everyday lives, and how their ideas and ways of being lived on in people and images in Mexico through their own creativity is still challenging because so many misperceptions, even misinformation, circulate about them.

To further undermine all the misinformation, this book has three goals:

- To provide a concise overview of Aztec history and civilization. It represents my attempt to make sense of their ways of being in a holistic way using the insights of a broad array of primary sources and scholarship (older and recent) – some of which emphasizes the economy, some of which highlights language, thought, and intellectual and artistic trends – to understand Aztec societies and its people, men, women, and children, commoner, and noble.
- To explain in some detail the great number and range of sources about these people but also to describe the limitations of this source base, especially when either the material or the cultural and linguistic is emphasized at the expense of the other.
- To reemphasize the way material life and the economy functioned relative to politics, philosophy, religion, and

intellectual and artistic developments. Aztecs created *value*, material and symbolic worth, every day. That value allowed them to survive and thrive. Value was created through *transformations* of bodies, things, and ideas. The overall goal of value creation and transformation was to keep the Aztec world – the cosmos, the earth, its inhabitants – in *balance*. These three concepts, value, transformation, and balance, are key to describing their civilization.

In this book, I discuss both material and symbolic value. Aztecs created material value (*patiuhtli* referring to something that has a price or specific value) for use and exchange and clearly intended to do so.

> ### Molina's Dictionary
>
> How do we know what words of the Aztec language, Nahuatl, mean? Our best source goes back to the sixteenth century and was written by Fray Alonso de Molina. He produced the first dictionary of the Nahuatl language, the *Vocabulario en lengua castellana y mexicana y mexicana y castellana*. This dictionary represents the essential foundation for the translation of Nahuatl, the language spoken by Aztecs. Born in 1513, Molina came to New Spain as a child where he learned Nahuatl. He died in 1579. One of the great early linguists among the Franciscans missionaries, he wrote a Spanish–Nahuatl dictionary published in 1555 and republished as an enlarged, more detailed edition in 1571, that included a Nahuatl–Spanish section. Other dictionaries exist and are discussed in the Bibliographic Essay.

They bartered, used money, and sought profits. Not to be mistaken for a nascent capitalist society, the Aztec economy nonetheless was partly market based, with the creation and exchange of material value an important activity for men and women. For Aztecs, symbolic value involved accruing and using sacred power. It was also useful for demonstrating, maintaining, or improving social status. Aztecs paid a great deal of attention to the transformations that unfolded in human, plant, and animal life. Cosmic time, history, and sacred forces were rooted in transformations of energy, humans, food, and weather. People could change into spirits, animals, or deity forms, and deities manifested themselves in many different ways. Raw materials could be transformed into everyday and luxury items. Value creation, transformation, and never-ending cycles of cosmic creation and destruction fueled the Aztec search for order, harmony, and balance. The Aztec world sought to find a balance between order and chaos. Falling (to fall, *huetzi*) and slipping (to slip or slide, *alahua*) conveyed disorder and loss of balance and were to be avoided physically, socially, and morally. Balance and reciprocity could also be maintained by debt payment or *nextlahualiztli* through offerings and sacrifice. Exchange, transformation, and reciprocity helped to maintain or restore order. Aztecs put vast effort into keeping their physical and spiritual world in balance, a balance that could only fleetingly be achieved.

    The chapters of this book feature these ideas. Before discussing its contents, I explain why they are important and what sources exist to document Aztec history. Then the introduction discusses who the Aztecs were and describes the terminology for referring to the peoples of the central region of what is today Mexico, especially the area known as the Basin of Mexico. It also reviews the earlier history of the Aztecs.

Why Are These Ideas Important?

First, two approaches have dominated Aztec studies over the past four decades. One approach, carried out mainly by archaeologists, examines the Aztec economy, how its market, trade, and tribute systems worked, and how these funded and empowered the political system of kingdoms, confederations, empire building, and war that characterized the late prehispanic-era central area of Mesoamerica. The other approach highlights language, writing, intellectual and artistic developments, religion, as well as sociocultural patterns, especially emphasizing gender and sexuality, done primarily by ethnohistorians working with texts rather than material remains. In actuality, value creation depended upon both economic activities and the ideas and beliefs about transformation and balance that gave the material realm meaning for Aztecs. A shorthand term for those patterned ideas and beliefs is *culture*.

Why try to examine the interplay of economy and culture? Material approaches help us understand how people *survive* in the world; cultural studies help us understand how people *perceive* their world. Material approaches do not always consider how people think, strategize, or create. Cultural studies often deemphasize the material and social and therefore give a misleading impression about everyday life and the critical role of the mass of population, non-elites or commoners, and how they lived. Cultural approaches need to recognize the importance of the material realm that provided the means through which Aztec religion, intellectual life, social statuses, and governance and war functioned. Recently, both more materially centered and culturally focused scholarship have begun to problematize the relationships among people, things, and thought through the materiality studies approach mentioned in the Preface and to which I refer in places in this book. It is important to acknowledge the interplay among objects, environments, language, and culture in shaping how Aztecs thought about, organized, and carried out the work necessary for familial, community, and state survival.

Second, a great deal of literature about the Aztecs, specifically about the Mexica of Tenochtitlan, the largest Aztec city-state in the Basin of Mexico, focuses on religion, especially their most spectacular practice, that of "human sacrifice." As a result, in both scholarly and popular literature, Aztecs are quite often seen as freakish and exotic, a perspective this book challenges. If native peoples are thought of as the "other," Aztecs are the *other* of the other. They are regularly trotted out as some humorous or horrifying human oddity. Here is just one example in the "humorous" mode: In his much lauded book, *The Secret History of Emotion*, which examines how seventeenth-century European philosophical rhetoric about feelings became part of common ideas about emotion, Daniel Gross says in the very first line, "If you are tickled to learn that Aztecs located passions in the liver ..." to make a point about something else entirely. The ridicule embedded in this throwaway line dismisses Aztecs as people and, at a minimum, treats their beliefs as ludicrous, placing them somehow outside the range of intelligent ideas about how emotions work. Hundreds, if not thousands, of horrifying examples exist, virtually all written to highlight the Aztecs' supposed propensity for human sacrifice. This term and the killing rituals connected to war and fertility Aztecs practiced will be discussed in later chapters.

Because so many colonial written sources describe Aztec religion, this has led to an outpouring of scholarship on that topic. A great deal of interest in human sacrifice as mentioned above – important though the topic is – has the unfortunate and unintended consequence of reinforcing a tendency to see the Aztecs as almost beyond the pale of human cultures. A religious practice that has taken on an almost unquestioned and definitional status, it became intertwined with the political and military goals of empire building of some Aztec groups and intensified as a result. While it appears bizarre and cruel to modern western eyes, Aztecs were far from the only Mesoamerican people to carry out ritual killings, and the world history of religion provides many examples of terrible violence performed either in ceremonial contexts or motivated by religious beliefs. Rather than engage in rationalization or the distancing scholars often do when describing Aztec religious beliefs and practices, I heed religious scholar Davíd Carrasco's call to examine such violence carefully and deeply to argue that these killings and Aztec religion more broadly must be placed in their historical, cultural, and everyday contexts. Only in that way can we achieve a fuller picture of a people who are often depicted as so odd, so appalling. Yet these same people played a critical role in world history, not only for their agricultural, architectural, and artistic achievements, but because of the way they encountered and responded to Europeans upon their arrival.

With some exceptions, surprisingly few scholars really focus on this issue of finding the humanity of the Aztecs. Inga Clendinnen, relying primarily on a source discussed in detail in this chapter, the *Florentine Codex*, highlights the alien and the bleak in her well-known, oft-quoted book, *The Aztecs*. This type of exoticizing description is unfortunately too common. A scholar who does better is Caroline Dodds Pennock. She writes in her book *Bonds of Blood* that her goal is "to reinvest the Aztecs with a humanity and individuality which has frequently been denied to them" because of the mortal violence in which they engaged. Theirs was a "culture of contradictions," bloody *and* beautiful. "Pity, sorrow, love, grief and joy were all deeply felt" and expressed in Aztec ways.

Whether drawing on material or cultural frames of reference to interpret Aztec history and culture, the immense source base they generated through their own writings, architectural presence, and art as well as through the ways they stimulated, even aided, Spanish writing about them has generated much attention. The Aztecs, in conjunction with their colonizers, created what is perhaps the largest written source base about any Native American people at the point of contact with Europeans and thereafter. However complex the task of interpreting the many different written texts that exist and which are complemented by a valuable but more fragmentary material base of archaeological remains, the fact is that written and archaeological sources offer an unparalleled amount of evidence about them.

Sources

The Aztecs are therefore intriguing not only because their civilization is complex and fascinating but also because the corpus of written materials directly concerned with their culture, history, and "conquest" is so remarkably deep. The clash between Aztec peoples and Spaniards, provoked by the Spanish invasion, gave rise to an immense number of written sources. If the archaeological material is not as rich as that which exists for the Maya, there is nevertheless an abundance of material remains, especially from outside of Tenochtitlan. But even for that *altepetl* (*altepeme*, pl., water-mountain, a city-state or kingdom, and the basin's largest) lying under today's Mexico City as it does, there is ancient material evidence that has been recovered. It is to the vast and intriguing written source base that I turn first.

While many written primary sources fall into two basic categories, Indigenous, native-language texts and Spanish-authored texts in that language, some represent what might be considered hybrids between the two. Consider Indigenous-authored texts: One important category of these consists of the pictorial codices, few of which actually date from the prehispanic period.

Codices

There are many codices relating to Aztec groups. In this book, I rely primarily on four that provide a great deal of information about prehispanic life and give an idea of the range of information available. The earliest is the *Codex Borgia*, believed by most investigators to be prehispanic. Its exact place of origin is unknown, but the eastern basin or areas to the southeast are possibilities. It consists of a deer-skin screenfold, meaning the panels have an accordion-like form whereby they fold out and in, with seventy-six leaves that represent a 260-day ritual calendar count (the *tonalpohualli*, discussed in Chapter 2) as well as sections covering prognostication for birth, marriage, climate, and ceremonies for a variety of deities (www.famsi.org/research/graz/borgia/thumbs_0.html).

Introduction

The *Codex Borbonicus*, with its thirty-six folded leaves, was likely produced just prior to or shortly after the Spanish victory over the Mexica, on Indigenous paper (*amatl*). It includes both a 260-day ritual calendar as well as a 365-day solar calendar and was done in the traditional screenfold form. Very beautifully drawn and painted, with quite limited annotations added in Spanish, it likely was created in an important basin altepetl, but which one is not currently identifiable (www.famsi.org/research/graz/borbonicus/index.html).

The *Codex Mendoza* is something quite different from the *Borgia* or *Borbonicus* that reveal little Spanish or Christian influence. This codex, seventy-one folios long, was created in 1540s Tenochtitlan for a Spanish audience to provide detailed information on Mexica rulers, their wars, and the tribute paid to the Mexica from the tribute-paying regions. It also includes an ethnographic section showing the life cycle of Mexica men and women, likely intended to defend the Tenochca Mexica political system and moral code. The first two sections draw on prehispanic histories and tribute records (especially the *Matrícula de Tributos*, a possibly prehispanic text, of which the *Mendoza* could have been a copy). The third is a more colonial creation, though it, too, may draw on prehispanic forerunners, books of prognostication in which morality and proper behavior are depicted. The *Mendoza's* content shows the strong influence of its Mexica artists, at least two, operating within Mexica artistic and intellectual traditions but created in conjunction with one or more Spanish scribes who did the annotations. Done in European book form, it is an early example of what I will call hybrid sources, discussed below (https://digital.bodleian.ox.ac.uk/objects/2fea788e-2aa2-4f08-b6d9-648c00486220/).

The *Codex Telleriano-Remensis*, also a colonial production, is a lengthy, complex text painted in Aztec style in book form on European paper. With its fifty folios (a small number are missing), it has multiple sections that include a calendar of the eighteen solar festivals of the solar year, a *tonalamatl* or divining handbook (like the *Borgia*) based on the 260-day calendar, and an historical section detailing migration histories, dynastic histories of several basin altepeme, along with colonial events up until 1562 in annals, or year count, form, recounting major events year by year. Multiple annotators commented upon the drawings and supplied information and misinformation. The paintings likely were done in the mid-1550s, the commentaries added up to the year 1562. Like the *Mendoza*, the *Telleriano-Remensis* combines both prehispanic and colonial elements and tries to render Aztec time-keeping and the recording of history in a way that would be comprehensible to Europeans. It nonetheless retains artistic elements rooted in the Aztec visual vocabulary as it existed prior to the arrival of Spaniards (https://gallica.bnf.fr/ark:/12148/btv1b8458267s).

Most consist of often-modified copies of now-lost prehispanic codices. Codices cover a wide array of topics about the economy and tribute, rulers and their kingdoms, religion and calendars, family relations and naming patterns, even health and medicine. Scribes, usually native (*tlacuiloque*, *tlacuilo*, sing., the word for painters and writers), included handwritten explanations in Nahuatl and/or Spanish as well as sections treating the period when Spaniards violently encountered the Aztecs and its aftermath, adding a strong element of polyvocality to these writings. Tlacuiloque drew the pictorial images according to Aztec artistic and historical traditions, though Aztec imagery would come to be influenced by European imagery over time.

Written texts and documents in Nahuatl exist as well. Some are annals histories such as the chronicles of don Domingo de San Antón Muñón Chimalpahin Quauhtlehuanitzin.

Introduction

Chimalpahin

The man who became known as don Domingo de San Antón Muñón Chimalpahin Quauhtlehuanitzin, having styled himself as such, was born in May of 1579, a descendant of the founding ruler of Tzaqualtitlan Tenanco, a subdivision (*tlayacatl*, explained in Chapter 3) of the Chalco region. Not a noble himself, he was nonetheless literate and had access to his maternal grandfather's collection of pictorial histories of the subdivision of his birth. Domingo Francisco moved to Mexico City as a young adolescent where he lived at the church of San Antonio Abad and began to write histories in annals form, of Chalco and several other altepeme. Truly learned and deeply read in Indigenous sources, he also drew on Spanish authors and history and was familiar with the ideas of classical writers like Sophocles and St. Thomas Aquinas. He made observations about far flung places such as China, Egypt, and Haiti, knowledgeable as he was about ancient and world history. Chimalpahin even copied and annotated an important Spanish-language text, Francisco López de Gómara's *Conquista de México*. But his most important writings were in Nahuatl. In them, he chronicled the histories of his beloved Chalco and other altepeme, covering almost a thousand years of Aztec history from 670 CE into the first third of the seventeenth century. A devout Christian, he took enormous pride in Indigenous history and drew attention to the early migrations and founding of altepeme, the great rulers of the past, as well as how the loss of Indigenous sovereignty led to a less orderly world in which a racial hierarchy was beginning to emerge. Chimalpahin's greatest emphasis was on the Chalcan world of his ancestors. He also had a special interest in the role of women in the founding of altepeme, their dynasties, and the role royal women played in maintaining rulerships when a male heir could not succeed as the ruler or *tlatoani* (pl., *tlatoque*) The author of rich political and social histories, Chimalpahin stands virtually alone among colonial Indigenous authors writing under his own name in his own language.

Others consist of narrative histories such as the *Crónica mexicana* by Hernando Alvarado Tezozomoc, likely drawing on the same Indigenous source that the friar Diego Durán used as a basis for his much-read history (described below). Alvarado Tezozomoc's chronicle provides a historical perspective reflecting that of the former ruling dynasty of Tenochtitlan to which he was related as a grandson of the second Moteuczoma as well as those of a number of Aztec altepeme. Another Nahuatl-language source consists of the speeches, *huehuetlatolli* – old words or words of the elders – preserved in a variety of texts, especially Book Six of the *Florentine Codex* (see below). Poem-like songs by Aztec authors, many translated into Spanish by the esteemed Mexican anthropologist-historian-linguist Miguel León-Portilla as well as into English by the North American folklorist John Bierhorst, have also survived. Finally, there is a wide array of civil judicial records written in Nahuatl – wills, censuses, town council minutes, petitions, and contracts. These records were often part of the documentation for lawsuits over land or other property, governance, or labor exploitation.

There is also an abundance of Spanish-language material. The eyewitness accounts of the Spanish war against the Mexica, the best known by Hernán Cortés and Bernal Díaz del Castillo, as well as lesser known but revealing texts by participants such as Andres de Tapia and Fray Francisco Aguilar and early colonial chronicles and histories, many by Spanish friars such as Toribio de Benavente, known also by the Nahuatl word for poor, Motolinia, Gerónimo de Mendieta, and Juan de Torquemada. These writings offer vital information about Aztec civilization as well as Spanish reactions to what they saw and experienced. Civil officials also wrote narratives about Aztec history and government. One of the most read of these is Alonso de Zorita's *Breve y sumaria relación de los señores de la Nueva España*. The *Relaciones geográficas*, another Spanish-language source, consists of answers to a royal questionnaire collected between 1578 and 1585 to collate information on population, economy, and governing structures as well as geography. Many of the reports for individual communities contain maps. These texts, although in Spanish, are polyvocal too. Spanish chroniclers relied heavily on Indigenous scholars and writings for information they incorporated, thus Indigenous intellectuals contributed to these texts with their knowledge as well as writing and artistic skills. And legal cases heard in early colonial Spanish-organized courts encompass complaints, pleadings, and testimony of Indigenous litigants. They may include maps and drawings, genealogies, wills, and testimony of hundreds, if not thousands, of colonial Indigenous individuals; much of this evidence is in Spanish (though some, described above, was rendered in Nahuatl).

Native-language documents provide an immense amount of information about Indigenous languages – in this case Nahuatl – and prehispanic ways of living. But they do not offer an unaltered pathway into prehispanic Aztec life. As Nahuatl came into contact with the Spanish language and began to be written in the Roman alphabet, its vocabulary and, eventually, even grammatical structure changed somewhat. Furthermore, the Christian influence of the Catholic Church on the education of Aztecs literate in Nahuatl, Spanish, and sometimes Latin rendered their writings a product of an on-going contact between languages, forms of intellectual and creative expression, and ways of organizing societies. The turn toward emphasizing Nahuatl-language documentation has immeasurably deepened our understanding of Aztecs both before and after Spaniards arrived. These invaluable and numerous texts are polyvocal. They capture the multiple voices of their creators as well as those depicted, and they allow for a much richer, more nuanced investigation into how Aztecs and Spaniards influenced each other.

Finally, several kinds of sources fall into the category of hybrid sources. Some are by authors who were *mestizos*, individuals of Indigenous and Hispanic heritage, so were themselves hybrid in their origins and, more important, in their social and linguistic identities. Men such as Juan Bautista Pomar and Fernando Alva de Ixtlilxochitl, both fluent in Nahuatl, wrote chronicles in Spanish in the late sixteenth and early seventeenth centuries that dealt with the Indigenous history of the kingdom of their ruler ancestors, Tetzcoco. Another such chronicler was Diego Muñoz Camargo from Tlaxcallan who strongly identified with his conqueror father and his Spanish heritage. Yet these particular texts were written to provide the history of the city-state from which each came and to promote the rights of that place and its ruling dynasty in the new colonial political system. Other hybrid sources were constructed by both Indigenous writers, informants, and/or artists in conjunction with Spaniards. One example would be the famous, most often used source for this period, the text that goes by the name *Florentine Codex*.

Sahagún and the *Florentine Codex*

Still the single most important source for studying the Indigenous societies of the Basin of Mexico area, the *Florentine Codex* was compiled by the prolific Franciscan friar Bernardino de Sahagún. Remarkably adept in the Nahuatl language, he came to Mexico Tenochtitlan in 1529 and ministered in at least two altepeme before becoming a Latin teacher in the Colegio de Santa Cruz de Tlatelolco. By the late 1540s, he had already collected forty of the huehuetlatolli which would later make up Book Six of what has become known as the *Florentine Codex*. He also set down on paper a Tlatelolca-based account of the events of the Spanish-Mexica war in the 1550s. Originally called the *Historia universal de las cosas de la Nueva España*, in 1558 Sahagún was commissioned to write a general description in Nahuatl about Indigenous religion and ways of life. Researched with Aztec elders and intellectuals and composed in three altepeme – Tepepolco, Tlatelolco, and Tenochtitlan – between the commissioning of the project and 1569, the writing of what became the *Florentine Codex* went through several stages, the first of which resulted in the *Primeros memoriales*, researched in Tepepolco and based on interviews with the ruler and leading elders. Both this text and the *Florentine Codex* depended on collaborative investigation and writing by four trilingual co-authors – Antonio Valeriano of Azcapotzalco, Alonso Vegerano of Cuauhtitlan, Pedro de San Buenaventura of Cuauhtitlan, and Martín Jacobita of Tlatelolco – who were fluent in Spanish and Latin as well as, of course, Nahuatl. Both works included not only copious text but also drawings illustrating much of the written information. Whereas the *Primeros memoriales* has four sections (Gods; Heaven and Underworld; Rulership; Human Things), the *Florentine Codex* has twelve (Gods; Ceremonies; Origin of the Gods; Soothsayers; Omens; Rhetoric; Sun, Moon, Stars, Binding of the Years;

Kings and Lords; Merchants; The People; Earthly Things; Conquest of Mexico). Almost certainly influenced by medieval encyclopedias, the *Florentine Codex* is a linguistic treasure trove reflecting Sahagún's goal of providing information to help fellow friars in the conversion project. However, that project also included suppressing what he viewed as pagan beliefs, revealed by examining some of the editing which can be detected in the choices of wording and corrections, cutting, and pasting that took place as the volumes were prepared. By considering this text as a material object, close study of the physical properties of its folios provides an example of the materiality approach mentioned in the Preface. Sahagún's co-writers were themselves Christians, whose beliefs shaped the way they viewed Aztec religion so these works must be evaluated carefully despite the rich reporting they contain about many aspects of Aztec life. Before and during the compilation of the *Florentine Codex*, Sahagún compiled or wrote additional texts including sermons, songs, a guide for missionizing, even a re-written version of the invasion account that emphasizes Spanish, rather than Aztec, perspectives. A Spanish version, published as the *Historia general de las cosas de Nueva España*, part translation, part paraphrase, part commentary based on the Nahuatl, has been separately published in multiple editions.

Another such text, mentioned above, would be the *Historia de las Indias de Nueva España e islas de Tierra Firme* by the Dominican friar Diego Durán.

Durán and His Hybrid History

Born in Spain, Durán came to New Spain at the age of seven, learned Nahuatl as a child in Tetzcoco, and then moved to Mexico City. He joined the Dominican order in 1556 and served in several monasteries near the Basin of

Mexico, like Sahagún becoming steeped in Aztec culture. Again like Sahagún, he came to believe that learning about that culture was necessary to evangelize and stamp out the idolatrous practices he thought continued to exist. The product of years of observation, reading, and writing, his *Historia de las Indias de Nueva España e islas de Tierra Firme* represents his deep knowledge gained through extensive interaction with Aztec elders and scholars who could help him interpret the pictorial codices upon which he also relied. His history was composed between about 1574 and 1581 and comprised three sections: a history from the migration period through the first years after the defeat of the Mexica, a book about the gods and rites, and one covering the ancient calendar, each with illustrations. In the historical section, while drawing on an Indigenous source, Durán frequently interjects his own observations about Aztec history, religious practices, and daily life. He refers at times to his belief that the Aztecs could be compared to Hebrews, conjecturing that perhaps they were descended from the lost tribes of Israel. While reflecting his use of annals histories, Durán produced a fully narrative history, one with vivid characters – mainly rulers as well as Tlacaelel, a personage of great importance to the political development of the Mexica (described in Chapter 3) – and an epic, ultimately tragic scope as he described the arrival of the Spanish and the war that followed.

The *Historia* is a hybrid text because, while written in Spanish, Durán makes clear throughout that he used as his most important source an Indigenous-authored annals history which up until now has not come to light (the Mexica-centered, so-called *Crónica X*, also used by Hernando Alvarado Tezozomoc as his main source). Both Durán and Tezozomoc provide clues to the annals history and Nahuatl terminology upon which they were drawing.

Other Spanish friars worked with native scribes to produce Catholic catechisms, sermons, plays and other conversion-related documents, written in Nahuatl, for teaching and preaching purposes. Yet the re-casting of Christian ideas in Nahuatl vocabulary, sometimes had the effect – as anthropologist Louise Burkhart has so eloquently argued – of "missionizing the missionary" and reinforcing many Aztec religious ideas, even producing what another scholar, Ben Leeming, calls "counter-narratives."

This abundance of textual sources is a gift for scholars and students, but like all historical documentation, these materials must be used with analytical rigor. All written records are created for specific reasons for particular audiences and reflect the culturally-rooted assumptions of their authors. Readers must always consider what the intended purposes were and who the intended audience was. Meticulous historian though he was, Chimalpahin's relaciones for instance, offer a defense of the culture of his Chalcan ancestors, especially their rulers and polities. This defense is embedded in his histories, designed consciously or unconsciously to bolster the status of those ancestors' descendants. Cortés' letters quite obviously were no objective account. He represents specific points of view intended to justify and glorify himself and misrepresents or leaves out other points of view. Durán and Sahagún lived among Aztecs in order to missionize. The question of how much can we generalize from information that is specific to a particular time and place arises, as well as the fact that this documentary record is fragmentary and can sometimes be unclear and difficult to interpret.

Why? Ancient documents sometimes simply are hard to read, either because of their handwriting or their condition of preservation, but also due to the language used. This is true for both the archaic Spanish and colonial Nahuatl. Such texts present challenges for translation and interpretation for English- and Spanish-speakers alike. Another difficulty of these sources for contemporary readers is a fundamental characteristic of Aztec history in which conscious rewritings and multiple versions of the histories of dynastic families and their altepeme abounded. These versions then became subject to colonial revisions due to native political interests increasingly expressed in ways intended to appease Spanish officials. Aztecs reshaped their histories in a context of colonial power relations. Their texts embody both ancient sociocultural patterns and emergent political interests. Achieving a neat, linear, chronologically accurate historical reconstruction therefore may simply not be wholly possible.

Material remains also exist and provide richly detailed evidence for understanding the Aztecs of a pre-European time. These remains consisted of architecture and artifacts, monumental public buildings and their decorations – temples, palaces, ball courts, shrines, and altars – in both Tenochtitlan and elsewhere in the Basin of Mexico and beyond, along with housing, including the homes of both ordinary people and the palaces of elites. Urban layouts suggest the grand scale of ceremonial centers and the care with which Aztecs designed them. Cities and towns always had a central area, especially huge in Tenochtitlan, which contained rulers' palaces, and ceremonial, political, and economic structures. Surrounding that central area would be residential areas, often divided into discrete neighborhoods and outlying small areas, called *calpolli* (big house, ward, local community) or *tlaxilacalli* (ward, local community) in Nahuatl. Encompassing the housing of commoners and minor elites, some of these peripheral communities lay at some distance from an altepetl's urban core. The remains of public and household structures from both urban areas and outlying neighborhoods offer evidence about building periods, materials and techniques, layout within buildings and room function, and astronomical orientations, which for public buildings carried spiritual and political meanings.

A question archaeologists have tried to answer through material remains and historians through early colonial documents is just how many Aztecs were there just prior to the arrival of Europeans. The first answers about population were relatively low because early twentieth-century scholars believed Aztecs represented a simpler kind of society that could not generate large, dense populations. As scholars began to look carefully at more data and understand better how complex Aztec societies were, their answers to that question became higher both for the Basin of Mexico and its most populous altepetl, Tenochtitlan. The low count estimates for the basin are less than a million inhabitants versus higher counts as high as 30 million. For Tenochtitlan, estimates ranged from 60,000 to 300,000. Contemporary estimates based on synthesizing textual and archaeological evidence suggest that the basin had a population of about 1.5 million people, and if surrounding areas are added in, the total Aztec population in 1519 would have been between 3 and 4 million. For Tenochtitlan, estimates still range widely, from as low as 72,000 all the way up to 300,000. Given that early descriptions and sixteenth-century census-like documents do not provide consistent, reliable counts, careful scrutiny of the evidence that does exist suggests that an estimate of roughly 120,000–150,000 is reasonable. This estimate assumes a density of about 12,000 people per sq. km. or about 30,000 per sq. mile applied to the residential areas of the city, allowing for palaces of wealthy nobles and rulers as well as the homes of well-to-do merchants and skilled craftspeople to house larger numbers of people. Additionally, the city's temples and markets attracted large numbers of visitors for shorter or longer stays. The next largest altepeme housed populations of about 24,000 (Tetzcoco), 17,000 (Huexotla), and 11,000 (Otumba [Otompan]).

For Tenochtitlan and many other Aztec cities within the Basin of Mexico, another important kind of architecture had to do with water control, which was essential for supplying water for farming. Controlling water flows from the huge lake system, with its five lakes, in which sat Tenochtitlan and that so many mainland cities bordered, was critical. Inhabitants of this densely populated area needed access to drinkable water, and this lake water also supplied agricultural areas with the water needed to produce edible and usable plant life (see Map 1.2). But keeping cities and towns in and around the lake system from flooding also proved essential. Aztecs built and managed sophisticated hydraulic systems that included aqueducts, dams, canals, and hillside terracing for all these purposes.

As for artifacts, portable remains, archaeologists have recovered many different kinds. One category would be largescale sculpture – deities, sacrificial stones, and skull racks (*tzompantli*) were common across Aztec sites of much size. But for Tenochtitlan, its Templo Mayor site,

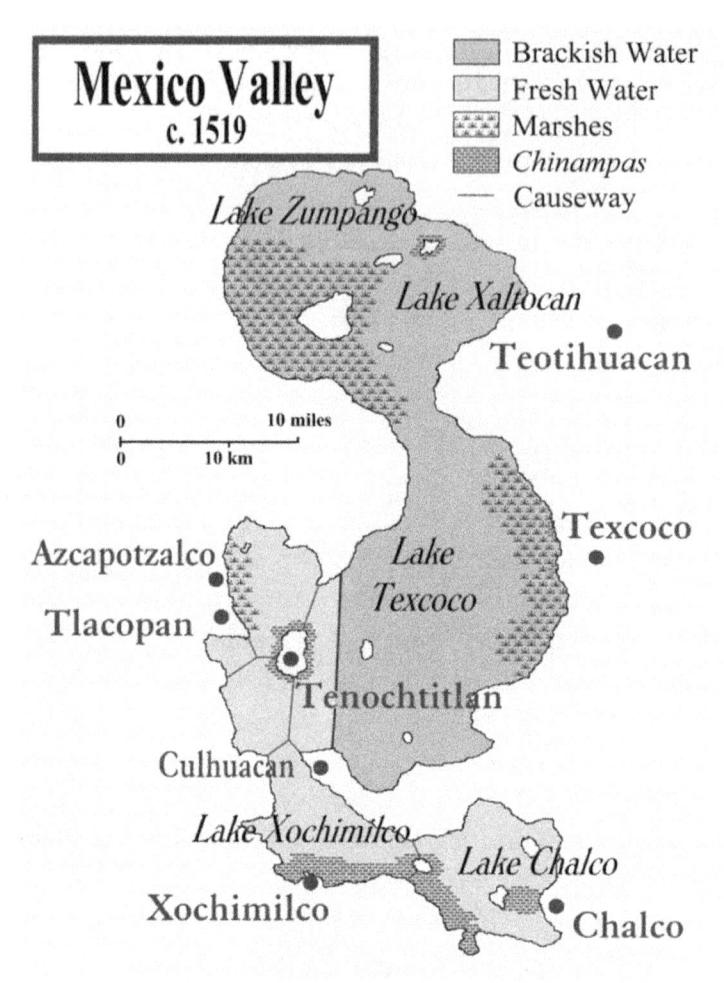

MAP 1.2 The five lakes in the Basin of Mexico, major altepeme near them, and chinampa areas
Public Domain. Map made by Madman2001, GNU Free Documentation License
File: Lake Texcoco c 1519.png - Wikimedia Commons

the central area for state-sponsored religious activities, was especially large and dramatic and featured thousands of pieces of large- and small-scale sculptures in addition to its impressive architecture. Small sculptural pieces, especially deity figures made from stone, wood, or clay were common and found their way into the archaeological record. Stone blades, food-processing tools such as *manos* (grinding tools), *metates* (flat stone surfaces for grinding), and *molcajetes* (stone bowls), plates, and vessels for drinking and cooking have been excavated as well as smaller scale art works such as turquoise mosaics, feather work, and clothing and jewelry. Such remains provide insights into the lives of Aztecs of lower and higher strata. Rulers, and high-ranking nobles, many of whom were governing figures, had vast arrays of clothing and jewelry, some made with the gold and silver that Spaniards would find so alluring. Archaeological remains, especially spindle whorls, say a lot about kinds and amounts of textiles produced for commoners.

Archaeological remains are important. They are of prehispanic origin and less obviously biased in the way that historical documents are because they are the remains of daily life, providing information about people's everyday activities, where they lived, what they ate, how they worked, worshipped, and fought. Documents are more selective in what they say. But archaeological evidence presents its own problems of interpretation, especially that arising from urban archaeological projects, because material remains may occur in more or less accessible places and in greater or lesser quantities. For Mexico City, lying over the former Mexica altepetl of Tenochtitlan, that material which can be excavated relates mainly to elite political and religious activities, some of which is propagandistic, given the imperial goals of the Mexica ruling dynasty. Also, variable patterns of perishability influence what survives and what does not. And without words, the archaeological record can only tell us so much about ideas, beliefs, social patterns, and cultural production.

A third kind of evidence consists of studies of the cultures of living peoples who are descended from the Aztecs, known as *ethnography*. While living peoples have experienced 500 years of history that deeply influenced their languages, beliefs, and cultural practices, decades of ethnographic research has demonstrated that continuities with ancient ways of life exist. Even with all the changes colonialism, the development of nationhood for Mexico, and the technological changes the modern, industrial world brought, family and kinship organization, tool use, curing practices, and important conceptions about the cosmos, spiritual beings, and conceptions of identities have survived. However, before we can explore who the Aztecs are in today's world, we should examine who they were and how such peoples came to be.

Who Were the Aztecs?

The name "Aztec" gets used in a variety of ways. Sometimes it is used to refer to the Mexica who called themselves "Azteca" early in their history but then were commanded by their patron deity, Huitzilopochtli, to change that name, as Chimalpahin recounts, explaining that when the people first known as Aztec left Aztlan, they were not yet called Mexica. "They all called themselves

Azteca. And we say that later they took their name, they called themselves Mexitin." The ethnonym "Mexica" is the most accurate name for the peoples of Tenochtitlan and Tlatelolco, but late colonial and nineteenth-century writers like Francisco Javier Clavijero and William Prescott popularized the use of "Aztec." "Aztec" has also been used to refer to the peoples encompassed by the city-states that would include the Triple Alliance confederation, the Tepaneca, the Acolhua, and the Mexica, or even more broadly to all the linguistically related peoples who spoke Nahuatl dialects in and around the Basin of Mexico, a usage I follow. From here on, for colonial and contemporary Nahuatl-speaking peoples, I use the term "Nahua." For contemporary Nahuatl-speaking peoples, this is a term they occasionally use for themselves. More often, however, today's Nahuatl speakers use "Mexicano" or "Mexicanero" as their ethnonym. They may also use "*masehuali*" (pl., *masehualmej*), which comes from the prehispanic Nahuatl term for commoner (*macehualli*) and refers to Nahuas or Indigenous people generally.

Aztec peoples created the material remains and historical records that still exist. They bequeathed language, ideas, and customs to contemporary Nahuatl-speaking peoples as well as ideas about those ancient societies that shape today's discourses in Mexico and beyond about those peoples and their descendants. To trace the origins of Aztec peoples and the Mexica, one must rely on ancient material evidence and colonial era pictorial and alphabetic sources that combine elements of history and myth. Many written and material sources enshrine, however, a Mexica rewriting of history that occurred in the mid-fifteenth century that obscures the earlier histories of the peoples of the Basin of Mexico, complicating and fragmenting what we can understand from colonial-period versions of codices. Nonetheless, the Aztecs developed out of early Mesoamerican peoples whose histories help explain the cultural traditions Aztecs drew upon as they created their societies and ways of living.

Spanning from northern Mexico to much of Central America, ancient Mesoamericans, who included the Olmecs, Mayas, Teotihuacanos, Toltecs, Mixtecs (Ñudzahui, the ethnonym they use for themselves), Zapotecs (Benìzàa), and Otomis (Hñahñu) spoke many different languages but shared similar, though not identical, features. These included ways of keeping time, uses of writing, obsidian tools and ceramic pottery, ideas about deities and ceremonies, reliance upon trade and markets, intensive agricultural techniques, and house building patterns. Aztec groups built upon older templates that gave rise to the societies and ways of living Europeans came upon in the Basin of Mexico region at the end of the Postclassic period that spanned the centuries from 900 CE to 1521 CE.

The Olmecs of the Gulf Coast region pioneered an early template for Mesoamerican civilizations during the Middle and Later Formative periods (about 1200 BCE to 150 CE) that included urbanism, a widespread art style, and a commanding ruling group influencing the Mesoamerican civilizations that followed. Classic-period (about 150 CE–650 CE; hereafter I dispense with CE, Common Era, as all dates refer to this expanse of time) Mayas of southern Mesoamerica and Teotihuacanos of the Basin of Mexico built large cities, immense pyramids, and developed highly productive agricultural and craft-based economies, with powerful ruling classes. Teotihuacan, in particular, housed a large population and created trade networks that operated across a broad swath of Mesoamerica. The site lay in ruins by the time of the Aztecs, having fallen around the mid-seventh century. It loomed large in their story of the sun's and moon's origins and led to a brief period called the Epiclassic (650–900) during which a variety of regional centers emerged in central Mexico and Maya kingdoms began to suffer from environmental and political stresses. The sun and moon narrative told of the rise of the Aztec epoch, what was called by the Mexica the age of the Fifth Sun, which came after the early Postclassic (about 900–1200). During those centuries, the next Basin of Mexico center, Tollan (located within today's Tula), grew into a large, powerful center, not the equal of Teotihuacan, but one that Aztecs imagined as the center of the creation of a later Mesoamerican template where writing, calendrics, and luxury crafts, in particular, began. In reality, much of that template had older Olmec roots.

Aztec histories then describe the migration of Chichimeca nomadic hunting peoples of the north coming into central Mexico and intermingling with settled, agricultural urban, Tolteca peoples of the center. These migrations likely took place in two waves, an earlier wave of non-Nahuatl speaking Chichimeca just before and as the city of Tollan, the Tolteca capital, was falling late in the twelfth century, and a second wave during the thirteenth century, after Tollan's fall, by Nahuatl speakers, also labeled Chichimeca. These later migrating peoples settled in the Basin of Mexico and nearby areas between 1200 and 1300 and in Tenochtitlan – the Mexica capital – around

1325. Better thought of as stereotypes, the terms "Chichimeca" (some of whom actually were agriculturalists) and "Tolteca" do not themselves represent Mesoamerican ethnicities. Rather, multiethnic and multilingual in origin, these were kinds of peoples with distinctive lifeways, some migratory and some settled – neither linguistically nor culturally unified – who came together to form the ethnicities of the Basin of Mexico region as these existed in 1519.

The women and men who were part of the second-wave migrations mainly spoke Nahuatl, most of Chichimeca *and* Tolteca origins. Their movements have been referred to as the "Aztlan" migrations, and codices and historical narratives say that those migrant groups began their journeys from Aztlan or Chicomoztoc. Combining with peoples of other linguistic and cultural heritages, including the Nonoalca, Olmeca Xicallanca, Otomi, and Matlatzinca, some indigenous to the central Mesoamerican region, others also migrants, they would go on to form the ethnic groups, about fifteen, that existed just before the arrival of Spaniards. Some of these were coterminous with an altepetl, such as the Xochimilca; others spread over a wider area, such as the Matlatzinca of the Toluca Valley or the Acolhua of the eastern Basin of Mexico, encompassing multiple altepeme. Pictorial and alphabetic texts explain how Basin of Mexico peoples migrated to their places of settlement where they then built their city-states and their ruling families. Most such accounts feature a place of origin, a place with both historical and sacred meanings, where a people emerge from caves called Chicomoztoc (Seven Caves).

Such sources describe multiple peoples emerging from Chicomoztoc and going on lengthy journeys, filled with challenges. The numbers and names of peoples and stages in the journeys differ across accounts. The Mexica accounts mostly emphasize their place of origin as Aztlan (Place of Whiteness or Place of Herons). What the migration narratives do agree on is that the Mexica were the last group to set out on a journey of migration and that they followed the guidance of their patron deity, Huitzilpochtli, on their journey to the place where they would build their capital city, Tenochtitlan. Because so many written sources describe the Mexica and their history, this book centers them, but the chapters that follow include information on other Aztec peoples as well.

The major elements of migration tales – whether rendered in pictures or words – feature several key points in the Mexica journey:

- Guided by their patron deity, Huitzilopochtli, these "Azteca," as they were then known, began a journey, organized into seven calpolli sub-groups and migrated southeast for a period during which they experienced many hardships. Departing Aztlan early in the twelfth century, the Azteca then stopped at Chicomoztoc and Mount Colhuacan. But Huitzilopochtli – usually referred to as a deity but sometimes appearing in sources about these early migrations as a human being, an early leader who over time became transformed into a deity – promised them an eventual better, wealthier, settled, more powerful existence and ordered them to change their name to Mexica.
- Conflicts developed and several splits occurred within the original migrating group. A particularly bitter split occurred when the Mexica abandoned followers of

Huitzilopochtli's sister, Malinalxoch, and both groups struggled to find places to settle. This conflict led into the next stage of the journey whereupon the Mexica arrived at Coatepec (Snake Mountain) where their deity Huitzilopochtli was reborn from a ball of feathers that had inserted itself into the stomach of his mother, Coatlicue. He then fought with another sister, Coyolxauhqui, who ordered their 400 brothers to attack Coatlicue before the birth could take place. Born with tools of war in his hands, Huitzilopochtli killed and dismembered Coyolxauhqui. The Mexica then recreated the watery environs of Aztlan at Coatepec, where they lived peacefully until another sister provoked another split within the group, and the main body continued on.

- The Mexica stopped at a number of places in the Basin of Mexico which by then they had entered. One of these settings was Chapultepec, now a beautiful park in Mexico City, but then the site of the remnants of a Tolteca community, where the Mexica tried to establish themselves around 1300. Attacked and driven from that place twice, the Mexica began to transform their political system, moving it away from the early pattern of collective leadership organized around four religious and fifteen to twenty calpolli leaders toward a single ruler, the first known as Huitzilihuitl. However, he was killed by enemy forces, the Tepaneca of the western side of the lake system, the dominant confederation at that time. The Mexica moved on, next begging the Tolteca-descended leaders of Colhuacan to settle in their altepetl. Sent by Colhuacan's rulers to the site of Tizaapan, a nearby rocky and snake-infested area, instead of disbanding or moving on as Colhuacan's leaders surely

Introduction

intended, the Mexica thrived. They farmed, hunted, and fished for food, and the Colhua began to interact with them more through trade and intermarriage. These intermarriages were important because through them the Mexica began to style themselves the "Colhua Mexica," claiming Toltec heritage. But the Colhua became worried by the increasing military skill of the Mexica. Because he believed Colhuacan was not to be their final settlement, their god Huitzilopochtli then commanded them to ask for a daughter of one of the rulers of Colhuacan, which the ruler Achitometl provided. Arriving at what he thought would be a wedding ceremony, whereby the beautiful young woman would become the wife of Huitzilopochtli, Achitometl discovered instead that his daughter had been ritually killed, her skin removed, then donned by a priest. As the priest appeared before Achitometl in a temple, the ruler cried out in abject horror. The Mexica time in the Colhuacan region had come to an end.

- They escaped and came to rest at the place that would become their final settlement on an island amid the basin's lake system. There they saw the sign Huitzilopochtli had told them to look for – a cactus growing from a stone with an eagle perched upon it – which the deity said to call Tenochtitlan, Place of the Stone Cactus. Most Aztec histories say this happened in 1325. While the island was scarcely developed, though it may have already had a small, probably Tolteca-remnant population, it held rich resources of swampy soil that could be developed into so-called floating gardens. They do not really float. Surrounded by water, these garden plots would be used to grow food and give access to the lake's resources, especially fish and birds that provided needed protein. Tenochtitlan's builders divided the island into four districts called *campan* or tlayacatl. These districts included subdivisions called calpolli early in the city's history and at first numbered seven, then fifteen to twenty by the late fourteenth century. The subdivisions later became known as tlaxilacalli that eventually numbered about 100 as the city grew dramatically in population over time. While beginning to flourish economically, the Mexica remained tributaries to the Tepaneca, whose capital at this time was the altepetl of Azcapotzalco.

- One last event would mark this foundational period and that is the settlement of Tenochtitlan's sister-island, Tlatelolco, around thirty years after the settlement of Tenochtitlan. The Mexica of each settlement experienced both conflict and cooperation with each other. Tlatelolco would prove central to the rise of Mexica commerce, eventually leading to the dramatic downfall of its ruler Moquihuix, vanquished by the Tenochca ruler Axayacatl in 1473. Tlatelolco would play an important defensive role in the Spanish-Mexica War.

Aztec communities memorialized the history of their migrations and how their kingdoms came to be located where they were as well as the histories of their ruling families in oral, pictorial, and written form. A characteristic of those histories, belief systems, and ways of living and acting in their world is that they often reflected and conveyed the idea that political activities, economic undertakings, and spirituality and worship were tightly linked together in the organization of community *and* household life as well as in the mentalities that underlay, shaped, and interpreted those experiences. The monumental architecture and sculpture of the ceremonial centers of Aztec altepeme – especially, but not only, the Mexica Templo Mayor – communicated the economic, political, and religious powers they asserted over both their own and other peoples and places. The texts and material remains of many Aztec cities and towns show how value creation in daily life allowed for political, economic, and religious transformation within altepeme and beyond as alliances formed and an imperial political organization grew. These transformations reinforced the Aztec desire to search for order, stability, and balance in a frequently chaotic world.

Keeping the Aztec integrated and holistic way of thinking in mind helps us to comprehend the Aztec world, to the extent we can, in a more Indigenous way. My goal is to bring together the two lines of thought and evidence mentioned at the beginning of this chapter, the economic and material, as focused on mainly by archaeologists, the other highlighting language and cultural traditions undertaken mainly by historians, art historians, and linguists working with written and pictorial texts. The synthesis of these approaches that this book aims for will show how in all areas of life the Aztecs relied on both material and symbolic elements to think about, organize, and carry out the tasks of governance, production, spiritual activities, and intellectual and family life. Through these activities, Aztecs created value, engaged in transformations, and sought balance between order and chaos, reciprocity and hierarchy, center and periphery, and male and female – paired ideas that expressed the balance they sought.

Both women and men created value, value that had uses politically, economically, socially, and symbolically. Throughout this book, I assess the integrated nature of Aztec ways of seeing the world, living in it, and the value that women and men produced. In Chapter 2 on religion, I argue that not only did religion have material significance, as a variety of scholars have shown, but that mythical transformations, deity beliefs, and ceremonial practices underlay both the hierarchical and egalitarian relationships around which Aztec political, economic, and social life was organized. In Chapter 3, I argue that altepeme, the kingdoms or city-states, were key to the organization of political and economic relationships across the Aztec region. These were also structured around local communities whose relationships of reciprocity and hierarchy between central places and outlying communities, peripheries, defined the internal structures of the localities and altepeme. In Chapter 4, I look at Aztec economic ideas and patterns of production, exchange, and consumption in more detail. These ideas of reciprocity and hierarchy were critical to the workings of Aztec economic activities. Labor, tribute, and commerce fed into a political and social organization that was becoming organized in more hierarchical ways. Nonetheless, throughout their history, Aztecs prized reciprocity because of the need to keep their world in balance. The household as an arena for economic, political and religious activities is explored in Chapter 5 as are marriage, family life, education, gender roles, and sexuality. Again, the concepts of value, transformation, and balance help us understand how Aztec women, men, and children shaped their daily lives. In Chapter 6, Aztec creativity and intellectual life come to the fore. Aztecs represented their ways of thinking and living to themselves and others through science, writing and literature, and art. Ultimately, these areas would play pivotal roles in their survival and resilience after Spaniards arrived. Chapter 7, the final chapter, considers how the Aztecs experienced what most commonly is referred to as the "Spanish conquest." The chapter describes how a civilization that most think of as extinct actually lives on in both its direct, Nahuatl-speaking descendants as well as through contemporary Mexican and even global ideas about Aztecs. While using a thematic organization for the chapters, I stress the historical relationship between hierarchy and reciprocity, how it changed over time in relation to the creation and use of value, the transformations involved in such changes, and the way the search for cosmic and worldly balance persisted.

2
Living in the Aztecs' Cosmos

One version of an Aztec creation story explains that first came the gods Tonacateuctli and Tonacacihuatl who lived in the highest Aztec upper world, a place of creation from where all life came. They had four sons who were representations of the omnipresent deity Tezcatlipoca – Red Tezcatlipoca, Black Tezcatlipoca, Quetzalcoatl (white), and Huitzilopochtli (blue). In addition to a color, each was associated with one of the four cardinal directions, thus defining the horizontal structure of the earth. Together, Quetzalcoatl and Huitzilopochtli went on a creation spree, generating fire, a half-sun, the calendar, the upper and lower layers of the universe including the earth and its waters, and the first man and woman, Oxomoco and Cipactonal, he to farm, she to spin and weave. They created the worker *macehualtin* (commoners; *macehualli*, sing.) upon whom so much of Aztec life depended. Other creations by the four Tezcatlipoca followed, including calendars and the lords of the lower world – Mictlanteuctli and Mictlancihuatl. Then they created other upper worlds and water. The waters held Cipactli, a large reptilian monster. After next creating the rain deity Tlaloc and his consort Chalchiuhtlicue, the four then created the earth out of Cipactli's body. Because creation was so important to the Aztecs – as creation and destruction played key roles in the cycle of transformation through which they understood life, time, and the earliest parts of human history – they told and represented their world through multiple stories that expressed their ideas of value, transformation, and balance.

After a brief review of creation narratives, this chapter considers Aztecs' concepts of time, space, and place, all of which provided context for the rich ceremonial life of the Aztecs. A spiritually enveloping, time-consuming, and value-creating set of activities, Aztecs centered these ceremonies on supernaturals who were powerful spiritual beings. They related to many key elements of the Aztec natural and built worlds that are described here along with the personnel, male and female, who served and often embodied them. Finally, the chapter covers ceremonies conducted for those beings, the offerings presented to them and exchanged or distributed during the ceremonies, and examples of power and energy that offerings, including offerings of living humans, represented. While not always easily comprehended by contemporary eyes used to a non-Indigenous split between the sacred and secular, a split that did *not* exist for the Aztecs, ceremony was a fundamental part of everyday life for Aztecs from the smallest villages to the largest, most urbanized altepeme.

Our knowledge of the religious realm of Aztec life is based on a wide array of textual and archaeological sources, a huge but incomplete record of beliefs. Textual sources provide detailed evidence about creation stories, calendrical and other ceremonies, the priesthood and education of its members, and the ideas about power, reciprocity, and value that religious ideology and practice represented. Both Sahagún's Indigenous coauthors and Diego Durán's textual researches resulted in the works with the most comprehensive descriptions of beliefs and ceremonies, with the accounts of rituals by the Franciscans Motolinia, among the earliest, and Gerónimo de Mendieta also informative. Works about Aztec religion created by or with Catholic priests betray Christian influence, which must be carefully considered when using these sources. Many codices provide images of calendrical accounting, deities, ceremonies, and the priests and priestesses and others who participated, as well as explanatory annotations in Nahuatl and Spanish. Among the most useful are the *Codex Borgia*, the *Borbonicus*, and the *Codex Telleriano-Remensis*, all described in the previous chapter. Text-based creation accounts in the *Historia de los mexicanos por sus pinturas*, the *Histoyre du Mechique*, the *Leyenda de los soles*, and the *Anales de Cuauhtitlan* provide insights into the ideas about creation and history of the universe, the earth, deities, and people; many of these works provide details about the offerings and ritual killings that were a part of Aztec religious practices. Other texts illustrate the local variations across Nahuatl-speaking areas that existed in deity names, calendrical reckonings, and emphasis on particular ceremonies. Archaeological evidence shows the design and placement of temples and other important spaces for ceremonies, the three-dimensional portrayal of deities, and the goods offered to gods, priests, and rulers during ceremonies. That evidence also allows an assessment of the place of ritual killing within the broad array of religious activities Aztecs carried out.

Stories of Creation

Aztecs narrated the beginnings of the universe, the earth, their gods, and human life through a variety of stories.

These stories – what anthropologist H. B. Nicholson called "cosmogonic myths" in his authoritative 1971 article on Aztec religion – covered long, long ago periods of time. They describe events going much farther back in time than the narratives of migration that explained where from the thirteenth century on Aztec groups originated and how they came to found the altepeme Spaniards encountered in 1519. These cosmogonic stories communicated descriptions and explanations of the Aztec natural, spiritual, and human-made worlds as well as ideas about the values Aztecs expected themselves and others to uphold and the obligations they expected all Aztecs to fulfill. The notion of human obligation is made especially clear in a narrative about the creation of the sun and moon in which the gods, as related in Book Seven of the *Florentine Codex*, had to decide which one would give himself up as an offering in order to create the sun. While a wealthy deity, Tecuciztecatl volunteered to leap into a cosmic fire, he was too cowardly to actually do it, so another deity named Nanahuatzin, poor and pockmarked, leapt into the fire and rose as the sun. Tecuciztecatl, shamed by Nanahuatzin's action, cast himself into the fire and rose as the moon. But astral bodies still needed to be put in motion, and the other deities offered themselves up for this purpose. But finally, it took the wind deity, Ehecatl, to blow on the sun to make it start to move. This action represents the idea that "sacrifice" or offering of that which was precious was essential to provide the energy that the sun required to stay in motion. Human hearts and blood, those very precious items, would be needed for that purpose. But the sun–human relationship did not flow smoothly.

For the Aztecs, it took four cycles of human creation to reach their "sun" or age, known to them as the Fifth Sun. Rooted in an older and widespread Mesoamerican cosmogonic myth, the Aztecs believed that four ages had preceded their own, each one troubled, having ended in a disaster particular to that era. Giants roamed the earth during the First Sun, Nahui Ocelotl (Four Jaguar), and ate acorns, then a jaguar came to devour them. The Second Sun, Nahui Ehecatl (Four Wind), saw humans living from piñon nuts, with hurricanes destroying the humans, turning them into monkeys. Four Rain, Nahui Quihuitl, in which humans ate aquatic plants, featured their destruction by a dramatic, fiery rain. The Fourth Sun, Nahui Atl or Four Water, saw humans transformed into fish by a deluge of rain after eating wild seeds. The Fifth Sun, Nahui Ollin or Four Movement, is our own age with maize-eating humans whose era will be ended by great earthquakes, according to Aztec narratives. In order for humans to come to exist in their current maize-eating form, another story tells how Quetzalcoatl journeyed to the underworld, Mictlan (Place of the Dead), where he gathered the bones and ashes of the previous Suns' imperfect humans. He and other deities ground the bones and ashes together with their own blood, creating first a male, then a female child. By bringing maize into being as the primary human foodstuff of the Fifth Sun, a source of material and symbolic value came into existence, one that would be involved in the cycle of obligation that the earth and its fruits underwrote between the gods and humans. Transformations that occurred as death and life endlessly recycled in a constant process of dynamic change across vertical and horizontal conceptions of space and over both cyclical and linear time also were important features of these creation narratives.

Time, Place, Space

Building upon an ancient Mesoamerican foundation of ideas about time, Aztec civilization focused its timekeeping on the notion of progressive ages, the idea of cyclical time, and two calendar systems. The calendars used two ways of keeping track of days and months and how these temporal units related to important ceremonies, calendrical and other, is described below. The *tonalpohualli*, or day count, was a 260-day calendar made up of twenty day names and thirteen numbers. Each day over the course of a 260-day cycle carried a unique sign and number beginning with the day Ce Cipactli (One Crocodile; see Table 2.1). After the first twenty day signs, those signs repeated, beginning with Eight Crocodile, and after day 260, the cycle began again with day One Crocodile. Aztecs apparently had no term for the thirteen-day periods, of which there were twenty. Spaniards referred to these as *trecenas*. Each had a ruling deity. There were also thirteen day gods or "lords" as the literature on religion refers to them and nine night lords. These signs, numbers, and deity associations allowed the priests who devoted themselves to reading the books that kept tonalpohualli counts, the *tonalamatl* (day book, such as the *Codex Borgia*), to predict the futures of newborns based upon the day they were born. The *tonalpouhque* (those who could read the tonalamatl) advised rulers, officials, communities, and families about consequential undertakings, agricultural, commercial, military, ceremonial, or familial.

Table 2.1 *The twenty day signs and thirteen numbers of the Aztec tonalpohualli*

Crocodile	1
Wind	2
House	3
Lizard	4
Snake	5
Death	6
Deer	7
Rabbit	8
Water	9
Dog	10
Monkey	11
Grass	12
Reed	13
Jaguar	1
Eagle	2
Vulture	3
Movement	4
Flint	5
Rain	6
Flower	7

Source: Boone, *Cycles of Time and Meaning.* (All sources for tables are fully cited in the Bibliographic Essay.)

Aztecs called their other calendar, a solar and agricultural calendar, rather than one of divination, the *xiuhpohualli*, or year count. The calendar was divided into eighteen segments of twenty days each, called in Nahuatl *metztli*, a word also meaning moon; Aztecs associated each segment with one or more ceremonies. In addition to the 360 days, this count included five extra days – the *nemontemi* – added at the end of the year and thought to be a dangerous, unstable time of the year before the solar calendar began again (see Table 2.2). The calendar was highly variable across the Aztec area with different starting months and deities celebrated in

Table 2.2 The eighteen months of the solar year

Month	Translation	Approximate Dates	Deities Celebrated
Atl caualo/ Cuahuitlehua	Water Stops/ Pole Raising	Feb. 13–Mar. 4	Tlaloc, Chalchiuhtlicue
Tlacaxipehualiztli	Men Flaying	Mar. 5–24	Xipe Totec
Tozoztontli	Little Vigil	Mar. 25–Apr. 13	Tlaloc, Centeotl, Chalchiuhtlicue, Chicomecoatl
Huey Tozoztli	Great Vigil	Apr. 14–May 3	Centeotl, Chicomecoatl, Tlaloc, Quetzalcoatl
Toxcatl	Dry Thing[a]	May 4–23	Tezcatlipoca, Quetzalcoatl
Etzalcualiztli	Eating Etzalli[b]	May 24–June 12	Tlaloc, Chalchiuhtlicue, Quetzalcoatl
Tecuilhuitontli	Lords' Little Feast Day	June 13–July 2	Xochipilli, Huixtocihuatl
Huey tecuilhuitl	Lords' Great Feast Day	July 3–22	Xilonen, Cihuacoatl
Tlaxochimaco/ Miccailhuitontli	Giving Flowers/ Small Feast of the Dead	July 23–Aug. 11	Huitzilopochtli, Tezcatlipoca, all deities
Xocotl huetzi/ Huey miccailhuitl	Xocotl (fruit) Falls Great Feast of the Dead	Aug. 12–31	Xiuhteuctli, Yacateuctli
Ochpaniztli	Sweeping the Way	Sept. 1–20	Teteo innan, Toci, Centeotl, Chicomecoatl
Teotl eco/ Pachtontli	Gods Arrive Little Moss	Sept. 21–Oct. 10	Tezcatlipoca, Huitzilopochtli, Yacateuctli, all gods
Tepeilhuitl/ Huey pachtli	Mountain Feast Day Great Moss	Oct. 11–30	Tlaloque, Xochiquetzal, pulque gods
Quecholli	Red Bird	Oct. 31–Nov. 19	Mixcoatl, Camaxtli

45

Table 2.2 (cont.)

Month	Translation	Approximate Dates	Deities Celebrated
Panquetzaliztli	Raising Banners	Nov. 20–Dec. 9	Huitzilopochtli, Tezcatlipoca
Atemoztli	Water Falling	Dec. 10–29	Tlaloque
Tititl	Stretching	Dec. 30–Jan. 18	Cihuacoatl, all gods
Izcalli	Growth	Jan. 19–Feb. 7	Xiuhteuctli, Tlaloc, Chalchiuhtlicue
Nemontemi	Useless days	Feb. 8–12	No rituals celebrated

[a] Durán translates this term in *Book of the Gods and Rites*.
[b] Etzalli was a paste or porridge made from corn and beans.
Sources: *Florentine Codex*, Book 2; Durán, *Book of the Gods and Rites*; Caso, "Calendrical Systems; Nicholson, "Religion in Pre-Hispanic Central Mexico"

various locales as well as different names for these periods. But the xiuhpohualli always allowed for calculation of the most appropriate times for planting, harvesting, and marketing in places with different local ecologies. An area of disagreement among scholars is whether Aztecs made an adjustment in their calendar for the fact that the solar year is in actuality 365 and a quarter days. The leap year of one extra day every four years is how we correct for the precise length of a solar year, thereby allowing for a fixed calendar in which a new year begins the same time of year every year. It seems both logical and likely that the Aztecs, intensely dependent on agriculture to feed the large, dense population, made some kind of correction, perhaps based upon alignments between the sun and the surrounding topography as well as human-built features. The sources on religion do not shed light on this matter, perhaps because chroniclers recording calendrical information did not fully understand how Aztec calendars worked nor how the solar calendar related to the mountainous landscape of the basin, especially to the east where the sun rises.

Each named month was associated with one or more patron deities. Aztec communities carried out ceremonies honoring the deities of each month. Those ceremonies marked periods of the agricultural cycle; they celebrated plant and human fertility and recognized the need for rain, the significance of war, the value of certain occupations, and the high status placed on rulers and nobles. Other ceremonies, held during specific months, occurred every four and eight years. For example, during the eighteenth month, Izcalli, the feast called Pillahuanaliztli (Festival of Children) took place every four years. Every eight years, the feast called Atamalcualiztli (Eating Water Tamales) took place. In addition, Aztecs undertook ceremonies for the day signs of particular deities. The *Primeros memoriales*, the *Florentine Codex*, and Durán's religious chronicle refer to these as "fiestas movibles" or "movable feasts" because they did not have a fixed day, neither during the divinatory nor solar year. Particular groups of Aztecs – men, women, warriors, seamstresses, merchants – would celebrate the day sign of their patron deities on these movable feast days. Other ceremonies also existed such as those for the death of a tlatoani, the naming of a new one, success in war, or the return of merchant expeditions safely, as well as life-cycle ceremonies for the stages of life. No matter one's status in any Aztec community, ritual participation took up a lot of time virtually every day as household ceremonies dedicated to the hearth and household altar brought worship out of temples and public spaces into every home.

One of the most important ceremonies that all Aztecs participated in was the New Fire ceremony (Toxiuhmolpilia; Binding of Years), a major ritual that occurred every fifty-two years when both the divinatory and solar calendars began anew on the same day, the day Ome Acatl (Two Reed). Archaeologists have shown that the ceremony dates back at least to the Early Postclassic with the Mexica refining it to emphasize *their* centrality to the maintenance of political and social order. That fifty-two-year period, the *xiuhmolpilli* (bundle of years), represented the Aztec century. Aztecs felt anxiety and fear as a xiuhmolpilli drew closer to its end because they had to await the beginning of a new fifty-two-year cycle, which – if it did not begin again – would signal the end of the Fifth

Sun. The ending of that age would throw their world into chaos. At the end of such a cycle, as evening approached, people put out all fires across the cities, towns, and villages of the Basin of Mexico – temples, palaces, workshops, homes. Deity figurines and ceramic pots were thrown away, pregnant women were masked and guarded so they would not become fearsome beasts, and as it became dark, priests known as "fire priests" (*tlenamacaque*) and others dressed as the deities, including Quetzalcoatl and rain, fertility, maize, and earth deities (Tlaloc, Xipe Totec, Centeotl, and Teteo innan). The priests left Tenochtitlan and walked to a hilly shrine to the south of the city, visible across the basin, called Huixachtlan (Thorn Tree Place).

Watching the movement of the cluster of stars we know as Pleiades, the Aztec priests looked for the constellation they called Tianquiztli (Marketplace) to reach the center of the sky. When that happened, a fire priest started a fire on the chest of a man to be killed, with the fire used to light a stack of firewood upon which the victim's heart was placed as an offering. By regenerating fire, the sun would continue its daily and yearly journey. Men, women, and children cut their ears in order to splatter blood in the direction of the fire at Huixachtlan. Priests and runners took fires back first to Tenochtitlan, then to other communities throughout the Aztec region. Within Tenochtitlan, after relighting the fire at Huitzilopochtli's altar at the Templo Mayor, discussed below, (see Fig 2.1), altar fires in other important buildings in the sacred precinct were relit. Priests then carried fire to the four quarters from where fire was transported to each neighborhood's local temple. Rejoicing, neighborhood

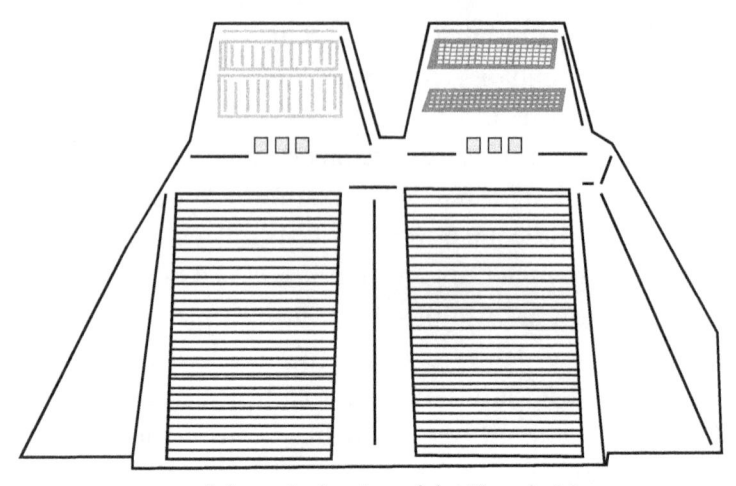

FIG. 2.1 Schematic drawing of the Templo Mayor
Public Domain. Creative Commons. https://commons.wikimedia.org/
wiki/File:Templo_Mayor.svg

residents delivered fire to their households. New household implements appeared; men, women, and children wore new clothing; and they offered incense and food to the newly lit household hearth. After fasting until noon, feasts were then enjoyed by all. We see in this ceremony not only a reverence for spiritual and secular (lived) time but also the Aztec reverence for space and place.

Places had widely shared sacred meanings, and just as Aztec chronicles of creation illustrate the significance of timekeeping, so do they illustrate the meanings of place and space. From the lowliest household to the most exalted temples and high mountain tops, sacred *places* were a part of the everyday Aztec spiritual world. Aztec homes had many sacred associations because they were places not only of social and economic activities but ritual ones also. The hearth with its three stones and their related female deities, one of whom was Chantico, an ancient fire goddess, held the fire used to cook and keep the central area warm. Fire was also associated with another ancient god, Huehueteotl (Old God), one of the oldest of the Aztec deities who they pictured as old and understood to be one among the deities of earlier Mesoamerican societies. The fires burning at the center of homes and temples kept this deity at the center of Aztec worship. Many women's activities in the home also had sacred associations beyond the work they did to produce or sell goods of household and commercial value. Sweeping and cleaning, thought of primarily as women's work, helped to keep household and cosmic order, with sweeping considered an offering to the gods. Many household rituals were carried out in relation to sweeping, cooking, and honoring the dead. As Louise Burkhart points out, cooking became sacred, associated with both household fire and hearthstones, with girls' umbilical cords buried "not just by the hearth but directly beneath the grinding stone." Homes held the burials not just of daughters' umbilical cords but also the ashes of dead household members who had been cremated and the placentas of children born to the women of the household. The energies released by those decomposing substances allowed the sun to remain in motion and transformed those substances into new life, human and plant.

Temples also were sacred places, from those in neighborhoods to the temples of the sacred centers of altepeme throughout Aztec-associated regions and Mesoamerica more broadly. Urban ceremonial centers contained large pyramids, likely modeled on mountains, that expressed reverence for those geological forms, a felt connection to the sun, moon, and stars as studies of archaeoastronomy have shown, as well as for the centrality that was a feature of Aztec spatial ideas. Tenochtitlan's great dual-chambered pyramid, the Templo Mayor featuring a design based on Aztec cultures prior to the Mexica, highlighted worship of two of the Mexica's most important deities. These were Huitzilopochtli, a warrior and solar patron deity especially associated with the Mexica, and Tlaloc, a rain deity worshipped widely by Aztec peoples. The foundations of this temple probably date back to the first half of the fourteenth century, but it – like many important Mesoamerican temple pyramids – took on additional levels and layers over time. While the Mexica copied earlier Aztec dual-chambered temples, the Tetzcoca copied the Mexica temple. As the Tetzcoca became more closely aligned with the Mexica under their ruler Nezahualcoyotl (that altepetl's ruler from about 1414–1472), their worship of Tonacateuctli and female goddesses, sisters of the sun and moon according to Alva Ixtlilxochitl, became downplayed in favor of Huitzilopochtli. Nezahualcoyotl built a dual-chambered temple like that of Tenochtitlan dedicated to Huitzilopochtli and Tlaloc.

Expressing another of the ideas associated with this particular structure, that of imperial growth, Tenochtitlan's temple grew most during the reigns of the tlatoani Itzcoatl, Moteuczoma Ilhuicamina, and Axayacatl, but the second Moteuczoma was still having the structure modified before Spaniards arrived. Rulers' coronation ceremonies and funerals took place, at least in part, at this pyramid, celebrating the place of Mexica rulers in Tenochtitlan and the Excan tlatoloyan. These increasingly elaborate ceremonies heralded the sacralizing of Mexica military and political power as did the placement of sculpture on and near the pyramid. Perhaps the best example is the bas relief sculpture of Coyolxauhqui (Bells on Cheek), one of Huitzilopochtli's sisters, which Aztec architects or sculptors placed at the foot of the stairs leading up to his temple. This dramatic sculpture, an image discussed in detail in later chapters, commemorates Huitzilopochtli's victory over her early in Mexica history as she is shown in a defeated, dismembered pose. This version of the stone, the one known today, commemorates the mythic event just mentioned and perhaps also a specific historical event, the ruler Axayacatl's defeat of the ruler of Tlatelolco, Moquihuix, which happened in 1473, and brought about Tlatelolco's subordination to Tenochtitlan thereafter. The Mexica often connected significant events of their earlier past with the achievements of later rulers as they memorialized them in sculptures that carried religious, historical, and political meanings.

This main temple pyramid, part of a ceremonial precinct that lay at the center of Tenochtitlan, represented Mexica spirituality, history, identity, and power. Its twin towers and deities brought together the two key components of Mexica identity – Chichimeca and Tolteca – so historically important as these identities came together during the migrations mentioned earlier in this book. Rulers broadcast their power by enlarging the structure and by hosting ritualized slaughters of captured enemy warriors after victorious campaigns of conquest. Some monthly ceremonies for Huitzilopochtli – those held during the months Toxcatl, Tlaxochimaco, Teotl eco/

Pachtontli, and Panquetzaliztli – also featured the Templo Mayor as a site of ritual activity. This was especially the case for Panquetzaliztli (Raising Banners) which celebrated this central site but also helped integrate the Mexica central sacred place with those of surrounding communities. During this month, an image of the deity Painal, related closely to Huitzilopochtli, was carried by a priest around a ritual circuit that included the island and several mainland cities on the western and southern sides of Lake Tetzcoco, beginning and ending at the Templo Mayor. After this procession, four slaves brought by merchants rising up in the merchant hierarchy were put to death at the temple.

Tlaloc, the other deity commemorated at the Templo Mayor, tended to be celebrated by the Mexica and other Aztec groups in many locations, often mountains, in and around Tenochtitlan. Six of eighteen months, one-third, celebrated him or closely related rain and water deities. While Huitzilopochtli had solar and sky connections, Tlaloc had mountain and earth associations, with beliefs about mountains closely connected to rain, water, and the earth because mountains were thought to contain water. Some of those months featured sacrifices of adults or children on mountaintops or in lakes at points north, south, east, and west of Tenochtitlan. Through these actions, Aztecs hoped they could create rain and encourage maize to grow. Aztecs also venerated salt water, salty lake and ocean water, represented by Tlaloc's sister Huixtocihuatl. During the month Tecuilhuitontli (Lords' Little Feast Day), a month that also celebrated maize, the sun, and social and cosmic harmony between the ruler and the ruled, Aztecs brought offerings to Tlaloc at the Templo Mayor and many other sites in and around the Basin of Mexico.

At the Templo Mayor, archaeological excavations show that Tlaloc received the largest number of offerings. While more ceremonies and ritual killings appear to have been carried out in worship of Huitzilopochtli at the main temple, both adult and child sacrifices that honored Tlaloc, water, and fertility occurred regularly. The ritual killing of children had the purpose of conjuring tears and rain and took place at the Templo Mayor and multiple other sites, especially mountainous ones. Along with these human remains, offerings to Tlaloc and water-related deities included deity sculptures, jade beads, ceramic objects featuring Tlaloc imagery, and sculptural images as well as the actual remains of fish, snails, tortoises, and crocodiles. These objects came from near and far, with many of the animal remains originating from the Gulf and Pacific coasts. Rain, mountains, rivers, lakes, and oceans – all water or containing it – came from Tlalocan. The earth as mentioned earlier, Aztecs thought, was a huge cipactli or crocodile floating on waters that emerged from Tlalocan, Tlaloc's domain – a level above the earth – from where it flowed under the earth into mountains and wherever it was found.

As hallowed a location as the Templo Mayor was, this place of offerings and sacred, though often politicized, violence intended to honor both the earth with its water and the sun with its vital energy was only one among many temples within and beyond Tenochtitlan that carried solemn meanings for the Aztecs. Late in the dry season (late April or early May), during the month of Huey Tozoztli (Great Vigil), four rulers – those of

Tenochtitlan, Tetzcoco, Tlacopan, and Xochimilco – traveled to Mount Tlaloc, east of Tenochtitlan, in the heart of the region known as Acolhuacan. Walking up to the pyramid at the top of this mountain, the rulers brought gifts, including clothing similar to that used to dress a new ruler during his coronation. Having symbolically become a ruler, Tlaloc would then bring rain, as the rainy season during the normal course of the Basin of Mexico's cycle of weather would begin around early June. But it was also the case that as this ceremony was happening, another ceremony was being carried out at the Templo Mayor.

Mexica priests erected a large tree, "Tota," or Our Father, surrounded by four smaller trees. A young woman representing Chalchiuhtlicue, Jade Skirt (a companion to Tlaloc), sat within this miniature forest. Once the priests learned that the rulers had carried out the Mount Tlaloc ceremonies, the living Chalchiuhtlicue and Tota were brought by canoe to Pantitlan, an island shrine to this goddess, site of a spring feeding Lake Tetzcoco. The priests then placed the tree, a tree of life symbolizing plant regeneration, near the spring and sacrificed the young woman. Her blood poured into the lake. Aztecs connected sacred places through their movements among those places as so many ceremonies were carried out across sites they connected through linear or circular movements of ritual participants. Such movements created a dynamic landscape across which values were exchanged, transformations of humans and substances occurred, and cosmic balance between center and periphery was achieved, at least momentarily. That balance could only ever be achieved temporarily because it was always threatened by chaos. All this movement took place across space, horizontal and vertical. These peregrinations tied together what David Carrasco, noted scholar of religion, calls the Aztec "ceremonial landscape."

Remembering that the earth, *tlalticpac*, was conceived of as a gigantic crocodile surrounded by water, with a center (*tlalxico*, earth's navel) from which the four horizontal, cardinal directions extended north, called Mictlampa, Place of Death; south, Huitztlampa, Place of Thorns; east, Tlapcopa, Place of Dawn; and west, Cihuatlampa, Place of Women. Aztecs associated each of these directions, including the center, with a deity, color, sacred tree, and bird. Tenochtitlan, like many altepeme, was divided into four parts that mirrored the four directions with a central, sacred place, the ceremonial precinct.

If we think vertically rather than horizontally, the earth as horizontal place lay between a series of upper layers perhaps numbering thirteen and collectively called Topan (above us), and nine under layers, Mictlan, with Tlalticpac being the first level of both. Aztecs associated a deity and bird with each of the upper levels, the under levels represented a place through which one of the souls or energies of the dead, discussed further in Chapter 5, passed before reaching the lowest level, Mictlan. While early colonial sources as well as scholarly literature often use the terms "heavens" to refer to the upper levels, I avoid the term due to its Christian associations. The thirteen-level upper schema may have been found predominantly in the Basin of Mexico, likely imposed by the Mexica late in Mexica and Excan tlatoloyan history. Aztecs in other areas described vertical space as divided into nine upper and lower levels. It is possible, however, as recent scholarship has argued, that the notion of fixed upper and lower levels is an idea heavily influenced by friars' descriptions of heaven and hell.

However local Aztec communities conceived of vertical space, horizontal space was thought of in the same way across much of Nahuatl-speaking areas with horizontal space and time closely related. Aztecs connected each of the four cardinal directions with five day signs, one of the days designating a thirteen-year segment of the fifty-two year calendar round. And as described above, a deity supported each direction, but these sky bearer deity identities varied regionally. The close connection Aztecs drew between timekeeping and deities brings up a question about how Aztecs thought about sacred power and those who held it, rooted in the idea of *teotl*, a word Spaniards translated as "dios" and scholars translate as god or deity.

The Deities and Those Who Served Them

Deities and priests have already been mentioned many times in this chapter; but the answer to the question of what Aztecs considered a deity is not so clear-cut because the word for deity or god, teotl, had multiple meanings. And what Spaniards took to be gods existed in *many* forms and variations. Father Molina, the learned early Spanish linguist who compiled the early dictionaries mentioned in the previous chapter, translated teotl simply as god. But the root term "*teo-*" appears in Nahuatl in a variety of contexts. It can refer to an anthropomorphized creature sculpted or painted with human-appearing faces and bodies and acting in or on the world as humans did – giving birth, speaking, and having family-like relationships as mothers, fathers, daughters, sons, sisters, or brothers. But these supernaturals could also take the form of weather, places, or inanimate objects and they could de- and re-compose in multiple forms. There was no overall pantheon through which all, or even most, *teteo* (plural of teotl) were related to each other. As supernatural figures, teteo were so flexible that whether they are gods in the fixed sense we mean by the term is open to debate; some scholars consider them manifestations of sacrality, the divine force mentioned below. The word also referred not only to sacred beings but also to hard-to-explain, even monstrous, things.

When attached to a word, teo- could modify that word's meaning as Molly Bassett, a scholar of religion, has shown. The word *teoxihuitl* meant "fine turquoise" and implied rarity, preciousness, and divinity. Aztecs did not use teo- as a modifier for all objects, only a small number. When they did, they used it to suggest special qualities of power, a divine, vital force. This force or energy imbued deity impersonators, living images known as *ixiptlahuan* (sing., *ixiptla*; sometimes clearly male, sometimes clearly female, sometimes gender ambiguous); elements of nature such as wind, sun, or bodies of water; or objects, naturally occurring or human-made, with a kind of energy or animacy. This animacy represented an empowering spirit or force in all things alive or not. The tonalamatl, for example, likely had a kind of animating power. Aztecs, thus, did not divide the world around them into supernatural and natural, sacred and secular – it was all *one* sacred field charged with that vital energy. They represented this animism in ways that expressed a dynamic and deep history through stories of creation describing supernatural actions that ordered and explained human relationships in a transitory, fragile, endangered world. Through these stories, the types of deities and forces Aztecs saw as affecting them past and present, forces they tried to keep in balance through sacred actions, became apparent.

The collectivity of Aztec supernaturals consisted of deities older, those that had existed at least from the time of Teotihuacan on, and newer, patron deities associated with altepeme and ethnicities that came into being during the later Postclassic period. The pantheon also grew to include the deities of people conquered by the Excan tlatoloyan and brought into its systems of worship. In his classic article on Aztec religion, H. B. Nicholson categorized Aztec deities as organized into three groups: celestial creativity-divine paternalism; rain-moisture-agricultural fertility; and war-sacrifice-sanguinary nourishment of the sun and earth. Working from these basic categories, I have organized them somewhat differently to emphasize the functions of this complex set of spiritual beings. Aztecs worshipped deities of the uppermost and lowest realms, earth mothers, gods of fate and destiny, founders and patrons, sky and fire gods, water, and maize and other plants (see Fig. 2.2). The deities of the uppermost sky (Omeyocan, Two Place) and the underworld (Mictlan) were both male and female. Creation and destruction thus had female and male associations, embodying the balance of sacred forces the Aztecs sought through their ritual practices. Earth, water, and plant deities often were female. Among the earth deities, female-gendered deities predominated, with water- and plant-related deities more gender balanced. These could

Creator Deities
Ometeuctli (M), Two Lord
Omecihuatl (F), Two Lady

Earth Mothers
Teteo innan, Gods Their Mother
Cihuacoatl, Woman Snake
Atlatonan, Water Our Mother
Chimalman, Shield Extended
Xochiquetzal, Flower Feather
Tonan, Our Mother
Yohualticitl, Night Doctor

Deity of Fate and Destiny
Tezcatlipoca, Mirror Smoking (M)

Founders, Patrons, and War Deities
Huitzilopochtli, Hummingbird Left (M)
Quetzalcoatl, Feather Snake (M)
Mixcoatl, Cloud Snake (M)
Camaxtli, God of Hunting (M)

Deities of the Sky and Fire
Tonatiuh, Sun (M)
Huehueteotl, Ancient God (M)

Water Deities
Tlaloc, Of the Earth (M)
Tlaloque, Rain gods
Chalchiuhtlicue, Jade Her Skirt (F)
Huixtocihuatl, Salt Woman (F)

Maize Deities
Centeotl, Dried Ear of Maize God (M)
Xochipilli, Flower Noble (M)
Chicomecoatl, Seven Snake (F)
Xilonen, Young Maize Ear Doll (F)

FIG. 2.2 Classifications of major deities and translations of their names
Sources: Molina, *Vocabulario*; Caso, *The Aztecs*; Nicholson, "Religion in Pre-Hispanic Central Mexico"

be represented by male or female gods, exemplified by the water deities, Tlaloc (Of the Earth), deity of rain, and his consort, Chalchiuhtlicue (Jade Her Skirt), goddess of lakes, the oceans, and other bodies of water. Maize deities were predominantly female, but other plant and flower-related gods could be male (for example, many of the *octli*, or pulque, gods) or female, such as Xochiquetzal (Flower Feather; goddess of flowers, grains, and the patroness of weavers). Related to earth mother deities, often shown in sculptural and painted images with similar features including skull-like heads, tousled hair, and claws rather than hands, are female spiritual beings known collectively as *cihuapipiltin* or *cihuateteo* (women nobles, women gods – these names used interchangeably for women who died in childbirth whose energies became transformed into these beings), and *tzitzimime*, what art historian Elizabeth Hill Boone has called "celestial monsters" who could harm or heal.

Two sets of deities especially signified war, hunting, and violence and were associated either with specific altepeme or certain social groups within them. The supreme patron deity of Aztec warriors, was the solar deity, Tonatiuh. Patron of the eagle and jaguar warriors, these men pledged to provide the deity with the hearts and blood needed to keep the sun in motion by capturing prisoners who would later be sacrificed. Huitzilopochtli, also a solar god, symbolized war generally and the bloody complex of ideas around it; he also served as an emblem of Mexica history and identity. Especially associated with that group, broader worship of Huitzilopochtli began later, after the rise of Mexica and Excan tlatoloyan imperialism and never spread much beyond the Basin of Mexico. Indigenous-descended historians of the early colonial period made clear the deep connection of patron deities to the people who worshipped them. These deities guided them to the places they settled and remained important in the spiritual lives of those peoples. Alvarado Tezozomoc described this connection for Huitzilopochtli and the Mexica; Alva Ixtlilxochitl and Chimalpahin did so for Tezcatlipoca and the Tetzcoca and Chalca respectively.

Another set of deities, what Nicholson calls the "Mixcoatl-Tlahuizcalpantecuhtli Complex," has characteristics that overlap with Huitzilopochtli in relation to war and the patron role. Mixcoatl – Cloud Snake – was the tutelary deity of Tlaxcallan. Of likely Chichimeca origin, he and his alternative form Camaxtli, represented hunting. Although hunting supplied a smaller portion of Aztec diets than it did in the Chichimeca past, the activity symbolized warfare and killing and still provided some food. We will see that the Tlaxcalteca were highly skilled fighters, who had a history of resistance against the Mexica and would eventually greatly aid the Spanish in their war against the Mexica. Hunting also provided blood for offerings – especially that of deer – important in several ceremonies, for example, the coronation rituals for supreme rulers.

Religious functionaries, *teopixque* and *cihuateopixque* (sacred guardians, male and female respectively), played a number of different roles in Aztec communities, with priests (*tlamacazque* and *cihuatlamacazque*) key to the ceremonies for the deities carried out in their temples (*teocalli*, god house) or in their names in the many other sacred spaces Aztecs used for worship. Most priests came from the noble class. The priesthood represented a commitment to spending time at the *calmecac* (a priestly school, primarily a school for some sons and daughters of the nobility) of major altepeme to become highly educated in the specialized knowledge that these functionaries of the divine were expected to learn, understand, and communicate. They tended to their responsibilities full-time. These duties included maintaining temples and their deity images, praying and giving offerings including their own blood, conducting sacrificial and other ceremonies at temples and around altepeme and beyond, reading and interpreting calendrical books, teaching initiates, curing, and supervising younger priests and priestesses and others who serviced the most important temples, which likely had a hierarchy of staff.

These men and women rose through the ranks from *tlamacazton* (lowest level priest/ess) to either Quetzalcoatl Totec tlamacazqui or Quetzalcoatl Tlaloc tlamacazqui (the high priest of Huitzilopochtli's and Tlaloc's temples, respectively), but priestesses do not appear to have reached the upper levels, nor did they necessarily dedicate their entire lives to serving as cihuatlamacazque. Those priestesses who advanced through the female hierarchy served as *cihuacuacuiltin* (*cuacuiltin*, a high rank for priests and priestesses). This level represented the highest rank religious women could reach. These particular women likely served for their adult lives and trained in the *cihuacalmecac* (women's religious school) associated with the Templo Mayor.

While "tlamacazqui" means priest, a possible etymology for the word is "giver of things." What did they give? Knowledge, morality, ideology in service of both temple and state. But priests also received food from lands dedicated to temples, the sacred lands, (*teotlalli*) worked by commoners; a share of state tribute; offerings to temples; alms for which priests at certain times of the year begged; and the right to steal, again during certain times of the year. All these activities and resources helped support priests and the deities' houses. Lay people also provided devotional labor for temples beyond the goods and agricultural labor Aztec commoner and noble households gave. For example, both women and men mostly from the noble class took vows to serve particular temples for specified periods of time, including the "older brothers" (*tiachcauh*) of Huitzilopochtli who served in his temple for a year. Young boys, and perhaps girls, from the calmecac of Tenochtitlan also provided labor – generally sweeping and cleaning – whether they intended to become priests or not. Even rulers and high officials, usually not themselves priests (though in Chololan the highest ranking priests participated in ruling that altepetl), bore ritual responsibilities to help maintain the altepetl and renew life, human and other, based upon their participation in calendrical ceremonies throughout the year. They prayed for rain, celebrated successful harvests, and took part in ceremonies brought blood to the earth and gods for the regeneration of solar energy, key to maintaining life.

Historian Lisa Sousa also reminds us that the female physician, *ticitl*, a gender-neutral term for female or male medical practitioners, cured people, sanctified the birth of a baby, and also participated in marriage and funerary ceremonies, especially the funerals of women who died giving birth, thus carrying out both medical *and* spiritual responsibilities. The speeches given by midwives and family members as a child was being born suggest the respect given to midwives arose not simply from their medical roles. They were also spiritually authoritative figures who could call upon powerful goddesses such as Cihuacoatl, Yohualticitl, and Chalchiuhtlicue to aid the birth and protect both the mother and child. Other practitioners – some priests, some not – engaged in divination, shape-shifting transformations into animals (the *nanahualtin*, sing., *nahualli*), and there were those who saw visions through magic or hallucinogens. Deities and ordinary people also could change form. Tezcatlipoca was especially known to have this capacity. These practitioners – and of course priests and priestesses – carried out state, neighborhood, and household rituals. The complexity of the Aztec spiritual world is hinted at in the *Anales de Cuauhtitlan* when the author treats spirit figures as historical personages, rather than as deities as they are depicted in the *Florentine Codex*. These figures took war captives to Tollan and initiated sanctified killings by arrows long before the appearance of any Aztecs or their communities.

Ceremonies

Ritual feasting and celebration, calendric and non-calendric, went on throughout the solar and tonalpohualli ritual year. Calendric ceremonies fell into two categories: fixed and movable. The xiuhpohualli structured the fixed ceremonies which consisted of eighteen festivals, eleven of which clearly related to the agricultural cycle. The festivals concerned themselves with water, plant growth, and/or harvesting. Seven of those directly involved Tlaloc; others featured fertility goddesses, maize deities, and earth and the deities of its products. The beginning of the Aztec year, between the second half of February and the first days of March, saw several months' ceremonies devoted to rain and agricultural fertility with Tlaloc, his female consorts, and plant deities celebrated through singing and dancing, offerings and blessings of flowers and plants, and the offering of children and deity embodiments, the ixiptlahuan.

The first month, Atl Cahualo (Water Stops), featured the decoration of poles erected for the festival with paper banners, offerings to maize deities, and the sacrifice of children on mountains and in lakes to make tears flow to encourage rain. During these ceremonies, the Aztecs celebrated Tlaloc, Chalchiuhtlicue, Quetzalcoatl, Chicomecoatl, and Xilonen, water, creation, and maize gods and goddesses. Other monthly festivals celebrated additional important supernaturals, especially Huitzilopochtli for the Mexica, hunting and hunting deities, rulers and the nobility, and the patron deities of particular occupational groups. The Toxcatl (Dry Thing) ceremonies, which took place during May, featured the worship of Tezcatlipoca, Huitzilopochtli, and Cihuacoatl, creator, patron-warrior, and earth mother deities. Beyond Tenochtitlan, other culture hero deities like Camaxtli in Tlaxcallan were celebrated during this month. This was a month of renewal ceremonies, with the making and eating of *tzoalli* or dough images of Huitzilopochtli, quail sacrifices, and food offerings that included corn and amaranth tamales. Aztecs decorated shrines and patios with branches and flowers. They feasted, bled children, and killed ixiptlahuan of Tezcatlipoca and Huitzilopochtli.

The ritual killing of Tezcatlipoca, among the most powerful of creator and patron deities, represented the culmination of a rite in which a handsome, youthful male captive, one who was thought to be as close to physically perfect as possible, lived for a year as Tezcatlipoca, partaking of music and tobacco. He went before the ruler who gave gifts to adorn him and help along his transformation from man to deity. Near to the time of his sacrifice, called a *nextlahualli* or debt payment, he was provided with four women, attired as the deities Xochiquetzal, Xilonen, Atlatonan, and Huixtocihuatl, goddesses of sustenance and the earth. Tezcatlipoca's ixiptla lived intimately with them. He traveled in and around Tenochtitlan with the women who distributed food and other gifts. At the end of Toxcatl he was taken to Chalco to a small temple there. He went up the stairs of the temple breaking the flutes and whistles he had been given, whereupon priests grabbed him, placed him on a sacrificial stone, and removed his heart. Coincidentally, Toxcatl feasting was the setting at the main temple for the slaughter of many high-ranking nobles by Pedro de Alvarado and other Spaniards during the Spanish-Mexica War, an event with disastrous, nearly fatal consequences for Spaniards, which will be discussed in Chapter 7.

Several ceremonies focused on the roles and responsibilities of rulers and nobles. These included the seventh and eight months in June and July, Tecuilhuitontli (Lords' Little Feast Day) and Huey Tecuilhuitl (Lords' Great Feast Day). Tecuilhuitontli featured ceremonies dedicated to the deities Huixtocihuatl and Xochipilli as well as Tlaloc; Huey Tecuilhuitl celebrated Xilonen, Cihuacoatl, and Chimalman. These mostly female deities signified flowers, plants, salt, and the earth. Ixiptlahuan of the goddesses were put to death, nobles provided feasts for commoners, and rulers had the obligation to distribute food to people in Tenochtitlan and other nearby altepeme. Demonstrating the tlatoani's role as conserver of cosmic order by taking the responsibility to oversee the community's well-being, the Mexica ruler showed his generosity and appreciation for commoners' labor and productivity through distributions of food as well as armaments for warriors. The required presence of rulers from surrounding communities' reinforced *their* subordination. While such distributions to commoners, especially of food, ameliorated poverty and reinforced a sense of an altepetl's identity, these ceremonial distributions also strengthened the nobility's superior position both within and beyond Tenochtitlan. Yet the themes of balance and reciprocity between the two classes – noble and commoner – played out, demonstrating how each needed and had obligations to the other.

Rulers played a role, too, in the last month of the year, Izcalli (Growth) when they participated in ceremonies for their patron deity Xiuhteuctli, another name for Huehueteotl (Fire Deity). But commoners also participated in this month's ceremonies in significant ways. This ceremony – along with those of the third, fourth, and fifth months, Tozoztontli (Little Vigil), Huey Tozoztli (Great Vigil), and Toxcatl respectively – overlapped with ceremonies that concerned the life cycle. Izcalli featured ceremonies to stretch children as well as every four years piercing their ears and assigning guardians, using the words for uncle (someone's uncle, literally), *tetla*, and aunt (someone's aunt), *teahui*. During this annual festival, households produced tamales and tortillas made of corn that were eaten, and amaranth-dough effigies of Xiuhteuctli were made and honored. The Izcalli ceremonies show the layers of participation in monthly ceremonies, from rulers to commoners, from major temples to individual households.

Preparations took place throughout each month for the eighteen feasting cycles culminating in the major ceremonies usually carried out at the end of each month. Some festivals emphasized the deities especially celebrated by rulers, nobles, and warriors, others featured commoners generally, artisans, and merchants celebrating the agricultural cycle, the deities of particular occupational groups, and the life cycle. Additional feasts highlighted Aztecs' special concern for the growth and well-being of children. As all-encompassing as the eighteen monthly ceremonies appear to have been, requiring much planning and preparation, many resources, and using household and public spaces from local temples to the temples of the ceremonial center as well as roads, fields, lakes, and mountains, other ritual cycles also existed. Especially significant were rituals connected to the 260-day calendar, the tonalpohualli. Each day, with its unique day and number designation, had a connection to a specific deity, some worshipped by entire altepetl, others by specific groups such as nobles, merchants, weavers, or fisherman.

While both calendric cycles involved extensive ritual preparation and activities, Aztecs also carried out similar activities – fasting, keeping vigil, ritualized bleedings, making offerings – as part of life-cycle celebrations. These included birth and naming, entering and completing education in the calmecac and *telpochcalli* (a school mainly for commoner boys where they received military training and performed public works), recognizing achievements in war, marriage, elevation to high military, commercial, or political rank or office, as well as death.

Fasting and other ritual actions also marked many other occasions. These actions included not only the daily household rituals that women of all households carried out at or near the home's hearth as well as the altar area of homes' patios and the frequent rituals farmers carried out at their fields, but also homecoming ceremonies for merchants and warriors that took place where and whenever appropriate. Civic ceremonies such as enthroning rulers, dedicating new religious or governmental structures or monuments before and after war, especially for important conquests, also meant undertaking feasting. These ceremonies featured offerings of sacred substances often derived from the ritual killing of animals and humans. Codices, annals, and descriptive texts in Nahuatl or Spanish make clear that all of these ritual activities entailed enormous economic investments in infrastructure, implements, costumes, jewelry, flowers, and food.

Many such ceremonies, sacred and civic, involved the deaths of human beings. The practice is undoubtedly what Aztecs are best known for. Reports by Spaniards of ritual killing, including of Spaniards during the invasion period, affixed a persistent image of them as irrational, bloodthirsty killers in the popular imagination as well as in scholarly discussions of them. But neither archaeological nor ethnohistorical evidence bears out the idea that Aztecs put to death anything like the thousands upon thousands of people that sixteenth-century writers reported. Even the 20,000 per year number that Aztec experts assert for the Mexica seems problematic when weighed again human remains and Nahuatl-language documentation, neither of which support such high figures. Fray Diego Durán's oft-repeated claim in his historical volume of 80,400 being put to death at the 1487 dedication ceremony held at Tenochtitlan's Templo Mayor under the ruler Ahuitzotl is almost certainly wildly inflated. The *Anales de Cuauhtitlan* and the *Historia de la nación chichimeca* of Alva Ixtlilxochitl both repeat Durán's immense figure. The *Codex Telleriano-Remensis* depicts the number of those killed at the event celebrating the Templo Mayor as 20,000.

What has also been called "ritual killing" or "ceremonial homicide" took place in several contexts but always as part of a broad set of beliefs and practices centered on the importance of the ideas of nourishment of deities, propitiation, atonement, consecration, and even the activity of accompanying a high-status deceased individual on their afterlife journey. The gods had offered themselves to create the sun and maintain its motion, and they had created humans. To honor those creations and to support human life, Aztecs frequently carried out rituals through which they honored the deities by bestowing offerings. The giving of offerings was an important activity carried out to recognize, celebrate, and appease those deities. Offerings both propitiated deities for their acts of creation, repaying the debt humans owed them, but they also reflected the hope that a deity might provide a benefit such as success in battle. Through these continuous reciprocal acts between humans and deities, Aztecs achieved a kind of balance between life and death, helping them to negotiate what they saw as a dangerous, highly unpredictable world. By giving things of material and symbolic value, as described above when discussing offerings at the Templo Mayor, Aztecs expressed their desire to achieve that balance.

Blood, which they considered divine, was the most valuable offering. It symbolized fertility and the continuity of human life, even though death was a certainty. Through "self-sacrifice" (also referred to as "auto-sacrifice"), Aztecs drew blood from ears, arms, thighs, and genitals. Priests frequently engaged in this practice, but all Aztecs drew blood, hoping for human and plant fertility, purification, and to nourish and repay the debt to the creator deities. Yet the greatest offering human beings could give to their divinities was to provide human lives to them, offering hearts and blood, and that they did. Aztecs carried out such ceremonial killings in various ways. Victims might be burned, drowned, shot with arrows, or have their throats cut, depending on the context, the deity, and the type of propitiation believed most appropriate. During several of the solar months, for example, Aztec priests drowned children to draw their tears, thought to bring on rain as mentioned. Death could also be used as punishment for certain crimes, particularly adultery and some types of theft. And merchants trying to move up their status hierarchy made vows to achieve safety and success by engaging in ritual killings to achieve a governing position in that hierarchy.

However, the most common form of such killing was removal of the heart. It and other forms of ritual killing took place in several different contexts. One such context occurred as part of the monthly ceremonies during which Aztecs offered blood and hearts to a particular deity, one who had been embodied by a living person, the ixiptla, who was then put to death to honor that deity. Aztecs also put warriors and slaves from defeated kingdoms to death during monthly and other kinds of ceremonies. This kind of highly ritualized killing held religious significance but also helped to broadcast and reinforce both Triple Alliance and most especially Mexica political dominance. It was in political contexts such as celebrating victory, enthroning a new ruler, or dedicating a monument that the greatest number of killings occurred, a practice that intensified in Tenochtitlan during the later fifteenth century. Both archaeological and ethnohistorical evidence suggest that for specific occasions Mexica rulers sought to use large numbers of sacrificial killings as a kind of terroristic propaganda. Tlatoque strove to enforce political order within the imperial realm and frighten those beyond it with a threat of the violence that could be brought to bear on enemy realms. But the accuracy of the most dramatic claims of high numbers simply cannot be demonstrated. In other settings during monthly ceremonies in which the numbers of people put to death were much lower over the course of a year, perhaps in the hundreds in the largest altepeme, the practice – one deeply embedded in Mesoamerican societies dating much further back in time – was intimately connected to the ideas of balance, reciprocity, and the felt need to regenerate life by making offerings of precious, sacred substances, the blood, hearts, other body parts, skin, and skulls, obtained through death.

There is no doubt that such ceremonies inflamed Spaniards who used their disgust at them to justify their own murderous behavior, empire-building project, and emerging socio-racial hierarchy. But because Spaniards failed to grasp the meanings of ceremonial killing and often greatly exaggerated the numbers of "human sacrifices," does not mean Aztecs neither observed the practice nor conveyed some of its meanings to themselves and others. In thinking about the Aztecs, even as scholars and readers interested in this civilization attempt to understand the numbers accurately and consider the meanings of ritual killing, we must remember that violence has long been a part of the sacred in world religions, its "heart and secret soul" as religious scholar René Girard observed. We need to confront the idea that Aztec ritual killings are hard for us to envision. They indeed killed, removed hearts, and in the case of one monthly ceremony, Tlacaxipehualiztli (Men Flaying), the second month of the year, they killed captured warriors and removed their skins. These were then worn by poor individuals who engaged in mock battles and collected alms as they wandered throughout Tenochtitlan.

During Tlacaxipehualiztli several kinds of ritual killing occurred. Men, women and children, and warriors and captives who had been made slaves were killed, Diego Durán says with the goal of creating "fright and horror," especially in foreign leaders who watched the killings being carried out at a temple in the main ceremonial precinct. Some victims became deity representations, living, for example, as Xipe Totec, Our Flayed Lord, in the city's neighborhoods, before being killed after enduring combat with several warriors. This ritual fighting was a part of a war-like killing, representing the fulfillment of a vow by a warrior to house and sacrifice a captive. The flayed body of the victim was taken first to a local temple, *calpolco*, then to a captor's home where parts of the body would be eaten by the captor's family.

The bloodiness and violence this series of killings entailed cannot be denied. Nor can it be denied that Aztecs and others put to death reacted to their fate in different ways, difficult as it is to tease out emotions from pictorial and written sources, ranging from acceptance, sadness, sometimes bravery, even rare attempts at escape. These rituals, nevertheless, display the central idea of value because the preciousness of blood offerings are emphasized in descriptions of these ritual killings and transformation as captives became deities, warriors wearing skins took on the power of warrior captors, and hearts and blood became a debt payment to Mexica deities. While the vivid nature of killing captured warriors and absorbing their energy through distributing and partaking of blood and body parts reveals "a story the Aztecs told to themselves about their triumphant wars," it also lays bare the very intimate connections between life and death experienced by every Mexica. The *Florentine Codex's* description stresses the community-wide nature of the ceremonies during Tlacaxipehualiztli. Everyone watched the goings-on as they occurred not only at the city's ceremonial center but also in each neighborhood. The ceremonies conveyed the idea of achieving a balance, however temporary, between humans and deities, life and death, to the entire populace. The communal nature of these ceremonies reflected an ancient and very widespread practice of flaying connected to the encouragement of agricultural fertility. The combat element, the war-related sacrifice that took place before rulers from many altepeme, began after a successful Mexica war around 1460 against the Huaxtecs. The militaristic aspects of this monthly ceremony undoubtedly reinforced imperial and Mexica dominance.

A similar flaying took place during the eleventh month, Ochpaniztli. During this month a female ixiptla of the goddess Toci was killed, decapitated, and then flayed to celebrate human and agricultural fertility. The *Codex Telleriano-Remensis* draws attention to the sweeping and cleaning aspects of the rituals of this month, especially the sweeping of houses and roads, and the fertility aspects of the month through veneration of plants. Many of the pages of this codex focus on the everyday rituals of the xiuhpohualli, suggesting that the most dramatic public killings had the greatest impact in Tenochtitlan and perhaps the larger Excan tlatoloyan cities, with residents, especially commoners, of other smaller altepeme attending more to local community and household practices and meanings.

Explaining such sacrificial practices highlights the story of debt payment to the gods that Aztecs told themselves combined with the rapid rise of the Excan tlatoloyan, an empire within which power dynamics changed over time. Yet despite material and written evidence that demonstrates that such killings occurred and had meanings within the Aztec religious system, there are writers who reduce these rituals to a need for protein or who dispute whether "human sacrifice" occurred at all. Focusing primarily on the Maya, archaeologist Elizabeth Graham argues that Spaniards created the idea that such killings related to warfare and its economic and ideological justifications much more than to gods' needs. She also applies this argument to the Aztecs despite a wealth of archaeological and ethnohistorical evidence showing that ritual killing indeed related not only to beliefs about the origins of their deities, the movement of the sun, and the relationships among life, fertility, regeneration, and death and degeneration but also to political and economic changes. Other writers assert either that the Aztecs were protein deficient and sacrifice helped to fill that need or that Spaniards made up their descriptions of Aztec ritual killing in order to justify their invasions and wars against the Aztecs, further arguing that archaeologists and historians take these claims at face value without further investigation or analysis.

Both material and written evidence from the Aztecs themselves show that they carried out these killings and that they intensified later in the fifteenth and early sixteenth centuries, especially among the Mexica. Mexican archaeologists, excavating the Templo Mayor found the skull rack, *tzompantli*, and associated towers, on which skulls were displayed. Most were from men, but some were from women and children. Some skulls stayed on the rack for long periods of time, others were removed, modified, and used as offerings and perhaps as decoration for the deity impersonators, the ixiptlahuan. Neither a mirage conjured up by Europeans nor the Rosetta Stone through which all of Aztec civilization can be characterized, any reading of the atrocities committed by Spaniards detailed at length by Aztec and Spanish chroniclers suggests that Aztecs had no monopoly on public killing or on the uses of death to encourage transformation, reinforce social hierarchy and order, and create feelings of fear and awe.

Conclusion

Much Aztec physical and spiritual effort went to support the vast array of priests, temples, and ceremonies described in this chapter. The chapter also shows the links Aztecs, especially the Mexica and the Excan tlatoloyan populace more broadly, drew among their spiritual beliefs, political actions, and economic activities. Deities needed to be propitiated every day. From the smallest household to the largest city – and at every political level in between – ceremonies of offering took place as Aztecs sought water, food, the survival of human life, and balance in what they perceived to be an often chaotic Mesoamerican spiritual and material world. In their dynamic universe, deities and their human embodiments, priests, and rulers manifested great power. While we turn next to the workings of rulers' power in the realm of political organization and action, we should note that Aztec art, science, and writing and literature, all related to both the religious, political, and economic realms. These forms of knowledge, interweaving the sacred and secular, are discussed in Chapter 6 to highlight Aztec creativity, intellectual life, and forms of knowledge production. These activities helped to keep them alive as living peoples and as an idea important to Mexican and world history, topics discussed in Chapter 7. The ideas and practices related to worship, divination, and communicating deities' needs and desires described here in this chapter ultimately expressed the Aztec ability to use value to generate and regenerate life – plant, animal, and human – as they tried to balance the paradox they lived as death was transformed into life throughout the ritual and solar years.

3
Communities, Kingdoms, "Empires"

The Basin of Mexico and its nearby surrounding areas contained about sixty political units, each of which the Aztecs called an altepetl. The largest and most militarily, economically, and religiously powerful was Tenochtitlan, the Mexica capital city. The most common translations, city-state or kingdom, each capture something essential about these entities. They had urban cores, and they were ruled by supreme rulers, tlatoque, who came from dynastic families. The altepetl-centric focus of recent scholarship – archaeological and ethnohistorical – has, however, somewhat obscured the localities that constituted them, known as tlaxilacalli or calpolli. These smaller units, in many ways communities unto themselves, were of critical importance for the formation and functioning of altepeme. Even when altepeme eventually faded in importance in the colonial period, some of these localities survived into the national period, even beyond.

This chapter begins by examining the altepetl and its constituent parts – the internal organization as well as the rulers and other personnel who constituted Aztec governments. The chapter covers alliance-making, using the lens of the rise of the Excan tlatoloyan through wars of conquest and other means, and considers the uses of material and symbolic value in political transformations and the maintenance of political and cosmic balance to which rulers, nobles, and commoners, men and women, were crucial. Value was central to the region's political economy. Material value was based upon things Aztecs transformed to fulfill peoples' needs and nurture relationships between and among rulers and between rulers and the ruled. Symbolic value came into play through those relationships. Goods elevated powerful rulers, transforming them into semi-divine figures. Reciprocal, balanced relationships of production and exchange provided the items that sustained political relationships within a social system that was becoming more hierarchical over time. Because women were creators, symbols, and beneficiaries of material and symbolic value, their roles in Aztec governance helped organize those activities. Therefore, this chapter will highlight, among other themes, women's place in politics.

Political Organization from the Bottom Up

Sources from the Basin of Mexico, especially the Tetzcoco area, suggest that at about 1200 a new, more dispersed settlement pattern featuring the local governing institutions just described developed in the Tetzcoco/Acolhua region after the dissolution of the Tolteca empire. These became variously known as tlaxilacalli or calpolli. Compared to the previous more nucleated settlements of the Teotihuacan and Tolteca periods (during the Classic, Epiclassic, and early Postclassic periods), these were, as historian Benjamin Johnson explains,

> unique, spreading large and surprisingly autonomous populations over extensive territories to manage local ecosystems with much greater efficiency. Only decentralized local control

Communities, Kingdoms, "Empires"

allowed for the close-in, rigorous management that proved fundamental for the spread of human settlement across nearly all of central Mexico's varied ecosystems. Tlaxilacalli anchored people on the landscape in new and intensive ways.

They also allowed for the explosive population growth of the late Postclassic period. Growing crops, building infrastructure, and managing water, these localities – with their arrays of officials, male and female – would provide building blocks for the developing kingdoms, altepeme, across the Basin of Mexico. While the tlaxilacalli and calpolli may have had some continuity with earlier central Mesoamerican sociopolitical units, especially the Teotihuacan apartment compound, the altepetl appears to have been something new. These small kingdoms with their characteristic central areas that contained the palace of the ruler, a temple for the patron deity, a market, and multiple constituent localities, some closer to the center, others outlying and more dispersed, began to come together in the thirteenth and fourteenth centuries. Altepeme formed as migrant populations settled down and joined together with Tolteca-descended and other groups already present in this central region who provided legitimacy to the dynastic families that would emerge as paramount rulers.

While Aztec visual and written texts depict their origins as humble, they almost certainly were more sophisticated than they themselves depicted as they entered the Basin of Mexico. They proved quite capable rather quickly of building capital cities, war machines, and powerful confederations, especially the Excan tlatoloyan, that came to be the largest and most powerful in 1519 Mesoamerica. To tell this story clearly, we will first focus on the rise and political development of the Mexica specifically. Constituted by a number of subgroupings called calpolli early in their history, perhaps numbering seven as they migrated to and then settled Tenochtitlan and Tlatelolco, and "tlaxilacalli" later, the people who came to be called Mexica governed themselves through collective means with calpolli leaders and chiefly priests. The word calpolli would stay in use for temples and religious affiliations in the many neighborhoods spread across the urban areas of Tenochtitlan and Tlatelolco; it persisted in other altepeme. This representative governance was important in Tenochtitlan's early history. It allowed for local and higher-level collective governance by the various ethnicities that came together to form the Mexica. Even though virtually all colonial Mexica sources highlight the later royal and imperial phases of Mexica history, some aspects of collective governance persisted well into the colonial era.

The Indigenous-written histories of Tenochtitlan and many other altepeme show how important women were to the process of city-state and dynastic formation. A ruler's mother could ennoble a first ruler and the subsequent line, but many codices and histories also show founding couples, men and women, often pictured in or near cave or mountain images, designating the founding of that community, even perhaps shared rule of that community. A number of visual texts from Acolhua Tetzcoco – the *Codex Xolotl*, the *Mapa Quinatzin*, and the *Mapa Tlotzin* – depict such couples as does Fernando Alva Ixtlilxochitl's narrative of altepeme foundings and the political history of Tetzcoco. For the Mexica of Tenochitlan, Chimalpahin's relaciones as well as the *Crónica mexicayotl* provide similar narrative information, and two illustrations from Durán's texts show founding couples in the seven caves of Chicomoztoc. In addition to the role of founding couples, ancestors and rulers could be conceptualized as "fathers-mothers," embodying both genders. Proper governance among the Aztecs relied upon the idea that ruling, like parenting, embodied the gender complementarity that both parents together provided by nourishing, sheltering, and teaching.

After finally settling and developing the cities of Tenochtitlan and Tlatelolco, the Mexica grafted a kingly or royal rulership onto their governing structure. The first dynastic tlatoani, Acamapichtli, descended in part from Tolteca nobility through women, possibly from a woman named Ilancueitl (Old Woman Skirt). There are many varying accounts of how Acampichtli of Tenochtitlan came to be ennobled and the first legitimate, Tolteca-related, tlatoani of Tenochtitlan. A textual example that deemphasizes a precise genealogy of Acampichtli's mother or wife by never precisely identifying her relationships with him is the *Anales de Cuauhtitlan*. It stresses Ilancueitl's role in connecting the Mexica ruler to the descendants of the Tolteca through Colhuacan's ruling dynasty. The *Codex Telleriano-Remensis* shows this process of ennoblement visually, depicting Ilancueitl as connected to Acampichtli as mother or wife. The image is ambiguous because multiple versions circulated of just how early Tenochca tlatoque had tied themselves to the Colhua heirs to Tollan's ruling dynasty. These Mexica allied themselves as mercenaries to the Basin of Mexico power, the Tepaneca of the western mainland whose capital city was Azcapotzalco. The Mexica, however, grew tired of their servile position. Copying some of the arts of statecraft practiced successfully by Azcapotzalco's ruler Tezozomoc, they decided to use the Postclassic political strategy of alliance-making and their own martial skills to turn the tables and overthrow the Tepaneca. Two Mexica leaders played critical roles in this independence project, the tlatoani, Itzcoatl (Obsidian Snake), and Tlacaelel, his closest advisor and holder of the title *cihuacoatl* (Woman Snake). The two of them plotted the downfall of the Tepaneca, a project that succeeded around 1428. From that point on, the governing structure of the Mexica became more hierarchically and bureaucratically structured within and beyond Tenochtitlan. As that process played out, Tenochtitlan's ruler became referred to as a "*huey*" tlatoani (great or supreme ruler), and his power, status, and wealth grew alongside the growth of the altepetl and empire (see Fig. 3.1).

At some point early in Tenochtitlan's history, the tlaxilacalli, or neighborhoods, of Tenochtitlan became organized into four quarters, the campan or tlayacatl. The altepetl's political organization developed in relation to its large territorial size, increasing population, and emerging economic and social complexity. Another possibility is that these quarters began or functioned as altepeme or sub-altepeme with rulerships of their own as James Lockhart suggested. Because Mexica histories emphasize the dynasty of the huey tlatoque and downplay this level of governance, how the four quarters may have functioned earlier or later in the city's history is not possible to reconstruct with the texts that currently exist. What is clear is that the city's political and economic influence began to expand as a growing number of people and goods flowed in and out.

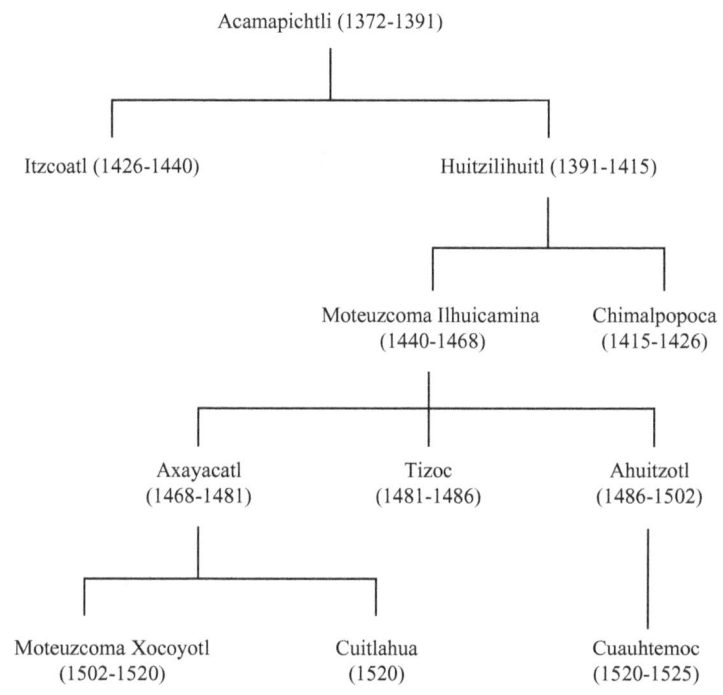

```
                    Acamapichtli (1372-1391)
                             |
         ┌───────────────────┴───────────────────┐
Itzcoatl (1426-1440)              Huitzilihuitl (1391-1415)
                                           |
                                  ┌────────┴────────┐
                       Moteuzcoma Ilhuicamina   Chimalpopoca
                            (1440-1468)          (1415-1426)
                                  |
                    ┌─────────────┼─────────────┐
               Axayacatl         Tizoc         Ahuitzotl
              (1468-1481)     (1481-1486)     (1486-1502)
                    |                              |
          ┌─────────┴─────────┐                    |
Moteuzcoma Xocoyotl       Cuitlahua           Cuauhtemoc
    (1502-1520)             (1520)            (1520-1525)
```

FIG. 3.1 Abbreviated genealogy and approximate dates of rule of Mexica tlatoque of Tenochtitlan
Sources for the genealogy include Hassig, *Aztec Warfare*; P. Carrasco, "Royal Marriages in Ancient Mexico"

Localities within the city were administered on a day-to-day basis by tlaxilacalli neighborhood officials called *calpoleque*, and leaders who oversaw labor organization for public works and tribute collection (*calpixque* and *tequitlato*). Two kinds of nobles made up the upper stratum of Aztec society, the *pipiltin* (sing., *pilli*), who were lesser nobles, some of whom held positions of authority over the tlaxilacalli and probably descended from an older calpolli elite, and the *teteuctin* (sing., *teuctli*), who were the holders of the highest governing positions and were closely related to the dynastic tlatoque. Nobles supervised the collecting of revenues, led the military, administered justice, taught the young, directed the complex spiritual practices of a deeply religious people, and at the highest level, advised rulers. The noble class, and especially the nobles most closely related to the ruling dynasty became much more powerful after the overthrow of Tepaneca domination.

A special feature of the higher-level Mexica political system was the division of power and responsibility between the huey tlatoani and the cihuacoatl, the former responsible for external affairs, especially war, and the latter, internal affairs. This system seems to have originated early in Tenochtitlan's history, under a leader named Tenoch. It may have grown out of a dual structure that organized the early calpolli and their leaders, those associated with the sun, sky, war, maleness, and the east and others associated with the earth, water, regeneration, femaleness, and the west. These early units may have been organized in this dual fashion reflecting the existence of a moiety, or dual leadership and kinship system, a kind of political and social structure common among many Indigenous societies of the early Americas. These calpolli associations became downplayed in Tenochtitlan's histories as the city grew more urbanized and Mexica rulers reimagined their people's history as one of imperial dominance in which neighborhood governance grew less powerful. Yet commoners still held influence and authority through governing councils, courts, and tributary collection processes. Even as memories of an older, more collectively organized governing structure faded, especially as represented in official histories, elements of that older neighborhood and leadership structure remained vital through neighborhood leadership positions, representation by commoners in higher levels of governance, and limits on the power of the highest leaders.

This more bureaucratic, eventually imperial, structure evolved too as the role of the cihuacoatl developed. This role existed in a few other of the larger altepeme but was not nearly as crucial to their governance. In Tenochtitlan, the role of the cihuacoatl grew more important due to the increasingly complex tasks associated with administering a growing city and empire and also because of the efforts of a remarkable cihuacoatl, Tlacaelel. Before discussing Tlacaelel in more detail and noting that the political office was held by men (though evidence mentioned below hints that early in Tenochtitlan's history at least one woman held the office), the naming of the office carries a gendered significance. Its existence with a name that is equivalent to a highly important goddess illustrates the impact of the notion of balance and complementarity in maleness and femaleness. These concepts permeated the organizational structures and ideologies of Mexica and other Aztec societies throughout the Basin of Mexico.

In Tenochtitlan, the cihuacoatl served with the tlatoani. On occasion, he dressed as the goddess in his role as representative of their deity in important ceremonies. He also conquered regions where the goddess Cihuacoatl served as a patron deity, especially Colhuacan and Xochimilco. These were fertile, green places that held a special importance in the history and economy of the Mexica: in the history, because these wars expanded Mexica power and access to tribute items; in the economy, for the intense *chinampa* agriculture, the garden plots or "floating gardens" by the edges of lakes and canals (discussed in more detail in the next chapter), that the Mexica would rely upon in those southern lake areas. For the Mexica and others, the goddess represented a major deity who simultaneously symbolized birth, work (principally agricultural), and war and destruction. The latter associations might have been strongest for the Mexica, especially among their high nobility, because she was associated with conflict that split the Mexica early in their history. In her guise as Coyolxauhqui, she symbolized defeat and the need to be fed by the victims of ritual killing. But for Aztec macehualtin, especially those commoners living outside of Tenochtitlan, Cihuacoatl was a healer and patroness of midwives whose images lacked the negative features seen in the Mexica imagery of codices and sculptures. Female deities and historical figures could be creators and alliance makers; but they could also be figures linked to conflict, "Women of Discord" as archaeologist Susan Gillespie called them. Another such woman, the elder sister (*hueltiuhtli*) of the Mexica patron deity Huitzilopochtli, Malinalxoch, founded the polity of Malinalco after feuding with and being abandoned by her brother early in the Mexica migration period.

Who was Tlacaelel, this particularly important cihuacoatl? A younger brother of Moteuczoma Ilhuicamina, the fifth tlatoani, Tlacaelel, was an experienced warrior who proved to be a powerful second in command to several rulers. While his main responsibilities included advising the tlatoani on Tenochtitlan's governance, taking the tlatoani's place when the ruler was absent, meeting with visiting diplomats and delegations, and administering the city's cycle of calendrical and other rituals, he also acted as a judge, usually for crimes committed by those of high rank. These largely city-related responsibilities eventually gave way to more war-related responsibilities as building and defending the emerging imperial structure marked each tlatoani's responsibilities from Itzcoatl, who ruled from 1426 to 1440, on. Although the cihuacoatl was not in the direct line of command for war, he nonetheless advised a series of rulers about military actions. Four leaders – including the *tlacochcalcatl* (armory person) and *tlacateccatl* (people lord), the two highest-ranking councilors to the ruler who also served as generals in the military command structure – as well as two other officials performed leadership roles in war. According to the *Florentine Codex*, one of these officials, the tlacateccatl, received his education at the telpochcalli and was not of noble origins, representing a commoner role in military decision making that continued despite a shifting power structure, one becoming more hierarchical as power at the top became more concentrated.

Tlacaelel's rise and consolidation of power occurred not only because of his own qualities of wisdom and boldness combined with a longevity that allowed him to accrue power, wealth, and rulers' respect, but also because of the development of an imperial power structure. That process meant that the tlaxilacalli and their leaders, the latter of whom may have represented an older noble group coming from Tenochtitlan's founding calpolli, were losing power and position to an increasingly dominant upper, dynastic nobility. In that more highly ranked nobility, close relatives of rulers carried expanded responsibilities and brandished more authority in offices. They functioned through councils including a supreme council, with its four highest-ranking officials, as well as others including the *tlatocan*, which was a general ruling council, and a war council. These bodies advised the ruler about matters of governance, internal and external to Tenochtitlan. Noblemen also served on courts at the calpolli and state level. For the latter, there were two courts, the *teccalco* that heard cases involving commoners and the *tlacxitlan* that heard all cases pertaining to nobles as well as the most serious matters in which commoners were involved. Merchant and military tribunals also existed on which noble *and* commoner judges served. For Tenochtitlan, councils and high courts had rooms in the huey tlatoani's palace (see Fig. 3.2).

The practices involved in the lower levels of tlaxilacalli legal practice are harder to reconstruct. Nevertheless, tlaxilacalli officials, noble and commoner, adjudicated disputes, and the *telpochtlato*, or ruler of youth, judged young men who misbehaved in the telpochcalli. Both provide examples of commoners' roles in judicial processes. For Tetzcoco, in addition to a supreme legal and governing council (probably called the *tlatocaicpalpan*) and a war council, other councils existed. These included a treasury council with representatives of merchants and tribute collectors, a council concerned with art, music, and the supernatural that was governed by priests with expertise in writing, history, and calendrics, and a *teoicpalpan* (sacred tribunal) that dealt with the most serious offenses punishable by death. These councils all participated with the ruler in governance. Commoners served on some of these councils and participated in lower level judicial decision making.

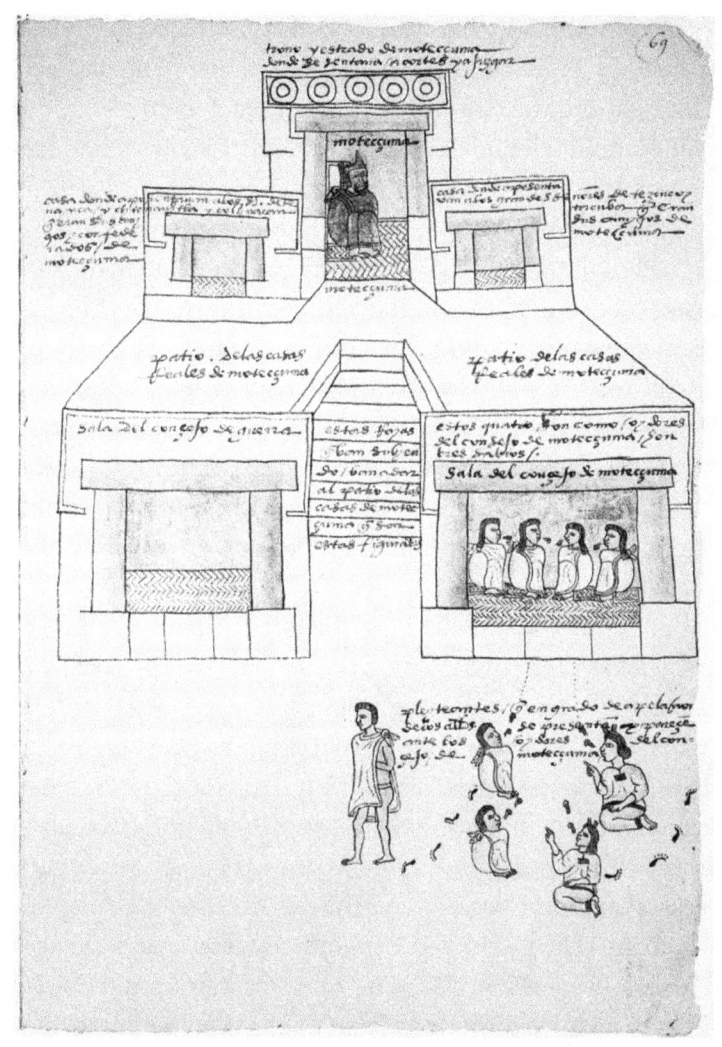

FIG. 3.2 Moteuczoma Xocoyotl's palace with council meeting rooms and courtrooms
Codex Mendoza, fol.69r. Courtesy of the Bodleian Libraries, University of Oxford, Ms. Arch. Selden A.1, Creative Commons License CC BY NC 4.0

As centralization of legal and other bureaucracies occurred in the larger altepeme, especially Tenochtitlan, Tlacaelel and the tlatoque with whom he served placed an ever increasing emphasis on capturing enemy warriors for ritual killing. Further buttressing rulers' fame and power as well as that of the Mexica state, the changing patterns of such killings played a role in the development and history of the Excan tlatoloyan. However, the Mexica political structure should not be understood as the only model for the political structures that existed across the Basin of Mexico or its nearby areas. While altepeme had features – both in physical layout and political organization – in common, there also was diversity in size and organizational structure among them. Variations on an altepetl theme existed.

For features in common, as Michael E. Smith has shown archaeologically and Mary Hodge and James Lockhart ethnohistorically, altepeme contained core areas with a palace for the tlatoani, a pyramid temple structure, and a market. This core area would be surrounded by the residential areas mentioned above – the calpolli or tlaxilacalli – along with dispersed rural subdivisions. These more distant areas sometimes became intermixed because the ruler to whom macehualtin owed tribute and labor could change due to shifting alliances among rulers or warfare and therefore lacked clear boundaries. The agriculturally based economies of the Basin of Mexico supported altepeme, though many people, whether rural or urban, produced utilitarian and specialized goods that flowed across and beyond the Basin of Mexico through both tribute and a vast trade and marketing system discussed in more detail in the next chapter. Organizationally, tlaxilacalli and altepeme were characterized by political and social hierarchies entailing tribute and labor along with ceremonial and military obligations that flowed from commoners to nobles. But because a great deal of political volatility existed among altepeme with relations often shifting between alliance and conflict, the military responsibilities of the neighborhoods carried real importance. The highly ritualistic and polytheistic Aztec religious system reinforced the power and authority of rulers and the military and is another example of the close integration of politics, religion, and economic organization for the Aztecs.

But the actual organizational structure of rulerships, bureaucratic councils and offices, the roles of nobles and commoners in governance, and the extent of domination by nobles over both material and symbolic resources for governance varied. Codices and early histories make clear that political and social organization differed across an east/west axis, with the east characterized not by calpolli or tlaxilacalli but by a unit called the *teccalli*, (lord house, a unit of political and social organization) to which nobles and commoner followers were attached and for which commoners labored. In the west, the house of a high noble was called a *tecpan* (lord place) and was fully integrated into the neighborhood tlaxilacalli or calpolli structure. Recent studies show that in addition to this east-west distinction, at least four different forms of Aztec political organization existed in and around the Basin of Mexico.

Much of the basin as well as the area corresponding to the modern state of Morelos follow the pattern as laid out for Tenochtitlan and the Mexica, but some altepeme had complex structures. These always included multiple altepeme. A few altepeme – Chalco being the best example – maintained the level of political organization known as the tlayacatl between an altepetl and the tlaxilacalli or calpolli, mentioned earlier for Tenochtitlan. The ruler of each constituent altepetl (often called a "tlayacatl altepetl" by the Nahua writer Chimalpahin) largely ruled his own altepetl though frequent consultation occurred among these tlatoque and one might serve as a ceremonial leader of the whole complex unit. Elsewhere political structures differed even more.

Organized as an altepetl, two priestly rulers and a council governed the altepetl of Cholollan. Neither Huexotzinco nor Tlaxcallan, still farther east, fit the altepetl model well, based on ethnohistorical and archaeological evidence. Both of the latter political systems feature rulerships, *tlatocayotl* in the case of Huexotzinco, *teuctli* in the case of Tlaxcallan, and noble houses, teccalli, with few or no calpolli or tlaxilacalli. Tlaxcallan, in particular, appears to have had the least monarchical, least centralized political system in central Mexico. Its archaeological remains suggest at best a diffuse urban center, with the area integrated through roads and plazas rather than the palace-temple-market cores that characterized the more urbanized centers. Tlaxcallan governed itself and conducted warfare with the Mexica – whose immense machinery of war and imperial governance failed to conquer it – through a council system. Council members held a noble title, "teuctli," but they gained that title based upon achievement not birth. Archaeologists who have worked intensively in the region question whether this area was organized into altepeme at all. Despite its far less centralized form of government, Tlaxcallan's highly capable military organization affected the Mexica and then the Spanish.

Warfare

The history of Mexica warfare takes us back to a crucial figure in their history, Tlacaelel. It was he, in conjunction with the rulers who built the Aztec imperial system, Itzcoatl and Moteuczoma Ilhuicamina (who ruled from 1440–1468), who strengthened central leadership, strategized to overthrow Tepaneca domination, and reinvigorated the Mexica military. Aztec war practices broadly relied upon structure and discipline, weaponry, the pursuit of captives, and the vanquishing of enemies who would then provide material wealth in the form of everyday and luxury items paid as tribute to the imperial powers.

Aztec militarism developed out of an ancient history. While the Olmec – whose Formative period cultural florescence saw their art style and technology spread across many areas of Mesoamerica – were not themselves an imperial power, they developed weaponry including obsidian projectile points, spears, clubs, and slingshots that they used to defend their communities and trade routes. This array of weaponry persisted as types of weapons used by Mesoamericans for centuries to come even as Aztecs further developed their own weapons of war. The Mexica and other Aztec groups built on earlier Mesoamerican traditions of armed conflict for both defensive and expansionist reasons as evidenced by the warfare associated with both Teotihuacan and Tollan. The early Mexica fought as mercenaries in the frequent wars that took place among the altepeme of highland central Mexico. Their later expansionist military goals, therefore, built on this ancient Mesoamerican expansionist tradition and their own early history.

Trained and recruited into the lower fighting units through the telpochcalli, these warriors, from the four tlayacatl of Tenochtitlan as well as those from other towns and city-states whose rulers answered the call from a Mexica huey tlatoani, would gather supplies of food and weaponry for wars of conquest or "angry wars" (*cocoltic yaoyotl*) as they were called in Nahuatl. While spies and scouts preceded Aztec armies, once the decision to conduct a campaign had been made, a hierarchically organized army would begin its march. The armies fielded by the Excan tlatoloyan could vary in size, reaching one hundred thousand or more men at a time. The *xiquipilli* (unit of 8000 men, something like a battalion) was the unit through which the smaller groupings were commanded. The xiquipilli could itself constitute an army, or multiple xiquipilli could be combined into larger armies. Lacking a standing army, each tlaxilacalli or calpolli had to supply 400 men commanded by the local community or neighborhood's war leaders, and they were probably further subdivided into units of 100–200 men. When the tlatoani himself led a campaign, he came richly arrayed in clothing, feathers, gold, and silver, and carrying weaponry a day after priests who bore deity images on their backs had set off. Generals, members of the high-ranking military orders, and veteran fighters accompanied him. Then came Tenochtitlan's warriors followed by the fighters from Tlatelolco and the other Triple Alliance altepeme as well as allied altepeme. Marching last, fighters from conquered altepeme followed. They participated as a kind of tribute payment.

The invading army used its size to strike fear into the ruler and populace of an altepetl under attack and the forms of fighting, including shock charges, fierce hand-to-hand combat, and individualized battles between the most skilled fighters served the same function. Aztecs used offensive weaponry effectively. Their array of weaponry included bows (*tlahuitolli*), arrows (*yaomitl*), darts (*tlacochtli* and other names), swords and clubs (*macuahuitl*), and spear throwers (*atlatl*). Wearing plumes, cotton armor, and animal skins and carrying a variety of shields that glowed or shone, soldiers voiced loud taunts, boasts, and threats by yelling, whooping, or howling – all this sound accompanied by noise from conch shell trumpets as armies faced each other.

In battle, such cacophony came from both sides as fighters began to go at each other and projectiles began to be launched. Each line of soldiers then advanced and hand-to-hand combat broke out. But opposing armies had rarely, if ever, seen such large armies as those fielded by the Excan tlatoloyan. Their war paraphernalia and the loud, raucous sounds their fighters produced impressed enemy soldiers and induced fear. With so many skilled fighters and such concentrated determination to gain captives and reach an altepetl's central area where the main temple – dedicated to its primary deity – would be set on fire as the symbol of defeat, Excan tlatoloyan units often achieved success. As wars ended, victorious forces often pillaged enemy communities, taking the last captives that they could, then stealing and destroying property. The ruler of a defeated altepetl might be killed or he might be allowed to live to oversee a feast in which he and his lieutenants listened to the victors gloating. On this occasion, the defeated ruler learned of the tribute his now-conquered subjects would be required to pay. Soldiers and their captives then marched back to Tenochtitlan. There, those captured would meet their fate on Tenochtitlan's main pyramid, with their bodies decapitated, their hearts removed, skulls placed on the tzompantli, and body parts taken by captors for a celebratory feast in their households through which the victor's family celebrated the victory by consuming the body parts. The victor did not himself partake of his captive's flesh because the captor saw himself as having a ritualized, fictive kinship relationship with that captive as father and son. Captors and their families celebrated the fearsome power of Huitzilopochtli and other war deities as well as the courage of enemy warriors.

But Mexica armies and those of other altepeme did not always emerge victorious from their military campaigns. The Aztecs relied on both actual power and perceptions of power, but such strategies met with varying success. Sometimes they lost; sometimes they fought in a semi-ritualized form of battle in which victory took decades or never occurred at all. This was certainly the case during the prolonged Mexica war against Chalco, a city bordering the southern-most lake sector of the lake system at the center of the Basin of Mexico in which this complex kingdom either vanquished or fought Mexica and Excan tlatoloyan armies to a standstill multiple times. The alliance finally defeated the Chalca in

1464. Characterizing the wars against Chalco, but even more prominently the military engagements between Tenochtitlan and Tlaxcallan, to the east of the Basin of Mexico, was a style of warfare usually referred to in English as "flower war/s" (*xochiyaoyotl*).

This unusual form of warfare involved a specific set of enemies: Chalco for a period of time, then Tlaxcallan, Huexotzinco, Chololllan, and Tliliuhquitepec, all mainland communities to the east or southeast of Tenochtitlan. These were wars with very specific rules of engagement characterized by a ritualistic formality in which battles were fought on a sacred space set aside specifically for them, the *cuauhtlalli* (eagle land) or *yaotlalli* (war land). Capturing warriors for ceremonial killing was certainly a prominent objective. In fact, Tlacaelel himself announced this goal. Another purpose of this type of warfare included wearing down enemies as well as providing or keeping soldiers in training. Mexica leaders likely viewed such wars, therefore, as wars of attrition in which an enemy state could be depleted to the point of eventual victory, especially when carried out over the long term. This strategy was successful with Chalco; it was not – to the ultimate dismay of the Mexica – with Tlaxcallan.

While annals, colonial histories, and anthropologists' and historians' writings all emphasize angry and flower wars as the sole province of men, war represented an arena of Aztec life in which men and women, noblemen and commoners all had different experiences and goals. Commoners fulfilled responsibilities to altepeme and their rulers and sought material and social rewards, especially land and goods along with increased status through participating in warfare. Nobles and the states they led had numerous objectives – conquering, gaining administrative control and access to resources, and enhancing wealth and status. Through warfare, nobles, rulers, and their states acquired rights to land and achieved the extraction of tribute payments. Rulers and military leaders loomed large as strategists looking for victory and prestige; ordinary soldiers hoped for victory but also wished to gain social mobility and material rewards. The repercussions of the wars men fought also differed by class as injuries and deaths occurred more often among macehualtin who fought on the frontlines and with less armor.

Likewise, Aztec men and women experienced war differently. Looting, sacking, and slaughter were regular features of the angry wars the Aztecs fought to gain tribute, land, and political control in many parts of Mesoamerica. The impact of it fell heavily on women, men who did not fight, children, and the elderly. Any of these people could be killed or taken prisoner. Those who were younger often experienced enslavement or were forced to labor to pay tribute after defeat. Durán, Alvarado Tezozomoc, and Chimalpahin all record the destructiveness of Excan tlatoloyan wars, with Alvarado Tezozomoc especially emphasizing the bloodiness of the campaigns. He describes in vivid detail a war undertaken against two altepeme in a formerly Tepaneca area of what is now the state of Guerrero, in which the tlatoani Ahuitzotl ordered the killing of all residents, except for young men and women who would be taken to Tenochtitlan and other nearby altepeme. He also demanded the razing of both communities. The chroniclers all make the point that Aztec warfare affected the *entire* populace of a targeted altepetl or region, not just its soldiers. The cruel impact of these wars on local populations is well documented.

Women could be killed, captured, raped. Sometimes women were subjected to attacks to provoke or express tensions between altepeme. This happened both early in Aztec history as when Tepaneca warriors attacked and raped Mexica women at Chapultepec during their migration period or when women of Cuauhtitlan were attacked and violated during the period of the Tepaneca War in the late 1420s. Tlacaelel ordered men, women, and children to be killed in Azcapotzalco as the Mexica fought to overcome Tepaneca domination. Mexica market women and tribute collectors (*cihuatequitque*) were killed at various times as tensions ratcheted up between the Mexica and other groups they sought to conquer. Fighters from Cuauhtitlan specifically took women prisoners from Huexotzinco around 1508.

While men dominated the military decision making and fighting forces of the Aztecs, there are examples of women's participation in fighting. The known examples of women's participation show it to have been unstructured and informal, an irregular aspect of Aztec military organization. The most dramatic example of women's participation in warfare is that of the Tlatelolca women who, Durán and Alvarado Tezozomoc tell us, desperately sought to fight off conquest by the Tenochca Mexica in 1473. The Tlatelolca women exposed their genitalia and stomachs and squeezed their breasts, producing milk, which they threw on their enemies. Accounts by Alva Ixtlilxochitl and the *Anales de Cuauhtitlan* suggest that Tolteca and Tepaneca women participated in battles in the eleventh and early fifteenth centuries respectively.

Women of Tlatelolco also fought against the Spanish. As the Tenochca Mexica withdrew, the Tlatelolca women refused to surrender and kept on fighting. This more unstructured participation in war does not equate to women having no role in or little influence on war efforts. Women's textile making, food preparation, and performance of household rituals critical to war efforts across the Aztec world provided crucial support to armies. Their lesser participation in fighting the near-constant Aztec wars meant, however, that women did not participate in one of the key pathways of mobility for men, commoner or noble. This exclusion has been seen as marginalizing for women, downgrading the influence of women's sphere of activities.

Yet the ideology of gender complementarity and the symbolic value of female identity remained strong throughout the period before and after the arrival of the Spanish. Altepetl and confederation expansion relied upon communal, collective efforts, male *and* female. Through childbirth, women supplied future soldiers, and the labor they contributed through household-based tasks produced food and other needed military supplies. Their sweeping and praying protected men at war. The parallel rituals for women and men at the beginning and end of life as well as the parallel treatment of women who died during childbirth, because Aztecs considered that type of death equivalent to that of men who died in warfare, reinforced the idea of the complementarity and interdependence of male and female domains and activities.

Furthermore, goddesses such as Cihuacoatl, the earth and warrior deity who symbolized creation and destruction as well as victory and defeat, embodied the Mexica desire for war, conquest, and subjugation of enemies from the time of Itzcoatl to the second Moteuczoma. She and other female deities had a spiritual association with conflict and war that reflected power women did have. While warfare reinforced a gendered militaristic symbolism that associated women with defeat, it also created a powerful need for women's labor, practical and spiritual. Through their creation of value, material and symbolic, female labor played a role in the creation of a confederation and imperial configuration that was founded and reinforced through war. But women, as wives and mothers, played another kind of role in alliance and confederation building as well.

Was There an Empire?

Whether a flower war or an angry war, violence was a key part of Aztec political culture and state and confederation building in the late Postclassic period. Inter-altepetl relations took place, furthermore, within a context in which the Excan tlatoloyan sought aggressively to enlarge its domain of control, becoming an expansive confederation. Those relations at times depended upon marriages among rulers and nobles. The comportment of elite women could help create, reinforce, or undermine those relations. Ethnohistorian Pedro Carrasco showed how different elite marriage patterns structured inter-altepetl political relations, with the daughters of rulers often marrying higher or lower status rulers to create or maintain alliances between city-states. But he treated women as pawns of rulers, whereas ethnohistoric sources and recent scholarship demonstrate the roles mothers and wives could play in negotiating, reinforcing, or undermining intra-dynastic and inter-altepetl relations. Indigenous and hybrid sources, for example the annals of Chimalpahin and the chronicles of Alvarado Tezozomoc and Alva Ixtlilxochitl, narrate the histories of political relations and confederation building of the Mexica, the Tetzcoca, and the Chalca. These are family histories as much as they are political narratives that show women to have been partners to men in dynasty and altepetl creation.

Such texts as well as others show how early noble-women ennobled the first rulers of altepeme, a few even served as rulers themselves, usually early in a polity's history or in place of a male ruler too young to take his position. A few sources including a fragmentary text known as the *Fragment de'l Histoire des Anciens Mexicains* and the *Historia de los mexicanos por sus pinturas* hint, for example, that Ilancueitl from Coatlichan (in these sources said to be the wife of the first Mexica tlatoani, Acamapichtli) actually herself ruled either Coatlichan or Tenochtitlan or served as cihuacoatl. While the *Anales de Cuauhtitlan* does not refer to Ilancueitl as a ruler, it treats her as someone powerful, someone who could summon powerful men and choose a ruler for Colhuacan. This same source brings attention to another role of women in claiming and settling territory. It discusses the Chichimeca who first settled Cuauhtitlan. Describing a culture hero and deity like Huitzilopochtli, but in this case a woman named Itzpapalotl (who is described as a deity in the previous chapter), she is said to have told her people whom to choose as a ruler and directed them to claim territory by shooting arrows to the east, north, west, and south.

The same text names women and men who helped to seat and legitimate an early ruler and also mentions that Cuauhtitlan had three female rulers between 866 and 1372. The annals of Chimalpahin offer several examples of women ruling for their young sons in the altepeme of the Chalco region. And the royal wife of Xolotl, founder of the Tetzcoca dynasty, a woman named Tomiyauh, was said to have been ruler of provinces to the east of the Basin of Mexico, perhaps in the Huastec region. Alva Ixtililxochitl implied she ruled with Xolotl. Women also expressed political agency by pushing forward claims to rulership for their sons. Wives' and concubines' loyalty to their partners or lack thereof also at times disrupted dynastic relations within or between altepeme, leading to what historian Camilla Townsend has called "civil wars" within them. In the case of the Excan tlatoloyan, marriages made and unmade, played a role in the war between Spaniards and the alliance in the early sixteenth century.

Did the confederation that made up the Excan tlatoloyan form an empire? This point has been much debated. There are those scholars who downplay or reject the idea that an empire structured around three altepeme – Tenochtitlan (Mexica), Tetzcoco (Acolhua), and Tlacopan (Tepaneca) – existed. Others argue that such a confederation not only existed but constituted an empire. Ross Hassig argues forcefully, from an anthropological perspective, that the "Aztec empire" was of a hegemonic rather than territorial nature. For him, this empire was one in which the imperial system was based more on strong influence and persuasion, undoubtedly with coercive elements, than outright domination over territories. What was its nature and what roles did ideology and economics play in it?

Confederations, often structured around three capital cities, had a history dating back to at least the early Postclassic period and probably further back to Teotihuacan and the Maya city-states of the Classic period. More complex structures with four or more allied polities also existed, especially during the later Postclassic. Through warfare, propaganda, and diplomacy, Mexica rulers and their close allies created the most powerful confederation of the late Postclassic period. In 1428, after overthrowing an earlier confederation centered upon the Tepaneca capital, Azcapotzalco, the Mexica began a campaign of expansion unlike any seen before during the Postclassic. The defeat of the Tepaneca of Azcapotzalco by the allied forces of Tenochtitlan and Tetzcoco set the stage for an alliance with the Tepaneca of Tlacopan, with these three sometimes undertaking wars together, at other times carrying out campaigns of conquest on their own. They conquered much of the basin region by 1480. Within and just beyond the basin, each of the three powers dominated different areas, the Mexica the south, the Acolhua the northeast, and the Tepaneca, the northwest. Particular territories, however, were frequently intermingled due to the complex nature of land distributions after wars and the ways that wars and shifting alliances could change which ruler had access to which lands, tribute payments, or laborers. The Excan tlatoloyan then set out on campaigns of further expansion that lasted until the Spanish arrival put an end to those expansionist efforts.

For a time, the rulers of three polities, Tenochtitlan, Tetzcoco, and Tlacopan, cooperated in conquests within and beyond the Basin of Mexico. Whereas the Mexica of Tenochtitlan and Acolhua of Tetzcoco started out in the first half of the fifteenth century as relatively equal partners, with the Tepaneca subordinate to the other two, three Mexica tlatoque in particular, Moteuczoma Ilhuicamina, Ahuitzotl, and Moteuczoma Xocoyotl, increased the size of territory dominated by the Excan tlatoloyan. The Mexica then became the dominant partner. After 1428, the Mexica used their growing power to gather warriors, equipment, and labor for militarily needed public works to be turned over to the tlatoque of the three major centers for the conduct of warfare. This imperial formation made use of economic strategies to capture wealth and bring it into the three leading altepeme and political and military strategies to influence governance and control borders across a realm that expanded during the fifteenth and into the sixteenth centuries. The payment of tribute, meeting irregular demands for labor or additional goods, including providing still more war supplies beyond those delivered as part of required tribute payments, constituted the major economic strategies imposed across many regions of Mesoamerica, spanning thirty-eight tribute-paying provinces. The political and military strategies involved protecting the expanding borders of Excan tlatoloyan states from surrounding states never subjugated by the Triple Alliance polities through colonizing or building and manning garrisons and forts. The local populations, constituting "strategic provinces," a phrase used by Michael E. Smith, that built such fortresses also provided goods not considered tribute but similar to the tributary war supplies delivered by the tribute-paying provinces. They also sometimes fought in frontier battles.

The political and economic strategies, thus, can be understood as parallel, but different, imperial strategies, each depending on the other to function. The increasing militarization of the Triple Alliance altepeme and power of their armies can be traced textually in sources such as the histories of Alvarado Tezozomoc and Durán. This history can also be traced graphically. The tributary section of the *Codex Mendoza* shows that by the last decades of the Excan tlatoloyan most tributary provinces provided shields and warriors' clothing. In its historical section, the *Codex Telleriano-Remensis* shows warrior costumes becoming a more important aspect of tribute payments, and Mexica warriors are represented in increasingly elaborate arrays of clothing and weapons.

From Itzcoatl's efforts to the south with Chalco to the second Moteuczoma's campaign into Mixtec and Zapotec regions of today's Oaxaca as well as a campaign far to the south to conquer Xoconochco, rich in cacao, the Triple Alliance expanded to cover much, though by no means all, of Mesoamerica (see Map 3.1). Many defeated city-states and regions became tribute-paying provinces. Although each one of the three leading altepeme oversaw its own area of influence from which tribute flowed primarily into that altepetl's coffers, some sources indicate that when tribute was divided among the three, the formula used was 2:2:1 – two-fifths to Tenochtitlan, two-fifths to Tetzcoco, and one-fifth to Tlacopan. More wealth eventually accrued to Tenochtitlan and the Mexica over the course of the empire's history. While the Excan tlatoloyan

Communities, Kingdoms, "Empires"

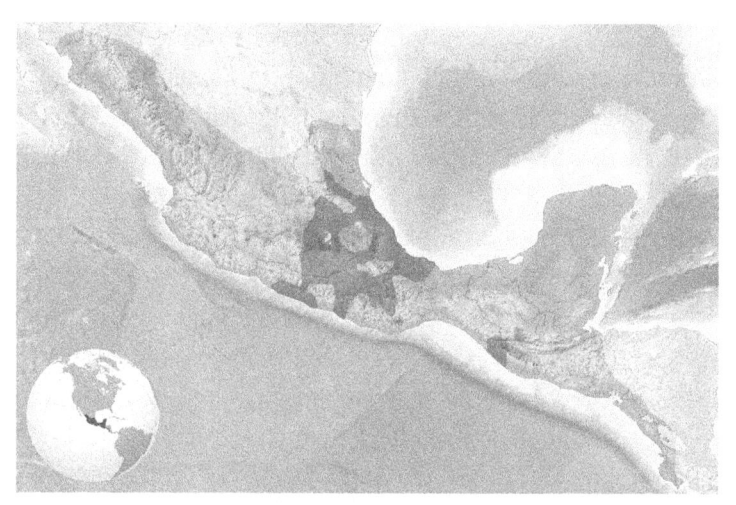

MAP 3.1 Map of the extent of the empire at the height of Moteuczoma Xocoyotl's reign. Created by Aldan-2. File: Aztec Empire under Montezuma II.png. Wikimedia Commons. Public Domain, CC Atribution-Share-Alike 4.0. International License

imposed this tributary structure over defeated kingdoms in which a tribute collecting hierarchy oversaw the extraction of wealth, it also created military garrisons and colonies to strengthen the borders along the boundaries of this complex imperial formation and to enforce order within outlying localities.

Confederations and empires, particularly hegemonic empires, can be more fragile than the word "empire" implies. They often do not persist over the centuries; the Excan tlatoloyan lasted less than a hundred years. While the Spanish were ultimately responsible for its demise, it had difficulties managing far-flung linguistically and culturally different regions, with rebellions against imperial authority not altogether unknown. The theorist of empire Ann Laura Stoler has argued that empires are subject to "processes of decimation, displacement, and reclamation," a description that fits the Triple Alliance. Empires are perhaps best understood as a set of governmental processes rather than a *thing*, easily defined and unchanging. I use the term "imperial formation" in places in this book to draw attention to this idea. Through these political and economic structures, not only goods, but land and laborers, came to be held by rulers, their relatives, rulers of allied cities, high achieving warriors, and even the tlaxilacalli and calpolli that had sent soldiers.

Given that war was such a prominent part of political action and daily life across Mesoamerica in the late prehispanic period, the motivations that lay behind the technologies and processes of warfare must be considered. For the Aztecs, especially the Mexica of Tenochtitlan, ideological motivations played a major role in their desire to carry out warfare and the ways they conducted it. But other kinds of motivations drove the pronounced tendency not only for political violence during the Aztec period but also the rise of the Triple Alliance confederation and especially the Mexica within it. Many writers – scholarly and popular – see religion as *the* motivating factor that lay behind Aztec political history. It played an important role undoubtedly, but economic and political motivations also lay behind the extreme political violence of the late Postclassic period.

Warfare, "Human Sacrifice," Tribute

Even if Spanish accounts highly exaggerated the numbers of victims of ritual killings as seems very likely, with Diego Durán having provided the spectacular figure of 80,400 men being put to death upon the order of the tlatoani Ahuitzotl at the dedication of the Great Temple as discussed in the previous chapter, the need to capture enemy warriors fueled Aztec warfare, especially that of the Mexica. In Tenochtitlan, these sacred yet politicized ceremonies by the Mexica related to their expansionist goals. While such killings – public, highly ceremonial forms of violence – undoubtedly took place, the existing evidence, especially archaeological, does not support such numbers, even as the political uses of these public killings increased concurrently with the escalation of the militarism of the Triple Alliance and the Mexica. As the Excan tlatoloyan confederation developed and tlatoque from Axayacatl on tried to strengthen their own position vis-à-vis other rulers and other altepeme, Mexica rulers and priests promoted an ideology of war. They expressed this ideology through the importance they placed on their patron deity Huitzilopochtli, who combined elements of a culture hero, perhaps based on stories about an early priestly leader and pre-Aztec deities who symbolized warfare and the sun. This ideology, really a form of Mexica propaganda, prompted soldiers up and down the warrior hierarchy as well as the populace of Tenochtitlan to support the costly war aims of the altepetl's ruling officials.

Two narratives, briefly mentioned in the first and second chapters, structured around the meaning and importance of ritual killing and the birth and characteristics of the deity Huitzilopochtli expressed the central tenets of this ideology and reflect the intertwining of politics with religion. The story of the creation of the sun and the moon – which the Mexica believed occurred at Teotihuacan – emphasized the self-sacrifice of two deities, Nanahuatzin, and Tecuciztecatl, becoming the sun and moon. This story, which included the idea of the immolation of other gods as well, became part of a belief system in which prisoners of war captured in Mexica and Triple Alliance wars would have their lives taken in order to provide energy to keep the sun in motion.

The other narrative describes the birth of the Mexica patron deity, Huitzilopochtli, during the period of migration from Aztlan. As his mother Coatlicue (Snake Skirt, an important female deity) swept, she became impregnated by a feather which enraged her daughter Coyolxauhqui and her 400 brothers, the Centzon Huitznahua (400, or innumerable, Stars). With Coatlicue attacked and decapitated by these children, Huitzilopochtli – born fully armed before his mother died – destroyed the stars and then dismembered his sister. Mexica sculptors captured the image of her dismembered body in a huge stone monument that lay at the base of the Templo Mayor (see Fig. 3.3).

Such mythical histories suggest that religion indeed motivated wars, that disruptions around women of discord – deity or human – could lead to battle. These ideas shaped the way wars were fought to emphasize obtaining captives, especially by the Mexica, among whom ceremonies that glorified warfare occurred at the state, neighborhood, and household levels. While Tlaxcallan also seems to have celebrated and justified warfare in a similar way, many other Aztec communities emphasized agricultural cults and ceremonies concerned with insuring the abundance of rain and agricultural yields over the Mexica cult of war, though they too sometimes carried out these war- and Huitzilopochtli-glorifying ceremonies. Yet capturing some of those agricultural yields as well as valuable

FIG. 3.3 Coyolxauhqui relief image
Ancient Mesoamerica 18 (2007), p.15; by permission of Emily Umberger and Cambridge University Press

commodities was a practical matter that very much motivated the violent conflicts characteristic of the Excan tlatoloyan.

After an altepetl experienced conquest by this alliance, the usual practice was for that now-subject population to pay tribute to one or more of the allied powers. Localities, especially those closest to an Excan tlatoloyan altepetl, paid tribute in basic food and other items. These included maize, squash, beans, fruits, honey, salt, and sometimes cotton and cochineal (a dye made from insects that live on the prickly pear cactus). More distant regions tended to supply the more valuable and luxury items Aztec elites coveted: cotton, jade, cacao, precious feathers, shells, even gold. Manufactured items given as tribute included cotton blankets, warrior clothing, feathered shields, reed mats and seats, and pottery of various types, coming from areas near and far. Central needs and local ecologies shaped tribute payment patterns, but some provinces made payments in goods not actually locally produced, enmeshing them in their own elaborate tributary and commercial arrangements.

But the transfer of wealth did not stop with tribute; control over land and labor also flowed to the center. Within the Basin of Mexico, rulers of the three great powers appropriated lands that they gave to themselves, other high nobles, warriors, and to tlaxilacalli or calpolli. To make such lands productive, labor – agricultural and other kinds of service, particularly for public works – also was owed. Military service might also be demanded as could work on special projects such as efforts by Tenochtitlan to control flooding, building projects, or the coronation or funeral of a ruler. But war produced other kinds of value besides rights to goods, land, or labor. It produced influence, honor, and prestige, in other words, symbolic value.

While bearing many costs, nobles and commoners also benefitted from Excan tlatoloyan warfare and empire building. A ruler accrued value, material and symbolic, in a variety of ways. He had access to wealth through tribute as well as through access to lands and labor. But beyond becoming wealthier, he could use that wealth to bind other rulers and nobles to him through his ability to bestow gifts at feasts that accompanied major events and calendrical ceremonies. Such happened with the ruler

Ahuitzotl at the dedication of the Templo Mayor in 1487. Not only did the largesse, pomp, and violence of such special events as well as the coronations and funerals of Mexica tlatoque encourage loyalty from attendees at such feasts, these events also served to reinforce the overwhelming dominance of supreme rulers. Royal celebrations served to legitimate their rulerships at the cost of the prestige of other rulers, both allied and defeated. Select commoners also attended as guests such as elite warriors and singers. These macehualtin would have gained some material and symbolic benefits from their presence. Such ceremonies often coincided with major religious festivals during which large numbers of ritual killings of war prisoners took place, further embellishing the stature of the Mexica supreme ruler.

This was a very real dynamic during the period of Moteuczoma Xocoyotl's reign, for example. His power increased beyond that of other rulers of the Excan tlatoloyan, thereby costing Nezahualpilli, the ruler of Tetzcoco (who ruled from 1472–1515), power and prestige. The same was true for the tlaxilacalli and calpolli, whose leaders had lost some authority through the process of dynastic formation and imperial consolidation. Tlatoque increased their control over military units, sometimes sending them into battle against the desire of tlaxilacalli leaders, even though these units had traditionally selected, ordered, trained, equipped and united troops when needed. Thus, war provided material and symbolic benefits to rulers. As a ruler wielded his own symbols of office and wealth – special jewelry, clothing, and other decorations including precious feathers as well as living in a large palace that served dual functions as a place of administration of governance and his home – he sent visual messages about his power and prestige. By distributing food to laborers and the poor from Tenochtitlan and surrounding altepeme at such ceremonies, tlatoque reciprocated the energy and goods workers and fighters provided.

War therefore provided benefits and value, both material and symbolic, to rulers and nobles. It did so for commoners as well. When victorious rulers distributed resources the material benefit was clear. But the taking of prisoners provided status rewards, material and symbolic, for both noble and macehualtin fighters. The taking of from one to four or more captives resulted in rewards that included special garb and possibly higher status positions and arms. Very skilled warriors, generally but not only nobles, could become members of prestigious military orders, most often the eagle and jaguar orders (*cuacuauhtin*, *ocelome*, respectively). But other, even higher status, orders existed, the *otontin* (Otomi) and *cuahchique* (shorn ones). The latter had the highest status, and the highest military commanders belonged to it. Their high position was marked by their appearance, involving special hair styles, body paint, and clothing that were reserved for them as well as certain types of weapons. The military represented an arena to achieve and display wealth, power, and status, thereby enhancing the prestige of rulers, nobles, and those commoners who achieved the status of *cuauhpipiltin* (lit. eagle nobles, commoners who attained a quasi-noble status through achievements in warfare). Seeking to maintain authority over a growing nobility in his own altepetl and an ever-growing but fractious imperial formation, the second Moteuczoma bestowed many privileges upon nobles at the expense of commoner officials of tlaxilacalli, building on the legacy of his grandfather or great-grandfather, Moteuczoma Ilhuicamina, who had promulgated laws intended to differentiate between the nobility and the macehualtin. Nonetheless, because tlatoque depended upon commoners for food, tributary goods, and a wide array of services, especially military, the skills of the cuauhpipiltin still had to be respected, and tlaxilacalli heads even then had to be consulted late in the Excan tlatoloyan's history.

Conclusion

The Aztec era was one marked by political transformations away from more collective forms of governance toward a more powerful dynastic, ruler-centered form of governance, although elements of that more representative system persisted through and beyond the era of violent contact with Europeans. In the decades before Spaniards arrived, a tlatoani commanded the greatest prestige and symbolic value. His control over the symbols of office and the exalted status of his person through jewelry, clothing, and a special throne symbolized and reinforced his place in the political and sacred realms. Not himself deified, the Mexica and other rulers nonetheless led the propitiation of major deities by acting in priestly roles, participating in publicly viewed ritual killings, and dancing dressed as deities. The Mexica tlatoani led pilgrimages around the Basin of Mexico such as that to honor Tlaloc, the rain god, and in war, wore military regalia that symbolized deities, especially Xipe Totec, a deity of vegetation and the life cycle of plants. Not only did a tlatoani command material resources through land and labor attached to both his office and his dynastic family, but the political economy of tribute and market underlay a ruler's access to power, status, and prestige. Aztec tlatoque, Mexica and others, used their sweeping authority to develop, expand, defend, and change the structure of the Excan tlatoloyan, as it became more Mexica-centered. Similar processes of change affected other confederations of altepeme within and around the Basin of Mexico. The economy that supported such nearly continuous war efforts was powered by commoner labor and gendered through the organization of work, access to wealth, and the conceptualization of parallel roles of women and men in the symbolic sphere. That conceptualization explained, justified, and reinforced an ideology of complementarity, yet violence, imperial growth, and increasing inequality also influenced relations between the higher and lower classes and between women and men. The next chapter explores the growth of the Aztec economy and how that economy related to a political system structured around both balance and hierarchy.

4
Creating Value
Producing, Exchanging, Consuming

∼

Any number of writers consider the central paradox of Aztec civilization to be that of the contrast between what is often seen as an obsession with war, killing, and death through "human sacrifice" in contrast to ideas about beauty, time, and existence expressed through art and oral literature, but perhaps another paradox is even more central to the principles of organization and ways of living of these peoples. That paradox is the contrast between balance and hierarchy. While Aztec forms of governance and the creation of value supported the increasingly rigid forms of hierarchy that developed after the rise of the Excan tlatoloyan, the maintenance of that hierarchy relied upon a rapidly expanding economy rooted in forms of labor and the production and circulation of goods. That economy featured reciprocal exchanges of energy and goods among humans and between humans and the earth. Through those exchanges, interdependence and life as Aztecs knew it could be maintained. Using the concepts of value, reciprocity, and balance, this chapter discusses Aztec working women and men. It describes how they produced everyday and luxury goods and the land and commodities they used to do so, as well as the value they created by transforming resources into items with material and symbolic value. Aztec leaders, local and state, used the value workers created to underwrite both balance and hierarchy.

Working Men and Women

Aztec women and men worked hard. This was true both for commoners and nobles. Their labor fed the millions of people living in and around the Basin of Mexico, produced goods those people bartered or bought in the many marketplaces of the region, and made or collected goods for the tribute system into which altepeme subjugated to the Excan tlatoloyan paid. Workers also provided service labor for public works, civil and religious, and the commercial labor that got goods to marketplaces for barter or sale. Because the inhabitants of most Aztec households farmed and participated in craft production, both women's and men's work proved essential to meeting both family and community needs. Historian Arnold Bauer estimated that the labor needed to grind corn and make tortillas for family food consumption, work done by women, took up to five to six hours per day. Tortilla production alone could represent at least thirty-five hours of work each week. I mention this point to begin a theme threaded through this chapter about the material *value* that women created and its centrality to the Aztec economy, political system, and religious ideas and activities.

Early colonial texts such as the *Historia de los mexicanos por sus pinturas* and the *Leyenda de los soles* stress the fundamental nature of the gendered division of labor, tracing it back to the first humans and diviners, Oxomoco and Cipactonal. They gave birth to the macehualtin whose responsibility it then was to undertake labor. In a different sense, labor originated within each Aztec household as children learned the basics of the work in which their families engaged from their parents and other relatives. Households were the key to the Aztec economy – complex though this economy was – because of the way they produced food, a wide variety of goods, both utilitarian and luxury, and distributed those goods through tribute and commercial exchange. Thus the socialization of children into their work roles within the household made up a major aspect of family life.

From birth on, Aztecs closely associated childhood, gender, and work. The Aztec midwife, quoted in Book Six of the *Florentine Codex*, addressed both female and male children with words about work and adult responsibilities. She told girls that they would produce daily sustenance and that "sweat, weariness, effort" (itonalli, ciaviztli, tlapaliviztli) would be needed to provide food, drink, and clothing. The physician/midwife told boys that their military service would contribute nourishment to the gods. The socialization and education of children involved more than instruction in learning how to work. This was so because living up to the Aztec moral code, undertaking ritual responsibilities, and for boys learning the military arts were all expected in the Aztec world. They looked to children not only to learn specific work tasks but to be diligent in performing them. Children needed to become excellent workers because work, *tequitl*, provided sustenance for humans and deities. The concept of tequitl was broad, implying ideas about duty, serving, and obligation to provide labor through service, which included rotational service work known as *coatequitl*, or tribute. Written and visual texts show that boys learned to fight, farm, hunt, or fish, to make pottery, obsidian blades, and other manufactured goods such as working fine feathers into beautiful mosaic-like designs, or to exchange goods in markets near and far from home; noble boys would be educated for administrative or priestly occupations. Girls at all social levels learned to spin, weave, cook, and grow or use plants, and if they had been born into a craft-producing or trading and marketing family, they learned to produce, market, and keep track of the value of such goods. Careful investigation of textual, material, and ethnographic evidence shows that Aztec women's roles were and are actually even more expansive.

The complexity of tasks expected to be performed increased with age, with girls, for example, learning to spin between the ages of four and seven and weaving when they were about fourteen. Aztec parents, mothers and fathers, used verbal admonitions and physical punishments to reinforce skills because sloppy work or negligence were not acceptable. That work ethic allowed households, communities, and altepeme to survive and flourish. Once they reached adulthood in their mid- to late-teenage years, Aztec women and men undertook the many different kinds of labor just mentioned to support their own households; nobles' and rulers' palaces and families; administrative, military, and legal bureaucracies; marketplaces; and temples and other ritual settings that accommodated the near-constant ritual cycle through which material and symbolic value was created and circulated.

Beyond the tasks most basic to Aztec gender identities, both women and men produced an array of everyday and elite craft goods, and carried out the work of collecting, trading, and delivering goods – raw and finished – to marketplaces and tribute collection points. Women, like men, farmed, sold, or exchanged goods in the many marketplaces of Aztec cities and towns, and they participated in craft production. They worked as midwives, healers, and matchmakers as well as teachers and priestesses in song houses (*cuicacalli*, explained further in the next chapter) and temples. Some became administrators, even leaders, in merchant and governing hierarchies, serving also as tribute collectors. While, as already described, women rulers were rare among the Aztecs, they certainly existed. And whether she ruled or not, the primary wife of a tlatoani, the *tlatocacihuatl* (female ruler) had her own set of responsibilities. She was a "woman ruler, governor, guide, an organizer, giver of orders" (ca cioatlatoani, tepachoani, teicanani, tetlataluiani, tlanaoatiani) as described in the *Florentine Codex*. Women's responsibilities, whether noble or commoner, included significant amounts of work and even economic management of the often large, complex households they co-headed with their husbands. What did all the labor that women and men performed produce?

The Foods Aztecs Ate; the Goods Aztecs Made

Agriculture provided the food needed by the 3–4 million or so people living in and around the Basin of Mexico when the Spaniards arrived. Most Aztecs performed at least part-time agricultural activity, growing the corn, beans, squash, chiles, chia, and amaranth that people ate. Both women and men prayed to the female and male deities of earth, water, and plants – especially maize – through times of plenty and times of hardship. Another important plant Aztecs cultivated was maguey, grown for the plant's sap that was used for the alcoholic drink *pulque*, the leaves pulped to make paper, and fibers used for clothing, rope, and some of the cloth-based armor used in war. Beans, tomatoes, squashes, peppers, nopal cacti, were all cultivated as were amaranth plants, used in rituals or eaten. Among rural Aztecs, men cleared fields, planted, and harvested. Women helped with planting, they cleaned and harvested grains, and they prepared foods for families to eat. In addition to seeds and plants, different types of land and water sources constituted the raw materials necessary for the highly productive techniques Aztec farmers used.

They grew plants in highly diverse microenvironments differentiated by elevations that occupy three levels – *tierra caliente* (hot land, 0–1000 meters; or 3281 ft.); *tierra templada* (temperate land, 1000–2000 meters; or 6562 ft.), and *tierra fría* (cold land, 2000 meters or 6562 ft. and above). Amounts of rainfall and access to other water sources (lakes, rivers, swamps, and lagoons), and the many types of soil for which the Aztecs had a sophisticated system of classification also helped to determine the ways land could be used. The wide array of microenvironments across ancient Mesoamerica led to the development of several kinds of agricultural techniques. These included slash-and-burn, terracing, irrigation, and for the Aztecs, chinampa-based agriculture, an intensive form of agriculture based on using raised garden plots along watery environs for cultivation.

Often known as the Valley of Mexico, geologists know the most densely populated Aztec region as the Basin of

Mexico. Bounded by dramatic volcanic mountains to the south – Popocatepetl (Smoking Mountain) and Iztaccihuatl (White Woman) – and to the north by the rolling hills leading into the drier areas making up the Central Plateau, of which the basin is a part, its key feature was the large lake system that sat at its center. Five interconnected lakes made up this system, so crucial for farming in and around the basin (see Map 1.2). Draining to the interior areas of the Central Plateau (meaning no drainage from the lakes reached the Atlantic Ocean, thereby making it a basin) and fed by rainfall, springs, and rivers, Lakes Zumpango and Xaltocan lay to the north, Lake Texcoco to the east, and Lakes Xochimilco and Chalco to the south. The latter two lakes contained the freshest waters. Lake Texcoco's water was salty due to evaporation and did not allow for much agriculture on its shores. The lakes to the north tended to be brackish but still provided water for farmers, especially those planting chinampas (*chinamitl* in Nahuatl). The southern-most lakes offered abundant waters for chinampas and also nourished the rich aquatic life found in that zone – fish, turtles, frogs, and insects and their eggs – as well as providing important commodities such as reeds and salt. These waters, in combination with the moisture afforded by a rainy season lasting from about June or July to January of each year, along with the rich soils of the basin, allowed for agricultural productivity at a level that could support the million or so Aztecs who lived in the basin and the millions of Aztecs and others living in the other valleys of the Central Plateau.

Slash-and-burn agriculture was practiced in lowland areas, especially in regions south and east of the Basin of

Mexico where Aztecs grew crops, received tribute from subordinated Aztec altepeme or other groups, and traded for coveted foods such as cacao and vanilla. Aztecs and other Mesoamericans cleared and burned areas of land, seeded it, tried to control weed growth, and then harvested crops over several growing seasons. Then they left the fields to regenerate their fertility, moving on to farm other areas, later returning to re-start the cycle after several agricultural seasons.

In highland regions, terracing, irrigation agriculture, and the growing of needed crops in and around urban areas on chinampas along canals and lakeshores constituted the main Aztec forms of agriculture. In those areas where farmers could depend mainly on rainwater, Aztec farmers used hillside terraces to contain that water and stop soil erosion. Low earthen walls known as berms topped by agave or maguey plants, could surround other plantings such as corn, squash, fruit trees, or beans or trap precious water. This method, *metepantle*, kept soil from eroding and is still in use today in some areas. At lower elevations, Aztecs also used drainage ditches to catch water for dams, canals, or aqueducts to move water to where it was needed. In valleys and at the bases of mountains, they employed irrigation, sometimes simply collecting runoff water at higher elevations. As the numbers of people and settlements grew, more complex irrigation techniques spread throughout many parts of the Basin of Mexico. Some areas employed extensive systems of canals and aqueducts, examples of the sophisticated waterworks Aztec engineers developed to carry and distribute water.

In and around larger towns and cities of the mainland area and the populated islands of the lake system, Aztecs relied also on house land or plots (*callalli* or *calmilli*) as well as the chinampas mentioned above. Chinampas are still worked on by farmers in what is today the southern-most part of Mexico City known as Xochimilco. Beds built up from the swampy soils around the Basin of Mexico's huge lake system, they were found at the northern but mostly at the southern ends of these interconnected lakes. These shallow but extensive plots, averaging 300 feet in length by about fifteen to thirty feet in width, were surrounded by swampy water and filled with nutrients created by rotting leaves and organic fertilizers. Such plots produced crops year round, helping to feed the large populations of Tenochtitlan and other cities. Among the crops sown on chinampas were corn, chiles, tomatoes, tomatillos, squash, and many different kinds of flowers that Aztecs used for food, worship, healing, and decoration. Farming technologies – for chinampas and other kinds of fields – required land. Those lands were administered and used by various groups and individuals, with collective labor organization common.

While Aztec women and men created a highly commercialized economy, one in which governments regulated but did not control trade and exchange and individual and family initiative played a strong role, land ownership was an altogether different matter. For the most part, ownership was corporate with land holding groups having the right and responsibility to reallocate land. These groups or the nobles who oversaw them granted access to cultivable lands through use rights or through a form of servitude somewhat similar to the feudal serfdom of medieval Europe, though with greater mobility for laborers to move among estates. Leaders of the tlaxilacalli or calpolli granted use rights to the lands of an altepetl (*altepetlalli*) to macehualtin members of these units who worked lands known as *calpollalli* or *tlaxilacallalli*. The laborers tied to and working for a noble family or palace were called *mayeque* (dependent farm laborers, though there were other terms too as explained below). Evidence suggests that some lands and houses could be sold, but allocation and reallocation as a political and corporate process was much more common than sale. Other land categories included *tecpantlalli* or lands of the palace, *tlatocatlalli* (lands of the tlatoani), *pillalli* and *teuctlalli* (lands of nobles and subordinate rulers), *teotlalli*, and *milchimalli* (land of the gods and temples; military lands). Lords and rulers appear to have had access to both palace and lordly lands, worked mainly by mayeque, the former tied to the institutions of leadership, the latter bound to individuals or family lines, with lordly lands heritable and perhaps able to be sold, at least to a limited extent. It is possible that teotlalli and milchimalli consisted of certain lands of the calpolli or tlaxilacalli designated for the support of temples, feasting, and war efforts.

That calpolli or tlaxilacalli lands could be heritable, even on rare occasions sold as just described, also appears to have been the case as the earliest Nahuatl-language colonial wills made by Aztecs, noble and macehualli alike, suggest. While most agricultural land was under some type of corporate control, households nonetheless thought of themselves as having a least semi-permanent use rights signified by the existence of such terms as callalli and *huehuetlalli* (old or inherited land) that could be passed on. Another category of land, *cihuatlalli* (women's land) might have referred to lands given by rulers and wealthy nobles as dowry or to land owned by or that came to a household through a woman. While ownership of lands by nobles, communities, and commoners became hotly contested, and a trend toward privatization developed during the colonial period, ownership may not be the most accurate term to understand pre-European-influenced Aztec landholding patterns. These patterns seem to have been most connected to rights and obligations to work land and use what it produced. Ownership may have been a more abstract concept residing at higher levels with the gods and altepeme. Given that altepeme and the tlaxilacalli, and calpolli associated with them saw themselves as connected to a divine entity who was a part of their origin story, lands may well have been seen as a resource originating from the gods. Such a complex and layered concept of ownership shows again the interconnectedness of religion, polity, and economy.

Land and its uses for agriculture were the subject of various kinds of ritual designed to confirm use rights and to insure the water needed for successful growing seasons. Claiming territory and the founding of an altepetl by migrating groups involved ceremonies. Sometimes these included walking boundaries a group claimed, shooting arrows north, south, east, and west, dividing a core area into several districts, or providing a home for a patron deity by building a temple, palace, and other essential buildings. When Aztecs transferred houses and lands in the late prehispanic and early colonial periods, they threw stones in the four directions. They also used stones, trees, or other properties to set the boundaries of household plots and agricultural fields. Aztec groups also carried out other rituals to celebrate sacred landscapes and encourage rain to fall for bountiful harvests. As Chapter 2 described, ceremonies connected to rain, corn, and the agricultural cycle occurred throughout the Aztec solar year. The sacrifice of women and children, linked to ideas about fertility, the earth's regenerative powers, and rain took place during these ceremonies that also celebrated mountains and the life-sustaining water contained, Aztecs believed, within them.

Laborers making the goods that Aztecs used also drew connections among work, spirituality, and ceremonial life through calendrical and other rituals carried out by specific occupational groups. When Book Nine of the *Florentine Codex* discusses the production of gold, stone, and feather items, the writers specifically mention the deities worshipped by each group of workers. They describe the ceremonies and goods used in those ceremonies for patron deities as offerings and adornments. While the obligation to work came from the gods, it was also a fundamental part of everyday life, something owed to family and community. Many workers were farmers, some of those farmers also produced the material items needed for everyday life as well as luxury goods for elite use, and some workers, especially in cities, worked full-time to produce such items and/or trade and sell them.

Whether they worked as part- or full-time artisans, Aztecs were incredibly skilled craftspeople. Among the items produced by Aztec women and men were textiles (for which women were the main producers) and pottery (men may have produced most ceramic items). But whatever the predominant gender division of labor for a particular type of craft production, because so much work was performed at the household level, it may not have been unusual for men and women to work together to manufacture particular types of goods by performing complementary tasks.

Producing obsidian tools and other objects was also quite important. Aztecs used this volcanic glass to make knives, projectile points for weapons, scrapers, as well as mirrors and adornments, and used other types of stone for everyday items such as mortars, pestles, drinking, cooking, and serving implements. Given the frequency of wars fought by the Excan tlatoloyan and other altepeme, the production of blades for weaponry, often in workshops, illustrates how crucial just this one stone, obsidian, was to the Aztec economy. In addition to weapons, Aztecs made many others kinds of things from obsidian including the tools for food and craft production such as wood, metal, stone, and feather working. Obsidian workers also made implements used for rituals including knives and points for auto- and human sacrifice as well as some of the jewelry that adorned individuals and even art pieces, such as small sculptures of animals. Other stone workers made utilitarian items, for example, for cooking and also fashioned fine stones for jewelry as well as adornments like masks, small sculptures, musical instruments, and implements for healing, divination, and protection and celebration during or after war.

Aztecs also made use of metals – gold, silver, and copper. They used metal for bells, axe monies, body adornments, musical instruments, dishes, and images of all sorts of plants and animals displayed prominently in the palaces of rulers, especially in the zoo of Moteuczoma Xocoyotl. He had placed images of Mesoamerican plants and animals there, crafted from metal as well as feathers.

As the priestly chronicler Motolinia, wrote about Aztec metalworking skills:

... they could cast a bird whose tongue, head, and wings move, and they could mold a monkey or other monster that moves its head, tongue, feet and hands, and in its hands they put little toys, so it appears the figure is dancing with them, and even more remarkably, they can make a piece half in gold and half in silver and cast a fish with its scales in gold and silver, alternating.

Working feathers was another Aztec fine craft specialty. While for Europeans, feathers communicated ideas about Aztec and Indigenous otherness, wildness, and a barbaric connection to the natural world, for Aztecs they had utilitarian and symbolic value, signaling wealth, power, and privilege. Feathers could be placed on or worn as clothing, used as parts of armor and weapons, or appear in artistic pieces decorating deities, venerated especially by nobles and rulers. Far from a simple craft, feather working entailed great skill, and Aztecs highly valued objects made of and with feathers. Feather workers produced their goods in households but also labored in neighborhood workshops or those attached to palaces (those workshops called *totocalli*, bird houses).

Prehispanic Aztec luxury artisans obtained feathers, especially the exotic ones from hummingbirds and quetzals, through markets, connections to long-distance traders (the *pochteca* discussed below), or through their ties to elite patrons. Known as *amanteca* (with luxury craftworkers generally known as "tolteca," including gold and fine stone workers), in Tenochtitlan and Tlatelolco, as well as in Tetzcoco, they lived in separate tlaxilacalli. In Tlatelolco, their neighborhood was called Amantlan, which had its own calmecac, as well as a temple. Feather workers thus worshipped together, and they carried out group-specific ceremonies. These neighborhoods were close to merchant areas and near or in palaces, with men and women who performed this labor doing so full-time. Later chapters of Book Nine of the *Florentine Codex* provide an in-depth description of the tools amanteca used that included obsidian blades and copper knives and the many steps needed to produce feathered items including warriors' garments and shields, garments worn by rulers and high nobles, and other kinds of elite and warrior insignia such as headdresses. Some items were constructed like mosaics for which feather workers produced patterns and glued brightly colored feather pieces (most natural, some dyed) to a harder, framed surface to produce images of plants, flowers, animals, or other designs. Another kind of feather work consisted of tying feathers and then sewing them together to create fans, bracelets, tassels, or other sorts of decorative ornamentation. Many of the objects created were worn by rulers, but some items, no doubt very valuable, were sold by amanteca.

As the empire and its noble elite grew larger later in the fifteenth and early sixteenth centuries, the array of high-quality luxury commodities, the demand for luxury goods, and the workers to produce them all increased, thus requiring full-time work organization especially in the larger cities, although parents remained the primary educators of work skills. While luxury production was concentrated in those cities, both everyday and some fine goods could be produced in smaller altepeme and rural areas. Households there tended to be less specialized and women and men performed a variety of kinds of work, producing food, textiles, pottery, rope and mats, paper, and other goods. But depending on the commodities in which particular regions specialized, neighborhoods even in smaller altepeme could contain workshops of artisans producing specific types of goods. Archaeologists Cynthia Otis Charlton and Alejandro Pastrana have both shown this to be the case for the altepetl of Otompan, northeast of Tenochtitlan, where significant amounts of obsidian were mined and many obsidian items produced. For particular obsidian goods, they might begin to be fashioned in an Otompan workshop, then finished in another one, likely also in Otompan. Then such goods would be traded far and wide across Mesoamerica. All this production of obsidian and other items, luxury and utilitarian, depended upon the collection, trade, and working of specific commodities. These included obsidian, of course, but also feathers, raw cotton, textiles, metal used for bells, jewelry, or as currency, greenstones, turquoise, obsidian, pottery, and salt.

The trading, production, and use of such goods relied on a gendered division of labor. While some women worked in luxury craft production like feathers, with the feather worker parents of a girl asking that their female children be skilled at choosing colors, buying feathers, and embroidering, virtually all women – noble, commoner, and slave – wove. Aztecs presented infant girls with weaving implements at birth, and tools for spinning and weaving were shown as part of the arrays of several important goddesses, notably Cihuacoatl, Tlazolteotl, and Xochiquetzal. A spiritual guardian of weavers, Xochiquetzal served as a patron for a number of artistic activities including embroidery, painting, working silver, and sculpting.

Creating Value: Producing, Exchanging, Consuming

Aztec girls learned to weave beginning between the ages of four and five. Noblewomen made the most elaborate, highly decorated garments worn by other nobles, male and female. Noblewomen weavers had access to the widest array and highest quality raw materials, especially fine cotton and feathers, and worked with the finest tools. Commoner women also wove with cotton, but they usually made and wore plain garments made from maguey or yucca. Textiles, clothing and other woven commodities served many functions in Aztec society. Worn as *huipilli* (blouse or shift for women), *maxtlatl* or loin cloths (for men), or woven into capes (*quachtli*), textiles could also be offered to deities or by parents as gifts at the dedication of youths to their schools. Merchants made cloth offerings during neighborhood feasts. Rulers did the same on a larger scale to create or maintain alliances through which cloth served a diplomatic function as a symbol of alliance, domination, or subjugation. The range of clothing produced by Aztec weavers and bought in markets or given as tribute was actually quite broad as shown in Fig. 4.1. In her book *Indian Clothing before Cortés*, anthropologist Patricia Anawalt discusses the forms of garment construction that include draped, slip-on, open sewn, and closed sewn items. The technology of clothing production remained similar across much of Mesoamerica, consisting of spindles, bowls, battens, and backstrap looms, though types of thread and the cloth produced, designs used, and skill levels all varied. Women's attire varied in quality but the huipilli and the skirt, the *cueitl*, were worn by all women. The *quechquemitl* appears to have been an older style of clothing worn by Aztecs in rituals, but not part of everyday dress. Men wore the maxtlatl, but used

Technique	Name	Definition	Gender	Example
Draped	Maxtlatl	Loincloth	M	Maxtlatl
	Tilmatli	Cape	M	
	Cueitl	Wrap-around skirt	F	
Slip-on	Quechquemitl	Slip-on upper garment	F	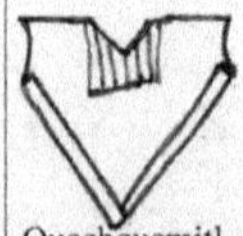 Quechquemitl
Open-sewn	Ichcahuipilli	Quilted shirt-like cotton armor	M	Xicolli
	Xicolli	Sleeveless jacket	M	
Closed-sewn	Ichcahuipilli	Ichcahuipilli with front sewn	M	Huipilli
	Huipilli	Sleeveless shift	F	

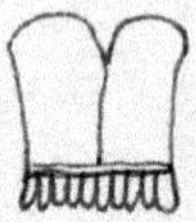

FIG. 4.1 Major categories of Aztec clothing
Drawings by author based on images in the *Florentine Codex*. Courtesy of the University of Utah Press

specialized garments, the *ichcahuipilli* for example, in war, and the *xicolli* in rituals.

In addition to clothing, textiles could be used as decorations or awnings for market stalls, temples, or palaces. They could serve as wrappings for the deity bundles known as *tlaquimilolli*, or for human bodies being prepared for cremation. They also served as a kind of money for exchange. Overstating the socioeconomic significance of Aztec textile production really is not possible. By the sixteenth century, Aztecs provided nearly 280,000 textiles as tribute each year; about 240,000 of these textiles were woven pieces used in the religious, commercial, or ceremonial settings mentioned above. The rest was clothing – loincloths, shifts, skirts, and protective clothing for war. Careful examination of quantities of cloth production, based largely on information in the *Matrícula de Tributos*, demonstrates the tremendous material and symbolic value of women's labor across the Aztec world.

The crops and goods Aztecs produced sustained them and their gods. Because they created so much value, it is worth exploring the setting for the enormous quantity of craft goods made by Aztec workers across the central region of Mesoamerica. For the most part, that setting was the household, often complex in structure (to be discussed in the next chapter), where both craft and agricultural activities were organized and carried out. Household members undertook a variety of economic activities to support themselves and meet their work and tribute obligations. While crafts work could be carried out in workshops tied to rulers' palaces and sometimes in markets, most of it took place within homes in which residents employed diverse strategies to support families and other residents and meet community obligations. Even in the years when needed rainfall fell short, when floods might adversely affect chinampa output, or war interfered with production, transportation, or market functions, the production of craft goods for tribute or trade had to continue. It was the case, however, that most wars took place from the late fall through the spring, which made up the majority of the dry season, when male farmers could devote time to the war units in which they fought if called up to serve.

The foods, crafts, and commodities Aztecs produced, especially those intended for others besides household members, needed to be transported and distributed.

In other words, goods had to circulate in order to be used. They did so throughout the Aztec world. In circulating, they gained value, with transportation a critical element for creating that value. With no domesticated pack animals or wheeled vehicles, human carriers moved most of those goods over long distances. Across the Basin of Mexico, in addition to human porters, called *tlamemeque* (sing., *tlameme*), Aztecs used canoes to move goods across the lake system and along navigable rivers. Carrying loads of up to about 160 pounds, tlamemeque placed goods in baskets or on carrying frames called *cacaxtli* and carried them by using a tumpline, a strap placed around the forehead that allowed porters to balance loads on their backs rather than their shoulders and walk long distances, usually traversing about thirteen to eighteen miles per day. Low-status work, this occupation nevertheless experienced increasing demand as the economic reach of the Excan tlatoloyan grew. Tlamemeque, predominantly even probably overwhelmingly male, likely began their training at age five, having been born into families that did such work, though some porters performed this labor as tribute payment. There were altepeme, for example that of Tepeaca, that owed this kind of labor to Tenochtitlan as part of its tribute assessment. Other men turned to this work because of poverty and landlessness. Tlamemeque provided service labor but they did not organize trade or tribute. Rulers and others of a higher class status did that.

Class and Tribute

One of the key markers of commoner status was the payment of goods and provision of service to local and

Creating Value: Producing, Exchanging, Consuming

imperial rulers. For the Excan tlatoloyan powers, especially the Mexica, tribute payments from conquered peoples demonstrated rulers' authority and reinforced the reverence with which rulers were to be treated. Despite the earlier history of collective governance, the importance of the idea of balance, and the practices of reciprocity between rulers and the ruled mentioned in the previous chapter, the idea of different kinds of access to wealth and power has appeared frequently on the pages of this book and in this chapter. Social and economic inequality was a key aspect of Aztec society. This inequality was rooted in the lengthy history of class difference in Mesoamerican societies that was characteristic of Aztecs as well. While comprising a very small proportion, perhaps about 2 percent, of the Aztec population, rulers and nobles controlled most land and wealth in the forms of labor, tribute, and luxury items obtained from markets or long-distance traders. It is too simple to say that the distinction between nobles and commoners rested solely on who paid tribute and owed work to whom – commoners to nobles. The obligations of commoners varied in how tribute and work were provided to the nobility, and lesser nobles paid tribute to higher ranking nobles and rulers.

Despite the hereditary nature of noble status, strata existed within that group as it did among macehualtin. Ranging from pipiltin who were born into the nobility but did not hold high positions and teteuctin who held important administrative positions within altepeme, to tlatoque who were rulers of altepeme, and culminating in the supreme rulers, the huey tlatoque, of the Excan tlatoloyan powers, at each level the nobility held greater power and more wealth. Excavations of noble palaces across many altepetl show how closely their size and opulence correlated with the standing of communities they governed. Such excavations as well as descriptions in texts demonstrate that the goods owned by Aztecs differed along class lines. From cloth to pottery to obsidian, nobles and rulers had access to a wide array of finely crafted items that commoners did not. Commoners, for example, wore coarse, maguey-fiber clothing much more often than they did apparel made from cotton. Such was true in war and peace as noble fighters wore better protective and decorative costuming. In peace, nobles had access by law to finer clothing, jewelry, and footwear. Even two-story housing was restricted to "great noblemen and valiant warriors," as Fray Durán puts it.

While the vast majority of commoners, the macehualtin, farmed and/or produced goods for the markets of many areas within the basin and across Mesoamerica and owed tribute and labor to the lords who administered their communities as well as to altepeme and imperial rulers, other statuses existed within the commoner class. A variety of regional terms described people who directly depended upon nobles, worked their lands, and performed services for them. Mayeque (sing., *maye*), tlalmaitin (sing., *tlalmaitl*) and -*tech pouhque* (*pohua*, to count or assign something), all were terms referring to these people and refer either to the idea of laboring by hand, *maitl* being the Nahuatl word for hand, or being assigned or belonging to someone. Those directly subjugated to a noble appear to have been less well off than those with access to corporately administered lands, but beneath those dependent commoners lay yet another strata, that of the *tlacotin* (sing. *tlacotli*), or slaves. These unfortunate people had been captured in war, assigned the status as punishment, or they had fallen into this stratum due to an accumulation of unpayable debts. Even circumstances such as famine could throw someone into a situation of overwhelming hunger or debt whereupon an individual would sell themselves or others, including children. Given as tribute or sold in markets, tlacotin often labored in nobles' palaces, with female slaves especially valued for the quachtli they wove. The tlacotli status was not heritable and was not always permanent. Slaves nonetheless were destitute, almost wholly dependent on others for survival, and some number – especially war captives – were put to death as part of calendric celebrations or other kinds of public ceremonies.

A small but significant middle stratum of people – about whom historians have pondered whether they constitute a middle class or not – represents a complexity of the Aztec social system. For example, as already described, commoner men could achieve high rank through the Aztec military. The cuauhpipiltin were the warriors who achieved a quasi-noble status through their achievements in battle. Having risen through military ranks by taking large numbers of captives, these men's higher status was designated, Ross Hassig explains, "by the honors one received, the way one's hair was worn, the jewelry one was entitled to wear, the clothing one wore in peace, and the arms, armor, and insignia one wore in war." One very valuable privilege they attained was that they no longer had to pay tribute. Cuauhpipiltin participated in the war council, and rulers rewarded them with lands. Furthermore, they could be elevated to the high military orders, but they could *not* wear the same kind of special war suits as pipiltin nor could they sell the lands they were given as a reward by the tlatoani. They were barred, therefore, from claiming full noble status through the ways sumptuary laws, laws that governed consumption, reinforced the Aztec class hierarchy.

These laws, concerned with housing, clothing, war insignia, and jewelry, made the distinction between nobles and commoners clear, though they changed over time among the Mexica. The first Moteuczoma codified such rules; the ruler Ahuitzotl loosened them to reward commoner soldiers, and Moteuczoma Xocoyotl greatly tightened them to exclude commoners from positions within the palace and to fortify class distinctions among those appointed by Ahuitzotl. Another kind of high-ranking commoner were wealthy pochteca, who could amass great fortunes. Living in their own neighborhoods, policing themselves through their own governing hierarchy, and serving both rulers and their own family interests, they had access to power, wealth, and privileges. But like the cuauhpipiltin, Aztecs placed limits on the status of merchants. When those from Tenochtitlan returned home after a successful expedition and unloaded their valuable goods, they did so at night so as not to attract undue attention. While they displayed their wealth in their homes and at the banquets they held to celebrate their successful journeys, they did not flaunt their riches widely beyond their own households to avoid provoking undue ire of other commoners and nobles who might view them with jealousy. Like other commoners, even the luxury artisans who had connections to rulers, nobles, and merchants paid tribute and displayed subordination to the elite, ruling class.

Nearby subject altepeme paid tribute in foods grown on tlaxilacalli, calpolli, or teccalli lands to be consumed in elite palaces and commoner households. Both nearby and far-off communities paid tribute in a wide array of other items – textiles, warrior arrays, pottery, obsidian blades, reed mats and baskets, paper, as well as copper, gold, and paper items. While in larger cities like Tenochtitlan, Tlatelolco, and Tetzcoco, full-time specialists produced such goods, in smaller cities, towns, and villages, men and women farmed *and* produced the craft items that they provided for tribute payments or sale in markets. Both female and male labor provided tribute goods, but because so much tribute came in the form of cloth used for clothing, shields, cotton armor, and even as a form of currency (the plain woven cotton textiles called quachtli, already mentioned), women's work was critical to tribute flows. As Frances Berdan has pointed out, after a defeat by Triple Alliance fighters, it was in fact common for tribute levies to emphasize the textiles woven by women. That was because the frequent wars that preceded tribute imposition often led to the depletion of male workers. However, tribute streams returned to their regular patterns as more usual gendered production levels once again emerged. Macehualtin also provided services to the ruler and his palace in public works needed for an altepetl, or in war, giving military service. Tribute and service labor might also be needed at special times. A ruler's coronation or a special construction project such as the aqueduct that the Mexica ruler Ahuitzotl commanded be built required so many laborers that they looked like "ants on an ant heap." Drawn from any number of altepeme beyond Tenochtitlan, according to Fray Durán, this project flooded Tenochtitlan, meaning that yet more laborers were required to repair all the damage. Later, Moteuczoma Xocoyotl demanded special purpose laborers numbering 10–12,000, according to the Mexica chronicler Alvarado Tezozomoc, again from numerous altepeme, to move a large stone in order to carve a new *temalacatl* (a round stone used for war-like ritual killings) for the Tlacaxipehualiztli rituals.

Imperial rulers demanded and obtained large amounts of goods and services both regularly and through these extraordinary requests. Rulers extracted significant amounts of material and symbolic value beyond what macehualtin owed to the ruler of the altepetl in which their tlaxilacalli or calpolli was located. A hierarchy of tribute-collecting officials carried out the task of collecting tribute assessments. They served within localities and altepeme, and also at tribute collection centers designated by the Triple Alliance powers. These were located across the tribute paying areas, mentioned in the previous chapter, of the Excan tlatoloyan empire. Some areas, however, did not pay tribute. Instead, these regions, lying near enemy polities, especially the Tlaxcalteca to the east and the Purepecha (popularly known as Tarascans) to the west, played an important border protection role. Such communities, the strategic provinces, provided protection for the borders of the Excan tlatoloyan empire.

Collection and distribution was overseen by local tribute collectors, tequitlato, at the community level and by regional or imperial-appointed *calpixque* at the regional and Excan tlatoloyan level. Many tributary items went directly to Tenochtitlan. Mexica officials then redistributed items to the other powers. The delivery of imperial tribute frequently involved ceremonies meant to embellish the status of imperial rulers and remind subordinate rulers of their lower position. Diego Durán describes the Mexica tlatoani Ahuitzotl demanding tribute from all subjugated kingdoms be brought before him in order to display his "grandeur and power to the enemies and guests and foreign people and fill them with bewilderment and fear. They saw that the Aztecs were masters of the world."

Imperial and local rulers, nobles, and priests also received service labor from farmers tied to corporately-held or noble-held lands, artisans attached to palaces through royal workshops, and young people providing services to temples for a year-long period. While many goods and services flowed to nobles and rulers through these tribute and labor arrangements, more goods – raw, finished, and luxury – likely flowed through markets, helping to provision the thousands of households of the villages and cities of the Aztec empire. Market items also sometimes supplied tribute goods when the assigned items were not locally available. Cotton provides a good example. Few areas actually grew the cotton needed to produce the cotton textiles that women wove for paying tribute from many communities that owed cloth to the Excan tlatoloyan. The same was true for elite-prized items, such as gold, turquoise, or tropical feathers.

Markets and Commerce

One of the distinguishing characteristics of Aztec civilization was its extensive market system. Marketplaces existed throughout Aztec-controlled regions across Mesoamerica, with exchanges carried out through barter or the use of money within and beyond markets – in neighborhoods, on streets, or in homes. All this negotiation and exchange of value reinforced the importance of commerce in Aztec society. Less controlled from above than land transmission or labor organization, commerce nevertheless featured some administered elements. Rulers and nobles directly oversaw the uses of labor and land and thereby derived substantial amounts of wealth, which reinforced their power. Thus, land and labor cannot be considered to have been commodities in a modern, capitalist sense, and the Aztec market economy was not an example of emerging capitalism. The Aztec economy, nevertheless, featured entrepreneurship and elements of a profit motive that made the value created through labor and exchange crucial to the workings of the economy and the political and religious systems as well. Dynamic patterns of exchange among Aztecs and with others created material and symbolic value that tied the nobility and commoners together in reciprocal and hierarchical relations.

So much activity, selling and other, went on in Aztec markets – and every altepetl had at least one – that along with households and temples, marketplaces were critical settings for Aztec daily life. While markets likely were ancient institutions in Mesoamerica, especially in what became Aztec-controlled areas, the rapid population growth across the Basin of Mexico, the increasing interdependence among rulers, nobles, merchants, and luxury-producing artisans, and the special nature of Tenochtitlan and Tlatelolco as island cities that could not feed themselves, promoted the development of a vast and sophisticated market system. Much of this growth occurred throughout the fifteenth century. In this expansive, fluid commercial system, women and men participated as producers, sellers, traders, and consumers within and beyond Tenochtitlan, extending across many parts of Mesoamerica.

Every town or city of any size had a marketplace, though the largest – the marketplaces of Tenochtitlan, Tlatelolco, Tetzcoco, and possibly Tlaxcallan – occurred on a daily basis. Most market activity elsewhere occurred every five days, but other marketing patterns of nine, thirteen, and twenty day cycles also existed, the latter three coinciding with regional calendrical celebrations. Spaniards were impressed by the numbers of markets, the vast array of goods to be found in them, and the numbers of people they observed participating in commercial transactions. Hernán Cortés famously described Mesoamerica's largest marketplace located in Tlatelolco, saying: "The city has many open squares in which markets are continuously held and the general business of buying and selling proceeds. One square in particular is twice as big as that of Salamanca and completely surrounded by arcades where there are daily more than sixty thousand folk buying and selling."

The largest markets attracted buyers and sellers from their own and other altepeme, with many different kinds of goods on offer: foodstuffs, raw and prepared; craft and textile items and some of the raw materials such as cotton dyes or obsidian needed to produce them; medicines and herbs; and luxury items like feathers and gold. Craftsmen produced some goods such as obsidian blades in markets, and service providers including barbers, pharmacists, scribes, and sex workers offered their skills. Workers for hire for the day, such as tlamemeque, also could be found.

On any given day, anywhere from 20,000 to 60,000 people may have participated in Tlatelolco's huge market. Markets in other communities were smaller, with some more specialized, selling goods, including slaves, that they were known for featuring. In the larger markets, the huge number of people buying and selling so many different kinds of goods and services meant that regulation of marketplaces was needed to keep order. Market judges and administrators, *pochtecatlatoque* and *tianquizpan tlayacanque* worked to maintain order, ensuring fair prices, the quality of goods, and severely punishing theft. Both women and men served as tianquizpan tlayacanque, checking goods and making sure measures were accurate.

For fair assessment and honest exchange of value to take place, an orderly system of payment was needed. Barter and money provided the means through which exchanges of valued goods took place in marketplaces across Mesoamerica, including in central Mexico. Nahuatl speakers used words for barter (*patla*), buying (*cohua*) and selling (*namaca*). Early colonial sources suggest that barter was the most common basis for exchange. But money – goods that could be exchanged based upon a commonly accepted value – also existed, with Aztecs commonly using cacao beans and the white cotton textiles called quachtli as currency. Other forms of money Aztecs used included copper axes and gold dust. Cacao beans continued to be used as money into at least the late sixteenth century, with exchange values somewhat standardized, although they could vary somewhat among regions and different Aztec groups. For example, in Tlaxcallan one cacao bean could buy a large tomato and sixty-five beans could purchase a small quachtli cloth.

Creating Value: Producing, Exchanging, Consuming

Table 4.1 *Some price equivalencies in the sixteenth century*

Item	Value in Cacao Beans
Turkey hen	100
Turkey cock	200
Rooster	20
Large rabbit	100
Small rabbit	50
Avocado, just picked	3
1 cacao bean	20 small tomatoes
Local green chile just picked	2 for 1 cacao bean
Prickly pear cactus	1
Tamale	1

Source: "List of market prices established by judge, Tlaxcala, 1545" in Anderson, Berdan, and Lockhart, *Beyond the Codices*

Table 4.1 shows some additional very early colonial exchange values from that same place. Buyers and sellers sought fair exchanges with sellers looking to make a profit (*tlaixnextiliztli*). Who were the sellers and traders who performed the commercial work underlying Aztec ways of accessing and consuming goods?

Archaeologists have shown that from at least the fourteenth century on, commerce within and beyond the Basin of Mexico increased, resulting in the sophisticated production and marketing system observed by Spaniards early in the sixteenth century. Many elements of these systems lasted throughout the sixteenth century and beyond. Descriptions of the Aztec economy often focus on long-distance trading by the pochteca and *oztomeca* (the spying and long-distance merchants). In fact, trading ranged from producer-sellers who sold goods in local marketplaces (the seller called *tlachiuhqui*), others known as *tlamanacac* (a small-scale merchant), and the *tlanecuilo* (a merchant retailer), to the more illustrious pochteca and oztomeca. These merchants traveled to far-off regions of Mesoamerica to obtain luxury goods with high material value. Both food producers and craftspeople, often one and the same, frequently sold their wares in local markets. Other craftworkers sold their goods to the tlanecuilo who traveled among markets or had permanent stalls at larger urban markets. Peddlers, the tlamanacac, who moved among smaller markets, along roads, or sold house-to-house in rural areas also sold such goods.

Both women and men produced and sold, but most peddlers and the true long-distance merchants of the Aztec world who traveled the farthest within and beyond the Basin of Mexico, sometimes far beyond, were men. Women certainly trekked locally among communities around the lake system, walking in groups to sell products from the lakes and other goods. Women from long-distance trading, pochteca, families served as trade administrators and investors. But the merchants who traveled the farthest distances – the oztomeca – brought with them the most coveted goods and carried out reconnaissance, essentially spying missions for rulers, those merchants were men. Yet women were and are key actors in trade among the Aztecs, contemporary Nahuas, and across Indigenous Mesoamerica. The most detailed source on Aztec, particularly Mexica, commercial patterns, Book Ten of the *Florentine Codex*, shows in its illustrations women and men to have made up equal shares of market sellers, men associated more with luxury goods and women with food, textiles, and tobacco (see Fig. 4.2).

At least twelve basin altepeme housed neighborhood areas in which long-distance merchants resided. These twelve

Creating Value: Producing, Exchanging, Consuming

FIG. 4.2 Women selling goods in a marketplace
Florentine Codex, Book 10, Images 124 and 125. Courtesy of the
University of Utah Press

included Tenochtitlan, Tlatelolco, Tetzcoco, Huexotla, Coatlichan, Chalco, Xochimilco, Huitzilopochco, Mixcoac, Azcapotzalco, Cuauhtitlan, and Otompan, lying to the north, south, east, and west of Tenochtitlan and Tlatelolco. Macehualtin entrepreneurs, many of the merchants from these altepeme nonetheless were wealthy, sophisticated traders who lived in their own enclaves and experienced a kind of social mobility that no one else but the most successful warriors did. Pochteca traded within and beyond the Basin of Mexico, bringing in high-value items, usually low-bulk goods, such as gold jewelry, fine feathers, precious stones, even slaves, in contrast to tlanecuilo who traded in valued bulk commodities like cotton, cacao, salt, and chiles as well as pottery and baskets. These merchants carried goods for themselves as well as nobles and rulers, with traders from Tenochtitlan and Tlatelolco carrying goods for Tenochtitlan's rulers, meaning pochteca could engage in private commercial ventures while representing imperial rulers.

Other pochteca traveled far afield to many of Mesoamerica's regions including places like Xicalanco on the Gulf Coast and Xoconochco on the Pacific Coast, both international trading areas located among Maya-populated areas. The oztomeca, in particular, disguised themselves and used their language skills and trading activities as a way to spy on far-off rulers and to learn about their political and military strengths or weaknesses. These merchants also assessed economic conditions in far distant regions. Dressing and speaking the languages of groups such as the Otomi or Maya peoples including the Chontal (lowland) or Tzotzil (highland), the disguised merchants took enormous risks to obtain goods and knowledge, even sometimes guiding military campaigns. These were dangerous activities indeed. Rulers of such far-off places did not appreciate the presence of these stealthy merchants. Clearly, long-distance traders understood they could provoke trouble as they traveled. They carried arms and moved around in large groups. When attacked, they responded. But an attack on them carried risks for distant rulers and their kingdoms. War and conquest of the aggressor group could be the result.

With a strong sense of identity among themselves, bolstered by living in particular tlaxilacalli or calpolli enclaves in the altepetl in which they resided and worshipping a particular deity, Yacateuctli, as their patron deity, merchants reinforced that identity by carrying out ceremonies particular to their professional group. These included rituals to prepare for travel, to ward off danger while on an expedition, and to commemorate safe returns from commercially successful expeditions. In addition to Yacateuctli, merchants honored other deities including Xiuhteuctli (Fire God), Tlalteuctli (Earth God), as well as patron deities of their home altepetl, for example, Huitzilopochtli, the patron deity of the Mexica, for merchants of Tenochtitlan and Tlatelolco.

The most spectacular merchant feast known as the Tealtiliztli, or Bathing of Slaves, a ceremony that featured the killing of slaves purchased at one of the main slave markets at Azcapotzalco, was carried out by Mexica merchants during Panquetzaliztli, the fifteenth monthly ceremony. Such ceremonies allowed merchants to venerate Yacateuctli and Huitzilopochtli, express gratitude for their successes, and to assert and reinforce status within and beyond the merchant community. This was particularly true for a merchant *tealtianime* (bather of slaves) who sponsored these sacrificial ceremonies, a high status sought by merchants, difficult to achieve. By providing blood for the gods at the time of year when the sun needed renewal, the winter solstice, merchants asserted a warrior-like importance through the nourishing of the god with blood and other offerings. This ceremony had, therefore, both material and symbolic meaning as it featured value that merchants generated and shared in both realms. By inviting high status Aztecs, giving away gifts to other merchants as well as to high military and government officials, a few particular merchants achieved near-noble status. Illustrating the close connections Aztecs drew among war, tribute and commerce, and religion, the Tealtiliztli ceremony signifies how Aztecs created and used material and symbolic value.

Conclusion

Both women and men created value. This is so because in addition to the productive labor of men, women's labor and skill fed and clothed ordinary families, Aztec armies, and royal palaces. Their cooking and weaving labor had material significance, symbolic value, and cosmic implications because one of the ways Aztecs imagined the cosmos was as woven. The special province of women of all social levels, their work created the most common and among the most valuable of tribute items, woven cloth. With quachtli and clothing given as tribute in huge amounts, these items were also bought and sold in markets and redistributed through lifecycle ceremonies, religious rituals held in households and temples, and political occasions of celebration or mourning.

Women's work, therefore, supported Aztec life by creating wealth and providing a means to obtain and assert status and power. Aztecs made, wore, and used large amounts of woven cloth. That cloth allowed many to trade goods they produced or collected; it covered Aztec deities, marked the status of rulers and warriors, and enfolded the sacred mortuary bundles, the tlaquimilolli, of rulers and deities. In a sense, women turned raw goods with material value into social and symbolic value upon which both hierarchy and reciprocity rested, creating a balance between the two. Even if merchant women did not carry goods long distances, they nonetheless sold goods for profit in markets, invested in long-distance expeditions, guarded the property of goods left in merchant homes and storehouses by male kin, and likely had a say over prices as goods went into markets.

The work of both genders fueled the increasingly sophisticated goods Aztecs produced, the large amounts of trade, and the increased commercialization that occurred across late Postclassic Mesoamerica. While a lot of the labor that went into all this output remained performed at the household level, workshops grew in number and craft production became more complex as population increased, political organization became more elaborate, and demand for both everyday and luxury items increased. The increasing output of Aztec producers and growing number of commercial endeavors engaged in by merchants underwrote an increasingly rigid hierarchy based on the transformation and trade of commodities with material and symbolic value. Aztecs also expressed ideas about balance – not only in the realms of politics and the economy – but through the beliefs and ceremonies associated with their gods and cosmos using goods they produced in large quantities. As we saw in Chapter 2, the gods gave humans life and humans owed the gods devotion and nourishment. Political, economic, and religious activities interacted with each other and suffused Aztec life. Aztec people began to experience these realms of life in the households of their local communities. It is to those households and the families who lived in them that the next chapter turns.

5

Sex and the Altepetl

Gender, Sexuality, and Aztec Family Values

The Aztec home provided a cradle for all the realms of Aztec life. Sheltering, nurturing, teaching Aztec children all took place within the home among family. From the home setting, children became connected to the wider world of neighborhood, village or city, and state. Notions of creation and use of value, the stories of transformation and the need to live a balanced life would be instilled and then, ideally, lived out across the arenas of economic, political, and religious activities within and beyond the home. But in order for the Aztec individual to come into being, she or he had to be created.

Aztecs thought substance from both parents came together to form new life. A father's semen impregnated and helped to fatten a woman as well as completing the baby's form, and both parents contributed "blood, color, and descent" (in motatzin, in monantzin in temezio, in tintlapallo, in timoxijo) according to the *Florentine Codex*. Given that the Nahuatl words for bone and semen were closely related (*omitl*, *omicetl* respectively), and Aztec myths about human creation involved blood and bones coming together, beliefs about the father's connection to creating a baby's skeleton seem clear. The father also provided warmth, *tonalli*, which allowed a fetus to develop in and balanced the cold, wet environment of the mother's womb. However, her role in providing shelter and substance during pregnancy as well as giving birth gave women a special role in the home and in the ceremonial realm. Carrying and birthing children connected women with powerful earthly forces and the female deities who represented them. Aztecs associated these forces with the transformation of substances into human beings, those deities holding the power to create or destroy.

Through *tlalticpacayotl*, or "earthiness," the term Aztecs used to refer to intercourse, substances came together. Providing shelter for a baby to form and grow, Aztecs also believed that too much intercourse would deplete a man's supply of semen, making pregnancy difficult or impossible. They acknowledged an infant's connection to living and deceased kin by way of its mother and father throughout life cycle ceremonies held during pregnancy, birth, and to greet, name, and begin to socialize a newborn. The newborn, thus embodied aspects of both mother and father through which the baby came to reflect positive and negative traits of the parents. After discussing sexuality, this chapter focuses on significant points in the life cycle to examine how Aztecs experienced the concepts of value, transformation, and balance in their daily lives.

Sexuality and Gender

Preaching moderation in sexuality did not prevent Aztecs from engaging in a wide array of sexual activities, both heterosexual and homosexual. Aztecs valued the pleasure sex brought to their lives, and moderation was, perhaps, more esteemed than lived. Young men had opportunities to engage in sexual relations before marriage through the schooling they received either in the calmecac, primarily for children of nobles, offering training for the priesthood and high office, or the telpochcalli, the young men's house, a school for commoner boys who received military training and performed public works. While parents and teachers encouraged chastity for young men and women, the number of accounts of punishment of young men for sexual contact suggests that sexual relations frequently occurred. Some young men of the telpochcalli, older adolescents, regularly engaged in intimate relationships with female companions.

Were the women, the companions (*inmecahua*) of young men in the telpochcalli simply young women of the neighborhoods in which the telpochcalli were located? Or did they come from another group of women, the *ahuiani*, or "pleasure women," women – often referred to as concubines or prostitutes – who sang, danced, and accompanied warriors and others in calendric rituals and who participated in private celebrations with rulers? The ahuiani also lived with rulers and high nobles in their palaces, part of a complex web of polygynous and sexual relationships in which nobles, especially rulers, could engage. Despite the existence of several kinds of intimate relationships, Aztecs expended effort to teach young women of their families and kin groups the importance of avoiding sex before marriage, not so much because chastity or virginity were highly valued in and of themselves but because sex – especially non-procreative sex – was seen as polluting, potentially excessive, and therefore harmful.

Both Indigenous and Spanish sources hint that same-sex interactions occurred in Aztec schools and temples, which were organized by gender, and perhaps in palaces, places where the rules for personal behavior that punished same-sex activity harshly were not always observed. Despite the existence of terms in Nahuatl that may have referred to male (*cuiloni*) and female (*patlache*) individuals who engaged in same-sex relations, there is little evidence that homosexuality or lesbianism existed as identities that defined specific people. While Aztec genders are widely seen as rigidly fixed social roles, gender identities and sexual activities combined elements of both fixity *and* flexibility because Aztecs saw human bodies as unstable and mutable. Infants' faces, even bodies, were transformable. Babies and young children could turn into mice or be born clubfooted if their mothers did such things as leaving the home during an eclipse of the moon or if the child fell asleep during the New Fire ceremony. A newborn's face would be permanently marked if the new mother burned a corncob. Adults and supernatural beings also could transform. Both women and men could turn themselves into animals; deities could take human form, male or female; and priests could transform into deity embodiments, the female or male ixiptlahuan so important in monthly rituals. Human forms were not stable, nor were gender identities.

Deities often took multiple forms, both female and male, and priestly cross-dressing and images of deities with female and male biological attributes and accoutrements were common. For example, earth mother deities who seem to have had a relatively fixed gender identity were depicted in images that frequently included male symbols, especially those relating to war. In the *Codex Telleriano-Remensis*, for example, Tlazolteotl – a goddess of sexuality, fertility, and confession – is shown partly

A Concise History of the Aztecs

FIG. 5.1 Image of Itzpapalotl (Obsidian Butterfly) *Codex Telleriano-Remensis*, fol.18v. Courtesy of the Bibliothèque nationale de France

covered with feathers and with a flayed skin draped around her. The sacrificial victims provided by wars often were costumed with feathers, which could have been an allusion to Quetzalcoatl or more likely to Tezcatlipoca, the patron of sorcerers who was associated with transgression, chaos, and confession, like Tlazolteotl. Also included in that codex is a striking image of the goddess Itzpapalotl (Obsidian Butterfly; see Fig. 5.1). Portrayed with skull imagery, eagle-like talons for her feet, an obsidian knife head ornament, and wearing both the skirt of female deities and a male loincloth, she was a fearsome ancient goddess, according to stories probably dating to pre-Aztec times. Associated with war, she met a violent end, shot with arrows or burned by the god Mixcoatl or spirits associated with him. Such gendered bodily confusion threatened cosmic and social order by reminding Aztecs of the chaos they tried to hold at bay, but gender ambiguity in rituals could also renew order by transforming chaos into stability to re-establish the social order.

In order to maintain balance and keep chaos from breaking out, Aztecs relied on ideas about binary pairs, including female and male, to reinforce social, political, and cosmic order. But these gender differences did not constitute inborn essences that simply unfolded over the course of the life cycle. They were identities that had to be created and reinforced, especially during childhood. Both Rosemary Joyce and Pete Sigal emphasize in their descriptions of Aztec gender roles that these roles, while defined in binary terms, were created and performed. This meant that while biology, based on gender assignment at birth, had consequences for the ceremonies performed at that moment and others that followed, an individual's gender identity came into being based more on ceremonies, parental teaching, and schooling than birth itself. It was signaled through clothing, hairstyles, bodily markings, kinds of work performed, and roles played in household and other rituals. Nahuatl kinship terms for a child, niece or nephew, or grandchildren were *not* differentiated by the *child's* gender, suggesting that Aztecs did not view early gender identity as immutably fixed. Instead, they were differentiated by the gender of the *speaker* (for children, nephews, and nieces), so – for example – a male speaker called a child a *pilli*, a female called a child *conetl*, regardless of whether the child was female or male. Aztecs, however, referred to adolescents as *ichpochtli* (young woman) or *telpochtli* (young man). By that time, the socialization process and ritual participation had, as Rosemary Joyce so wonderfully put it, "girled the girl" and "boyed the boy." What did these socialization processes, familial and institutional, look like?

Socialization and Schooling

Girl or boy, Aztecs raised their children to work hard and create value, obey the rules for proper behavior, and practice moderation in all areas of family and social life, including emotional expressiveness. Before and until shortly after birth, infants were treated as raw materials. Adults spoke of them as young maguey plants or thorns, feathers, precious stones, or bodily parts, especially hair or fingernails. While birth signaled the beginning of gender differentiation, with the umbilical cords of girls buried in the home and boys' at the battle field, it was the rituals to read the calendrical destiny of the child based on the day of birth and a bathing ceremony during which the infant received a name when a gender identity began to become assigned. Aztecs named children in gender differentiated ways. They also gave newborns female or male work tools and clothing, thus beginning the baby's transformation into a socially recognized person. From birth through bathing and naming, to dedication to a school, wider circles of kin and even non-kin participated, and gender identity continued to be taught and reinforced.

The next life cycle ritual, an ear piercing ceremony, took place every four years during the month of Izcalli and involved children from about age one to four. Aztecs stretched children's necks and pierced their ears, perhaps a sign of children beginning to mature into their social roles (see Fig. 5.2). While this ceremony did not rely much on gender differentiation in how it was carried out, it was at the age of four when the first socialization into gender differentiated work took place. Fathers and

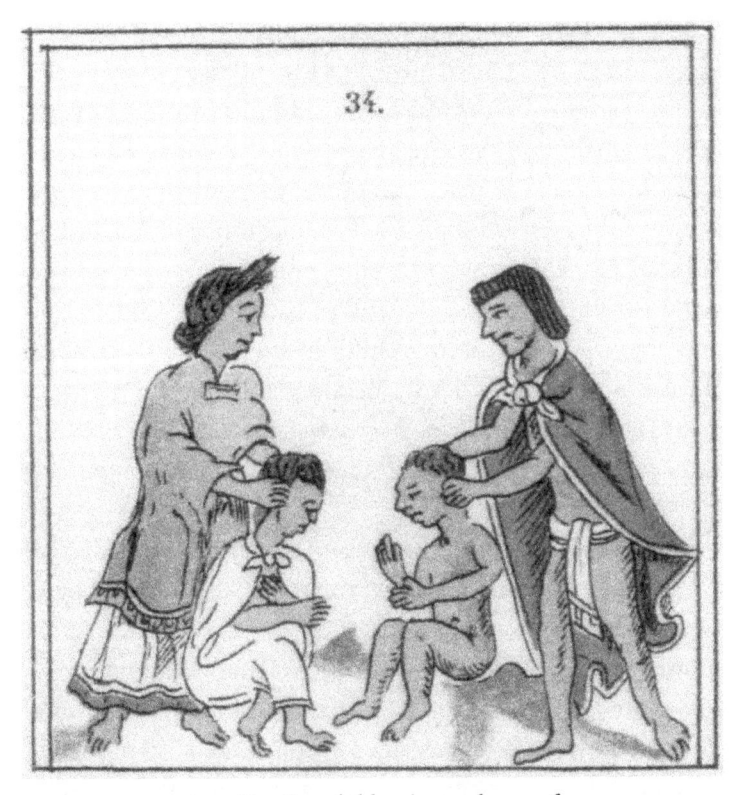

FIG. 5.2 Piercing children's ears by age four
Florentine Codex, Book 2, Image 34. Courtesy of the University of Utah Press

mothers played active roles in teaching their male and female children respectively how to perform the labor needed to maintain the home and community. As described in the previous chapter, for boys, farming, fishing, and the skills of a trade or commercial activities would be taught. For girls, mothers imparted the knowledge necessary for spinning, weaving, cooking, as well as female-associated responsibilities for craftwork or commerce. Just as the *Codex Mendoza* provides evidence of how children between the ages of four and fourteen were taught the skills for work required by their families and community, it also illustrates the intensity with which parents taught their children and the harsh punishments they used to enforce the proper performance of those skills with the diligence required to contribute to the family and wider community. It depicts sons being taught the specific skills of wood, stone, and silver working, mat making and decoration, as well as painting. Using thorns to pierce the skin, forcing children to breathe the smoke of burning chiles, inflicting beatings or a kind of banishment for a day, the *Codex Mendoza* shows all these repercussions for a lack of discipline for girls and boys (see Fig. 5.3).

After having been dedicated to either the calmecac or telpochcalli as infants, all boys and many girls would begin their training to contribute to the war-making capacity, political organization, or ritual life of their local community as well as the altepetl of which their community was a part. They were educated to do so in a gender-balanced way, so that at marriage, a couple would play the complementary roles needed by home and society. This training went beyond the family as every young man and woman

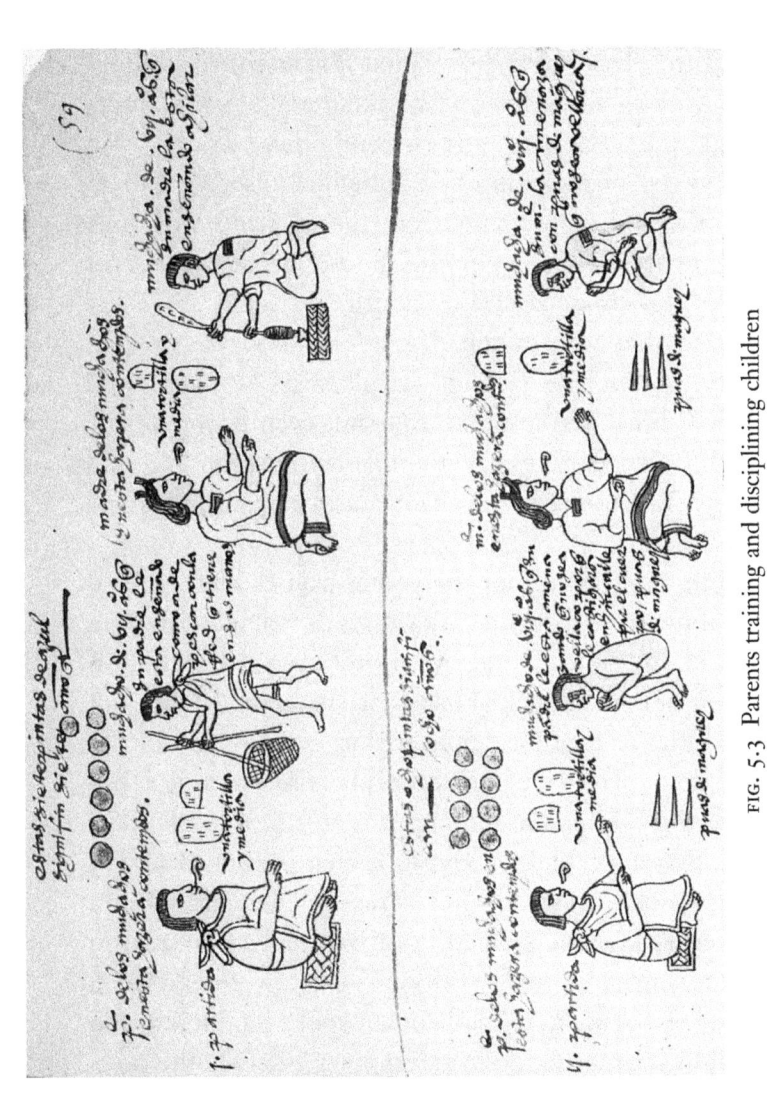

FIG. 5.3 Parents training and disciplining children
Codex Mendoza, fol.59r. Courtesy of the Bodleian Libraries, University of Oxford, Ms. Arch. Selden A.1, Creative Commons License CC BY NC 4.0

received some type of schooling. Attached to important temples, and likely numbering seven to ten in total, noble boys, the sons of wealthy merchants, and those commoner boys with a desire to live a religious life attended a calmecac. Learning about history, speaking and singing, interpreting the calendars, and writing, these young men experienced a harsh education, intended to separate them physically and emotionally from the comforts of home. There at the "house of crying, house of tears, house of sadness" (in choqujzcali, in jxalocali, in tlaoculcali), characterized that way in the *Florentine Codex,* young men learned to endure fasting, sleeplessness, hunger, and self-punishment in order to tolerate, even promote, the sacred violence necessary to maintain human life and mediate the forces of a chaotic and dangerous world and cosmos.

While the training for the young women who entered the calmecac to become priestesses is not described in detail in any source, they clearly received instruction in religion and the calendars so that they could carry out their duties to care for deities within temples and for the roles they played in the monthly rituals undertaken during the year and at important points in the life cycle. They, therefore, had an education that paralleled that of young men, even if not exactly identical to it. Furthermore, some women must have been educated in speaking, singing, and writing. We know that women worked as tlacuiloque, that women spoke eloquently and at length during life cycle ceremonies (such as the midwives who spoke at ceremonies around birth and priestesses who addressed young women entering the calmecac), and that women composed some of the songs

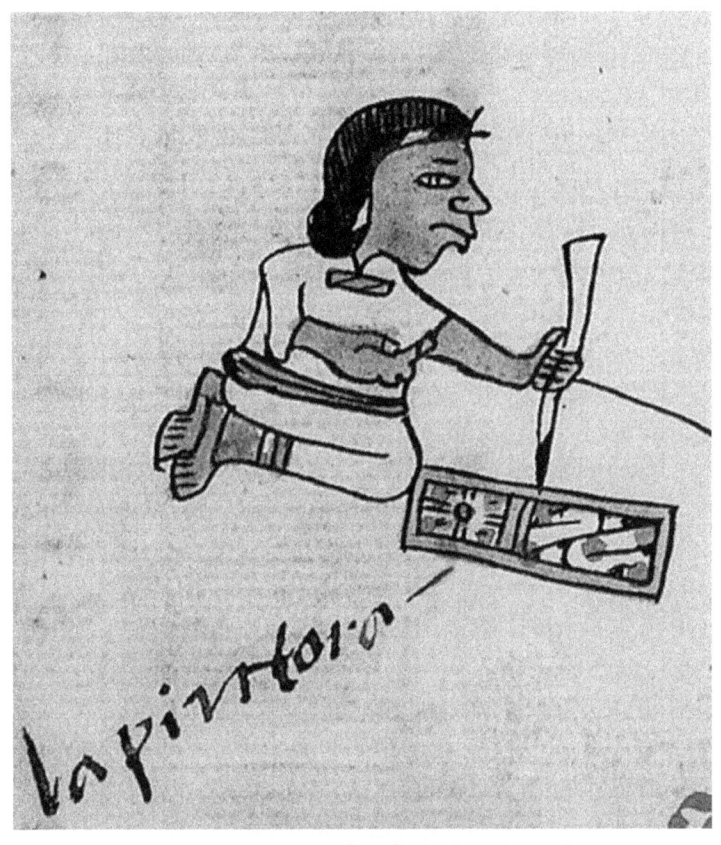

FIG. 5.4 A woman tlacuilo (painter/writer) *Codex Telleriano-Remensis*, fol.30r. Courtesy of the Bibliothèque nationale de France

sung on ritual or celebratory occasions (see Fig. 5.4). Fray Juan Bautista, writing in the very early years of the seventeenth century, described the education of Aztec women, saying that there were

> ... highly skilled and experienced matrons who educated the young girls with great care and taught and trained them in the understanding and worship of the gods and in other womanly

matters, especially in the profession of midwifery and of baptizing the newborn with much ceremony ... They also trained them in matters concerning marriage, in which the women always were the agents and marriage-makers.

Young men, mainly commoners, who did not attend the calmecac attended the telpochcalli, which existed in most, perhaps all, tlaxilacalli, at least in Tenochtitlan. This school emphasized warrior training and obedience to a teaching and warrior hierarchy for boys. Youth also participated in public works by working fields to support the telpochcalli, repairing roads or canals, and building and maintaining schools and temples. Other skills telpochcalli instructors imparted included the singing and dancing that were part of numerous ceremonies. For young men, however, the primary goal of the telpochcalli was to train them to participate in the military. As in the calmecac, discipline was instilled through teaching, fasting, and punishment, especially for drunkenness and sexual relations. The *Codex Mendoza* shows the punishments for youthful warriors and priests in training, illustrating young warriors pierced by needles and the beating of young priests with burning torches. The *Florentine Codex* describes the harsh discipline meted out for infractions. But attitudes toward sex in the telpochcalli were undoubtedly more lax, especially for older adolescent males. Sexual relations, as already mentioned, occurred regularly. After ritual singing and dancing at the end of the day, young men slept in the telpochcalli, with those with sexual experience, said to "already be men" (ie vel oquichtin) in the *Florentine Codex*, as sleeping there with partners. Echoing this practice but in a chapter on the worship of Camaxtli in Huexotzinco and Tlaxcallan, Durán states that a young man serving in his temple who was "undesirous of remaining as a minister of temple was allowed to live with a young woman, with whom he could live in free concubinage as long as he wished. She was given to him on trial; if she bore children and he desired to marry her later, he could do so. If not, he was allowed to abandon her and marry someone else."

The education of young men and women became complete by attendance at the cuicacalli, or song house, part of the tlatoani's palace, in which the girls and boys of about ages twelve to fourteen or fifteen were taught by female and male teachers respectively (the *cihuatepixque* and *tiachcahuan* or *teaanque*, women guardians and male teachers or guides) to sing, dance, and play musical instruments. The teachers instructed their students about the ceremonies of which the songs and dances were a part, reinforcing knowledge about Aztec creation narratives, gods, morality, and the social hierarchy. Aztec children and adolescents received instruction in work, values, and religious beliefs. Learning to create material value; watching the transformations of human bodies, animals, and plants and absorbing stories of transformations of deities, priests, rulers; and urged through speech and by action to strive for lives of balance, younger Aztecs experienced both hard work and the release offered by ceremonial life, not least through the rituals conducted in families and neighborhoods. In work, stories, and worship, gender roles were learned and lived. Those roles would further develop through wedding ceremonies and household formation.

Marriage

Aztecs recognized a variety of kinds of marriages. A lengthy process, formal marriages were set in motion by the groom's parents while their sons were still attending the telpochcalli or calmecac. Soon thereafter, while the beginning stages of what would culminate in a marriage ceremony went on, the bride's parents also became involved. A young man's parents discussed marriage with him after they decided he was ready. The parents also consulted officials of the school who would designate the young man as prepared to be married as well as seeking advice from neighbors, nobles, and other kin. While it was possible that a young couple could make a commitment to each other, perhaps meeting through their attendance at the cuicacalli, at the many public festivals that occurred throughout the year, or at markets or other public places, given the intense participation of parents' relatives, and the wider community throughout marriage ceremonies, it is likely that most marriages were arranged. The young age at marriage, especially for women, many of whom married between the ages of twelve to fifteen, with young men marrying at around ages nineteen to twenty, also makes it likely that a young man or women could only rarely choose his or her own partner, especially because the partners would not be recognized as adults until after marriage.

Once a young man was deemed ready to marry, his parents consulted kin and ritual specialists about whom he should marry. The Aztecs considered certain days as propitious ones for marriage, and tonalpouhque advised parents about whether a particular couple's marriage would be a satisfactory one based on their readings of a tonalamatl. The tonalamatl *Codex Borgia*, for example, has several leaves devoted to such marriage prognostications, either positive or negative. Once a potential wife had been selected, elderly women serving as matchmakers (*cihuatlanque*) approached the young woman's family with whom discussions went on for several days. If her family agreed, his family sought advice so that they could choose a propitious date for the ceremony. The young woman's family would then begin to prepare a feast for the ceremony to come and family, neighbors, teachers, local nobles and commoners would be invited. On the chosen day, guests arrived and were plied with food and drink (a lot of drink, it appears), tobacco, and flowers. As female guests arrived, they brought gifts such as cloaks and maize. Later in the day, the bride would be dressed and made up and seated on a mat at the front of the hearth of her home. Elderly men of the groom's family addressed her, telling her that now she must act as an adult, she should be circumspect in speech and behavior, perform her work with diligence, and live according to the teachings of her elders.

Elderly female relatives of the groom arrived to carry the bride to the groom's home. The young woman's female relatives briefly scuffled with the groom's relatives, perhaps to show how difficult it was to part with this precious young woman, and then a procession of the bride's and groom's female kin accompanied her to her destination. Then the bride and groom sat together on a mat in front of the hearth, and the mother of each presented gifts of clothing to her child's partner. After eating tamales, the couple adjourned to a sleeping room where

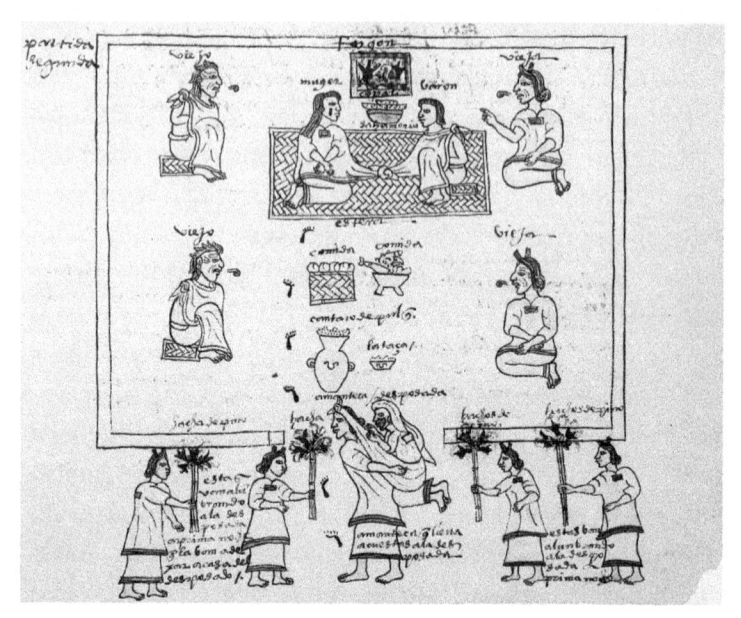

FIG. 5.5 Wedding scene
Codex Mendoza, fol. 61r. Courtesy of the Bodleian Libraries, University of Oxford, Ms. Arch. Selden A.1, Creative Commons License CC BY NC 4.0

they stayed for four days. The matchmakers guarded them, with consummation of the marriage said to occur at the end of the four-day period. On the fifth day, more festivities took place during which the new in-laws exchanged gifts, and relatives from both families again lectured the couple on their duties as partners in this new marriage (see Fig. 5.5). This new partnership represented the complementarity embedded in family life and thus expressed the gendered aspect of balance found in daily life across the Aztec world. It also provided the basis for the creation of material value because the married couple often worked together in complementary fashion to help support households, pay tribute to the community and state, and provide resources for the rich ceremonial life that took place within and beyond the Aztec household.

Before exploring the roles of wives and husbands in more detail, it is worth pointing out that the ceremonies surrounding marriage as described in both Motolinia's writings and the *Florentine Codex* and narrated here would have been challenging for poorer Aztecs to carry out. The ceremonies for high nobles and rulers, on the other hand, would have been still more elaborate. These marriages were subject to even more consultation, negotiation, and finessing because of the political nature of rulers' marriages as the story of one of Nezahualcoyotl's marriages to a young Mexica noblewoman, Matlalcihuatzin, shows. She had been promised to another man, but Nezahualcoyotl (who ruled from 1418 to 1472) maneuvered to marry her after having arranged to have her betrothed killed in war. The ceremony itself was also quite intricate, attended by the tlatoque of Tenochtitlan and Tlacopan, among others.

Noblemen also partook of alternative kinds of amorous relationships supposedly forbidden. Yet the frequent mention of adulterous relationships among nobles, defined as relations outside of marriage by a husband or wife for both nobles and commoners, suggests that such relationships were not so unusual. The fact that commerce and war took young and middle-aged men out of their communities allowed many opportunities for sexual contact outside of marriage to occur, despite the stringent penalties for adultery that existed. Even with those strict penalties, including death for adulterers, many men had on-going sexual relationships with multiple women, especially rulers. Women, too, apparently had adulterous relationships, but Aztecs considered those women scandalous. The unsparing penalties for male adultery applied to them as well. While Aztecs considered some extramarital relationships to be adulterous, others clearly were not. Several kinds of legitimate on-going heterosexual relationships were, in fact, recognized by Aztecs for older students in the telpochcalli as already mentioned and for nobles and rulers.

Rulers and wealthy nobles lived in large palaces called *tecpan* that also housed large numbers of women and children. Many of the women were servants or slaves, but others carried a higher status as secondary wives. Several versions of how the early Mexica tlatoani, Acamapichtli of the late fourteenth century, came to be the first tlatoani stress not just his descent from Tolteca-related women but also his polygynous relationships through which a dynastic line was born, from which all succeeding rulers descended. Having married Ilancueitl, who was descended from Tolteca nobility, this marriage ennobled their descendants. But some versions describing this marriage mention that she was sterile, and it was through secondary wives from leading Tenochca calpolli that children were born, although the populace was told the children were Ilancueitl's.

This narrative provides evidence of the political nature of royal polygynous marriages – a ruler would have a primary wife, with the terms *–namic* (spouse) or *–cihua* (woman) referring to that primary wife. This woman was often the daughter of a close ally of a ruler with whom good relations needed to be developed or maintained. Tlatoque also undertook secondary marriages with the daughters of other allies or with wives of enemy rulers who had been seized after a defeat. Aztecs referred to these wives as *cihuanemactin* (given women). Tertiary marriages with women also occurred. Some enslaved, some free, the *tlacihuaantin* (taken women) came to a ruler via war through capture. But whether the latter category of women should even be considered wives, especially when they were women who had been seized during combat aimed at subjugation, is difficult to say. This category of "minor wife," the tlacihuaantin, could well have overlapped with another category of women, the ahuiani, mentioned above, who participated in on-going relationships with married rulers, living in their palaces.

The women of royal palaces did not, however, easily navigate the emotional dynamics of polygynous relationships. Despite experiencing a kind of sisterhood by being bound together through work, living in close quarters in palaces, perhaps sharing childrearing and other kinds of interactions including joking about, even mocking, the men they shared their lives with, competition and jealousy existed in polygynous marriages. Wives knew they could be easily displaced and replaced as the focus of a ruler's affections. When they sought to promote the interests of their sons in negotiations over succession and perhaps over daughters' potential marriages, wives' statuses could rise or fall. As political alliances waxed and waned, so did personal relationships. Yet attraction, even love, existed within marriages, and affectionate relationships co-existed with relationships of political convenience.

While most Aztec marriages likely were monogamous, there is some evidence that even among commoners, a few men had two or more wives. Given the wealth of merchants and some luxury artisans, this is not completely surprising. In addition, imperial tribute demands created a great need for labor. Although early census data does not show many polygynous marriages to have existed among macehualtin, this need might also explain the existence of some of this type of household among some commoners. Descriptions of Aztec marriage practices, however, emphasize that the husband-wife couple formed the conceptual and actual foundation of the household; the complementarity of women's and men's roles was crucial to the success of marriage. The pairing was essential to the functioning of the household for work, tribute-paying, rearing children, and connecting the household to kin, the local community, and the altepetl for economic, religious, and political purposes. Farming, craft production, and commerce all relied on the physical and administrative skills of both women and men. Tribute payment, children's socialization within the household and the schools Aztec children attended, community and temple administration, even the reinforcement of moral standards for children *and* adults, relied on those skills. Images and descriptions of marriage show the monogamous couple to represent the ideal marriage, even if reality was, indeed, messier and more variable.

Housing and Residence Patterns

Housing patterns reflected the importance of the labor and other functions married couples fulfilled within households. The term "house compound" has been used to describe Aztec housing. Rectangular rooms (*calli*, a word that can mean house or room) that opened onto an inner courtyard or patio (*ithualli*) constituted the basic Aztec home. Many of the rooms around the patio area served as sleeping, laboring, and eating areas. However, work, consumption, and worship also took place in the patio area or in specialized rooms. Calli could house a person, a couple, a couple with children, a parent and child, or some other small number of people, with from two to six such family groupings often housed in the compounds. The walled house compounds sometimes contained rooms that Aztecs used for specific purposes such as storage, religious worship of deities important to the household, including craft workshops; and many houses had a room called the *cihuacalli* (women's room or house), probably used by women for performing some of their household duties. The density of such housing, usually single story, was greater in larger cities, especially Tenochtitlan. In other areas, communities featured larger numbers of houses made up of a single room, what the *Florentine Codex* refers to as *xacalli*. Even smaller cities and towns featured larger, prominent housing for their noble inhabitants, the tecpan, or palaces (see Figs. 5.6 and 5.7).

Commoner housing varied in size from the one-room houses found in rural areas to the much larger houses, with multiple rooms, of wealthy commoners such as elite merchants of Tenochtitlan or Tlatelolco. Also varying in size, the tecpan showed the wealth that some Aztecs experienced by being born into the noble class. Across the Basin of Mexico, some 500 tecpan existed by the late prehispanic era. Most were administrative palaces in which rulers and nobles lived and carried out their governing, religious, and judicial functions. Living with their wives, children, servants, palace functionaries such as

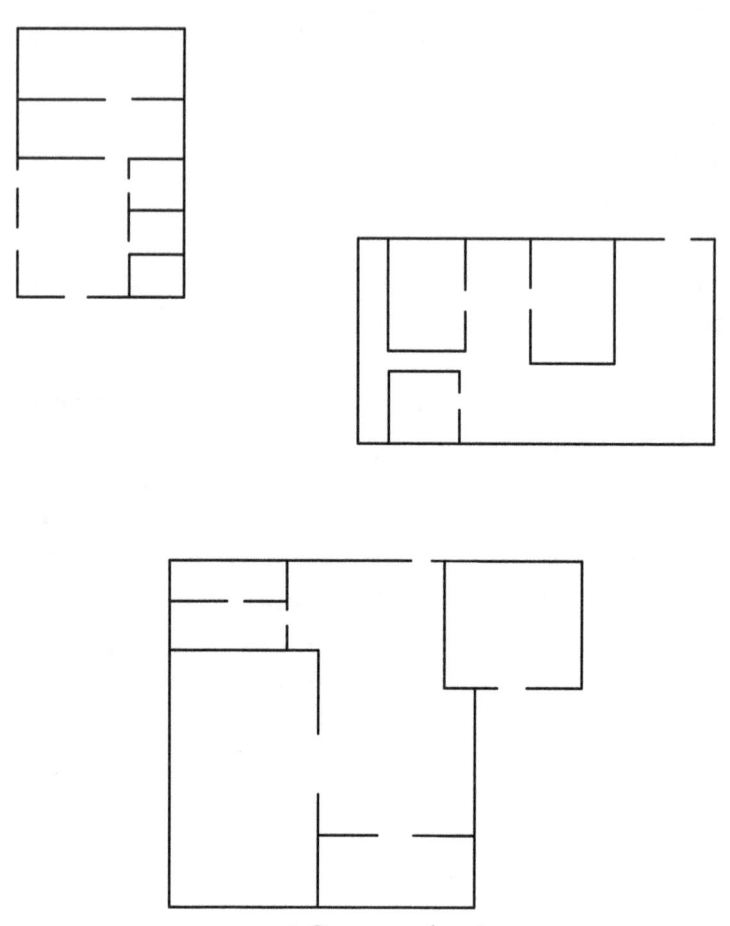

FIG. 5.6 Commoner housing
Drawings by author and Agnes Zakaria

bureaucrats, artisans, and hangers-on of various sorts, palaces were lively, busy, multifunctional places. A smaller number were what archaeologist Susan Evans calls "pleasure palaces." Often located in the sumptuous gardens that the most elite rulers of the Excan tlatoloyan built for enjoyment and relaxation, storage of tribute goods, and performance of religious rituals to celebrate

FIG. 5.7 What a tlatoani and his palace might have looked like
Drawing by Felipe Dávalos, with permission of artist and Mexicolore

agricultural fertility, they also served as a means of showing off the immense wealth of huey tlatoque. Book Eleven of the *Florentine Codex* acknowledges that palaces were places of importance, even honor, but that transgressive behaviors and intoxication also occurred there as this chapter and Chapter 6 will show.

Like commoner housing, however, the size and sumptuousness of noble palaces varied greatly in relation to the status of the noble or ruler who resided in a particular palace. Similar to the multi-room, multi-family houses found in many cities and towns across the Basin of Mexico, palaces featured large numbers of rooms and platforms built around an interior courtyard. They could range in size from about 4,300 square feet to the huge imperial palaces of rulers such as Nezahualcoyotl of Tetzcoco or Moteuczoma Xocoyotl whose palaces may have been as large as about 27,000 square feet. But even the lowliest palace of a local noble or pilli proved superior to commoner housing in both construction as well as the number, range, and quality of artifacts found within the elevated rooms, built on platforms, of palaces. Michael E. Smith excavated the small palace of a fifteenth-century lower-status noble of the town of Cuexcomate and found that palace to be larger than other residences with more high quality goods associated with it.

While both noble and commoner housing often featured multiple families living in house or palace compounds, house styles, construction materials, kin relationships, and patterns of labor organization could vary between communities and over time. Smaller houses or compounds allowed people to live closer to agricultural fields yet still provided sufficient space for craft production to meet household needs. At least some of that work might have been done outdoors. Climate could also have been a factor that influenced the organization of labor and household size, with the warmer, semi-tropical climates to the south encouraging Aztecs there to work outdoors, whereas the denser housing often found in the Basin of Mexico, especially its larger cities, reflected the greater tendency to work indoors due to cooler climate conditions. More complex forms of craft production and sometimes greater gender differentiation in labor patterns such that specialized rooms for female and male activities existed in urban housing also influenced the tendency toward denser settlement and larger house compounds.

The site of Xaltocan, a small island altepetl located in the northern Basin of Mexico, shows that housing patterns could vary over time within a single community. It provides an ideal site to study household and community organization because it was continuously occupied from 900 until well into the colonial period. The site allows archaeologists to intensively study change over time. Xaltocan's types of housing became modified as standards of living rose and fell in relation to growing or declining wealth due to success in exploiting and marketing local resources as well as the experience of war and subjugation to an imperial power. For Xaltocan, conquest by the Tepaneca in 1395 and later integration into the Excan tlatoloyan economy in the next century led to a transition from multi-room house compounds to a greater number of one-room houses. A decline in the standard of living for commoners and a change in craft production patterns away from production of salt and obsidian tools to greater production of cotton cloth occurred. These shifts related to changes in the ethnic makeup of the community as the original Otomi population declined and the Aztec population grew, as well as increased tribute demands first by the Tepaneca, and later by the Excan tlatoloyan.

What were the family and kin patterns that shaped the residence choices Aztecs made before Europeans arrived? A constellation of relatives – people connected through blood, marriage, or sometimes through fictive ties – influenced the residence patterns displayed by Aztecs. Other factors such as local topographies and climate, the resources environments offered, and occupation, also affected family and residence patterns. Four characteristics of the kinship and residential system stand out: first, descent from ancestors, often three to five generations above an individual or married couple, helped to define the universe of relatives with whom an individual had familial and residential relations. This grouping was often referred to by the term *tlacamecayotl* (literally, rope of people, descent line). While rulers and nobles placed the greatest emphasis on tracing descent from ancestors, commoners also remembered the relatives through whom status and property flowed in order to claim the right to live in a particular house compound or use certain lands to farm. Second, the Aztec person, male or female, lay at the center of a web of relations defined equally through her or his mother and father. This kinship system balanced a focus on descent from and through male and female relatives with individual or ego-centered bilateral relations with people of prior, one's own, and subsequent generations. These were the relatives, usually spanning no more than four generations, with whom an individual was most likely to interact. Third, the universe of kin terms in the Nahuatl language focused on the gender of individuals *to* whom a person traced and activated kin relations as well as ages and generations, along with the gender *of* an individual tracing a relationship to a kinsperson. Fourth, sibling and cousin terms were differentiated by age, so that birth position among siblings proved important. Elder siblings, both brothers and sisters, carried special responsibilities. Age as conveyed through terms for preceding generations as well as sibling terms could be extended to distant, fictive, even non-kin to convey respect, the status of a person being addressed, or to remind an individual of his or her responsibilities to others within and beyond the household.

How did kinship help influence the household residential choices Aztecs made? Some people lived in nuclear or consanguineal arrangements, with these households made up of parents or parent and children. Others lived in joint family arrangements organized either generationally around grandparents, even great-grandparents, their children, and children's children or around a groups of siblings and their descendants. In some communities, nuclear family arrangements predominated. In others, joint arrangements did, and these variations existed geographically and over time as household developmental cycles and events played out. Many factors beyond patterns of kin relationships shaped household structure and its variations across Aztec Mesoamerica – economy and environment, including labor organization; point in the life cycle of household members; and the class position of households as noble families often contained men with more than one wife and larger numbers of children and other relatives, as well as workers and servants.

Key to these structures was flexibility, with marriage a crucial point in the life cycle when couples and their families made decisions about residence. Because most households in the more densely populated areas, all noble and many commoner, were joint in structure, decisions about which household a new married couple would live in had to be made. As mentioned, available resources, class position, even where space existed or could be added on all played a role. Narrative sources depict the new wife moving to the household of the husband as the norm, but like with the diversity in the predominance of joint versus nuclear household structures, there was variation. Husbands, at times, moved to the household of the wife's parents or close relations. For communities where very early colonial records of household residents exist dating to the 1540s, couples lived with wives' parents or relatives between twenty and twenty-five percent of the time. Because married couples tended to marry within their tlaxilacalli or calpolli, women who moved to the husband's household did not actually live far from their relatives. A young wife also could have some of her relatives come to live with her. The new wife often easily remained in close proximity, geographically and emotionally, to her own relatives. However, for women captured in war or those married to nobles or rulers, that situation did not always occur. Those women often lived far from the relatives who then could not offer the familial support proximity allowed.

Given the tremendous flexibility and variability of Aztec household arrangements, while descent and marital choices help explain their makeup, especially nobles and those who were wealthier undoubtedly conceived of the household as something complex with a kind of unity that could last over generations. This pattern of kinship and household organization is referred to as a "house society." Such a system is less about genealogy and more about everyday decision making about residence, wealth accumulation, and social identity, though genealogy had practical implications for property rights and interpersonal interactions. It is important to remember that, as Pedro Carrasco long ago pointed out, the words Aztecs used for family refer to the physical structure of the house or house compound *and* the people who resided there – *cencalli* (one house), *cemithualtin* (literally, one patio, but Molina defines the word as "one family"), *techan tlaca* (people of the home), and *cenyeliztli* (one being). These words reference *where* family life took place and also allude to the *oneness* of those residing in the household.

Regardless of whether couples lived in joint or nuclear family arrangements, upon marriage, women and men took on the complementary tasks that supported households, neighborhoods, and communities. The tools given to newborns suggest the household-centered nature of women's work – cooking, sweeping and cleaning, spinning and weaving, while men fought and farmed. In reality, however, each gender performed tasks within *and* beyond the household such as farming, crafting, fishing, child rearing, healing, selling in markets, and in ceremonial life. Governance, too, had a household-based element, even for the most supreme of rulers of the Excan tlatoloyan. Rulers' palaces provided settings for diplomatic, administrative, legislative, and judicial tasks as well as a setting for the daily lives and socialization of those who lived there. Socialization was not solely a maternal or female responsibility, neither in homes nor schools. Fathers, noble and non-noble, and other male relatives played crucial roles in children's upbringing in teaching and discipline. Women and men played important roles in household-based life cycle and other ceremonies as descriptions of birth and marriage rituals described earlier in this chapter show. The married couple provided the kinds of labor already discussed in the previous chapter and paid tribute. Each partner toiled and made decisions as adults who could make choices in a consultative way, based on their complementary roles. What happened to the married couple as they aged? And what about another kind of life cycle ceremony, the funeral?

Death

Loss of family members must have been a frequent experience for Aztec families, often due to warfare. Funerals, therefore, were quite common. Female family members played important roles in them. For Aztecs, life and death provided two poles in an unending cycle of transformation of bodies and energy. Humans, in their present form, were created from bones and blood. The gods offered themselves to create the sun that provided the warmth and energy that sustained life. The Aztecs, thus, exalted death at least in a symbolic sense, because life led to death and death regenerated life. And certain kinds of death, especially the sacrificial deaths of warriors and the godly embodiments, ixiptlahuan, an identity often filled by prisoners of war, provided substances, hearts and blood, which sustained the energy exchanges necessary to maintain life. But death as an actual experience, rather than an abstract one, meant emotional pain. Feelings of grief and loss emerged, as did concerns rooted in the practical considerations for a household if someone who had performed vital labor died.

After a person passed away, the treatment of the body depended upon the cause and location of death. How a person died determined the final resting place for her or his body and "soul" (though archaeologists find more variation than text-based information suggests). Upon death, for most people, the body would be washed, dressed, and laid facing north toward the final resting place of the body's released energies, Mictlan. Water was then poured on the head and a precious stone for nobles or a rock for commoners placed in the mouth.

Offerings and personal effects would be situated with the body. These goods of course were especially luxurious and large in number for nobles, particularly rulers. The bodies, with these goods, would then be burned and ashes buried in the home or at the local temple. The energies released from the body then began a journey.

For those who died what Aztecs considered "watery" deaths, dying from drowning, lightening, or from diseases they associated with water such as gout or leprosy, or for women who died in childbirth, their bodies would be buried instead of being cremated, generally under house floors. The bodies of women who died in childbirth would be buried in a temple dedicated to the cihuapipiltin, goddesses derived from the energies of these deceased women. The energies from individuals Aztecs buried journeyed to Tlalocan, a watery level above the earth's surface. The energies of those who were cremated journeyed to Mictlan, perhaps an underworld. For infants who died, a third final resting place for their energies existed, an upper world that was the home of Tonacateuctli, Deity of Sustenance. There infants sucked at the milky branches of the Chichihualcuauhco, a milk-giving tree, pictured in the *Codex Vaticanus 3738* with its breasts dripping milk, to await re-birth. The energies of warriors who died in battle as well as those of women who died in childbirth went not to Tlalocan, but to a different upper region, Tonatiuh Ilhuicatl or Sun Sky. The bodies of those warriors would not be returned to their families if they had died far from their home altepetl, instead an image would be made and used in funerary ceremonies. In the Sun Sky, these men's and women's energies, thought of as spirits, accompanied the sun on its daily journey.

But before cremation or burial, four days after death, the washing and preparations began, thereby giving the mourners time to gather for the beginning of the funerary rites at the homes or palaces of the dead. After this washing, ceremonies to honor the dead unfolded. The texts that describe funerals in detail emphasize the weeping, mourning, and cremations or burials of rulers, nobles, and warriors, with female relatives chanting and crying. Widows did not wash themselves for eighty days, after which a priest relieved women of their dirt and sorrow, freeing them from their period of mourning. This was not, however, the end of memorializing the dead. A family's dead relatives would be remembered several times a year, and as many as seven of the solar festival months had elements of commemoration. For example, on the eighth day of the last month of the year, Izcalli, a month dedicated to growth of children, water and agriculture, fertility and the restarting of fires, family members buried under houses would be celebrated through offerings of tamales at the beginning of one of the feasts of that month. The dead were also remembered during the ninth and tenth months, Tlaxochimaco (also known as Miccailhuitontli) and Xocotl uetzi (also called Huey Miccailhuitl), with the alternative names emphasizing celebrating the dead, the Little and Great Feast of the Dead respectively, when households commemorated deceased children and adult relatives. Deceased kin mediated between humans and the supernatural as the ceremonies included worship of and offerings to deities relating to the earth, food, or water. Aztecs sought resources, gave thanks for those resources, or hoped to garner protection from calamities through these acts of propitiation.

While Aztecs lived among the remains of the dead and conducted numerous ceremonies for them, even as many people died in their prime, especially men who had been in battle, others lived to be elderly. Aztecs respected the elderly and granted them special privileges. Treating them as carriers of tradition who taught and upheld the moral values of Aztec society, newborns were viewed as the "representation and substitution" (timixiptla, timpatillo) of family elders. The families and neighbors of elders treated them well. Infants, as we have already seen, were greeted with joy and loved as precious gifts of recycled substances. And just as newborns were not gender differentiated at first, kin terms for elders also made no gender distinctions, expressing symmetry and a kind of balance Aztecs kept between past and future kin. This kinship terminology spanned a total of seven generations and included an uppermost level, the great-great-grandparents of a person and the lowermost, that person's grandchildren. Those terms, *mintontli* and *ixiuhtli* respectively, were not gender differentiated. While elders retained respect and influence, this stage of life was one when certain pleasures forbidden to others could be enjoyed such as that of partaking of pulque, an alcoholic drink made from the agave, or maguey, plant. The *Codex Mendoza* explains that old men and women could enjoy drinking alcohol to the point of intoxication. Respected, even sometimes revered, Aztecs, nevertheless, also saw the elderly as decrepit, childlike, even senile, as they approached the time when their bodies would help regenerate the earth with substances that could provide sustenance and energy for new human life to come into the world.

The process of decomposition was a bodily, material process, but decomposition also involved transition for "souls," better thought of perhaps as energies rather than souls in a Christian sense. Three that shaped an Aztec's personhood have been identified, the *tonalli*, *ihiyotl*, and *yolia*. Each energy was said to reside in an organ of the body. The tonalli, associated with the sun, heat, and the fortunes of the day a person was born on, was said to dwell in the head; the ihiyotl to be connected to the liver, and influence strong positive or negative emotions; the yolia tied to the heart. The yolia energy traveled to the destinations previously mentioned, depending upon the type of death described above. It too connected to emotions such as affection as well as the qualities of vitality and intelligence – at least such is the argument Alfredo López Austin made that has influenced so much scholarship on Aztec religion and death. More recently, it has been suggested that yolia was neither a spirit nor soul and that its definition as such was not an Indigenous concept. Possibly introduced by Spanish priests who applied the word yolia (from "*yoli*," a word that Molina says in his dictionary refers to something alive or to live) to the Christian idea of a soul, this naming offers an example of how the training in Christian precepts of Aztec scholars who aided the friars in their research and writing makes it difficult to tease out pre-Christian beliefs about bodies, energies, and afterlives.

Tensions in Aztec Life

The tonalli, which greatly influenced the personality and fate of a person, affected the way an Aztec person experienced family and neighborhood relationships. Some individuals experienced the life cycle in the ideal way that the ticitl, an infant's parents, and relatives spoken of in the orations, the huehuetlatolli, spoken before and after birth. These teachings helped families guide infants to become a girl or boy, woman or man. But some people experienced disruption and unhappiness. They lived more chaotic, difficult lives. Certain of the day signs predicted strongly negative, grueling lives. To take just one example, those born on the day Two Rabbit were fated to be heavy drinkers who could not function in society. Unable to work, sustain a family, care for themselves, or stay away from crime, they became especially prone to commit adultery. While the chapter of Book Four in the *Florentine Codex* that describes the fate of the poor souls born on Two Rabbit as men, the next chapter about the different kinds of alcoholics and alcohol-influenced behaviors that occurred makes clear that this fate could befall men or women. Both chapters show that excessive drinking by those not allowed to consume deeply disrupted family life. Those who were ill-fated would be unable to parent, nor could they experience a calm, peaceful family life. They might even have no home at all, living on the streets.

Aztec narratives, historical and legal, also illustrate the kinds of relationships, ideal and real, that families experienced. Elder siblings, especially brothers, were expected to guide and lead those who were younger. The term for the elder brother (tiachcauh) could be extended to refer to teachers in the telpochcalli, male and female (*tiachcahuan, cihuatetiachcahuan*). While sibling groups frequently owned houses and land together, tensions existed in sibling relationships. The stories of migration that were described in the first chapter show that conflicts between brother-elder sister deities led to intra-group splits and the formation of new groups and eventually altepeme. These divine elder sisters were only one manifestation of a role that existed in Aztec myths in which they also served among the god carriers during migration before founding a new altepetl, or as literal elder sisters who, if one was the sister of a ruler, could be married to the ruler of another group for political purposes.

Not always harmonious, sibling groups, especially among nobles, might be torn apart by competition over succession to high office and access to resources, with polygynous marriages and the multiple mothers and their offspring fueling competitive strife. When rulers' wives or consorts living in tecpan lobbied for one son over another at moments when succession to the rulership was an issue, they could create real conflict. The history of the last native ruler of Tetzcoco, Nezahualpilli, suggests such tensions. Chosen at a very young age to succeed as tlatoani, selected in place of four elder brothers, despite maternal lobbying, those brothers were most displeased. Nezahualpilli had to be hidden and protected until he could take his position, with the eldest brother eventually agreeing to serve as regent. Furthermore, conflicts over inheritance among siblings or the descendants of siblings, sometimes dating back to events before Spaniards arrived, were not uncommon in the early colonial era.

The parent-child relationship could also be one where tensions and difficulties manifested themselves despite the stress on parental obligation and child obedience expressed by the huehuetlatolli. We have already seen that alcohol abuse could interfere with parenting and undermine the values placed on stability and obedience that child socialization practices expressed and emphasized. The harsh punishments used by parents of children who failed to display the proper devotion to assigned work tasks that images of socialization in the *Codex Mendoza* reveal hint that parent-child relations did not always flow smoothly. Rulers, in particular, punished sons and daughters unsparingly, including with loss of life for crimes such as adultery. Rulers of Tetzococo for example, had sons, even a daughter, executed for such crimes. Alva Ixtlilxochitl also provides an example of parent-child tensions around succession in the very early colonial period, when he describes how the mother of a close ally of the Spanish, Ixtlilxochitl, great-great-grandfather of the writer Alva Ixtlilxochitl, failed to support him in his quest to become ruler after Nezahualpilli's death. When he pressured her to convert after the evangelization efforts began in Tetzcoco, she refused. Ixtlilxochitl then threatened her with death.

Just as parent-child relations did not always flow as smoothly as the proscriptive sources like the huehuetlatolli speeches around birth recorded in the *Florentine Codex*, other sources suggest that husband-wife relationships, too, experienced tensions. Unlike in the eyes of the Catholic Church, Aztec marriages could be dissolved through a rarely used but legitimate process. If a husband or wife were lazy about their responsibilities, argumentative, or physically abusive, divorce could follow. If a woman could not have children or had committed adultery, those incompatibilities also could lead to the end of a marriage. Judges who heard divorce cases counseled couples to remain together:

They harshly scolded the guilty party, and they asked the pair to recall the good will with which they had entered into marriage; they urged them not to bring shame on their parents and relatives who promoted the marriage; the judges also reminded them that people would point the finger of blame at them, for it would be known that they had been married. Many other things the judges said in order to reconcile them.

But married couples did not always stay together; unhappy parties sometimes did divorce. Given that when a couple married, the Aztec version of a prenuptial agreement was created as lists of property were kept by tlaxilacalli or calpolli heads so it could be redistributed if a marriage fell apart, the idea of separation of couples and their property clearly existed.

It is, however, in the histories of altepeme and their rulers that the most evidence of marriages coming asunder is to be found. Tales of courtship and love certainly exist. Sometimes these have a Pygmalion-like quality such as when, according to the *Anales de Cuauhtitlan*, an early Tetzcoca ruler, Quinatzin, "found love" (yn oquittac quitlaçotlac) with Chimalxoch, a young war captive. She refused to marry him until after she had completed a vow to a deity, but marry and have children they did. Another story, this one recounted by the chronicler Chimalpahin, tells of the early Mexica ruler Huitzilihuitl and his pursuit of the lovely daughter of the ruler of the altepetl of Cuauhnahuac, Miyahuaxihuitl. That tlatoani, Oçomatzin teuctli, refused the request. Eventually Huitzilopochtli, after being directed by a night deity, Yohualli, shot an arrow with a beautiful green stone he had placed on it into the palace courtyard whereupon Miyahuaxihuitl came upon the stone, swallowed it, then conceived one of the most powerful of Mexica rulers, Moteuczoma Ilhuicamina, and became one of Huitzilihuitl's wives.

But the family histories of rulers also tell us about bad love and marriages that came apart. It is hard to tell with these tales whether we are seeing sex rending empire or the reverse, empire rending sex. What does seem clear is that tlatoque used sex to stake out positions in the ever changing geopolitics of the Triple Alliance imperial formation. An early example comes from the *Anales de Cuauhtitlan* which describes a royal wife as an informant. The woman involved was a daughter of Cuauhtitlan's ruler Tecocoatzin, an ally of the Tetzcoca during a period of war against the Tepaneca and their allies in the late 1420s. She was captured by enemy forces from Toltitlan and then married that altepetl's ruler. She then proceeded to provide her father with information about the war plans of Toltitlan's ruler. When a battle between the opposing forces began, not only had she told her father about Toltitlan's plans, she set fire to its main temple, by which it was destroyed, a sign of the defeat of that altepetl. Another example involves the sister of the Tenochca tlatoani Axayacatl who married Tlatelolco's ruler Moquihuix. He treated the woman, Chalchiuhnenetzin, very badly, preferring other wives and palace women. Her complaints to her brother ostensibly provoked a war during which some Tlatelolca women tried to help their altepetl's failed cause by leaping onto roofs, exposing their genitals, and squeezing their breasts to produce milk and throwing it on their enemies' fighters. The *Anales de*

Cuauhtitlan treats this woman not simply as an aggrieved primary wife but as a political informant who passed on Moquihuix's war plans to her brother. Neither conventional nor unconventional approaches by Tlatelolco to the military clash succeeded. Moquihuix ended the war by throwing himself from Tlateloco's main temple. Chimalpahin rather poetically says "The Tlatelolca perished because of concubines" (*chahua*).

Perhaps tensions between the sister cities of Tenochtitlan and Tlatelolco and Tlatelolco's defeat were not solely reducible to the marital problems of its ruler. That Tlatelolco controlled the largest and most affluent market in all of Mesoamerica surely provided motivation for the Tenochca Mexica. But multiple sources demonstrate that Chalchiuhnenetzin played a role in the outbreak of war. And she was far from the only woman of discord to be found in the codices and chronicles relating altepeme histories from the Basin of Mexico. Another lurid story of a different Chalchiuhnenetzin, a daughter or niece of the tlatoani Axayacatl, got herself executed for her immoral behavior, provoking political tensions that would reverberate into the period of war with and colonization by Europeans.

Having been married quite young and assigned to live with her female servants in Tetzcoco until she was old enough to begin sexual relations with Nezahualpilli, this Chalchiuhnenetzin instead indulged in relations with several lovers who she then had killed. She had statues made of them, placing the images in her rooms. Having allowed three of the men to live, Nezahualpilli discovered her activities when he spied one of the men with a jewel he had given to this particular wife. He had her executed very publicly along with the men. People from towns all over the Basin of Mexico saw her execution, undoubtedly shaming the Mexica royal family very publicly. Nezahualpilli's relationship with the Mexica, especially with their ruler Moteuczoma Xocoyotl (Chalchiuhnenetzin's brother or cousin), never equaled the relationship his father Nezahualcoyotl had with previous Mexica rulers. When Nezahualpilli died and Moteuczoma inserted himself into the succession struggle and decided upon the ruler who would follow after Nezahualpilli's death, Tetzococo's ruling dynasty became deeply split. That altepetl, still an important member of the Excan tlatoloyan, never allied itself definitively with Tenochtitlan again. This mattered after 1519. These marital troubles and political conflicts were intimately related; sex undermined imperial ties yet helped create and sustain new ones. When Nezahualpilli had his Mexica wife executed, the tales told later about this event symbolized and justified Tetzcoco's emerging alliance with the Spanish, a partnership crucial to their military goals.

A less lurid story involving the Tetzoca ruling dynasty dates further back, again to the time of tensions between the Tepaneca and Tetzcoca in the first decades of the fifteenth century. Not only did the Tetzcoca ruler, an earlier Ixtlilxochitl, reject a marriage with a daughter of the Tepaneca ruler Tezozomoc, but a daughter-in-law, a royal Tetzcoca woman married to one of Tezozomoc's sons, fled back to Tetzcoco and took another husband after the mistreatment and death of her son. When Tezozomoc learned of this marriage, enraged, he ordered the murder of Tetzcoco's ruler, Ixtlilxochitl. This episode is recounted in the *Anales de Cuauhtitlan*, providing one more tale of a woman portrayed as causing conflict that provoked war and death. The politics of relations between the Tepaneca and Tetzcoca were complicated and related to the rise of the Mexica as a much more powerful altepetl, no longer subservient to the Tepaneca. The existence of stories about how women provoked political conflicts at the highest level early and late in Aztec history illustrates the way gender and political relations were deeply interwoven among them.

Conclusion

The family lives of rulers show in dramatic fashion that households, sex, and daily life were closely connected to the activities of founding and ruling polities, war, and ritual, even production and commerce as alliances made or broken affected tribute and trade. In noble and commoner homes, women and men played significant roles within and beyond the household. Both genders tied households to communal life and values through production, child socialization, and enforcing the moral values and behavior of household residents. While a senior man within the home organized labor and tribute payments, women could at times play this role. Furthermore, tracing house compound ownership rights as well as the beginnings of altepeme to founding couples demonstrates that such pairs provided a basis for household formation and community identity. The parallel organization of production and socialization in which senior men and women played leading roles reinforced the importance of male and female complementarity within and beyond the home. The couple at the head of a household mediated activities like working and passing on land, residence rights, labor for crafts and commerce, settling disputes, and carrying out the activities of worship of household deities within the home. These included praying for family members away at war, caring for sacrificial victims that tlaxilacalli or calpolli leaders or merchants brought into their households during certain monthly ceremonies, and conducting life cycle ceremonies for birth, marriage, and death. Women's and men's activities complemented each other. Because women and men both held hierarchically organized positions, this structure resulted in parallel lines of authority in governance, commerce, production, and schooling. What can be termed "gender parallelism" rooted in these co-existing lines of authority, was a significant component of the complementarity or balance that deeply influenced Aztec gender roles.

Through work, socialization, and spirituality, Aztec men and women transformed the infants they treasured into children, then adults, who created the material and symbolic value that sustained villages, towns, and cities, underwrote their activities of war and diplomacy, and defended confederations and imperial formations. Maintaining the Aztec world – writ small in the household, writ large in the altepetl and empire – in balance was the responsibility of both women and men. The complementary partnership that marriage represented provided one of the foundations upon which Aztec political, economic, and religious practices survived and became transformed both before and after the Spanish arrived. Aztec intellectual and creative activities were another foundation for both transformation and change.

6

Resilience

Part One: Aztec Intellectual Life

∽

Aztec ways of being have survived until today despite a variety of brutal assaults. War, disease, and colonial and national rule all led to changing landscapes, technologies, laws, means of communication, and identities. Science, writing and literature, and art all provided resources through which the Aztec ideas of value, transformation, and balance would be remembered, modified, and serve as resources for cultural resistance and resilience. As Aztec people, their families, and communities coped with new forms of change, the "globalized present" referenced in the first chapter eventually came into being. Medicine, the written word, and images all played significant roles in the survival of descendants of the Aztecs as well as how they have come to be seen by others. Their intellectual and creative projects, linked to religion, yet constituting activities in some ways separate from it, are the subjects of this chapter. War, change, and survival are the subjects of the next.

Science

Aztecs were brilliant scientists, writers, and artists. Highly skilled at using math and science in architecture, engineering, and astronomy for buildings, urban planning, and waterworks, they used the sky and stars for many purposes, especially for keeping track of time for ritual and practical matters. These included: to orient their buildings and cities; to use the growing season to its best advantage; to organize tribute collection; and to live in and worship the sacred world. Their engineering of water control infrastructure helped supply sufficient food for the large, dense populations of the Basin of Mexico and protected altepeme from flooding. Aztec knowledge about health, medicine, and illness was likewise deep and rested on the foundation of the desire to maintain the human body and society at large in a state of equilibrium or balance. How the Aztecs practiced medicine provides the example of their scientific knowledge for this chapter.

In order to consider how Aztecs treated diseases, sometimes through treatments that are still in use today within *and* beyond Indigenous communities, it is important to establish what Aztecs thought caused disease. While Aztecs were relatively healthy and well-nourished for a preindustrial people, they nonetheless were well aware that diseases and wounds occurred. They developed a wide range of ideas about the causes of illness, both practical and supernatural. War and the wounds it caused of course undermined health for men, women, and children and could lead to illness as could changes in temperature, actual changes as well as metaphorical imbalances between substances thought to be cold or hot, famine, or accidents. Supernatural causes of disease included both divine forces and human magic. Deities and sorcerers such as the *teyollocuani* (heart eater) could both cause and cure diseases. Failure to live up to Aztec moral standards also could lead to disease, and one's date of birth could incline a person to suffer from certain diseases as well.

Just as deities could bring about disease, they could help cure. Tlaloc and associated rain deities caused diseases such as leprosy, gout, rheumatism, or dropsy, but they also could cure these and other afflictions. During the month of Tepeilhuitl during which rain and mountain deities were celebrated, for example, Aztecs made tzoalli dough representations of mountains which were decapitated, the dough then distributed to those suffering from water-caused diseases. The families of those who had died from those illnesses also made the images to honor their deceased relatives. Other deities could provoke diseases. Xipe Totec, for example, could give people skin and eye diseases, but if vows were made or offerings given to him, he could cure those same afflictions.

Priests, priestesses, and temples were involved in curing, but Aztecs had a wide array of healers beyond priests who treated diseases. Treatments often combined sacred and empirical knowledge. Priests dedicated to deities who caused diseases could also aid in curing them. The most commonly used term by Aztecs for a doctor – someone with specific and practical knowledge about healing – was ticitl, a word that referred to those women and men who provided medical treatments. Medical specialists focused on specific areas of the body, healing through plants, setting broken bones, or dealing with the soft tissues of the body. Others dealt with eye diseases or provided expertise in the medical properties of an immense number of herbs. Their practices intersected with the spiritual realm because religion, magic, and ideas about dirt as physically and spiritually harmful played strong roles in disease causation and healing. But before healing could take place, a diviner needed to diagnose and identify the cause and prognosis of a disease. Was the cause supernatural, due to divine or magical intervention, or related to natural causes? Priests played a role in divination as did other practitioners such as doctors and other healer/diviners who would make determinations about the causes of illness before curing could be attempted.

The books priests specializing in the ritual calendar read to carry out divination, the tonalamatl, often contained sections covering healing and could be used to discover causation, diagnosis, as well as cures. Cipactonal and Oxomoco were the first human couple *and* the first diviners. They are shown in the *Codex Borbonicus* divining with maize kernels and were closely associated with the tonalpohualli, the 260-day ritual calendar described in Chapter 2, as well as with curing, having been the inventors of not just the books of days and divining but also medical knowledge. While practitioners of divining and curing overlapped, the ordinary person also played a role in health because men and women had a moral and social responsibility to live balanced lives. This entailed carrying out their duties to the gods, their families and communities as well as caring for themselves, responding to the people around them with respect, and practicing moderation in all things. But events – supernatural, human, natural – often intervened and caused sickness and suffering. Before Spaniards arrived, Aztecs, while generally healthy, suffered from viral and bacterial diseases such as dysentery, colds and influenza, strep or staph infections, tuberculosis, arthritis, and parasitic diseases. They also experienced bone breaks, wounds to the skin, and snake and insect bites. Because war was so prevalent, Aztec healers – women and men – displayed considerable expertise in treating bone and skin wounds, even engaging in surgical repairs.

Aztecs also dealt with women's health issues, in particular pregnancy and childbearing. Vigilance and hygiene were part of standard care for pregnant women, especially as they gave birth and then recovered. The attention by midwives to women giving birth has been described in the preceding chapter; they bathed women before giving birth as well as the infant after being born. During and after birth, women repaired to the *temazcalli* (bathing house), a stone structure in which attendants poured water on hot stones to produce copious amounts of steam. Temazcalli existed far back in Mesoamerican history and are still in use today in many parts of Indigenous Mesoamerica. Men, women, and children used sweat baths, but they were thought to be especially helpful to women after giving birth to help them regain energy or heat lost during the birthing process. In addition, the herb *cihuapatli* was also used by women to strengthen their contractions to help along a birth. Its use indicates another area, using plants as medicine, in which Aztec cures also excelled. Like temazcalli, some of these cures are still used today.

The importance of herbal curing to Aztec medical practices is undeniable. Some of these cures had magical properties, but many had chemically active properties that produce empirically observable positive effects. About 2000 medicinal plants were known to Indigenous healers across all of Mesoamerica before Spaniards arrived. One study of 118 plants known to be used by Aztec healers showed 85 percent of them to produce curative effects. Aztecs understood and classified plants according to whether they were cacti, magueys, shrubs, and herbs. They differentiated between flowering plants and those that bore fruits, and they also used aroma as a means of classification. They valued both aquatic plants and those grown in drier regions as well as plants grown in hotter or colder zones, a difference that correlated with elevations. Thus Aztecs – certainly their medical specialists – were knowledgeable botanists.

Aztecs associated plants they used for healing with deities and believed them to have divine properties. For example *ololiuhqui* – a kind of morning glory – and other plants with hallucinogenic properties were tied to Tlaloc because they grew in watery, humid places. The Catholic priest and extirpator Hernando Ruiz de Alarcón had a particularly harsh reaction to this medicine because of its hallucinogenic properties but also because of his belief that Aztecs thought of it as a deity. Other plants, for example *yolloxochitl* or heart flower, were believed to affect the organ or part of the body they resembled. Yolloxochitl, a type of magnolia, indeed does help the heart by strengthening it and helping to regulate the pulse.

Aztecs used plant medications in a variety of ways – as antidotes, purgatives, and to bring down fevers in addition to helping women give birth or to help overcome heart problems. They administered herbal remedies in many forms – as a decoction (or essence), an oil, a purgative, a tea, or a laxative. Although the introduction of Spanish medical ideas and cures would influence Aztec medicine, native plants and Indigenous curing methods have had a lasting effect on the practice of medicine in Mesoamerica.

Healing and medicines – particularly plants – were important enough to Aztec intellectual life to be painted and written about in their books. The *Codex Mendoza*, for example, contains many plant images often part of the written names for places or painted as images of plants provided as tribute items.

Writing and Literature

That Aztecs *wrote* is not widely recognized. The Maya are well known for their sophisticated hieroglyphic writing system; the Aztecs are not. A descendant of the writing of Teotihuacan, itself likely an outgrowth of earlier systems developed by Zapotecs and Mayas, Aztec writing is *not* merely pictography, or writing with pictures, it is something more complex and developed throughout the late prehispanic period and into the colonial period up to the early seventeenth century. An important characteristic of writing is that it is definitive in the ways it communicates meaning regardless of whether signs are letters as in our alphabet or phonograms (signs for sounds), syllabograms (signs for syllables), or logograms (signs for words), all three common in Aztec writing. It is intended to convey meaning so that "various individuals can read and utter a particular text in very similar if not identical ways," as archaeologist Karl Taube has explained. While images can form a narrative and tell a story, they are open to a much wider range of interpretation. Writing conveys names, places, and events or actions in more definitive ways.

What did Aztecs use writing for, and how did their system work? Because Spaniards destroyed so many Aztec books (what we now call codices for their highly pictorial content), very few prehispanic versions survived to the present-day. Perhaps only the *Matrícula de Tributos*, likely drawn very early in the sixteenth century, and the *Codex Borgia* (along with six other closely related codices) date back to before the arrival of Spaniards. That group of codices and very early colonial texts such as the *Codex Mendoza*, based on the *Matrícula* or a closely related text that both the *Matrícula* and the *Mendoza* drew upon, provide clues to the purposes to which Aztecs put writing and images. Certainly writing served the practical purpose of record keeping. The *Matrícula de Tributos* recorded a list of tribute goods provided either to Tenochtitlan's ruler or to the rulers of the Excan tlatoloyan over a certain period of time, perhaps a year. The *Codex Borgia*, probably originating in Aztec areas to the southeast of the Basin of Mexico, most likely the Cholollan-Tlaxcallan or Tehuacán Valley regions, and representing a specific art style, the Mixteca-Puebla style (discussed in more detail later in this chapter), offers a priest's manual covering a wide array of topics. These included the 260-day divinatory calendar, signs relating to birth, marriage, death and war, patron deities for the thirteen-day periods of the tonalpohualli as well as images of major Aztec deities and weather prognostications. From how and when to plant, when to get married, and the lives of deities and heroic figures of the earliest Aztec period, pictures and writing communicated the value of goods, the ways both objects and gods could transform into spirit beings or matter, and the effort to keep the earth and cosmic forces in balance so that the forces of chaos did not overwhelm that balance. Books also contained histories about the deepest past, the Aztec migrations, and rulers' genealogies. Writing and painting served, therefore, practical, spiritual, and historical purposes for Aztec priests, rulers, and intellectuals. It conveyed information in specific contexts through grammatical rules both particular yet flexible.

Aztecs used writing to name people, titles, places, and deities. Their system combined logograms and either phonograms or syllabograms. In addition to using such signs, rebus writing, in which a picture of a word represents the sound of that word, also appears. In contrast to our writing system, in which letter order is key to comprehending both sound and meaning, Aztec signs could be written in varying order, so that no fixed reading order existed. Aztec writers, the tlacuiloque, used several other signs to communicate or reinforce meaning when they wrote. These included using *connectors*, short lines meant to link a written name to an image of a person, place, title, or sometimes even a family relationship. Tlacuiloque also used *size* to communicate meaning as in using a larger sign to communicate the adjective for large size or importance in addition to meaning old, huey, as part of a place name, for example. They used *color* to convey color terms in personal or place names. *Complements* and *indicators* also served to enhance or reinforce meaning. Complements add information to a sign or sequence of signs; indicators reinforce information. A phonetic complement like *te-* (from *tetl*, stone, or teotl, referring to divinity) adds information in the writing of, for example, a name to provide clarity in meaning. A phonetic indicator helps in the reading of the intended sound in a word. In the *Codex Telleriano-Remensis*, as linguistic anthropologist Gordona Whittaker has explained, the name for Acampichtli's wife, Ilancueitl is indicated by an image of a

FIG. 6.1 Ilancueitl's name written in the Aztec writing system *Codex Telleriano-Remensis*, fol.29v. Courtesy of the Bibliothèque nationale de France

skirt (*cueitl*), tooth or teeth (*tlantli*), and a dangling cord with an image of a human liver hanging from it (*elli*). The liver sign was used for the sounds "el" and "il," and the cord as a phonetic indicator specifies that the correct reading is "il"—Il-an-cueitl ("il" from the word *ilpia*, to tie; see Fig. 6.1). This example shows the way Aztec writing could use phonetic signs.

All Aztec writing made use of such signs, but geographically varying patterns for the use of phoneticism existed.

These variations have been described as "scribal schools" by Alfonso Lacadena, a Spanish archaeologist-linguist-historian. He argued that at least two Aztec schools of writing existed (he thought more probably did as well), that of Tenochtitlan and that of Tetzcoco. The two schools shared most features of Aztec writing: the overall set of signs; the ways they were represented and used; the variable ordering of signs; as well as the naming, counting, and calendric functions of writing. Where the two schools differed was in how often they used phonetic phonograms and complementation, with the Tetzcoco style of writing consistently using both more often. It is impossible to definitively rule out influence coming from the arrival of the Spanish language on Tetzcoco writing because new names and titles required using sounds of the Nahuatl language written in glyphic form using phonograms. The presence of the Spanish language reinforced the phoneticism already present in Aztec writing. For example, the syllable "to" (pronounced "toe," from *tototli*, bird) used for the Spanish word for a nobleman, *don*, was shown with a picture of a bird (see Fig. 6.2).

Tlacuiloque adjusted their writing practices to new needs for record keeping. For example, Aztecs sought to protect communities' land and water rights because boundary and inheritance disputes broke out in great numbers, given intrusions and exploitation by Spaniards and sometimes other Indigenous people or communities. When writing documents in Nahuatl, or occasionally in Spanish, to be used in colonial legal contexts, the tlacuiloque adapted the Roman alphabet to Nahuatl. The many legal proceedings that occurred beginning in the 1530s led to such innovations. The Aztec writing system,

FIG. 6.2 Phoneticism in Aztec writing
Codex Aubin, fol.58v. © The Trustees of the British Museum

however, actually remained quite traditional because the readers were other Aztecs, *not* Spaniards. Spaniards did not understand this writing system and appear to have made no effort to, if other than a few even understood that Aztec books contained writing and not just pictures. Furthermore, the phoneticism of the Tetzcoca school remained characteristic of their writing from those documents produced shortly after 1521 to those produced in the late sixteenth or early seventeenth centuries. Understanding that Aztecs wrote, used their own writing system for a variety of purposes, and that the system survived beyond the sixteenth century likely until there were no longer readers or writers using Aztec writing helps us appreciate their intellectual pursuits, examples of which can also be found in Aztec literature, both written and oral.

The creativity found in Aztec literature shows the value they placed on skill with words, and also demonstrates the flexibility and regionalism we saw in the writing system. Aztecs used their writing system in combination with painting to produce books, those texts commonly called codices. When Fernando Alva Ixtlilxochitl, for example, described the sources he was using to produce his histories, he made very clear his preference for *Indigenous* texts, mentioning books that recorded Aztec annals; genealogies of rulers; maps of cities, provinces, and landholdings; and records of law, the religious calendar and ceremonies, and of science and song. Some of those books provided prompts for the singing, chanting, or speaking of hymns, secular songs, poetry, and histories.

Aztec books – *amoxtli* – took several forms: screenfolds, also called *tiras*; individual sheets used to record tribute records and maps; and large cloth pieces called *lienzos* that recorded altepeme histories and landholdings. The *amacuahuitl*, or fig tree, along with maguey plants and sometimes animal hides, provided the materials for the paper used for Aztec books. The Aztec process for making paper from fig trees consisted of boiling a tree's inner bark to obtain fig fiber, pounding the fibers together on a plank, smoothing the surface, letting it dry, and forming sheets of varying sizes. Paper of different hues was produced because differently colored species of fig trees existed. Aztecs greatly valued this paper which today is still made in some parts of Indigenous Mexico. Because the altepeme of the Excan tlatoloyan could not produce enough paper, given the many types of books they made and the other uses to which paper was put, it became a major tribute item. Paper had great material value that then could be converted into symbolic value in the political and religious contexts in which books and paper were used. Paper served to keep tribute records, decorate deity sculptures, or adorn sacrificial victims. For scholars it is a source of great frustration that so few Aztec books survived the Spanish-Mexica war. Adding to that frustration is the fact that the Mexica ruler Itzcoatl conducted his own book burning in the early fifteenth century to glorify his imperial desires and his period of rule, thereby erasing the histories of altepeme formation, earlier rulers, and neighborhood governance.

Nonetheless, we can reconstruct a lot about the types of books written and the literature Aztecs produced. Durán, in particular, emphasized that Aztecs had a writing system that recorded information in a long-lasting form:

All was written down, painted in books and on long papers, indicating the year, month, and date on which each event had occurred. Also recorded in these painted documents were the laws and ordinances, the census, and so forth. All this was set down painstakingly and carefully by the most competent historians, who by means of these paintings recorded extensive chronicles regarding the men of the past.

Motolinia also described the books that Aztecs wrote, emphasizing that there were five types, including books about the years; days and feasts; dreams and omens; baptisms and names; and ceremonies and prognostications for marriages. He also mentions that records were kept about succession to rulerships, wars, and disease.

Whether taking the form of screenfolds, sheets, or lienzos, several regional styles of writing and painting can be discerned in Aztec books. Lacadena, as noted above, demonstrated differences between the writing of Tenochca versus Tetzcoca scribes. Elizabeth Hill Boone, while acknowledging that an Aztec painting style influenced the regions the Excan tlatoloyan powers had subjugated, observes that the southeastern Aztec area and Tlaxcallan retained their own styles. Altepeme across the entire Nahuatl-speaking area thus retained local traditions in forms of expression before and after the arrival of Spaniards.

Many of the written and painted texts were intended to be recited, chanted, or sung out loud; in other words, writing and books, the written literature, provided the basis for Aztec oral literature. One class of that spoken literature that both Spanish chroniclers and contemporary scholars have been particularly fascinated by are their songs (*cuicatl*). Describing how Aztec youth prided themselves in their abilities to sing and dance, having been well taught in cuicacalli, Durán described some of the different kinds of songs:

[S]ome were sung slowly and seriously; these were sung and danced by the lords on solemn and important occasions and were intoned, some with moderation and calm, [while] others [were] less sober and more lively. These were dances and songs of pleasure known as "dances of youth," during which they sang songs of love and flirtation, similar to those sung today on joyful occasions.

He reminds us that for all the solemnity we find in Aztec literature and performing arts, that songs and dances could be "extremely gay, merry, and funny." Durán had, perhaps among Spanish missionaries, the most humane response to Aztec songs, declaring that he saw no need to stamp them out because the words, the way they were written, were largely admirable. Others sought to prohibit and repress what, to their minds, were dangerous ideas. León-Portilla explains that for Sahagún, the purpose of having his native collaborators collect songs was to find and erase those dangerous ideas that the devil had implanted in them. That collecting project resulted in several assemblages that still exist and provide much evidence about the range and even time depth of Aztec songs.

One such collection appears twice in the works associated with Bernardino de Sahagún. It consisted of a set of twenty songs provided by Sahagún's partners in Tepepolco around 1558 compiled in the *Primeros memoriales*. These same songs appear as an appendix to Book Two of the *Florentine Codex*. Because obscure and archaic forms of Nahuatl appear in these songs, dedicated to Aztec deities and sung in their temples, the authors of that text refer to them as "songs of the devils" (jncuic catca, in tlatlacateculo). These pieces are almost certainly of prehispanic origin. The tlacuiloque associated with this project would have transformed the written and painted texts into alphabetized texts. Sahagún commented, however, on how difficult the songs were to translate. Other collections show greater Christian influence, including the *Cantares mexicanos* and the *Romances de los señores de Nueva España*. The former is the largest compilation of songs, some ninety-one, collected by anonymous natives working with a missionary friar. Many of these songs were older and had been adapted to the Christianizing context. Others were composed after the fall of Tenochtitlan and concern themselves with a wide variety of themes – springtime, flowers, birds, fish, orphans, lords, suffering, war, water pouring, women, doves, sexuality, and elders' songs. Conquest and Christian worship also appear as themes. The songs came from a variety of places across Aztec Mesoamerica and they were sung or chanted in local styles (such as those of the Otomi, Chalca, Mexica, and others as well). The bulk of this collecting probably took place in the 1560s.

Another compilation of sixty songs, the *Romances*, gathered by the mestizo writer Juan Bautista Pomar, was put together most likely in the 1570s as the text in which they were included was completed in 1582. Many of these songs were from his home altepetl of Tetzcoco, but others came from Tenochtitlan, Chalco, and Huexotzinco. Pomar made clear that he searched for ancient, that is prehispanic, songs, though some contain Christian references. Similar to the songs found in the *Cantares*, but not as thematically wide-ranging, the *Romances* provide a wealth of information about themes of concern such as divinity, friendship, war, and death. Some comment on Aztec, especially Tetzcoca, reactions to defeat, both by the Excan tlatoloyan and by the Spanish.

Other songs, or at least fragments of them, can be found in different textual sources. Among others, songs or fragments can be found in Books Three and Ten of the *Florentine Codex*, the *Historia Tolteca-Chichimeca*, and the *Anales de Cuauhtitlan*. A fragment of a funerary song or chant from Book Ten, perhaps first sung at Teotihuacan, addresses a dead woman:

> Wake up, it reddens
> The dawn alights
> The flame-colored birds already sing
> The flame-colored butterfly already flies

Some songs, like this fragment, arose from ancient traditions and were part of Aztecs' collective historical memories. They reflect inherited traditions and the Aztec interest in both their deep and more recent history, a pattern we will see again with art. Others had authors. In some texts or song annotations, there are attributions to particular people.

Who were the creators of songs of prehispanic origin? Many of the extant songs had anonymous authors and could have been the product of a kind of collective authorship because as the songs were sung, their context and content developed and changed over time. In some cases, authorship is attributed to rulers, the Tetzcoca ruler Nezahualcoyotl having been considered to be especially prolific, with several songs in the *Cantares* and *Romances* attributed to him, and the historian Alva Ixtlilxochitl remarking on his wisdom and compositional skills. After proclaiming him to be a great philosopher and astrologer, one who divined the existence of one true god – Tloque Nahuaque, Lord of the Near and Close – Alva Ixtlilxochitl says he was a historian and composer of songs, at least sixty of them, and that due to his devotion to learning and the arts, he created councils of science and music, among others. Whether he was truly the singular author of the songs attributed to him is unclear. Rulers had among their palace retinues singer-composers who memorialized leaders' great achievements, and could well have been the actual composers. But Nezahualcoyotl's concern with law, philosophy, and the arts was widely known. A singer-composer wrote *about* him in a piece collected in the *Romances*:

> On a flower mat
> You paint your songs, your words,
> My lord, you Nezahualcoyotl.
> Your heart is painted with many-colored flowers
> You paint your songs, your words,
> My lord, you Nezahualcoyotl

A song found in the *Cantares* in Nezahuacoyotl's voice expresses an idea found among a number of songs – that life on earth is sorrowful and transitory – as he expresses sadness for the loss of the noble Tezozomoctzin. This man was a singer or singer-composer for whose songs and presence the ruler grieved, "Çan nihualayocoya nicnotlamati" (I am saddened, I grieve). Time, existence, and beauty appear as themes in the compositions attributed to Nezahualcoyotl as do they in those attributed to his son, the Tetzcoca ruler Nezahualpilli.

While men seem to have dominated Aztec literary production, women are known to have composed songs and participated in Aztec intellectual life. Not only scribes, they also contributed to Aztec literature by writing songs. Alva Ixtlilxochitl gave one literary figure the name "Lady of Tula." One of the lovers of Nezahualpilli, a son of Nezahualcoyotl who ruled after him, this woman was one of 2,000 such paramours the chronicler informs us, the commoner daughter of a merchant. Thought to be the equal in intelligence to the ruler and his wisest advisors, she held Nezahualpilli in thrall with her brilliant poetry.

But it was Macuilxochitzin, a daughter of Tlacaelel, probably born around 1435, who left concrete evidence of her writing. Her name is also a day and deity name – Five Flower. This deity was a patron of music, dance, and games and shared a connection with nobles and their retinues. The one song attributed to her and included in the *Cantares* is called Matlatzincayotl Icuic or Matlatzinca Song. It tells the story of war preparations by Mexica tlatoani Axayacatl, the preparations being for a war in the Valley of Toluca against the Matlatzinca and Otomi in the 1470s. The song celebrates the war as an Excan tlatoloyan victory, but during the war Axayacatl was wounded by an Otomi fighter named Tlilatl. Tlilatl asked "his women" (*ycihuahuan*) to care for Axayacatl. These women, in turn, interceded with Axayacatl who, the song implies, spared Tlilatl's life.

Another song *about* women attributed to the nobleman composer Aquiauhtzin of Amaquemecan, an altepetl of the Chalco region, is one of the finest and most studied of Aztec songs. In addition to the surviving text of the song found in the *Cantares*, Chimalpahin's *Seventh Relation* includes a long passage describing a performance of the song – the Chalca Cihuacuicatl (Chalca Woman's Song) – for the Mexica ruler Axayacatl. The Mexica had long tried to conquer Chalco. Beginning about 1375, several rulers conducted wars against the complex altepetl of Chalco and their people, but the conquest of the region was not completed until 1465 when Moteuczoma Ilhuicamina oversaw a final victory. That long struggle left the Chalca subjugated to the Mexica and feeling embittered about that. Aquiauhtzin expressed that bitterness in the voice of a Chalca lover, one of Axayacatl's ahuiani. Performed by a male singer before Axayacatl in 1479, the song both flattered yet mocked the ruler and the Mexica. Acknowledging that Mocteuczuma Ilhuicamina conquered Chalco, it also derided Axayacatl, turning the war and Mexica imperial power into what Miguel León-Portilla called a form of "erotic siege," one in which the ahuiani seeks a more fulfilling relationship with the ruler, but at times belittling him. While the woman eventually acknowledges that she will not become Axayacatl's wife and is destined to remain an aging pleasure woman who can never achieve a more balanced relationship with him, she ends the song by saying:

> On your mat of flowers,
> In your usual place, little one
> Slowly go to sleep
> Relax, my precious child
> You, tlatoani Axayacatl

The composer is suggesting that the woman, the defeated one, nonetheless has subdued the tlatoani Axayacatl. Rather than be insulted by the political and sexual themes of the song, according to Chimalpahin, Axayacatl embraced the song, asking the warriors and people of Chalco who possessed the song to give it to him, which they did. He passed it on to his son, who then left it to *his* son. These men had the song performed in their palaces because it was a "wondrous song" (ca cenca mahuiztic yn cuicatl). Chimalpahin comments that the song extolled the greatness of Chalco Amaquemecan despite it having become a lesser altepetl by the time he was writing.

This song and others Aztecs wrote held symbolic value for them. Songs even had material value too as the passage from Chimalpahin indicates. Not only could songs transform experience and memory into political commentary and philosophical explorations, they could express balance through the symmetry of style found in many of these compositions. Most songs have even numbers of verses, often eight in total, with symmetry achieved through this structure and by the repetition of ideas within and among verses. The parts of songs cohere together by means of symmetrical and repetitively structured parts, a theme James Lockhart stresses across many domains of Aztec life including cultural expression. We also see these ideas of value, balance, and transformation in the artistic production of the Aztecs.

Art

The "figurative and decorative objects" that constituted Aztec art communicated ideas about spirituality, the natural world, hierarchy and power, and everyday life, according to renowned art historian Esther Pasztory. Aztec artists and artisans produced a dazzling array of works that embodied value, both material and symbolic. Art objects held material value because of the substances from which they were fashioned, because of the intense labor that went into them, and because of the great skill with which they were produced. They held symbolic value because they communicated status, Aztec beliefs, and in the case of art coming out of the Excan tlatoloyan capitals, especially from Tenochtitlan, these creations broadcast propaganda about the power and dominance of this imperial configuration. Art also communicated history and identity, with regional styles and recognizable historical events depicted. Yet Aztec artistic endeavors could express some degree of subversion of dominant ideas. We should be careful not to allow Aztec – especially Mexica – propagandistic art to blind us to the human propensity to use art to mock, question, even reject dominant cultural ideals. We also should remember that on occasion Aztec artists expressed themselves idiosyncratically. Much, perhaps most, of what artists created tied together the everyday and the sacred, the natural and the supernatural, but some objects had more idiosyncratic, even personal, meanings and messages. Identifying those objects and decoding them, however, is no simple matter.

Something art historians and archaeologists can decode without great difficulty is the longer history of art in Mesoamerica that Aztec artists appreciated and emulated. They were heirs to central Mexican traditions; at the same time, they also innovated. Long after the Olmecs, the originators of Mesoamerican sculpture, the Aztecs became the greatest sculptors among later Mesoamerican peoples. Brilliant producers of both smaller-scale sculptures as well as massive stone heads, much Olmec sculptural production likely represented deities, perhaps rain and maize gods, although the huge stone heads they are known for probably represented rulers. There is no evidence to suggest that Aztecs were influenced by this early sculptural style. They had, however, some interest in it. They collected art objects from a wide variety of places, some of which they venerated, others they had conquered, taking objects from Teotihuacan, Xochimilco, and Tollan but also from Mixtec, Huastec, and Maya sites, even a greenstone Olmec mask. Although Olmec sculptural art did not directly influence Aztec artists, as consumers and purveyors of earlier history and cultural production other later art styles *did*.

Three art styles in particular influenced their art, especially in sculpture, those of Teotihuacan, Xochicalco, and Tollan, as art historian Emily Umberger has demonstrated. These artistic styles influenced the development of Aztec style not only because earlier concepts and forms permeated their art, but also because Aztec artists sometimes purposely imitated the art forms of prior civilizations. They used their archaeological investigations of Teotihuacan, Xochimilco, and Tollan to emphasize those particular peoples, copying their styles, thereby highlighting the deeper cyclical history lying behind the event for which a particular object was created or building constructed. The Aztecs revered Teotihuacan as the place where gods transformed themselves into the sun and moon. While that city's primary art form was its large, colorfully dramatic murals, its monumental architectural style and relief-style sculptural adornment of buildings are well known. A few monumental sculptures from Teotihuacan exist, at least two of which were goddesses. Perhaps these were foremothers of Aztec earth goddesses such as Cihuacoatl or Coatlicue. In addition to being influenced by Teotihuacan's use of monumentality to convey the idea of overwhelming power, the Mexica either reused or copied Teotihuacan sculptures, possibly of several Teotihuacan temples, sculptures, or images. Teotihuacan's influence – political, economic, and cultural – was very widespread across Mesoamerica, so it is not surprising that the Mexica copied aspects of their art style. They or at least their rulers viewed Teotihuacan with reverence, seeing it as important to the history of civilization in the Basin of Mexico area.

A post-Teotihuacan site, Xochicalco, also had historical and religious significance to the Aztecs, especially the Mexica. Located south and west of Teotihuacan, near today's city of Cuernavaca in the state of Morelos, the site dates to sometime between about 700 to about 900. Xochicalco may have been the place that Aztecs called Tamoanchan – a place name of possible Maya origin – with an artistic style that mixed Gulf Coast, Mixtec, Maya, and most obviously Teotihuacan influences. Like Tollan, Tamoanchan was thought of as a place of invention of learning and wisdom where the "books of days, years, and dreams" (quijiocuxque, in tonalpoalli, in xioamatl, in xippoalli, in temjc amatl) came to be, according to the *Florentine Codex*. Several Mexica monuments purposefully copied Xochicalco style dates yet also seem to reference the New Fire ceremony that took place in 1507, the last before Spaniards arrived. Xochicalco was one of the sites the Aztecs viewed as the birthplace of their calendar system, and 1507 represented the first year the second Moteuczoma held that ceremony in a different year and place than expected to avoid celebrating during a year of famine. Xochicalco, among other Epiclassic sites, may have played a role in the emergence of the Mixteca-Puebla style. This style, found in codices, wall paintings, pottery, and the fine crafts of turquoise mosaics, feather work, and gold, would influence Aztec art. But fuller development of the Mixteca-Puebla style would not come until after the fall of Tollan, another place of learning and art production with great historical significance to the Aztecs.

At Tollan, much of the decoration of its monumental structures consisted of large stone sculptures. This artistic medium strongly influenced Aztec art. Tolteca sculptors created relief carvings there along building walls, stairways, stelae, and their artisans made many stand-alone carvings such as chacmools. These are reclining figures that include bowl-like middle sections used as receptacles for extracted hearts and also created standard bearers for banners, and the famous Atlantean figures. Much of this art represents warriors or relates to sacrificial violence. Less sophisticated than Aztec sculpture, Tolteca sculpture was eclectic, showing influence from Maya art as well as that of Teotihuacan and Xochicalco, yet the Aztecs saw the Tolteca as their most direct artistic forbearers. The Aztecs portrayed the Tolteca as highly skilled architects, finders of precious stones, skilled feather workers, inventors of the year and day counts who understood astronomy and wrote the finest songs.

Aztec architects undoubtedly excavated and took art pieces from Tollan. Several Tolteca ceramic pieces were found in areas of the Templo Mayor, but it was more common for Aztec artisans to copy their forms and add identifiable Aztec motifs of dates, deities, or costumes. Several structures in the Templo Mayor complex resemble and pay homage to Teotihuacan- or Tollan-type platforms or rooms. Active archaeologists and art historians, Aztecs consciously produced objects that reflected the place of Tollan in their history. As rulers accumulated wealth and dominated larger swaths of Mesoamerica through their military successes, Mexica sculptural art increasingly blended deep, cosmic history with historical peoples and events. These structures constituted an homage writ large to Aztec political and religious ancestors. They demonstrate how the Mexica mined the central Mesoamerican past to bolster their sense of legitimacy and project their power. The Tetzcoca and Tlaxcalteca likewise showed a similar reverence for the art and architecture of the Tolteca.

Another later and crucial set of influences reflecting a widespread art style and iconographic system would influence Aztec writing, book production, pottery, and smaller-scale crafts. This is the style known as Mixteca-Puebla, named after the area where it likely began late in the Epiclassic and where it remained influential, especially for codices, murals, and pottery. Today known as the Postclassic International Style because of its widespread nature, the networks of exchange crisscrossing Mesoamerica allowed this style to expand and diversify geographically, leading to complex patterns of creative development. Sites in Puebla, Tlaxcala, the Mixtec area, and the Valley of Oaxaca all played a role in the early development of the Mixteca-Puebla style. As the Postclassic International Style evolved and as deity images frequented the codices being produced, the ways costumes and paraphernalia of the gods were painted became increasingly standardized, as did animal, floral, celestial, and sacrifice-related elements. Depicted very precisely, sometimes with an almost abstract quality, the elements of the style – symbols, emblems, and images – became quite recognizable. The Aztec variant, however, featured more emphasis on naturalism for human and other figures, principally in codices.

Aztec art, with its multiple influences, would over time manifest itself across the Basin of Mexico and to the south and east in a wide variety of media. Among these were: architecture; monumental and small-scale stone sculptures; books; precious stones and gold work found in mosaics and jewelry; textiles; dough sculptures; and paper. Artists combined particular icons – especially symbols of water, flowers, fire, stars, hearts, and motion – into iconographic units art historians call emblems. The emblems depict several symbols that typically occur together and include images such as solar disks, earth monsters, sky bands, and feather or fire serpents. These symbols and emblems, along with deity figures, conveyed major themes in Aztec art: sacrifice by gods and humans, the cycle of life and death, sacred and human war, rulers and rulership, and men and women as workers, transgressors, or sacrificial victims.

Many of the meanings embedded in Aztec art lay not so much in particular images, though these had meaning, but in the complex juxtapositions of symbols, emblems, and figures shown in images. By balancing opposed images, Aztec artists referenced transformations – time and the four or five ages of earth's history, day into night, the rainy into the dry season, or life into death. The attention paid to both balance and transformation becomes very apparent in the highly symmetrical and technically sophisticated realm of Aztec sculpture that developed over time. Pasztory identifies several stages of sculptural development for the Mexica. She shows that development from simpler pieces in the 1420s to a later period in the first two decades of the sixteenth century in which archaizing of the styles of the earlier civilizations mentioned occurred as more sophisticated three-dimensional items came to dominate Mexica art. Across these periods,

Mexica and other Aztec sculptors produced large numbers of deity figures, male and female, and other sculpture in the round, as well as relief carvings. Many were realistically sculpted in human form, though some combine realistic depictions with fantastical elements, skulls carved in place of faces, for example. Most male figures were either nude or almost nude figures. These might have been adorned with varying costumes and other accoutrement so as to represent various deities not just one, H. B. Nicholson explained. Sculptures of earth-fertility deities – mostly female – were even more numerous and represented earth, maize, water, and rain deities.

An important goddess statue is that of Coatlicue (Snake Skirt). The Coatlicue piece provides an example of a deity sculpture that combines realistic with fantastical elements (see Fig. 6.3). An earth deity who was the mother of Huitzilopochtli, Coatlicue likely was a Mexica version of the goddess Cihuacoatl who represented, as discussed, a war-like mother figure for the Mexica. On the bottom of the statue a sculptor carved a Tlaloc figure, and the two deities, Tlaloc and Coatlicue, together show a balance of male and female forces. They convey ideas of fertility, regeneration, and destruction and could also refer to the Mexica twin temples at the top of the Templo Mayor, uniting themes, Esther Pasztory suggests, of "the old and the new, war and fertility, life and death, Mexica and Toltec, conqueror and conquered."

While distinctive and prevalent among that type of sculpture, deity figures represent only one class of sculptures in the round. Other kinds include: animal figures, usually carved in a naturalistic style; human masks; chacmools; standard bearers; warrior figures; serpent heads

FIG. 6.3 Drawing of Coatlicue statue
From Herbert Joseph Spinden, *Ancient Civilization of Mexico and Central America* (NY: American Museum of Natural History, 1943). File:Ancient civilizations of Mexico and Central America (1943) (18199726095).jpg - Wikimedia Commons. Public Domain

FIG. 6.4 The Calendar Stone and its images of time and space Fanny Chambers Gooch, *Face to Face with the Mexicans* (NY: Fords, Howard, and Hulbert, 1887). Public Domain

and skulls, often placed as architectural decoration; and objects that are copies of objects made of other media such as drums or war shields. Another important class of Aztec sculptures are those in relief, that is, sculptures that are carved into a background medium, often floors, walls, or even carved into sculptures in the round. Found along with the Coatlicue statue, the Calendar Stone, also known as the Sun Stone, represents one of the highest achievements of Aztec sculpture (see Fig. 6.4). Carved from basalt probably sometime after 1502, it featured a central area with the face of either Tonatiuh, the sun deity, or Tlalteuctli, an earth deity from whose body the earth had been formed, concentric circles that refer to the twenty-day signs of the tonalpohualli ritual calendar, the four preceding suns, fire serpents who symbolized sacred warfare, as well as pointed rays that lead to the four cardinal directions. At the top, the date 13 Acatl (Reed) appears. This was the year of the creation of the Aztec era, the Fifth Sun, as well as the year when Itzcoatl, the early empire builder, took the Aztec throne even though these events happened in different eras of Aztec history. Correlating cosmically important dates with historical dates of significance to the Aztecs was common on their monuments, especially those of the Mexica. This immense piece also embodies the Aztec idea of the interrelatedness of time and space and that the Mexica, through warfare, perhaps especially those wars carried out by Moteuczoma Xocoyotl, dominated their historical era and all directions in space.

The stone images of Coatlicue and the Calendar Stone sculpture are dense with meaning, open to a variety of interpretations. The famous relief sculpture of Coyolxauhqui appears simpler to interpret. She was, as described in previous chapters, a sister of Huitzilopochtli; her name means Bells on Cheek. She plotted with her numerous brothers, the 400 sons of Coatlicue, to kill their mother because she had become pregnant from a ball of feathers that fell from the sky while she was sweeping a temple. As she was being attacked, she miraculously gave birth to Huitzilopochtli. Born fully armed, he killed Coyolxauhqui and chased away her brothers, thus becoming the warrior patron deity of the Mexica. According to early Aztec history, these events occurred at Serpent Mountain, Coatepetl, which the Huitzilopochtli section of the Templo Mayor commemorated. A large statue in the round of Coyolxauhqui's head was placed at the foot of the stairs leading up to Huitzilopochtli's shrine. This image may have been created under tlatoani Ahuitzotl's patronage in 1487 as part of the Templo Mayor dedication, perhaps to visually retell the history of Huitzilopochtli's birth and his emergence as the Mexica patron deity.

Even more well known than the Coyolxauhqui figure in the round is the relief carving of her found in the flooring in front of the Huitzilopochtli side of the Templo Mayor (Fig. 3.3). A stark depiction of a partly naked, decapitated, and dismembered woman, the image clearly portrays defeat, an image interpreted as referencing women's subjugation. Not just depicting defeat, given the earth mother images carved at Coyolxauhqui's knees and feet, the figure alludes to the chaos that could come from a war of total destruction. With no date glyph carved into the stone, determining when the sculpture was created has been quite challenging, although it is almost surely earlier than the carved head. One suggestion has been a date between 1468 and 1481, an important period of temple construction. More precise dates of 1469 or 1473 are also possible, relating to the death of the first Moteuczoma, a great warrior ruler who defeated a number of important altepeme, or the death of Moquihuix, ruler of Tlatelolco, killed in spectacular fashion after being stabbed and his body hurled off Tlatelolco's main temple. Whatever the date of its creation, while the relief image relates to defeat, its ruinous representation could well have served to send a number of messages. Perhaps the Mexica were marking the passing of a great warrior ruler who had enlarged Tenochtitlan's domain, a great defeat that they had inflicted, or they were reminding other powers that even the powerful could suffer a humiliating defeat at Mexica hands. This sculpture could well have been intended to send more than one of these messages.

The image must have served as a reminder of the fate awaiting the defeated; but the image also undoubtedly embodies a reference to the power earth mothers wielded. If total destruction was Coyolxauhqui's fate, her image reminded viewers of the discordant and destructive power of earth goddesses and that Mexica victories did not and would not come easily. That a work of art that seems relatively legible to modern, non-Aztec eyes might contain multiple messages tells us that Aztec art, especially sculpture, embodied and disseminated varied meanings. Works of art often do not have a single or simple meaning. Given that the messages of Aztec sculpture were complex and multilayered, one question to be asked is: Did Mexica art, in particular, serve as an imperial art form?

The answer is yes, but when we broaden the viewpoint to other places and forms of artistic expression, some complexities of Aztec art come into focus. Within the Basin of Mexico, the Mexica, along with the artists mobilized by the rulers of Excan tlatoloyan cities, used art – architecture, sculpture, and clothing – as an imperial strategy to convey power, control, and status. The Coyolxauhqui relief is instructive in this regard. The belt, a masculine piece of clothing seen on the relief figure, could refer to male identity and power transformed by defeat into a female identity.

Because rulers of nearby and distant provinces came to Tenochtitlan for important ceremonies, such sculptural propaganda almost certainly conveyed Tenochtitlan's rulers' sense of themselves as emperors of their universe. Projecting themselves as the inheritors of the political and cultural legitimacy and power of Xochicalco, Teotihuacan, and Tollan, they used the Templo Mayor area to convey Mexica military and sacred power. Paradoxically, across the farther reaches of the Excan tlatoloyan imperial formation there may have been less use of art, especially sculpture and architecture, to convey such messages. While imperial influence on ceramics and book production does appear to have been widespread, this may also represent the spread of the Postclassic International Style and not just imperial influence. Nonetheless, some appropriation of later Aztec styles and iconography occurred, given the widespread political and economic influence of the Excan tlatoloyan powers. But with sculpture and architecture, where we might expect the greatest presence of influence, the propagandistic influence does not appear to have been strong. A rigorous survey of the evidence from material remains by Umberger suggests complexity and paradox.

While outlying kingdoms' rulers or nobles likely commissioned highly trained sculptors from Tenochtitlan or other artistic centers in the Basin of Mexico to copy Mexica or other basin altepeme art styles, artists from those outlying areas could have received training in the center, or perhaps they copied forms with which they became familiar through travel to Tenochtitlan or other Aztec city-states. What is more surprising, however, is that regions known to have imperial colonies do not show much evidence of significant Aztec influence. Other areas, with less evidence of imperial colonization sometimes seem to show more. The Excan tlatoloyan imperial governing style relied heavily on elite-to-elite and tribute relationships for its dissemination, and the overall late Postclassic economy and cultural system depended upon market exchange and networks of communication that were broad geographically and socially. Triple Alliance elites influenced but did not solely control these networks. Elites and artists of distant regions may have used art to convey alliance and loyalty.

While the imperial art of Tenochtitlan told its rulers and inhabitants that they dominated their world, it also said the Mexica must always work to maintain their position by appeasing their deities and keeping the sun in motion. It also broadcast and propagandized to visitors of all classes and diverse ethnicities those same messages. Perhaps Excan tlatoloyan rulers chose not to invest in widespread propagandistic sculptural art due to cost constraints, believing that because outsiders regularly came to their centers, art within the imperial capitols effectively reinforced the messages their armies spread through force.

Aztec art of altepeme large and small embodied the ideas of value, transformation, and balance that I have stressed as so key to the imperial project *and* to everyday life. While Aztec art often carried messages about the divine and there is no doubt that for imperial powers, propaganda played a role in the making and placement of art pieces, art embodied other meanings as well. Art carried *value*. Objects carried great symbolic value given the meaning of deities represented, the deep histories, both cosmological and archaeological that art objects commemorated, with the size, beauty, and skill art represented reinforcing symbolic value. Art also carried material value. Artists used turquoise and greenstone, or other precious materials that they fashioned into jewelry or small carvings such as masks, figurines, animals, or plants. These objects conveyed not only the piety of elites but also their wealth and status. Aztecs also viewed feathers as precious commodities that could convey power, wealth, and status. Feathers carried the idea of civilization. Colonial historical codices pictured Chichimeca wearing animal skins; the Tolteca wearing feather-decorated garments.

Spaniards were astounded by Aztec wealth and artistic skill. Rulers and nobles lived in palaces decorated with art, filled with valuable items, materially and symbolically. Cortés saw these scenes with his own eyes, shocked that a ruler he considered barbaric could have art and jewelry made of such lavish materials and of such high quality. Bernal Díaz also went on at length about the opulence of Moteuczoma's lifestyle – the magnificent objects on display made of silver and gold. He also described the precious stones, feathers, and textiles he saw along with the animals the huey tlatoani kept in a zoo, and the surrounding gardens filled with trees, flowers, herbs, and fountains.

Because of the power imbued and wealth invested in Aztec art – an art that referred to *transformations* such as the creation of the sun, moon, and earth, an animal or human turning into a deity, or the transitions of the eras to the Fifth Sun – we might assume that Aztecs behaved as divinely motivated automatons. But while balance and symmetry dominated their literary and artistic cultural expressions, idiosyncrasy and resistance were also part of their world. Even though rituals sought to maintain both personal and community behavior in the balance necessary to maintain their world, people did not always live up to Aztec moral standards. Some Aztecs broke laws and transgressed. While usually unsuccessful, sacrificial victims sometimes rejected their fate; slaves sought to free themselves; communities revolted against imperial rule. Some Aztec art captures idiosyncrasy, even resistance.

A female figure known as the "Venus of Texcoco" exemplifies idiosyncrasy in Aztec art (see Fig. 6.5). Goddesses usually were presented clothed; if this figure is a deity image, there is little indication. Naked, with more expression on her face than the usually impassive deity figures convey, she is a perfectly proportioned female figure, looking like a human woman, not an otherworldly figure of often destructive power. Perhaps a representation of a living Aztec woman, the figure has an appeal very different from many other female images sculpted, painted, or crafted from clay. If, on the other hand she represents a deity, it could be that the figure represents a local Tetzcoca style, or perhaps it is an idiosyncratic piece whose meanings for the artist we cannot discern. Whatever messages the sculptor intended to convey, she is markedly different from other Aztec sculptures of female deities.

Even though the male bias inherent in descriptions of rituals in Indigenous- or Spanish-authored texts makes assessing women's roles and the way images of women would have been used in public rituals difficult, it does appear that men played the more apparent roles in religious practices outside the home. Within the home, women maintained household altars, officiated life-cycle rituals, and kept order in that space. Household rituals, however, reinforced community and state values, as these

FIG. 6.5 The Venus of Tetzcoco
DEA/Archivo J. Lange via Getty Images

rituals promoted social and cosmic order as well as abundance of plants and water. But household rituals had another side, displaying local variation and even contestation of state or male domination.

Archaeologist Elizabeth Brumfiel argued, based upon figurine collections at three communities outside of Tenochtitlan but in the Basin of Mexico, that the large numbers and imagery of female figurines reflect an ideology of resistance against an official gender ideology of male dominance. To her eyes, Mexica images of goddesses – especially Coatlicue and Coyolxauhqui – represent mutilation and subjugation. She argues that the kneeling posture of women found in small stone sculptures and codices also articulates an ideology of female subjugation. Figurines, on the other hand, rarely depicted kneeling or mutilated women; often their maternity is emphasized as female figures often hold one or two children in their arms. Asserting that female figurines suggest rejection of official ideology, Brumfiel concludes that such opposition suggests a kind of popular resistance.

Analysis of spindle-whorls from communities within or around the Basin of Mexico, implies something similar. Spindle-whorls were objects used to help turn fibers into thread for weaving textiles. The size of spindle-whorls provides information about the type and quality of thread, maguey or cotton, produced, with a transition to smaller sized whorls an indication of a shift toward more cotton production during the late Postclassic following increased tribute demands from the Excan tlatoloyan. The quality of thread spinners turned out suggests resistance to the increasing tribute burdens in a variety of basin communities. Like from Aztec communities in the basin, many from the altepetl of Chololllan have also been collected and analyzed. They reveal images related to women's activities, power, and sexuality. Aztecs associated the plant and flower images carved into them with medicine and sexuality. The birds and feather images might well have related to women giving birth, which ticitl likened to battle, comparing birthing mothers to eagle or jaguar warriors in their discourses. The cloth women wove from the thread they produced played important roles in family and community economies as it did in implements of war. Did women want to remind the rulers of their own altepeme or those of the imperial formation that they could themselves cause conflict?

Resistance to official discourses could well have occurred also in ceramics but in a different context, that is, with the invasion by the Spanish. The period of European arrival and subsequent war led to innovation in Aztec art. Even as some art forms were repurposed to support missionary aims or over time ceased to exist after the imposition of colonial rule, pottery continued to be made with Indigenous techniques. Manuscript painting also continued for the production of books. Architecture became transformed, especially religious architecture. But several unique Mexica ceramic pieces that likely date to the period when Spaniards invaded and brought new types of war with them show stress and resistance to Spanish conquest efforts by commemorating the Mexica and Aztec pasts. Fig. 6.6 shows an Aztec tripod plate similar to ones produced during or just after the Spanish-Mexica war. Such plates had images of eagles or jaguars, a reference to Mexica military might. Esther Pasztory indicates that such pieces recalled that military

FIG. 6.6 Aztec tripod plate
Courtesy of Yale University Art Gallery.
Gift of Peter David Joralemon, B.A. 1969, M.Phil 1974

might with their allusions to celebrated warrior orders. The brutal period of war that ensued after the Spaniards invaded Mesoamerica as well as the traumatic imposition of colonial rule brought many changes to Aztec life. Yet Aztecs survived as did the ideas of value, transformation, and balance, changed in certain ways, but persisting nonetheless.

Conclusion

Aztec writing embodied, and communicated value. It was used to create books such as the tonalamatl and made possible written records of tribute payments, histories, and census information as Motolinia, Durán, and Alva

Ixtlilxochitl all indicated. Colonial tlacuiloque used the Aztec graphic communication system, employing images and their writing system, to convey information about many facets of Aztec life for Europeans but also for themselves and their communities. They used alphabetic writing in Nahuatl for those same purposes. Given that the Indigenous graphic communication system was key to the way Aztecs remembered and communicated their histories and literature, its use must have facilitated learning and writing with the Roman alphabet. The use of images and production of texts in alphabetic Nahuatl greatly aided the creation of colonial books covering many subjects and containing a vast array of information about life in the Aztec world.

In the areas of health and art the existence of this incredible array of texts – many hybrid, containing images, Aztec writing, and alphabetic writing in Nahuatl and Spanish – and objects allows us to decipher some of the meanings embedded in the words, stone, and other materials used in Aztec artistic production. Decoding the meanings Aztec women and men communicated through their creative, aesthetic, philosophical, and intellectual endeavors helps us grasp some of the material and symbolic value Aztecs placed on the practices that have survived. Some texts, as discussed earlier in this chapter, convey a lot of information about Aztec health beliefs. This information allows historians, anthropologists, botanists, and linguists, Nahua and non-Nahua, to study the history of their healthcare practices to know more about which practices have survived despite the experiences of war, colonial, and national rule. Recognizing that

Indigenous communities experienced many forms of exploitation and exclusion makes Nahua resilience after 1521 all the more remarkable. Maintaining balance through transformative historical periods and within a challenging contemporary world has been key to that resilience.

7
Resilience
Part Two: Trauma, Transformation, Tenacity

~

The invasion of Mesoamerica – set off by the arrival of Hernan Cortés and his followers – was neither peaceful nor simple. The advent of Spaniards' presence brought different kinds of transformation than Aztecs likely envisioned. The Spanish military, political, and religious presence challenged Aztec ideas of value and balance. Transformations in Aztecs ideas took place as did many aspects of daily life. Before considering the destabilization brought about by that invasion and the re-stabilization that followed, it is necessary to consider the events that played out and the people involved after Spaniards came to Mesoamerica.

Encounter, Invasion, and War

The arrival of Spaniards in Mesoamerica was a direct extension of Spain's activities in the Caribbean that had begun with Columbus's expeditions starting in 1492. Exploration of Mesoamerica's southeastern coastline began early in the sixteenth century. Expeditions that landed in the Yucatán Peninsula headed by Francisco Hernández de Córdoba and Juan de Grijalva took place in 1517 and 1518. By 1518, the Mexica ruler Moteuczoma knew of the arrival of a bewildering people, and he made several efforts to understand who they were before ever encountering them. But it would be the invasion in 1519 that would be transformative. Having learned of the wealth of the Aztecs from encounters with coastal Maya groups, an expedition headed by Hernan Cortés began to move west, setting off a complex series of events. These events played out in three phases between February 10, 1519, when the expedition left Cuba and August 13, 1521, when the Mexica tlatoani, Cuauhtemoc, was captured. When this force left Cuba, it comprised 450 men and equipment that encompassed eleven ships, ten large cannons, four smaller ones, and sixteen horses. After this fleet landed in the Yucatán, Cortés and his men searched for two Spaniards who had been shipwrecked and thought lost. One, Gerónimo Aguilar, spoke a Maya language and became a translator for Cortés. The other, Gonzalo Guerrero, refused to rejoin the Spanish and returned to his Maya family. Mayas whom the Spaniards encountered led Cortés to believe that a powerful, wealthy group existed to the west, and he and his men set about to find and conquer them.

In a sense, the Mexica inadvertently supplied some motivation for the events that followed by sending gifts at huey tlatoani Moteuczoma's behest. The offering included items made of gold that whetted Spanish appetites for the great wealth of which Spaniards had learned. The Mexica reinforced this desire to find the source of gold objects that had been gifted when the Mexica governor of the central Veracruz region, inhabited by the Totonaca and where the invaders built their base settlement, again brought gifts including gold objects. This governor, Tentlil, and the Spaniards were each trying to learn about and assess the other. Tentlil's name, rendered differently in a variety of texts, in Nahuatl might have been Teotlilli, Sacred Black Ink, giving a hint of his high status. Aztec tlacuiloque drew images of Spaniards as well as of their armaments, ships, horses, and dogs for Moteuczoma, and he sent still more gifts including gold, turquoise, and the arrays of several deities including Quetzalcoatl. This act has given rise to the idea that Mexica, particularly Moteuczoma, believed Cortés and other Spaniards were deities.

Some sources, especially the *Florentine Codex*, suggest that Moteuczoma indeed saw Cortés as a god. Scholars have been vigorously debating this point, trying to understand how or why Moteuczoma and other Mexica might have viewed him as a teotl. But beyond referring to deities, it is important to remember that the word teotl carries several meanings as explained in the second chapter, and could refer to puzzling, frightening, and even monstrous things as well as to a vital energy that animated a variety of beings and objects. Spaniards had to be fitted into Aztec ways of thinking about and classifying people, spirits, and things, and several relatively early texts, dating to both before and after the *Florentine Codex*, show Mexica referring to Spaniards as teteo, though Cortés himself never made such a claim. Kevin Terraciano points out that Sahagún observed in the Prologue to Book Twelve that it was being composed while eyewitnesses to the violence and upheaval of the war between the Mexica and Spanish were still alive in order to argue that Moteuczoma and others around him indeed saw the first Spaniards as deities. It is also just as likely that Mexica leaders as well as the populace saw these first Europeans as something anomalous that did not fit easily into their worldview.

The notion of Spaniards as deities likely did not last long if it ever really existed, and there is another way to think about Moteuczoma's actions. Even as he considered the strange qualities of Spaniards, Moteuczoma may well have been announcing his superior status by giving generously, an action intended to create awe and fear among Spaniards, something he had done regularly with visiting rulers from nearby and subjugated altepeme. Moteuczoma made diplomatic efforts to assess who the Spanish were and to convince them to stay away from Tenochtitlan. At the same time, he also invoked sacred powers, sending nanahualtin and other sorcerers to the coast, a further effort to keep Spaniards away from Tenochtitlan. *If* the idea that the Mexica believed Spaniards to be divine was not a wholly colonial notion, with the powers both positive and negative that divinity implied, it certainly provided a convenient framework for Spanish and Indigenous writings after the war. It allowed Spaniards to glorify not only what they saw as their own superior fighting capabilities but also their more advanced intellects and morality. But for Nahuas, perhaps the idea had some utility as well. It helped to explain a painful defeat and also the early development of a Nahua Christianity, especially among elites for whom conversion became a politically and socially useful means to survive and maintain political power.

Whatever Moteuczoma's motivations, he had provided evidence for great wealth that lured Spaniards on, with ultimately disastrous consequences for his own rulership and for the Mexica. Cortés himself had also learned by May of 1519 that the Mexica had enemies with whom alliances could be created. The building of ties with allies, both Aztec and other ethnicities such as the Totonaca, would prove crucial to the Spanish victory over the Mexica. During this first phase, Cortés concentrated on cementing his standing with the King of Spain, Charles V, after exceeding orders for exploration, not invasion or military confrontation, from Diego Velásquez, the governor of Cuba, and creating alliances with Indigenous groups. Through both diplomacy and war, he and his lieutenants aimed to establish relationships that would prove crucial to the outcome of this war with the Mexica's fiercest enemy, the Tlaxcalteca (see Fig. 7.1). However, the diplomacy needed to forge alliances strong enough to take on the Mexica was enabled most of all by a woman, Malintzin, both famous and infamous.

As described in Chapter 5, the exchange of women was a common feature of Aztec diplomacy, a gendered act that created and reinforced alliances. Having been given a group of twenty women by the Chontal Maya after defeating Mayas in battles at Potonchan and Tzintla, Cortés learned that among this group was a woman known to the Spanish as Marina, doña Marina, or Malinche and to the Aztecs as Malintzin. Her life circumstances and intelligence endowed her with linguistic capabilities that proved to be crucial to Cortés's project. Born among Nahuatl speakers along the Gulf Coast to a noble family of that area, she was either given away or sold into slavery among the Chontal Maya who then passed her along to Cortés as one among those twenty women. Whereas Gerónimo de Aguilar's Mayan language skills had proved sufficient in the Yucatán, as the invaders moved west beyond that area, Malintzin's Nahuatl-Maya bilingualism became invaluable. After she learned Spanish, she became Cortés's primary translator before and after the defeat of the Mexica.

FIG. 7.1 Tlaxcalteca leader meets Cortés in the *Lienzo de Tlaxcala*
https://commons.wikimedia.org/wiki/File:Xicotencatl-Cortes.jpg.
Public Domain

Viewed by many Mexicans as the definition of a traitor for her role in the Spanish-Mexica war, exemplified by her actions during the Spanish massacre of the Chololtecas which is discussed below, she lived a difficult, often brutal, life. Married by Cortés to two different Spaniards as well as having a child with Cortés himself, surviving records, none of which are in her own voice, offer no clarity about the motivations for her loyalty to the Spanish cause. Did she love any of those men? Is that even an appropriate question given that Aztec and European patterns of emotion and emotional display were different? Did she resent the imperial domination of the Mexica over her own community of origin or did she simply have a pragmatic desire to survive? What is clear is that her life experiences, especially being passed from man to man, reflected the transitory and exploitative relations among many Indigenous women and Spanish men during the collision of worlds occurring across the Americas from the late fifteenth century on. Whatever her reasons, Malintzin's vast linguistic and diplomatic skills set her on a course in which she played a prominent role in the events of the Spanish-Mexica war, starting with events crucial to the Spanish-Tlaxcalteca alliance (see Fig. 7.2).

FIG. 7.2 Malintzin translating
Florentine Codex, Book 12, Image 54. Courtesy of the University of Utah Press

Having been pointed in the direction of marching through Tlaxcallan to reach Tenochtitlan by his Totonaca allies, the Tlaxcalteca attacked the Spaniards, an effort they kept up for days, displaying discipline and their tremendous skills in war. Over several days of battle, the Tlaxcalteca exacted a cost in lives, arms, and food from the Spanish. Had the Tlaxcalteca tried to annihilate the Spanish at this moment, they might well have succeeded, but they too were suffering casualties, and internal divisions were developing among what was at best four confederated political units. Their leaders may well have assessed an alliance with Spaniards as the most promising way to effect a change in the balance of power between themselves and the Excan tlatoloyan. By late September of 1519, this crucial connection through which the Spaniards would enhance their numbers by several thousand fighters had been agreed upon by both sides.

The Tlaxcalteca then advised or persuaded Cortés to travel through the altepetl of Cholollan to reach Tenochtitlan. An important Mesoamerican pilgrimage center, Cholollan had recently shifted alliances away from the Tlaxcalteca to the Excan tlatoloyan and was located at a critical site between Veracruz and Tenochtitlan from where Cortés and his men received supplies and communicated with allies in Cuba. Both Cortés and Bernal Díaz claim in their writings that the Chololteca sought to draw them into their altepetl to ambush them. The Tlatelolca authors of Book Twelve of the *Florentine Codex* assert that the Tlaxcalteca encouraged the events that took place. Having asked the Chololteca leaders to assemble in a courtyard, the Spanish massacred the political and military leadership, killed more of the populace, and looted the community.

The slaughter must have deeply disheartened Moteuczoma whose diplomacy and supernatural efforts failed to keep the Spanish from entering Tenochtitlan. He also became increasingly aware that these aggressors now had meaningful alliances and that his own political standing within Tenochtitlan was beginning to weaken. It was at that moment that Moteuczoma greeted Cortés as he and the other Spaniards entered Tenochtitlan on November 8, 1519, bringing the first phase of what would become an all-out war to an end. After leaving Cuba, Cortés had created the necessary logistical base and legitimized his position as leader of his expedition. He had solved the problem of translation or, more accurately, had it solved for him by the knowledge and actions of Malintzin. He and his men also made use of one of their most important alliances due in large part to calculations by and decision making of the Tlaxcalteca leadership.

And so the second phase of the Spanish-Mexica war began with the arrival of the Spanish in Tenochtitlan and their imprisonment of Moteuczoma shortly thereafter. Trying to govern through Moteuczoma, Cortés exerted effort and some influence but not control. Moteuczoma attempted to maintain Tenochtitlan's role as the dominant altepetl it had been throughout his period of rule. But by early 1520 Moteuczoma's position became severely compromised. His efforts to force his own closest advisors and governing officials to swear loyalty and deliver tribute to the Spaniards created rifts within Tenochtitlan's government, yet the Spanish position also began to become threatened. The governor of Cuba sent an expedition headed by Pánfilo de Narváez to capture Cortés and return him to Cuba. Velásquez sent a large expedition of some

800 men, so large that Cortés understood the threat and left Tenochtitlan, taking about 275 Spanish fighters, augmented by Indigenous forces, with him to confront Narváez. Cortés defeated Narváez's force, imprisoned him, and supplemented his own forces with many of Narváez's fighters who joined with him. But back in Tenochtitlan, the situation of the Spanish, under the command of Pedro de Alvarado had weakened dangerously.

The main cause of the increasingly untenable situation of the Spanish left behind in Tenochtitlan was due to the murderous actions of those Spaniards who in late May of 1520 carried out a massacre of the Mexica leadership at the Templo Mayor. This period coincided with a major festival for the Mexica, that of Toxcatl. The *Florentine Codex* identifies Toxcatl as the most important Mexica feast. It honored Tezcatlipoca and to a lesser extent Huitzilopochtli and featured the death of an ixiptla of Tezcatlipoca. After the ceremony began, Spaniards blocked four entrances to the main temple. Book Twelve then narrates in vivid detail the slaughter that the Spaniards carried out, describing decapitations, stabbings, and blood running like water. According to Durán, thousands of Mexica nobles died, and at that point the populace of the city rose up against Alvarado and the men Cortés had left behind. Some Spaniards were killed, but those who survived the attack were forced to retreat back to their quarters and continued to be under violent assault.

The Mexica, even while besieging the Spaniards, were unable to overcome them. The growing disarray of the Mexica whose once all-powerful seeming ruler appeared ever weaker due to the loss of many military and civil leaders left the government debilitated and the populace grieving. Spanish armaments proved effective enough in combination with Tlaxcalteca reinforcements to allow Cortés to re-enter the city. But now the Spaniards were in real danger, Moteuczoma could no longer offer any protection or meaningful cooperation, and he was killed.

Indigenous sources largely emphasize that his death occurred at Spanish hands. Spanish sources, for the most part, say he was stoned to death, accidentally or purposely, by a Mexica crowd that gathered to hear him speak. Given the Spanish record of killing the major rulers of the Excan tlatoloyan, that *they* killed Moteuczoma seems highly probable. A younger brother of Moteuczoma, Cuitlahua, became tlatoani. He would die of smallpox in under three months. Running short of supplies, on June 30, 1520, the Spaniards fought their way out of Tenochtitlan during a bloody battle in which fighters on both sides died, with the Spanish and their Indigenous allies retreating to Tlaxcallan, bringing the second stage of what was to become a brutal, all-out war to an end.

At the start of the third phase of this war, both the Mexica and the Spanish faced grave problems. With Moteuczoma and many ruling nobles dead, the Mexica government was facing a chaotic situation. Cuitlahua never consolidated his position as ruler and was soon dead from smallpox. The rulers of Tetzcoco and Tlacopan also were dead, and pro-and anti-Spanish factions had developed within a number of the ruling families of altepeme in the basin. During this chaotic period, Cortés also played a role in choosing rulers to ascend to ruling positions. In Tetzcoco, where both Moteuczoma and Cortés intervened after Nezahualpilli's death, factional conflicts among the ruler's descendants played out both before and after this period of war. Several factors added to the situation of weakened leadership groups among a number of powerful altepeme. These included a growing number of factions within those communities and their leadership groups, the beginnings of the spread of new diseases, and the disruption of the tribute system and commercial exchange patterns upon which daily life so depended. All of these circumstances reinforced the disarray enveloping the Excan tlatoloyan powers. The Mexica and the Excan tlatoloyan could neither broadcast their propagandistic messages of power amid so much disruption of political and religious practices, nor could they back up their tribute demands or enforce the existing political hierarchy as they once had.

The invaders, too, faced challenges after the retreat from Tenochtitlan. Having suffered casualties and a lack of supplies, Mexica and their allies attacked the Spanish-Tlaxcalteca forces several times, and Cortés faced some dissent from within his own force, especially from soldiers who had first arrived with Narváez. But no Spaniards defected in order to form an alliance with the Mexica or with their remaining allies. With another new tlatoani, Cuauhtemoc, who would briefly serve as the last independent ruler of Tenochtitlan, the Mexica emphasized defending their altepetl rather than confronting the Spaniards and Tlaxcalteca. This strategy gave them the ability to maximize their resources in people and supplies and to limit the Spanish ability to attack the city because the Mexica controlled both the lake system and the causeways linking Tenochtitlan and Tlatelolco to the mainland.

Despite facing obstacles, the Spanish force was able to withdraw and then re-group in Tlaxcallan. Understanding how important undermining Mexica dominance over the lakes would be to any further effort to defeating them, Cortés had new ships built, having earlier destroyed those on which he had sailed to the Yucatán from Cuba to preclude any of his men from escaping back to Cuba. And he succeeded in delivering what would prove to be a fatal blow to the Excan tlatoloyan when the Tetzcoca installed a pro-Spanish ruler. Cortés was able to take advantage of an alliance that brought fresh reinforcements from Tetzcoco and the altepeme subordinated to it.

With the Tetzcoca alliance in place, Cortés set about to establish more alliances with mainland altepeme around and beyond the lakes. Some battles Spaniards won, others they lost to Mexica fighters and their allies. With new ships and dividing his force into three units, each one able to control a major causeway in and out of Tenochtitlan, the Spaniards and their allies began to cut off Tenochtitlan from supplying itself with food and fresh water. Fighting then moved into Tenochtitlan itself where the Mexica indeed held certain advantages, especially knowledge of the layout of the city, ability to use their weaponry from rooftops that they controlled, and skillful use of canoes to attack Spaniards and their allies on the causeway. Nonetheless, Spanish ships proved effective against Mexica tactics. And then disease and famine began to weaken Mexica resistance.

While the invaders suffered setbacks and losses of fighters and supplies, the Mexica never dislodged them from the basin. Spaniards maintained most of their alliances, while those of the Mexica waned. A growing number of areas within the city came under Spanish control, including even the Tlatelolco market area.

Eventually, despite desperate resistance, Spaniards captured and imprisoned Cuauhtemoc midway through August of 1521. Despite the defeat of the Mexica, the Indigenous allies continued fighting, sacking, raping, and killing in the twin cities of Tenochtitlan and Tlatelolco. Did Cortés allow his Indigenous allies to punish the Mexica for their determined resistance, actions that made sense in Aztec terms as punishment for prolonging the fighting? Or did Cortés not actually control events at this point?

Despite Mexica displays of agency and efforts to innovate as they worked to defeat Spaniards and their allies, adapting to both Spanish ships and weaponry (sometimes using the latter when they were able to capture some of those arms), a number of factors underlay the Mexica defeat. Beyond Moteuczoma's reliance on diplomacy and spiritual intervention which failed to cause the Spaniards to withdraw, guns, germs, hunger, and exhaustion all played a role. The Spanish thirst for riches certainly motivated their continuing efforts despite their own losses and setbacks. Ultimately, however, structural weaknesses within the Excan tlatoloyan that allowed Spaniards to form alliances were crucial. These allies wanted to join with Spanish forces to defeat the Mexica. In other words, for the Indigenous pro-Spanish fighters, the war represented a kind of anti-imperial uprising. The Tlaxcalteca, Tetzcoca, and other groups may have bargained that the Mesoamerican practice of swearing allegiance and paying tribute to a new imperial power would allow Aztec civilization to continue on much as it had before the arrival of Europeans, just not with Mexica overlords. In some ways, the idea that a different imperial power might allow life to largely continue would not prove to be wholly wrong, because Spanish efforts at conquest were incomplete.

Like the Mexica and Excan tlatoloyan before them, Spaniards learned that conquering and governing the area that became New Spain would be a protracted, expensive, compromised process. For example, military control in the core areas Spaniards governed came rapidly but was tenuous, and their efforts to conquer and control peripheral regions were highly contested. Spaniards depended upon Indigenous knowledge and labor and with an incomplete "spiritual conquest," Indigenous autonomy allowed for the survival of native societies and many aspects of their ways of life. Nahuas both accommodated and resisted Spanish rule. What Spaniards proclaimed as a conquest triumph was more illusory than real in any number of ways. Yet Aztecs and other Indigenous Mesoamericans would never again experience true sovereignty as transformations began after 1521.

Trauma

Within 100 years after the Mexica defeat, numerous aspects of Aztec/Nahua life had changed. But a deeper look at Spanish efforts to impose imperial rule, their impact, and Nahua agendas and responses suggests that as trauma and transformation occurred, tenacity did as well. Spaniards inflicted four very specific traumas with consequences for Nahuas after 1521, three of them purposeful: changes in political and economic organization; forced conversion; and alterations in the social fabric. One was not. That was the demographic catastrophe unleashed by the introduction of new diseases. The size of the total

Mesoamerican population in 1519, while a fiercely debated issue, was most likely about sixteen million, with Nahuas making up just under or about one-quarter of the total Indigenous population. By 1600, the *total* native population had been reduced to approximately one million. Waves of epidemic disease in the 1520s, 1540s, 1570s, and 1590s led to extreme population loss, due largely to the spread of previously unknown diseases such as smallpox, measles, and typhus. War, famine, enslavement, even diseases native to Mesoamerica that flourished under the extreme conditions of social and environmental change taking place also contributed to the shocking amount of death that occurred. Many economic, political, and social institutions became destabilized as a result. Other changes Spaniards introduced reinforced that destabilization.

At first, Spanish officials used Indigenous officeholders, tlatoque, and other traditional altepeme governing officials, to oversee labor organization for public and religious works at the altepetl and tlaxilacalli levels through *encomienda* (grants to Spaniards of tribute and labor) and *repartimiento* (rotational labor draft, which resembled the Aztec labor draft practice coatequitl). Later in the sixteenth century, Indigenous governance shifted to the Indigenous governors (*gobernadores*) and councils (*cabildos*) of local communities. As time wore on, more and more informal arrangements between Indigenous workers and Spanish employers emerged. Although native governance persisted, as encomienda and repartimiento were abolished, and more localized and individualized labor arrangements developed for both agriculture and mining, the functions of Indigenous community governance narrowed. These political and economic changes proved traumatic. The institutions put in place using important aspects of Indigenous institutions of governance and many of its personnel largely to extract labor became more exploitative over time. This was so because Spanish needs for agricultural, mining, and public works labor swelled due to the increasing presence of Spaniards and those of mixed ethnoracial heritage, along with the Crown's increasing demands for revenue to support Spain's imperial project.

Given that the Indigenous population declined sharply until it began to recover in the second half of the seventeenth century, native governance in many communities became disrupted. At times that governance was tumultuous as factions competed for positions, some of these factions related to former ruling dynasties, others not. Although the native population eventually began to increase, accounts of abusive and cruel behavior by Spanish and native officials as well as by property owners and manufacturers surfaced not just through chronicles by Spanish, Nahua, and mestizo writers but also through lawsuits brought by native litigants over sequestration, incarceration, labor demands, physical abuse, and property transfers.

Tribute amounts also became excessive, at first due to high demands by Cortés, other of his associates, and early *encomenderos* (holders of grants of tribute and labor). While the imperial tribute system melted away with the decline of Excan tlatoloyan governing structures, native elites – largely local tlatoque – continued their own demands. In addition, categories of macehualtin who Aztecs exempted in the prehispanic period and continuing for several decades into the early colonial years such as some merchants, craftsmen, and temple servants no longer were. Spaniards also began to impose new kinds of tribute payments to support the legal system, hospitals, and military expenses. While based in Aztec patterns of work, service obligation, and payments in valued goods, rising demands for goods and labor led to increased exploitation of native laborers. Indigenous governing officials who had to enforce the obligations of work and tribute payments, first in kind and then in money, faced impossible burdens with the rapid decrease of the Indigenous population during the sixteenth century.

Trends in land ownership reinforced the traumas induced by colonial rule. While many important Aztec land categories survived into the seventeenth century, some categories such as altepetlalli, teopantlalli, milchimalli, and cihuatlalli did not. Other categories lasted well into and in some areas to the end of or even past the colonial period, especially calpollalli and tlaxilacallalli as well as *tlalcohualli* (bought land). While population decline meant that for many communities, an adequate land base to support the community existed, over time pressure on the native land base and other resources increased. During much of the sixteenth century, Spanish efforts at wealth redistribution focused more on extracting labor and tribute; extensive land transfers had not yet occurred. Yet some land appropriation by Cortés and other Spanish officials happened early on and some grants to and purchases by Spaniards occurred. Although Indigenous communities had long redistributed lands after wars, deaths, or population movements, the increasing rate of population decline meant that as time wore on Spaniards could reclassify lands as empty and appropriate them through grants or forced sales. Forced relocations of people, even communities, occurred through a program of *congregación* in the late sixteenth and seventeenth centuries. This process, although never completed to the extent Spanish officials intended, contributed to undermining the Indigenous land base.

Within communities, conflicts between nobles and commoners emerged over land rights. Clashes between communities or between Indigenous nobles and Spaniards over land ownership and boundaries broke out. Land disputes were often adjudicated within the Spanish legal system. The later colonial period saw more conflict between Nahuas and non-Nahuas as Indigenous populations recovered and the loss of community lands threatened the survival of some communities. Disagreements over grazing and water rights also exacerbated those threats, and changes in land categories and the need to balance the labor and tribute demands of Spanish governments and the Catholic Church with individual enterprises like *haciendas* (large landed estates) became more pressing. These tensions flowed down through communities to households and reinforced changes in Nahua economic life that the introduction of new crops, new forms of currency, and new kinds of production (of cloth, for example) and tools was bringing about.

But perhaps no change induced greater trauma, especially for the generation of Nahuas who themselves experienced the Spanish invasion and the further colonizing efforts, than the introduction of a wholly new religion through a campaign of forced conversion. Even with the shared idea that a victorious power could impose its deity, the loss of temples, priests, deities, and ceremonies provoked a number of responses – grief, resistance, adaptation, and ultimately a profound interpenetration of Aztec and Christian beliefs. The words of Mexica priests, gathered by Franciscan friars in 1524, articulated the pain they felt as friars attacked Aztec gods and traditions. The Mexica priests defended their beliefs as rooted in ancient traditions that allowed for food, rain, and an orderly society to exist. That sixteenth-century Nahuas grieved for older ways and resisted the imposition of foreign ideas and practices can be seen in the actions by individuals who actively preached and beseeched Nahuas to reject the new religion. With time, however, pressure, persuasion, and punishment led to conversion, sometimes superficial, sometimes deeper as an amalgamation of two traditions eventually gave rise to a Nahua Christianity.

In religion, society, and identity, over the course of the sixteenth century, changes came about. Trauma gave way to adjustment, and an interplay of Spanish requirements and Indigenous actions and reactions shaped these adjustments and transformations. While political, economic, and religious institutions built on Aztec frameworks – using the altepetl and its structure of governance as the basis for colonial governing organization and institutions – transformation occurred. With religion as an example, evangelizing friars, Franciscans and others, depended upon altepeme as the basis of parish organization, and Nahuas provided personnel to staff churches below the level of the priest who nearly always was Spanish. Individuals descended from Aztec noble families often filled important lay positions within churches, especially that of the *fiscal*, the highest ranking native church official overseeing the day-to-day running and financial affairs of a church.

It is clear that as time passed many Nahuas accepted the authority of the Catholic Church. Native nobles, in defending their privileges, portrayed themselves as trustworthy, loyal Christians who embraced and helped promulgate the new faith. For example, the theme of the conversion of his ancestors and their efforts to persuade others to embrace Christianity runs through many of Alva Ixtlilxochitl's accounts of Spanish-Tetzcoca interactions for example. Accepting the new faith publicly, however, did not necessarily mean a total rejection of older forms of spirituality, with clandestine ceremonies, writings, and healing activities continuing in many parts of Nahua Mesoamerica.

Friars emphasized using the Nahuatl language as a tool of conversion, the better to explain Christian ideas and effectively use their Indigenous assistants. Many of those assistants became literate through having access to Christian education and would go on to write sermons and other religious texts. Ironically, this helped produce a Nahua-inflected Christian discourse that communicated new ideas yet reinforced old ones. Churches were constructed on the sites of old temples; processions, baptisms, and religious plays filled a longing for the rich ceremonial life that had characterized Aztec religion. The adoption of saints by communities and households served as a vehicle through which a local deity was worshipped in the guise of a saint. The veneration of miraculous images that could transform from inanimate to animate through the spiritual energy of a deity bolstered the place of saints in homes, communities and churches, and peoples' lives. Despite many aspects of their religious practices changing, Nahuas did not so much lose Aztec religion as they reinterpreted it, just as they did with Christianity. This hybrid Nahua Christianity gave voice to the ideas and concerns of the Indigenous population and provided a foothold through which concepts of value, transformation, and balance could persist. Yet beliefs and practices were lost, and coercion and punishment played a role in the transition to a Nahua Christianity. Other areas of Aztec social life became transformed as well – law, gender roles, and ethnic identities provide examples.

Aztecs, especially in the larger altepeme, had courts as a part of their system of governance, though it is likely that many lower level disputes – especially over property or marital and family conflicts – were handled by tlaxilacalli, calpolli, or teccalli officials. But Aztecs adjudicated an array of crimes at the altepetl level – drunkenness, robbery, adultery, bribery, fraud, and murder, with the military and merchant governing structures having some jurisdiction over crimes committed by their members as likely did the priestly hierarchy. After 1521, lower level officials of local governance within altepeme, carrying new titles but consistent with positions and responsibilities prevalent before the Spanish invasion, continued to deal with many offenses committed at the level of the local community throughout much of the colonial period. This practice related to the Spanish idea of respect for Indigenous legal traditions. It exemplifies a continuity that Spaniards fostered related to their own earlier history of governing religiously diverse areas on the Iberian Peninsula that influenced their thinking on matters of governance of Nahuas after 1521.

Spaniards, at least many early officials, came to the Americas with the intention of providing legal remedies for the Indigenous population they had colonized, seeing them as needing protection. These officials arrived as bearers of a history of the Spanish kingdom of Castile having accepted the laws and customs of non-Christian others except for crimes considered especially serious, but such a policy could not and did not hold. War, illness and death, economic exploitation, and the jockeying for position by Nahua nobles in a new governing system, however compatible that system was with previous Aztec governing structures, set off new kinds of disputes in the years after the Mexica defeat. These conflicts occurred in such large numbers that the colonizers found it necessary to create legal innovations. Nahuas found the new judicial system useful to adjudicate a wide array of legal conflicts, both civil and criminal. Disputes over land, water, labor, tribute, and criminal accusations of theft, adultery, and murder to name many of the categories of legal cases, raged within, between, and beyond Nahua communities. Many of these ended up in Spanish courts, civil, criminal, or religious.

This innovative embrace of Spanish legal institutions and ideas had several effects. It allowed Indigenous communities and individuals to defend themselves and often had the unintended consequence of reinforcing ideas of communal identity. Adapting to and using Spanish law also allowed colonial Nahua litigants to protest and seek redress for injustices and exploitation. But using this introduced system as a tool to address such a vast array of legal and social conflicts and problems also tied Indigenous communities and people to a colonial system in which Spaniards ultimately held greater authority and power. The reliance on this system inevitably led to transformation of identities as well, facilitating changes in, for example, both gender and ethnic identities.

Some aspects of women's roles remained similar to their roles before Europeans arrived, especially in the realm of work. Both within and beyond the household, cooking, cleaning, weaving, and marketing activities continued even as Aztecs adjusted materials, production techniques, and labor organization to accommodate transformations in agriculture, animal husbandry, and production of goods such as textiles. The escalation of tribute demands increased women's work burden, and they lost political standing. Their status as legal adults with agency within the legal system declined as men increasingly represented them within formal legal settings. Furthermore, a religious system that strongly emphasized ideas about monogamy, purity, and chastity undermined family and kinship structures that had supported gender parallelism. The shift away from parallel roles led to a weakening of women's authority and status. Most of these changes happened unevenly and to a greater extent in urban areas.

While it is difficult to say whether male-on-female gender violence increased during the colonial period, it is clear that during that time domestic violence within Indigenous communities frequently came to the attention of colonial authorities. A gendered code of behavior that stressed how women's language and behavior influenced the self- and community-perceptions of masculinity played a role as did near-constant economic pressure in the beatings, stabbings, and murders that occurred. Women mobilized a variety of familial and communal authorities to seek redress for violent actions that went beyond the bounds of what native communities defined as acceptable, thus they were not without agency in coping with violent incidents and patterns of behavior. But the underpinnings of women's authority were no longer as strong. The worship of powerful female deities declined, and many of the institutionalized roles of women in governance – civil and religious – either disappeared or became transformed in ways that emphasized male agency over female agency. Even when women continued to perform duties related to marriage, birth, or healing, they readily drew the attention of religious authorities who feared their power, thereby attracting accusations of idolatry.

Although Nahua women exercised authority in both their homes and a variety of settings beyond the home economically, politically, and religiously, some of the complexity and flexibility of the prehispanic gender system diminished over time. That is because while Aztecs differentiated between women's and men's roles in labor, language, and in clothing and hair styles, gender ambiguity and cross-gendering were – as we have seen – important components of gender ideology. Male priests could take on the identity of female deities; this kind of cross-dressing and taking on the persona of the opposite gender, was common in Aztec ceremonies. Female deities not infrequently bore symbols of male identity. In Aztec cosmology, representations of gender ambiguity could symbolize cycles of creation and destruction through which order was reestablished out of chaos. Women's power and agency came not just from the value they created through their marriages, the productive labor they performed within and beyond the household, and the administrative, ritual, and healing functions they carried out. It also came from their roles in Aztec narratives about their early history as powerful figures. Represented either as deities or as rulers' mothers, wives, or daughters, these women of discord created conflict that led, as we have seen, to the existence of new deities, historical cycles, and even new ruling dynasties.

Although colonial Nahuas recast the Virgin Mary as an intercessor and authoritative figure, she was not a symbol of food, water, fertility, or sexuality in the ways Aztec goddesses were nor did she represent the complex blend of creation and destruction that Aztec goddesses had. The powers inherent in deities changing genders or changing form from human to animal or vice versa became defined as sinful and heretical. The concepts of gender complementarity that supported gender parallelism and balance in women's and men's roles in Aztec belief systems lost their social and cognitive bases among colonial Nahuas. Yet as these gender roles and ideologies transformed, some forms of gender complementarity persisted as did some ideas about ethnicity, even as these too changed under the influence of a new legal system, religion, and new peoples with whom Nahuas increasingly interacted.

While Spaniards tended to see Indigenous peoples, Nahuas and others, as Indians, a vast people they categorized as fundamentally different from themselves, Indigenous peoples viewed their own identities in more complicated, often subtle, ways. How did native peoples, focusing here on the Aztecs, understand their identities and how did these change, given the many new influences directed at them and the new contexts in which they had to operate? Aztecs, neither before nor after the Spanish invasion, saw themselves as a unified grouping. They shared a language and many cultural similarities, but the Nahuatl-speaking peoples who lived in and around the Basin of Mexico were different peoples with different histories. Aztec groups rooted their histories in their migration narratives as well as the narratives of how they founded and governed their altepeme. James Lockhart called them ethnic states, to emphasize that Nahuas differentiated among them and seldom felt an identity beyond them. The Indigenous scholars who wrote the Nahuatl texts of the *Florentine Codex* differentiated between Mexicas and those they called Nahuas, these Nahuas seemingly equivalent to the Tolteca, not a larger ethnic grouping. On the other hand, several ethnic identities spanned multiple altepeme – Mexica, Tepaneca, Acolhua. These identities were regional and based in shared histories of migration and dynasty formation. Nonetheless, empires and confederations did not persist long before or certainly not after the Spanish invasion. It was the smaller altepeme that usually persisted throughout the colonial period and beyond.

Altepeme had a connection for Aztecs to their definition of ethnic identity, and community-based identities continue to survive in areas with dense Indigenous populations today. In addition, they connected language, other cultural characteristics, such as dress and jewelry, region, foods, and deities, to peoples they identified as aggregates different from themselves. They were happy to pass judgment on some others, especially the Otomi, whom they saw as ill-educated, and uncouth. Yet altepeme also could be multi-ethnic, multi-linguistic conglomerations. Indeed, some of them began through the coming together of ethnically and linguistically distinct peoples. Population movements in and out had occurred as had de- and re-population on occasion. Nonetheless, because political alliances could and often did shift, a sense of deep connection – identifying with – other communities, sometimes even nearby ones might not last very long at all.

Colonial rule served to sharpen the connection between altepeme and a sense of local identity because larger agglomerations, transitory as they may have been before Spaniards arrived, did not survive the process of invasion and defeat, let alone colonial rule. But beyond a heightened identification with the colonial version of the ethnic kingdom, a process of fragmentation within altepeme meant that their component parts – tlayacatl, tlaxilacalli, calpolli – began to separate from the larger units of which they were a part and stand on their own as independent communities. This process of fragmentation was complex. Subject units within altepeme sometimes sought independence; population loss destabilized the internal structures of altepeme enough at times to lead to projects of reorganization, and leaders within altepeme and their subject units competed for power, wealth, and status. While the term altepetl continued to be used in Indigenous-language documents, by the eighteenth century it increasingly referred to a jurisdiction colonial officials called either *cabeceras* (head towns) or pueblos (towns). The larger ones retained elements of their internal structure, with their sub-units' governance and social structures persisting in forms similar to those of the late Postclassic period at least into the 1820s. But there is no doubt that aspects of political organization and identity underwent a process of fragmentation that occurred over the course of the colonial period, encouraged in part by a legal system that reinforced the fragmentation. Local community identities thus became more important.

Given that Spaniards introduced the identity "*indio*" and it was ubiquitous in Spanish-language legal documents, what about identity at a more macro level? Did this pan-Indigenous conceptualization of identity influence how Nahuas thought of themselves? In colonial Nahuatl-language texts the word indio is rare. While many Spanish loanwords became commonly used in Nahuatl-language texts during the colonial period, that word never did. The locality predominated when an identification of communal or individual identity was needed in an official document. Over time, however, when a broader usage was necessary, in the sixteenth century the term *nican titlaca* (we people here) was used. By the seventeenth century, *timacehualtin* (we macehualtin), referring to Indigenous people, rather than commoners, in comparison to Spaniards began to show up. It appears in legal texts as well as historical writings such as those of Chimalpahin. Nahuas, certainly Nahua intellectuals, seem to have developed a broader notion of collective identity; whether other colonial Nahuas felt that collective identity is unknown. Even today, while Nahuas recognize a kind of larger grouping using words like Mexicano or masehuali as ethnonyms, their deepest affiliation remains with their local community.

What many scholars investigating Nahuatl and other Indigenous-language texts have found about colonial Indigenous ethnic identity is well summed up by historian Stephanie Wood in her book *Transcending Conquest*. However Nahuas made use of the Spanish language and the technology of alphabetic writing, they did so, she says, "to preserve their own paramount and still essentially indigenous concerns of territoriality and community autonomy." Some innovations, some transformations, served the purpose of maintaining Nahua ways of doing things. Language, lands, identities – greatly transformed first by a colonial, then modern, world – have made their impact felt on today's Nahua communities. Yet these pueblos sustain ways of life different from the mestizo communities around them and different from the ways of life other Mexicans experience in urban areas.

Tenacity

To close this book, I argue that an *idea* of Aztec has tenaciously survived. It exists in contemporary Nahua communities, it exists as an element of national history and culture in Mexico, and it exists as a transnational idea.

Spread throughout many parts of Mexico and well into Central America, now as in the Postclassic, the Nahuatl-speaking Mesoamerican population is concentrated in the central part of Mexico, in the Basin of Mexico and its surrounding areas, including therefore Mexico City and the state of Mexico as well as the states of Guerrero, Morelos, Puebla, Tlaxcala, Hidalgo, and Veracruz. While Mexico does not break down its census data by ethnicity, the census provides information about the numbers of Indigenous-language speakers. Nahuatl speakers constitute the largest number of Indigenous-language speakers in Mexico. They number about 1.7 million, according to Mexico's 2020 census. Many people who consider themselves Indigenous do not necessarily speak an Indigenous language, so the linguistically based census numbers should be considered reliable minimums. Modern Nahua communities live in highly varying environments and have experienced the transformations and disruptions of colonial and modern history in ways heavily influenced by local economic patterns, political issues, and types of sociocultural change.

The enormous amount of Nahua ethnography, much of it written from the 1960s on, shows that contemporary

Nahua communities vary in their local histories and socioeconomic profiles. That includes their religious orientation because in some communities evangelical Protestantism is significantly challenging Nahua Catholic beliefs, ceremonies, and community religious economies. Nevertheless, modern Nahua communities still share Aztec features. In diet and tools for cooking and weaving, some Aztec influence can be found. For example, the modern Mexican terms metate, *molcajete*, and *comal* come from Nahuatl words, *metlatl*, *molcaxitl* and *comalli*. These examples of ancient technology are still used in Indigenous and non-Indigenous households for grinding and grilling, especially by cooks who value these implements for the deep flavors they impart. This value is due to the way they are used and re-used over and over, though the back-breaking labor of the metate is definitely not as popular as it once was. Elements of beliefs, myths, and ritual practices also have survived to today. One example is a widespread Nahua belief in a layered universe. The modern conception has four components: *ilhuicatl* (sky), *tlalticpac* (earth), mictlan (underworld), and *apan* (watery place). Another is the influence of creation stories such as the story of the fashioning of the sun and moon by Nanahuatzin and Tecuciztecatl, echoed in narratives told among Nahuas in both Veracruz and the Sierra del Puebla.

Ideas about illness and healing practices are another area where Aztec influence has persisted. Imbalances between energies and between hot and cold are still seen as causing disease in Nahua communities as are spirit attacks and acts of disrespect leading to social disruption. While western medicine is available in Nahua communities, elements of Aztec curing methods have also survived. Care of pregnant women and new mothers and their newborns features bathing, including sweat baths, burial of the umbilical cord, and a focus on dangers to pregnant women and their fetuses that recall the ancient beliefs and rituals described earlier. Curers hold positions similar to some that existed in the Aztec world. And curers still use some plants identical to those used before Spaniards arrived, among them cihuapatli, even now used to help women with gynecological issues and *tepezcohuite*, used for burns and wound healing.

Beyond language, cooking technologies, and healing as areas in which continuities between Aztec practices and those seen to exist today by ethnographers working among Nahua groups, there are two additional areas of Nahua life in which some continuities can be found. One is in family life. Like in the distant past, households can be made up of nuclear or complex family units; the terms used for kin are largely similar to those used in the past. Marriage practices have been influenced by Catholic or Protestant traditions, but there are still communities where go-betweens – usually from the future husband's family – initiate discussion, gifting, and feasting. While wives typically move to the husband's residence, flexibility exists as it did in the past, and relations between mothers and daughters and among sisters remain strong, especially when they live nearby each other. The flexibility that is inherent in the Nahua bilateral system for reckoning kinship relations in which households and related groupings can be structured through ties to men or women has ancient roots. But colonial and modern economic, political, and legal influences impinge as do local ecologies, land shortages, and changing religious influences. The lure of cities and transnational migration have impacted rural Nahua communities too. All these factors influence Nahua community life today as well as individual and family decision making.

The other is in the area of emotional expression. Ethnographers studying contemporary Nahuas report observing a kind of reserve in which emotion in interpersonal relations is downplayed by avoiding expression of powerful emotions such as love, anger, envy, or jealousy. In images, drawn or sculpted, and text, Aztec sources betray relatively little about emotions; finding emotions-related vocabulary in Nahuatl texts is not easy. Emotions are pan-human so it is not that Aztecs and Nahuas did not and do not feel emotion. Rather, emotional expression was and is muted and controlled because emotion – especially strong displays – was and remains thought to introduce disorder and disequilibrium into relationships, events, and ceremonies. Instead, emotion often reveals itself in narratives past and present. Tonalamatl and the speeches known as huehuetlatolli illustrate how excessive expressions of anger, fear, or sexuality could provoke deities to cause disease, death, even the loss of a pregnancy or newborn. James Taggart says about the contemporary Nahua communities he studied that while people did not like to talk openly about their feelings, they were "forthcoming about envy and jealousy when telling anecdotal stories of a world filled with envious and dangerous living and dead people, night beings (*tayohualmeh*), and creatures who cause the frequently fatal disease of envy sickness (*nexicolcocoliz*)." The tenacity of the idea that excessive emotion can lead to disintegration of social units and cause imbalances between the social and natural worlds, a kind of chaos, points to the persistence of Aztec ideas.

With years of ethnographic experience among Nahuas of Guerrero, anthropologist Catharine Good Eshelman has argued that even after having experienced centuries of intense economic pressure and cultural change, the reality for Indigenous societies is that despite processes of change, Indigenous Mesoamerican ideas and social patterns have persisted and been passed on. For Nahuas specifically, she describes four cultural themes that have endured across time: first is a very complex idea about work, tequitl, a strongly felt obligation to family and community, in which the idea of work encompasses the use of all kinds of human energies to bring about a specific end. Second are the concepts of interchange and reciprocity that underlie Nahua cosmology and social organization. Third, among Nahuas there is an idea of force or vital energy that constantly circulates. Fourth is the Nahua consciousness of a continuous collective history. Good Eshelman finds that these themes underlie the activities of labor (especially in agriculture), child-rearing, relations between the living and dead, and are expressed in ceremonial life. Her ideas are not identical to the themes of value, transformation, and balance that I have emphasized, but they overlap. Work, which creates value, and child-rearing, two areas she pays particular attention to, require energy or force (*chicahualiztli*) to grow corn, to raise a child, to use ritual to bring about a desired goal. To bring about such a desired end implies the use of energy to achieve the transformation that results in the end goal. The reciprocity involved in work, child-rearing, and ritual reflects the stress placed on living life in a balanced way. But before I close with a final discussion of value, balance, and transformation, foundational Aztec concepts that have persisted, I want to say a few words about another way Aztecs have survived, and that is not only as people but as an *idea*.

The idea of Aztecs is important in today's Mexico. As the first group, the Mexica specifically, to be defeated by the Spanish they became linked to a powerful, persistent narrative of Spanish military might, Indigenous weakness tied to beliefs in superstitions, and in the case of Malintzin, even taking treasonous actions. The *indigenismo* (a political and social revaluing of Indigenous cultures) created by artists, writers, and government bureaucrats after the Mexican Revolution sought to radically change representations of Mexico's Indigenous peoples and past. The creators of indigenismo glorified the image of the Aztecs to formulate a new national identity by exalting the native and vilifying the Spanish, even though indigenismo as an ideology hardly valorized modern Indigenous peoples. Its proponents viewed Mexico's Indigenous citizens as obstacles to progress and as political and educational projects who have been subjected to multiple campaigns to acculturate them in order to bring them into a modern, mestizo nation. These acculturative efforts included bilingual educational programs that accentuated learning Spanish over preserving and expanding students' Nahuatl-language skills. But indigenismo undoubtedly had lasting effects.

A special focus on the Aztecs took material form through the brilliant work of Mexican archaeologists, supported by government funding, in uncovering and excavating the Mexica's Templo Mayor and the sacred precinct of which the temple is a part. While parts of the Great Temple had come to light through excavations in downtown Mexico City in the late nineteenth and first half of the twentieth century, archaeologists' aim to fully excavate the temple and explore the sacred precinct was jump started after the accidental discovery in 1978 by workers for Mexico's electric utility of the huge Coyolxauhqui relief sculpture described in the prior chapter. That discovery led to a lengthy program of excavation and archaeological analysis that has added immeasurably to contemporary knowledge about the Mexica, their religious beliefs, and ceremonial practices. In addition to these archaeological efforts, the Mexican government also invested in a Templo Mayor museum that opened in 1987, which today is one of the most visited museums in Mexico. It houses eight rooms that cover the finds of the ongoing archaeological project, major Aztec deities, as well as their environment and economy.

The idea of Aztecs has a transnational resonance as well. Some Mexican Americans, for example, assert that because it is possible that Aztlan was located somewhere north of the Valley of Mexico, perhaps as far north as the US southwest, this region is a homeland for them, and that geographical possibility underlies their Indigenous Aztec identity. This identity claim through which the negative – discrimination and lack of historical recognition – to which Mexican Americans have been subjected is turned into something positive has proven to be a persistent idea underlying a sociopolitical identity that expresses an embrace of Indigenous identity and cultural creativity.

Like the twentieth-century Mexican art of the indigenismo movement – especially of the muralists and Frida Kahlo – in which Aztec deities and symbols are common and used to valorize Aztec culture, contemporary Day of the Dead ceremonies, often seen as descended from Aztec rituals, feature altars erected to honor dead family and friends. These celebrations and altars are becoming more and more common across the United States. Having experienced such altars in places in the southwest where I have lived, I have seen reverence, longing for family and now-distant homes, and even expressions of happiness to celebrate loved ones gone with a community of family, friends, and those wanting to partake of this kind of memorialization. Mournful, yet celebratory at the same time, these altars, Davíd Carrasco says, "emphasize the Aztec image of death and regeneration rather than the contrary image of sacrifice and conquest."

From using Aztec-related designs, iconography, or place names, films, to podcasts, video games, Twitter feeds, even sports teams and a rock band name, transnational claims of Aztec association or identity abound. Another way Aztec identity is also being claimed and revitalized is through dance, the Danza Azteca. This term refers to Aztec dances and dancers found in Mexico, the southwest US, in other parts of Latin America, as well as in Europe, including Spain. With complex roots in Mexican colonial Indigenous dance traditions as well as in Mexican and US-based student movements, the dances and dance groups have spread far and wide. They express a celebration of Aztec spirituality, cultural practices, and performance history. Learning the Nahuatl language through university classes, books, or online also is another way for Mexicans and others to connect to this language and to Aztec history, cultural beliefs, and ethnicity. Claims of identity and feelings of solidarity are deeply meaningful because they are rooted – as all ethnic identities are – in assertions of sameness with some people and difference from others. The context of such assertions changes over time, their ubiquity does not. Those professing Aztec heritage are laying claim to the histories, ways of being, and civilizational contributions of the Nahuatl-speaking peoples of Mesoamerica who developed distinctive ways of being with many persistent commonalities described in the chapters of this book over space and across time.

Final Thoughts

The ideas of value, transformation, and balance underlay the commonalities. These themes manifested themselves in the spirituality, political and economic organization, and the social, scientific, literary, and artistic lives of Aztecs as their civilization developed over time within and beyond the Excan tlatoloyan. The regeneration of life out of death was a very basic idea of the Aztec sacred. Rooted in transformation of substances and energy, the related concepts of value and balance helped weave together the Aztec sacred and secular. Gods and goods transformed or were transformed by women and men to create material and symbolic value. Those values underwrote the reciprocity and balance evident in Aztec economic, political and social domains, even as hierarchy became a more prevalent feature of the Aztec world. For all the emphasis on the themes of value, transformation, and balance flowing through Aztec life, it remains important to remember that idiosyncrasy, resistance, even rebellion by individuals and communities occurred.

Ultimately, however, balancing opposing forces kept the Aztec world going, even after the arrival of Spaniards, although value and transformation would come to have different meanings and consequences, as value became monetized and notions of transformations narrowed. Nonetheless, Nahua narratives about the sacred, ideas of disease causation, and the roles of curers suggest that ancient ideas of transformation have persisted in several realms of modern Nahua life. Perhaps the most significant concept that underlay Aztec religious life and the domains of politics, economics, and societal organization with each domain infusing the other, was balance. The struggle between opposed forces created a kind of equilibrium or balance, but the forces of chaos, excess, even joy and pleasure endangered it. Transformations brought about a balancing of opposed forces, but those same forces threatened any permanent state of equilibrium. In this dynamic, the search for balance underlay Aztec work activities in which one kind of substance was transformed into another, an emphasis was placed on the center and centering as opposed to disruptive or dangerous peripheries, and symmetry in architecture, economic exchanges, political dynamics, and literary and artistic expression was sought. Many rituals – from those held at the household to the state level – aimed to maintain the Aztec world by keeping the sun in motion and the forces of chaos at bay. Thus order, equilibrium, or balance could never be peaceful, permanent states, past or present.

GLOSSARY

This glossary emphasizes Nahuatl terminology; terms in Spanish are identified. Organized chapter by chapter, terms only appear in the listing for the chapter in which they first appear.

Chapter 1

Alahua   to slip or slide
Altepetl   water-mountain, a city-state or kingdom (pl., altepeme)
Amatl   indigenous paper
Aztlan   Place of Whiteness or Place of Herons
Calpolli   big house, ward, local community
Campan   district
Chicomoztoc   Seven Caves
Excan tlatoloyan   Tribunal of three, Triple Alliance
Huehuetlatolli   old words, words of the elders
Huetzi   to fall
Manos   grinding tools [S]
Masehuali   modern Nahuatl term for Nahuas (pl., masehualmej)
Metates   flat stone surfaces for grinding [S]
Molcajetes   stone bowls [S]
Nextlahualiztli   debt payment, offerings and sacrifices
Patiuhtli   price, value
Teuctli   lord (can also be part of deities' names)
Tlacuiloque   painters, writers (sing., tlacuilo)

Tlatoani   rulers (pl., tlatoque)
Tlaxilacalli   ward, local community
Tlayacatl   subdivision within an altepetl
Tonalpohualli   260-day count
Tzompantli   skull rack

Chapter 2

Atamalcualiztli   Eating of Water Tamales
Calmecac   priestly school
Calpolco   local temple
Cihuacalmecac   women's religious school
Cihuacuacuiltin   high ranking priestesses
Cihuapipiltin   women nobles; term referred also to women who had died in childbirth who were deified
Cihuateopixque   sacred women guardians
Cihuateteo   women gods; term referred also to women who had died in childbirth who were deified
Cihuatlamacazque   women priests
Cipactli   crocodile
Cuacuiltin   high ranking priests
Fiestas movibles [S]   movable feasts
Ixiptlahuan   living embodiments or representations of a deity (sing., ixiptla)
Macehualtin   commoners (sing., macehualli)
Metztli   moon, one of the eighteen twenty-day segments of the solar calendar
Mictlan   Place of the Dead, underworld (modern Nahuatl)
Nahui Ocelotl, Ehecatl, Quihuitl, Atl, Ollin   Four Jaguar, Wind, Rain, Water, Movement
Nanahualtin   priests or sorcerers who could transform into animals or other beings (sing., nahualli)
Nemontemi   the five days added onto the solar calendar

Octli pulque
Pillahuanaliztli Festival of Children
Teahui someone's aunt
Telpochcalli school for commoner boys where they received military training and performed public works
Teocalli god house or temple
Teopixque sacred guardians
Teotl deity; vital force; strange, anomalous things (pl., teteo)
Teotlalli sacred land or lands
Teoxihuitl fine turquoise
Teteuctin nobles holding high governing positions
Tetla someone's uncle
Tiachcauh "older brothers" providing service work in temples
Ticitl medical practitioner
Tlalticpac earth
Tlalxico earth's navel
Tlamacazque priests (sing., tlamacazqui)
Tlamacazton lower-ranking priests
Tlenamacaque fire priests
Tonalamatl day book for the 260-day count
Tonalpohualli day count
Tonalpouhque priests who could read the tonalamatl, soothsayers, or diviners
Toxiuhmolpilia Binding of Years
Trecena thirteen-day period in the 260-day ritual calendar [S]
Tzitzimime harmful or healing deities associated with fertility
Tzoalli dough used to make images for rituals
Xiuhmolpilli bundle of years
Xiuhpohualli solar year calendar

Glossary

Chapter 3

Atlatl   spear thrower
Calpixque   officials who oversaw tribute collection
Calpoleque   commoner neighborhood officials
Chinampas   raised plots used for cultivation (sing., chinampa) [S]
Cihuacoatl   name of a deity, title of a Mexica high official
Cihuatequitque   female tribute collectors
Cocoltic yaotl   angry war
Cuacuauhtin   eagle order of elite soldiers
Cuauhchique   shorn ones, high order of soldiers
Cuauhpipiltin   eagle nobles, commoners who became quasi-nobles through participation in warfare
Cuauhtlalli   eagle land, land set aside for flower wars
Hueltiuhtli   elder sister
Huey tlatoani   great or supreme ruler
Macuahuitl   sword
Ocelome   jaguar order of elite soldiers
Otontin   high order of soldiers named for the Otomi
Pipiltin   upper nobility (sing., pilli)
Pulque   alcoholic drink made from maguey leaves [S]
Teccalco   Mexica court hearing commoner legal cases
Teccalli   lord house, unit of political and social organization
Tecpan   lord place, palace
Telpochtlato   ruler of youth who passed judgment on young men in the telpochcalli
Teoicpalpan   sacred tribunal
Tequitlato   official overseeing public works
Teteuctin   holders of high governing positions (sing., teuctli)
Tlacateccatl   people lord, a high ranking member of ruler's council, military leader
Tlacochcalcatl   armory person, a high ranking member of ruler's council, military leader

Glossary

Tlacochtli dart weapon
Tlacxitlan Mexica court hearing nobles' legal cases
Tlahuitolli bow
Tlatocan ruling council
Tlatocayotl rulership
Tlatoicpalpan governing council
Xiquipilli a fighting unit of 8000 soldiers
Xochiyaoyotl flower war
Yaomitl arrow
Yaotlalli war land

Chapter 4

Altepetlalli land of the altepetl
Amanteca feather artisans
Cacaxtli carrying frame
Callalli house land or plot
Calmilli house plot
Calpixque tribute collectors at regional and imperial levels
Calpollalli calpolli land
Chinamitl raised plot used for cultivation
Cihuatlalli women's land
Coatequitl rotational labor draft
Cohua buying
Cueitl skirt
Cuicacalli song house
Huehuetlalli old or inherited land
Huey tlatoque supreme rulers (sing., huey tlatoani)
Huipilli blouse or shift for women
Ichcahuipilli cotton armor, male clothing
Maitl hand
Maxtlatl loin cloth, male clothing
Mayeque dependent laborers who worked land (sing., maye)

Metepantle agricultural method using stone terraces around vegetation
Milchimalli military lands
Namaca selling
Patla barter
Pillalli noble land
Pochteca long-distance traders
Pochtecatlatoque market judges
Oztomeca long-distance traders who spied
Quachtli large cotton cloaks used as tribute or trade items
Quechquemitl women's slip-on upper garment
Tealtianime bather of slaves
-Tech pouhque dependent laborers who worked land
Tecpantlalli palace land
Temalacatl round stone used for war-like ritual killings
Teotlalli lands of the gods
Tequitl work, obligation
Teuctlalli lordly land
Tianquizpan tlayacanque marketplace administrators
Tierra caliente hot land [S]
Tierra fría cold land [S]
Tierra temporada temperate land [S]
Tilmatli cloak
Tlachiuhqui producer-seller
Tlacotin slaves (sing., tlacotli)
Tlaixnextiliztli profit
Tlalmaitin dependent laborers who worked land (sing., tlalmaitl)
Tlamanacac peddler
Tlamemeque human porters (sing., tlameme)
Tlanecuilo merchant retailer
Tlaquimilolli deity bundle
Tlatocacihuatl woman ruler

Glossary

Tlatocatlalli ruler's land
Tlaxilacallalli tlaxilacalli land
Tolteca luxury craft workers ; also refers to settled inhabitants of the Basin of Mexico region who came together with Chichimeca migrants to form later Postclassic Aztec peoples
Totocalli bird house, feather workshop

Chapter 5

Ahuiani pleasure women
Calli house or room
Cemithualtin one patio, family, household
Cencalli one house, family, household
Cenyeliztli one being, family, household
Chahua companion, concubine
Cihua woman (can also refer to someone's wife)
Cihuacalli women's house
Cihuanemactin given women
Cihuatepixque women teachers, guardians
Cihuatetiachcahuan women teachers
Cihuatlanque matchmakers
Conetl child (female speaker)
Ichpochtli young woman
Ihiyotl energy or spirit connected with the liver
Inmecahua female companions
Ithualli inner courtyard or patio
Ixiuhtli grandchild
Mintontli great-great-grandparent
-Namic spouse
Omitl bone
Omicetl semen
Pilli child of a male speaker (also means noble)

Glossary

Teaanque guardians or teachers
Techan tlaca people of the home, family, household
Tecpan palace
Telpochtli young man
Tiachcahuan male teachers
Tiachcauh elder brother
Tlacamecayotl rope of people, descent line
Tlacihuaantin taken women
Tlalticpacayotl earthly pleasure, sexual intercourse
Tonalli warmth from the sun, energy or spirit associated with the head
Xacalli single room house, shack
Yoli something living
Yolia energy or spirit emanating from the heart

Chapter 6

Amacuahuitl fig tree
Amoxtli book
Cihuapatli herb used by women for childbirth
Cuicatl song
Don term of nobility, high status [S]
Elli liver
Huey large, important, old
Ilpia to tie
Lienzos large cloth pieces for keeping records [S]
Ololiuhqui plant with hallucinogenic properties
Temazcalli bathing house
Tetl stone
Teyolloquani heart eater, sorcerer
Tiras Aztec screenfold books [S]
Tlantli teeth
Tototli bird
Yolloxochitl heart flower, plant providing heart medication

Chapter 7

Apan   watery place
Cabeceras   head towns [S]
Cabildos   town councils [S]
Chicahualiztli   energy, force
Comal   griddle [S]
Comalli   griddle
Congregación   forced relocation [S]
Encomenderos   holders of a grant of tribute or labor [S]
Encomienda   grant of tribute or labor [S]
Fiscal   native church official [S]
Gobernadores   governors [S]
Haciendas   large landed estates [S]
Ilhuicatl   sky
Indigenismo   political and social revaluing of Indigenous cultures [S]
Indio   Indian [S]
Metlatl   grinding stone, mortar
Molcajete   bowl for grinding [S]
Molcaxitl   bowl for grinding
Pueblos   towns [S]
Nexicolcocoliz   envy sickness
Nican titlaca   we people here
Repartimiento   rotational labor draft [S]
Tayohualmeh   night beings
Tepezcohuite   plant that aids healing from burns
Timacehualtin   we macehualtin, Indigenous people as a group
Tlalcohualli   bought land

BIBLIOGRAPHIC ESSAY

This essay emphasizes both older, canonical works on the Aztecs that set forth arguments contemporary scholars either accept or still reckon with, and newer works that illustrate the current state of the field; it follows closely the organization of each chapter. I try to demonstrate the historiographical development of Aztec studies but cannot do so comprehensively. While the *Handbook of Middle American Indians* has become progressively out of date, some essays in Vol. X (*Archaeology of Northern Mesoamerica*; Gordon F. Ekholm and Ignacio Bernal, eds., Austin: University of Texas Press, 1971), especially those by Pedro Carrasco, Alfonso Caso, and H. B. Nicholson, remain valuable as do volumes XII through XV that list and describe many different ethnohistorical sources, those known by the time the volumes were published between 1972 and 1975. *The Oxford Encyclopedia of Mesoamerican Cultures*, 3 vols. (Davíd Carrasco, ed., Oxford: Oxford University Press, 2001), and *The Oxford Handbook of the Aztecs* (Deborah L. Nichols and Enrique Rodríguez-Alegría, eds., Oxford: Oxford University Press, 2017) offer more recent synthetic articles on a wide array of Aztec-related topics. For archaeological perspectives, *The Oxford Handbook of Mesoamerican Archaeology* (Deborah L. Nichols and Christopher A. Pool, eds., Oxford: Oxford University Press, 2012) also contains pertinent essays.

Preface

A few readings that provide insight into intellectual trends mentioned in the preface include Matthew Restall, "A History of the New Philology and the New Philology in History," *Latin American Research Review* 38 (2003), pp.113–134; Cynthia Robin, "Archaeology of Everyday Life," *Annual Review of Anthropology* 49 (2020), pp.373–390; Lisa M. Johnson and Rosemary A. Joyce, eds.,

Bibliographic Essay

Materializing Ritual Practices (Louisville, CO: University Press of Colorado, 2022); and Nancy Shoemaker, "A Typology of Colonialism," *AHA Perspectives on History* (2015), www.historians.org/research-and-publications/perpectives-on-history/october-2015/a-typology-of-colonialism. For an introduction to the idea of many voices in texts – what I call polyvocality, or what Mikhail Bakhtin, a brilliant literary and cultural theorist of the early twentieth century, called polyphony – see his *The Dialogical Imagination: Four Essays* (Michael Holquist, ed., Caryl Emerson and Michael Holquist, transls., Austin: University of Texas Press, 1982). The extracted quotation appears in Kay Almere Read and Jason J. González, *Handbook of Mesoamerican Mythology* (Santa Barbara, CA: ABC-CLIO, 2000), p.4. The significance of the front cover image is explained on the back cover. Doris Heyden discussed some of the meanings of sand in "Sand in Ritual and History," in Eloise Quiñones Keber, ed., *Representing Aztec Ritual: Performance, Text, and Image in the Work of Sahagún*, (Louisville, CO: University Press of Colorado, 2002), pp.175–196.

1 Introduction

Among the best overviews of Aztec culture are Jacques Soustelle, *Daily Life of the Aztecs on the Eve of the Spanish Conquest* (Stanford: Stanford University Press, 1961) and Frances Berdan, *Aztec Archaeology and Ethnohistory* (Cambridge: Cambridge University Press, 2014), the former for its beautiful writing and sensitive rendering of Aztec thought; the latter for its thorough treatment of scholarship on a wide range of topics. For a more archaeologically focused and geographically diverse overview, readers should consult Michael E. Smith, *The Aztecs* (Oxford: Blackwell, 3rd ed., 2012). Chronologically focused histories include Nigel Davies, *The Aztecs: A History* (Norman: University of Oklahoma Press, rev. ed., 1980) and Camilla Townsend, *The Fifth Sun: A New History of the Aztecs* (Oxford: Oxford University Press, 2019), the latter rooted in her deep knowledge of Nahuatl-language historical texts from a variety of altepeme.

Bibliographic Essay

For translations of Nahuatl-language terms, the text to start with is Alonso de Molina's *Vocabulario en lengua castellana y mexicana y mexicana y castellana* (Mexico City: Editorial Porrúa, 1971 [1555–1571]). Rémi Siméon's dictionary translating Nahuatl into French, *Dictionnaire de la langue nahuatl ou mexicaine* (Paris: Imprimerie Nationale, 1885), is also very useful as is Frances Karttunen's *An Analytical Dictionary of Nahuatl* (Norman: University of Oklahoma Press, 1992). The *Gran diccionario náhuatl*, put together by Marc Thouvenot et al., at https://gdn.iib.unam.mx, unites information from numerous early dictionaries and grammars. The excellent online dictionary available at https://nahuatl.uoregon.edu, organized by Stephanie Wood, or others available through www.lexilogos.com/english/nahuatl_dictionary.htm, will also be helpful to readers interested in both colonial and modern Nahuatl.

For Aztec thinking and the organizing concepts of value, transformation, and balance, works by Louise Burkhart, *The Slippery Earth* (Tucson: University of Arizona Press, 1989), James Maffie, *Aztec Philosophy: Understanding a World in Motion* (Boulder: University Press of Colorado, 2014), and Kenneth Hirth, *The Aztec Economic World: Merchants and Markets in Ancient Mesoamerica* (Cambridge: Cambridge University Press, 2016) have all been enormously useful in thinking about religious, philosophical, and economic domains of Aztec ideas. Also key to my thinking on value are essays by Frances Berdan, "Material Dimensions of Aztec Religion and Ritual," in E. Christian Wells and Karla L. Davis-Salazar, eds., *Mesoamerican Ritual Economy: Archaeological and Ethnological Perspectives* (Boulder: University Press of Colorado, 2007), pp.245–266, who points out how integrated Aztec thinking about economy, ritual, and politics was, and John M. Watanabe, "Ritual Economy and the Negotiation of Autarky and Interdependence in a Ritual Mode of Production," in that same volume, pp.301–322. Watanabe writes that "ritual reaffirms the value of the values it materializes, and through its often costly materializations it actualizes – and thus makes powerful in this world – the sacred powers to which it is dedicated," p.303. Perhaps I would put it: ritual reaffirms the *meaning* of the

Bibliographic Essay

values it materializes, but Watanabe's statement explains something important about Mesoamerican – and Aztec – societies, which is that the sacred and the secular cannot really be separated because they are so deeply intertwined, and the intertwining involves their ideas and actions around value. Aztec ideas about transformation are explored by Kay Read in *Time and Sacrifice in the Aztec Cosmos* (Bloomington: Indiana University Press, 1998) and on balance, not only by Burkhart but also by Agnieszka Brylak, "Hurtling off a Precipice, Falling into a River: A Nahuatl Metaphor and the Christian Concept of Sin," *Ethnohistory* 66:3 (2019), pp.489–513. On debt payment, nextlahualiztli, see both the *Primeros memoriales* and *Florentine Codex*, cited below.

For an overview of Aztec studies, see Deborah L. Nichols and Susan Toby Evans, "Aztec Studies," *Ancient Mesoamerica* 20 (2009), pp.265–270. Caroline Dodds Pennock does an excellent job of rendering the complexities of Aztec daily life in *Bonds of Blood: Gender, Lifecycle and Sacrifice in Aztec Culture* (Houndmills: Palgrave Macmillan, 2008). Inga Clendinnen's *Aztecs: An Interpretation* (New York: Cambridge University Press, 1991) offers a beautifully written if perhaps overly exoticized rendering of Aztec life and thinking. Geoffrey W. Conrad and Arthur A. Demarest discuss the relationship between Aztec ritual killings and the rise of empire in *Religion and Empire: The Dynamics of Aztec and Inca Expansionism* (Cambridge: Cambridge University Press, 1984). Davíd Carrasco considers the distancing Aztec scholars often do when thinking and writing about "human sacrifice," and pairs that with a call for scholars to examine religious violence more deeply and carefully, in *City of Sacrifice: The Aztec Empire and the Role of Violence in Civilization* (Boston: Beacon Press, 1999).

The codices on which I primarily rely have entries in *The Oxford Encyclopedia of Mesoamerican Cultures* that discuss the contents, dating, and significance of each of these texts. In addition, the introductory essays in Vol. I of Frances F. Berdan and Patricia Rieff Anawalt, eds., *Codex Mendoza* [CM hereafter], 4 vols., (Berkeley: University of California Press, 1992 [ca.1540s]) as well as Eloise Quiñones Keber's introductory essay to the *Codex Telleriano Remensis* (Austin: University of Texas Press, 1995 [mid-16th c]) provide essential information on the history and information embedded in these codices. It should be noted that the images for Figs. 3.2, 5.3, and 5.5 from the CM can be found online and also in Vol. III of the Berdan and Anawalt edition. Translations of the text with the images as well as of explanatory text the CM includes can be found in Vol. IV (3.2, p.143; 5.3, p.123; 5.5, p.143). Also on codices – historical, religious, and encyclopedic – the following works by Elizabeth Hill Boone are essential: *Stories in Red and Black: Pictorial Histories of the Aztecs and Mixtecs* (Austin: University of Texas Press, 1990); *Cycles of Time and Meaning in the Mexican Books of Fate* (Austin: University of Texas Press, 2007); and *Descendants of Aztec Pictography: The Cultural Encyclopedias of Sixteenth-Century Mexico* (Austin: University of Texas Press, 2020). A very recent set of essays written in conjunction with a new facsimile edition of the *CM* to be published soon offers updated interpretations, see Jorge Gómez Tejada, ed., *The Codex Mendoza: New Insights* (Quito: USFQ Press, 2022), https://read.amazon.com/?asin=B09SM72KBZ&ref_=dbs_t_r_kcr.

There is a very rich literature on the writer often referred to now as Chimalpahin (don Domingo de San Antón Muñón Quauhtlehuanitzin). In addition to Susan Schroeder's biographical sketch in *The Oxford Encyclopedia of Mesoamerican Cultures*, Camilla Townsend provides a biographical and historiographic overview, painting a vivid picture of his intellectual world in her *Annals of Native America* (Oxford: Oxford University Press, 2017). In addition, the volume edited by Clementina Battcock, Rodrigo Martínez Baracs, and Salvador Rueda Smithers, *Manuscritos mexicanos perdidos y recuperados* (Mexico City: INAH, 2019), contains multiple essays detailing his major themes and exploring the impact of his writings on colonial and later Mexican historiography. For Chimalpahin's writings about women, see Susan Schroeder, "Chimalpahin and Why Women Matter in History," in Gabriela Ramos and Yanna Yannakakis, eds., *Indigenous Intellectuals: Knowledge,*

Bibliographic Essay

Power, and Colonial Culture in Mexico and the Andes (Durham: Duke University Press, 2014), pp.107–131.

Important translations from Nahuatl of the largest collection of song-poems, the *Cantares mexicanos*, have been published in English by John Bierhorst, *Cantares mexicanos: Songs of the Aztecs* (Stanford: Stanford University Press, 1985) and in Spanish by Miguel León-Portilla, *Cantares mexicanos* (Mexico City: UNAM, 2011). Examples of both religious and civil hybrid texts can be found in Matthew Restall, Lisa Sousa, and Kevin Terraciano, eds., *Mesoamerican Voices: Native-Language Writings from Colonial Mexico, Oaxaca, Yucatan, and Guatemala* (Cambridge and New York: 2005).

Histories by Spanish friars and eyewitness accounts of the conquest era are cited in the primary source sections of later chapters. For Zorita, see Alonso de Zorita, *Life and Labor in Ancient Mexico: The Brief and Summary Relation of the Lords of New Spain* (Benjamin Keen, transl., Norman: University of Oklahoma Press, 1994 [ca. 1565]). The *Relaciones geográficas* are published under that title, 9 vols., (René Acuña, ed., Mexico City: UNAM, 1982). Many of the *Relaciones* contain maps done by Indigenous artist cartographers. On these maps, see Barbara Mundy, *The Mapping of New Spain: Indigenous Cartography and the Maps of the Relaciones Geográficas* (Chicago: University of Chicago Press, 1996).

Until recently, the publication to consult for Alva Ixtlilxochitl's texts has been *Obras históricas*, 2 vols., (Edmundo O'Gorman, ed., Mexico City: UNAM), 1975–1977. O'Gorman's introductory essay in Vol. I remains worthwhile. Also see Amber Brian, *Alva Ixtlilxochitl's Native Archive and the Circulation of Knowledge in Colonial Mexico* (Nashville: Vanderbilt University Press, 2016). Alva Ixtlilxochitl's famous "Thirteenth Relation" is available in English as *The Native Conquistador: Alva Ixtlilxochitl's Account of the Conquest of New Spain*, Amber Brian, Bradley Benton, and Pablo García Loaeza, eds. and transls., (University Park, PA: Pennsylvania State University Press [1608]). Also see his *History of the Chichimeca Nation: Don Fernando de Alva Ixtlilxochitl's Seventeenth-Century Chronicle of Ancient Mexico*, Amber Brian,

Bradley Benton, Peter B. Villela, and Pablo García Loaeza, eds. and transls., (Norman: University of Oklahoma Press, 2019 [1620s or later]). Manuscripts versions of his text are now available online as part of the *Codice Chimalpahin* at www.codicechimalpahin.inah.gob.mx. For other well-known writers of mixed Indigenous and Spanish heritage, see Juan Bautista Pomar, *Relación de Tezcoco: siglo XVI* (México: Biblioteca Enciclopédica del Estado de México, 1975 [1582]) and Diego Muñoz Camargo, *Historia de Tlaxcala* (Germán Vázquez ed., Madrid: Historia 16, 1986 [1585]).

A huge literature exists on the Sahagún corpus of texts. A useful bibliography of his texts can be found in H. B. Nicholson's entry on Sahagún in *The Oxford Encyclopedia of Mesoamerican Cultures*, Vol. III, pp.105–113. For biography and assessments of his life and writing, see Munro S. Edmonson, ed., *Sixteenth-Century Mexico: The Work of Sahagún* (Albuquerque: University of New Mexico Press, 1974); J. Jorge Klor de Alva, H. B. Nicholson, and Eloise Quiñones Keber, eds., *Bernardino de Sahagún: Pioneer Ethnographer of Sixteenth-Century Aztec Mexico* (Albany: Institute for Mesoamerican Studies, SUNY Albany, 1988); Walden Brown, *Sahagún and the Transition to Modernity* (Norman: University of Oklahoma Press, 2000); Pilar Máynez and J. Rubén Romero Galván, eds., *El universo de Sahagún: pasado y presente* (Mexico City: UNAM, 2014); Miguel León-Portilla, *Bernardino de Sahagún, First Anthropologist* (Mauricio J. Mixco, transl., Norman: University of Oklahoma Press, 2002); John Frederick Schwaller, ed., *Sahagún at 500: Essays on the Quincentenary of the Birth of Fr. Bernardino de Sahagún* (Berkeley: Academy of American Franciscan History, 2003); Jeanette Favrot Peterson and Kevin Terraciano, eds., *The Florentine Codex: An Encyclopedia of the Nahua World in Sixteenth-Century Mexico* (Austin: University of Texas Press, 2019); and Boone, *Descendants of Aztec Pictography*. The latter two publications are important not only for the recent and comprehensive scholarship but because they stress Sahagún's dependence on Indigenous writers and artists. They describe much more than ever before how substantial Indigenous contributions were and how the Indigenous writers and artists were themselves influenced by European art, religion, and intellectual trends of the early modern period. Such indigenous intellectuals contributed to a changing, hybrid literary and visual culture in early New Spain. Many of the essays in the Peterson and Terraciano volume bring much needed attention also to the over 2500 images that are a part of the *Florentine Codex*. On the images, also see Diana Magaloni Kerpel, *The Colors of the New World: Artists, Materials and the Creation of the Florentine Codex* (Los Angeles: Getty Research Institute, 2014). For the *Primeros memoriales* (PM hereafter), see Bernardino de Sahagún, *Primeros memoriales: Facsimile Edition* (Ferdinand Anders, ed., Norman: University of Oklahoma Press, 1993 [1558]) and *Primeros memoriales by Bernardino de Sahagún: Paleography of Nahuatl Text and English Translation by* Thelma D. Sullivan, *Completed and Revised with Additions by H. B. Nicholson and Others* (Norman: University of Oklahoma Press, 1997). While I have relied primarily on Arthur J.O. Anderson and Charles E. Dibble, transl. and eds., *General History of the Things of New Spain: Florentine Codex* [FC hereafter] (14 parts, Santa Fe and Salt Lake City: School of American Research and University of Utah, 1950–82 [1569]), subject to my own readings of the Nahuatl text, an online, paleographic version of the text that resides today in the Biblioteca Medicea Laurenziana in Florence, Italy is also available. The three volumes of this version can be found at www.loc.gov/item/2021667837. This link provides the first volume and links for the second and third. A useful addition to the FC is the 1585 revision of Book 12 on the Spanish-Mexica War: *Bernardino de Sahagún, Conquest of New Spain: 1585 Version* (Howard F. Cline, transl., S.L. Cline, ed., Salt Lake City: University of Utah Press, 1989).

The introductory essay to Fr. Diego Durán, *Book of the Gods and Rites and the Ancient Calendar* (transls. and eds., Fernando Horcasitas and Doris Heyden, Norman: University of Oklahoma Press, 1971 [ca. 1575]) holds up well as both biography and analysis of Durán's texts. For his historical text, see *The History of the Indies of New Spain*, transl., Doris Heyden (Norman: University of Oklahoma Press, 1994 [1581]). Boone's *Descendants of Aztec Pictography* analyzes both his texts and the images accompanying them. For the relationship between the historical texts of Alvarado Tezozomoc and Durán, in addition to the classic piece by Robert Barlow, "La Crónica X: versiones coloniales de la historia de los Mexica Tenochca," *Revista Mexicana de Estudios Antropológicos* 7 (1945), pp.65–87, see José Rubén Romero, *Los privilegios perdidos: Hernando Alvarado Tezozómoc, su tiempo, su nobleza, su crónica mexicana* (Mexico City: UNAM, 2003) and Sylvie Peperstraete, *La "Crónica X": reconstitution et analyse d'une source perdue fondamentale sur la civilization Aztèque, d'après l'Historia de las Indias de Nueva España de D. Durán (1581) et la Crónica Mexicana de F. A. Tezozomoc (ca. 1598)* (Oxford: Archaeopress, BAR International Series, 2007). Establishing the identities of and relationships among authors and their texts is not always simple nor is reconstructing an accurate timeline based on annals and codices as Camilla Townsend explains in "Glimpsing Native American Historiography: The Cellular Principle in Sixteenth-Century Nahuatl Annals," *Ethnohistory* 56 (2009), pp.625–650 as well as in *Annals of Native America*. For the use of the concept of "counter-narrative," in Nahuatl colonial religious texts, plays specifically, see Ben Leeming, *Aztec Antichrist: Performing the Apocalypse in Early Colonial Mexico* (Louisville, CO: University Press of Colorado and Institute for Mesoamerican Studies, 2022).

Michael E. Smith has discussed the structure, physical and organizational, of altepeme and their neighborhoods in *Aztec City-State Capitals* (Gainesville: University Press of Florida, 2008). While the etymology of the term "tlaxilacalli" has resisted interpretation, Louise M. Burkhart plausibly translated it as "row of houses" in "Mexica Women on the Home Front: Housework and Religion in Aztec Mexico," in Susan Schroeder, Stephanie Wood, and Robert Haskett, eds., *Indian Women of Early Mexico* (Norman: University of Oklahoma Press, 1997), p.29. On water management, so critical for rural and urban areas for the food supply, see Michael E. Smith,

Bibliographic Essay

Aztec City-State Capitals and Barbara Mundy, *The Death of Aztec Tenochtitlan, the Life of Mexico City* (Austin: University of Texas Press, 2015).

The extensive literature on the demography of the Aztecs as well as Tenochtitlan is covered in Lourdes Márquez Morfín and Rebecca Storey, "Population History in Precolumbian and Colonial Times," in *The Oxford Handbook of the Aztecs*, pp.189–200. Especially important publications on this major topic include Woodrow W. Borah and Sherbourne F. Cook, *The Aboriginal Population of Central Mexico on the Eve of the Spanish Conquest* (Berkeley: University of California Press, 1963) for a very high count. William Sanders, "The Population of the Central Mexican Symbiotic Region, the Basin of Mexico, and the Teotihuacan Valley in the Sixteenth Century," in William M. Denevan, ed., *The Native Population of the Americas in 1492* (Madison: University of Wisconsin Press, 1992), pp.85–150; and Thomas M. Whitmore, *Disease and Death in Early Colonial Mexico: Simulating Amerindian Depopulation* (Boulder: Westview Press, 1992). Sanders and Whitmore, using archaeological and historical evidence, come to similar lower, well-reasoned, estimates for both the basin as well as the larger Aztec area. For Tenochtitlan in particular, see Edward E. Calnek, "Conjunto urbano y modelo residencial en Tenochtitlan," in Woodrow Borah et al., *Ensayos sobre el desarollo urbano de México* (Mexico City: SEP, 1974), pp.189–204; Susan Evans, *Ancient Mexico and Central America: Archaeology and Culture History*, 3rd ed., (London: Thames and Hudson, 2013); and José Luis de Rojas, *Tenochtitlan: Capital of the Aztec Empire* (Gainesville: University Press of Florida, 2012) for medium, low, and high population estimates for the city respectively.

On Aztec artifacts, especially from the Templo Mayor, see Johanna Broda, Davíd Carrasco, and Eduardo Matos Moctezuma, *The Great Temple of Tenochtitlan: Center and Periphery in the Aztec World* (Berkeley: University of California Press, 1987), Eduardo Matos Moctezuma, *The Great Temple of the Aztecs: Treasures of Tenochtitlan* (Doris Heyden, transl., New York: Thames and London, 1988); and Leonardo López Lújan, *The*

Offerings of the Templo Mayor of Tenochtitlan, revised ed., (Bernard R. Ortiz de Montellano and Thelma Ortiz de Montellano, transls., Albuquerque: University of New Mexico Press, 2005).

Francisco Javier Clavijero uses the term "Aztec" in his important proto-national history, *Historia antigua de México* (Mexico City: Porrúa, 1964 [1780]) as does William Prescott in *History of the Conquest of Mexico* (New York: Modern Library, 1998 [1843]). Throughout this book I am using the ethnonyms commonly used in scholarly and popular literature to refer to Mesoamerican peoples, but those of the Classic, Epiclassic, and Postclassic periods must have had names for themselves different from what the Aztecs called them, for example, for those of Teotihuacan and perhaps Tollan as well. Such was also the case for many of their contemporaneous peoples who used names for themselves different from what the Aztecs used, but it is the names in Nahuatl that became standardized. Modern scholars tend to use the term "Nahuas" for colonial and contemporary Nahuatl-speaking peoples as I will do here, but their terminologies are more complex for themselves as Alan R. Sandstrom has discussed in his *Corn Is Our Blood: Culture and Ethnic Identity in a Contemporary Aztec Indian Village* (Norman: University of Oklahoma Press, 1991).

Book 10 of the FC documents the burning of older codices under the tlatoani Itzcoatl. Rudolph Van Zantwijk discusses how earlier history became subsumed in later Postclassic histories by Nahuatl-speaking peoples in *The Aztec Arrangement: The Social History of Pre-Spanish Mexico* (Norman: University of Oklahoma Press, 1985). Important discussions of Aztec ethnicities and their historical traditions can be found in Pedro Carrasco, "The Peoples of Central Mexico and Their Historical Traditions," in Vol. XI, *Archaeology of Northern Mesoamerica, Handbook of Middle American Indians*, pp.459–473; and Nigel Davies, *The Toltecs until the Fall of Tula* (Norman: University of Oklahoma Press, 1977). For a comprehensive overview of the archaeology of central and northern Mesoamerica, see Michael D. Coe, Javier Urcid, and Rex Koontz, *Mexico: From the Olmecs to the Aztecs*, 8th ed., (London: Thames and Hudson, 2019). Boone discusses codices and other sources on the Aztec migrations in *Stories in Red and Black*. Other important treatments of the Aztec and Mexica migrations include Michael E. Smith, "The Aztlan Migrations of the Nahuatl Chronicles: Myth or History?" *Ethnohistory* 31 (1984), pp.153–186; Federico Navarrete Linares, *La migración de los Mexicas* (Mexico City: CONACULTA, 1998); and Christopher S. Beekman and Alexander F. Christensen, "Controlling for Doubt and Uncertainty through Multiple Lines of Evidence: A New Look at the Mesoamerican Nahua Migrations," *Journal of Archaeological Method and Theory* 10 (2003), pp.111–164.

I consulted several historical primary sources for the historical overview section of this chapter, especially Fr. Diego Durán, *The History of the Indies of New Spain* (Doris Heyden, transl. and ed., Norman: University of Oklahoma Press, 1994 [1581]); Fernando Alvarado Tezozomoc, *Crónica mexicana* (Madrid: Dastin, 2001 [ca. 1598]); as well as Book 10 of the *Florentine Codex*, with its recounting of the histories of Tolteca, Chichimeca, Nahuas, and the Mexica as well as other peoples. Chimalpahin also wrote very important historical chronicles that are published as the *Codex Chimalpahin*, 2 vols., (Arthur J. O. Anderson and Susan Schroeder, eds. and transls., Norman: University of Oklahoma Press, 1997 [ca. early 17th c.]) and *Las ocho relaciones y el memorial de Colhuacan*, 2 vols., (transl., Rafael Tena, Mexico City: CONACULTA, 1998). Scholarly histories that I consulted include Nigel Davies, *The Aztecs*; Federico Navarrete Linares, *Los orígenes de los pueblos indígenes del Valle de México: los altépetl y sus historias* (Mexico City: UNAM, 2011); and C. Townsend, *The Fifth Sun*. For the internal organization of Tenochtitlan, in addition to Mundy's discussions in *The Death of Tenochtitlan, the Life of Mexico City*, see Alfonso Caso, "Los barrios antiguos de Tenochtitlan y Tlatelolco," *Memorias de la Academia Mexicana de la Historia* 15 (1956), pp.7–62; and Edward E. Calnek, "The Internal Structure of Tenochtitlan," in Eric R. Wolf, ed., *The Valley of Mexico: Studies of Prehispanic Ecology and Society* (Albuquerque: University of New Mexico Press, 1976), pp.287–302.

For extracted quotations, the quotes introducing the chapter come from Paul Chaat Smith, *Everything You Know about Indians Is Wrong* (Minneapolis: University of Minnesota Press, 2009), p.19 and Debra Nichols and Susan Evans, "Aztec Studies," *Ancient Mesoamerica* 20 (2009), p.265; Daniel Gross, *The Secret History of Emotion: From Aristotle's Rhetoric to Modern Brain Science* (Chicago: University of Chicago Press, 2007, p.1); Pennock, *Bonds of Blood, p.3; Codex Chimalpahin*, Vol. I, p.72.

2 Living in the Aztecs' Cosmos

Texts providing critical information about Aztec stories about creation include the *Historia de los mexicanos por sus pinturas* [HMP hereafter], https://archive.org/details/historia-de-los-mexicanos-por-sus-historias, an online version of an 1891 publication; the *Histoyre du Mechique*, "Histoyre du Mechique," *Journal de la Société de Américanistes de Paris* 2 (1905), pp.1–41; the *Leyenda de los soles*, and the *Anales de Cuauhtitlan*, the latter two published together by John Bierhorst, transl., *History and Mythology of the Aztecs: The Codex Chimalpopoca* (Tucson: University of Arizona Press, 1992). The HMP and *Histoyre du Mechique* came out of a lost work known as the *Tratado de antigüedades mexicanas* by Fray Andrés de Olmos, one of the early friars (though not among the first twelve), having arrived in central Mexico in 1528. Olmos, along with Molina and Sahagún, was one of the great linguists of the early colonial period. He wrote his great work in the 1530s. It was the product of his interactions with learned Nahuas in several important altepeme including Tetzcoco, Huexotzinco, and Chololan. The history of Olmos's writings is described in Georges Baudot, *Utopia and History in Mexico: The First Chronicles of Mexican Civilization, 1520–1569*, transls., Bernard R. Ortiz de Montellano and Thelma Ortiz de Montellano (Niwot: University Press of Colorado, 1995). The *Leyenda de los soles* is dated 1558 and likely presents a narrative from a prehispanic codex. It describes the ages before the Fifth Sun, other creation stories, as well as the fall of Tollan, and the Mexica migration period. The *Anales de Cuauhtitlan* was composed between 1560 and about 1570, probably by one or more of the men who worked with Sahagún to compose the FC. It represents an alphabetized version of an annals history likely derived from, or at least influenced by, a xiuhpohualli or year-count history for the altepetl of Cuauhtitlan, though the text ranges widely among important altepeme in the Basin of Mexico. Several codices, especially the *Borgia* and others of the Borgia group, which includes the *Fejérváry-Mayer* referred to in this chapter, provide evidence through their vivid pictorials on eastern and southern Aztec ceremonies, covering the Puebla, Tlaxcala, and Veracruz areas. Some Borgia Group codices show Mixtec influences as well. Also note that in addition to several books of the FC (1–3, 7), with this chapter relying especially on Book 2, the PM also provides rich, detailed information on Aztec ceremonies and beliefs. In addition to his writings on Aztec history, Fray Durán provided great insight and detail about Aztec religion. His *Book of the Gods and Rites* is indispensable. Fray Toribio de Benavente, who became known as Motolinia, was one of the first twelve Franciscan missionaries sent to New Spain. His writings are early (dating probably to between the 1530s and about 1560). His masterwork, which included texts that today are published separately, was lost. But it is reconstructed in Toribio de Benavente Motolinia, *El libro perdido: ensayo de reconstrucción de la obra histórica extraviada de Fray Toribio* (Edmundo O'Gorman, ed., Mexico City: CONACULTA, 1989). Having lived in Tenochtitlan, Tetzcoco, and Tlaxcala, his histories offer many insights into Aztec religious and social life, though like the writing of other missionary friars, his goal of conversion influenced his perceptions. The great chronicler of the Franciscan evangelization efforts in New Spain, Gerónimo de Mendieta, also described Aztec religious and social life, with the text – influenced by the works of Olmos and Motolinia – completed in 1596. See www.cervantesvirtual.com/obra-visor/historia-eclesiastica-indiana–0/html. Another Franciscan writer who knew a variety of Aztec intellectuals, Juan de Torquemada, incorporated the writings of a number of chroniclers – especially Olmos, Motolinia, Sahagún, and Mendieta. Perhaps the least original of the Franciscan writers, he also had access to Indigenous intellectuals. His great work is known today as the *Monarquía Indiana*, 3 vols. (Mexico City: UNAM, [1609–1612]). It is a voluminous chronicle of Aztec religion, political history, and social history based upon his interviews, readings and copying from fellow missionaries' writings, and his wide-ranging experiences in a variety of Indigenous communities in the basin and beyond. While not focused on religion, Fernando Alva Ixtlilxochitl on Tetzcoco, Diego Muñoz Camargo on Tlaxcala, and Chimalpahin on Chalco all provide observations about religious ideas and practices. They wrote from the late sixteenth century to the early seventeenth.

H. B. Nicholson's "Religion in Pre-Hispanic Central Mexico," in *Handbook of Middle American Indians*, Vol. X (Austin: University of Texas Press), pp.395–446 remains the place to begin when reading about Aztec religion. Another classic article in that same volume deals with Aztec calendars, Alfonso Caso, "Calendrical Systems of Central Mexico," pp.333–348. For other in-depth discussions of Aztec calendars, see Michel Graulich, *Ritos aztecas: las fiestas de las veintenas* (Mexico City: INI, 1999); Ross Hassig, *Time, History and Belief in Aztec and Colonial Mexico* (Austin: University of Texas Press, 2001), and Ana María Díaz Alvaréz, *El cuerpo del tiempo: codices, cosmología y tradiciones cronográficas del centro de México* (Mexico City: UNAM and Bonilla Artigas Editores, 2019). Specifically on the question of whether the Aztecs took into account that the year was actually longer than 365 days, in addition to Graulich, see Rafael Tena, *El calendario mexica y la cronografía* (Mexico City: INAH, 1987). Exequiel Ezcurra, Paula Ezcurra, and Ben Meissner explain how Aztecs likely kept an accurate calendar that accounted for the extra quarter day each year for agriculture without shifting months in "Ancient Inhabitants of the Basin of Mexico Kept an Accurate Agricultural Calendar Using Sunrise Observatories and

Mountain Alignments," *Proceedings of the National Academy of Sciences* (2022) 119, pp.1–8. The Mexica New Fire ceremony of 1507 is described in detail in Book 7 of the FC as well as in Davíd Carrasco, *City of Sacrifice: The Aztec Empire and the Role of Violence in Civilization* (Boston: Beacon Press, 1999). The ancient Mesoamerican roots of fire ceremonies, especially ceremonies of renewal, using archaeological and ethnohistorical evidence are recounted in Christina M. Elson and Michael E. Smith, "Archaeological Deposits from the Aztec New Fire Ceremony," *Ancient Mesoamerica* 12 (2001), pp.25–42; and Kirby Farah, "The Light Burned Brightly: Postclassic New Fire Ceremonies of the Aztec and at Xaltocan in the Basin of Mexico," in Nancy Gonlin and David M. Reed, eds., *Night and Darkness in Ancient Mesoamerica* (Louisville, CO: University Press of Colorado, 2021), pp.257–280.

Essays on space and place can be found in Davíd Carrasco, ed., *Aztec Ceremonial Landscapes* (Niwot: University Press of Colorado, 1991). An important question about Aztec conceptions of space is whether they conceived of vertical space in layers or not. A variety of early colonial sources state or imply that they did including the HMP, the *Histoyre du Mechique*, the *Codex Vaticanus 3738* (also known as the *Codex Vaticanus A* or the *Codex Ríos*), and Books 3 and 6 of the FC as well as others, though these sources do not agree on the numbers of levels (especially upper levels, numbering either thirteen or nine) nor on their names. A variety of essays in Ana Maria Díaz Alvarez, ed., *Reshaping the World: Debates on Mesoamerican Cosmologies* (Louisville, CO: University Press of Colorado, 2020) question whether Aztecs conceived of the cosmos in vertical terms at all and raise questions about the influence of Christian ideas. Alfredo López Austin strongly defended the authenticity of much of the abundant textual and archaeological evidence on Aztec conceptions of vertical levels of space in "La verticalidad del cosmos," *Estudios de Cultura Náhuatl* 52 (2016), pp.119–150. For the Templo Mayor and a concise discussion of the building stages and meanings attached to the building, see Eduardo Matos Moctezuma, "The Templo Mayor of Tenochtitlan:

Bibliographic Essay

History and Interpretation," in Broda, D. Carrasco, and Matos Moctezuma, *The Great Temple of Tenochtitlan*, pp.15–60.

Building on the ideas of Arild Hvidtfeldt about Aztec beliefs in a "vital force" that underlay their conceptions of deities in *Teotl and Ixiptlatli: Some Central Conceptions in Ancient Mexican Religion, with a General Introduction on Cult and Myth* (Copenhagen: Munksgaard, 1958), Molly Bassett expanded greatly the understanding of the meanings and usages of "teo-" and "teotl," in *The Fate of Earthly Things: Aztec Gods and God-Bodies* (Austin: University of Texas Press, 2015). A sophisticated discussion of past and present Aztec/Nahua beliefs about divinity and the ways their ideas of a divine and unified cosmos have survived can be found in Alan R. Sandstrom and Pamela Effrein Sandstrom, *Pilgrimage to Broken Mountain: Nahua Sacred Journeys in Mexico's Huasteca Veracruzana* (Louisville, CO: University Press of Colorado, 2023). James Lockhart argued that the semantic range of the word "teotl" was quite wide, including strange, inexplicable, anomalous things, in "Sightings: Initial Nahua Reactions to Spanish Culture," in Stuart Schwartz, ed., *Implicit Understandings: Observing, Reporting, and Reflecting on the Encounters between Europeans and Other Peoples in the Early Modern Era* (Cambridge: Cambridge University Press, 1994), pp.218–248.

On deities, Nicholson's comprehensive treatment in "*Religion in Pre-Hispanic Central Mexico*" should be consulted. Guilhem Olivier's *Mockeries and Metamorphoses of an Aztec God: Tezcatlipoca, "Lord of the Smoking Mirror,"* (Boulder: University Press of Colorado, 2003), on one of the Aztecs' most important deities, offers many insights on Aztec religion. Also useful for its concise discussion of deities is Alfonso Caso, *The Aztecs: People of the Sun*, Lowell Dunham transl. (Norman: University of Oklahoma Press, 1958). On female deities in particular, including the cihuapipiltin and tzitzimime, the reader should examine Cecilia Klein, "The Shield Women: Resolution of an Aztec Gender Paradox," in Alana Cordy-Collins and Douglas Sharon, eds., *Current Topics in Aztec Studies: Essays in Honor of Dr. H.B. Nicholson* (San Diego: San Diego Museum of Man, 1993), pp.39–64; "Fighting with Femininity: Gender and War in Aztec Mexico," in Richard C. Trexler, ed., *Gender Rhetorics: Postures of Dominance and Submission in Human History* (Binghamton: Medieval and Renaissance Texts and Studies 113, SUNY Binghamton, 1994), pp.107–146; "The Devil and the Skirt: An Iconographic Inquiry into the Prehispanic Nature of the Tzitzimime," *Ancient Mesoamerica* 11 (2000), pp.1–26; "From Clay to Stone: The Demonization of the Aztec Goddess Cihuacoatl," in Jeremy D. Coltman and John M.D. Pohl, eds., *Sorcery in Mesoamerica* (Louisville, CO: University Press of Colorado, 2021), pp.330–380; and Elizabeth Hill Boone, "The Coatlicues at the Templo Mayor," *Ancient Mesoamerica* 10 (1999), pp.189–206. On deities of hunting, see Guilhem Olivier, *Cacería, sacrificio y poder en Mesoamérica: tras las huellas de Mixcóatl, "Serpiente de Nube"* (Mexico City: UNAM, Fondo de Cultura Económica, and Centro de Estudios Mexicanos y Centramericanos, 2015).

No primary source account fully describes the priestly hierarchy, but both the PM and Book 2 of the FC provides a listing of priestly titles for many temples as does Fray Durán in *Book of the Gods and Rites* who also discusses training and responsibilities. Muñoz Camargo describes a simpler two-level hierarchy for Tlaxcallan in the *Historia de Tlaxcala*. The PM and FC have listings of functions that female practitioners fulfilled: healing (especially, but not only, children), divination using maize kernels or cords, and removing dangerous substances. On priestesses, see Pilar Alberti Manzanares, "Mujeres sacerdotisas aztecas: las cihuatlamacazque mencionadas en dos manuscritos inéditos," *Estudios de Cultura Náhuatl* 24 (1994), pp.171–217. Both L. Marie Musgrave-Portilla, "The Nahualli or Transforming Wizard in Pre- and Postconquest Mesoamerica," *Journal of Latin American Lore* 8 (1982), pp.3–62 and Anderson Hagler, "Exhuming the Nahualli: Shapeshifting, Idolatry, and Orthodoxy in Colonial Mexico," *The Americas* 78 (2021), pp.197–228 discuss nahualli. Lisa Sousa provides insights into the spiritual aspects of ticitl, the physician/midwives, in *The Woman Who Turned into a Jaguar and Other Narratives of Native Women in Archives of Colonial*

Mexico (Stanford: Stanford University Press, 2017). Edward Anthony Polanco also explores their roles in "'I am just a Tiçitl': Decolonizing Central Mexican Nahua Female Healers, 1535-1635," *Ethnohistory* 65 (2018): pp.441-463.

Johanna Broda discusses at length the relationships between power, ceremonies, and the redistribution of wealth in "Los estamentos en el ceremonial mexica," in Pedro Carrasco, et al., *Estratificación social en la Mesoamérica prehispánica* (Mexico City: SEP-INAH, 1976), pp.37-66. The relationships among the ritualized killings of human beings, agriculture, and war and empire are the subject of an extensive secondary literature. Leonardo López Lújan discusses the numbers question in "Water and Fire: Archaeology in the Capital of the Mexica Empire," in Warwick Bray and Linda Manzanilla, eds., *The Archaeology of Mesoamerica* (London: British Museum Press), pp.32-49 as does Caroline Dodds Pennock, "Mass Murder or Religious Homicide? Rethinking Human Sacrifice and Interpersonal Violence in Aztec Society," *Historical Social Research/Historische Sozialforschung* 37 (2012), pp.276-302. Important general works on ritual human killings include Yolotl González Torres, *El sacrificio humano entre los mexicas* (Mexico City: INAH, 1985); D. Carrasco, *City of Sacrifice*, which covers the Tlacaxipehualiztli killings in detail; Ximena Chávez Balderas, "Sacrifice at the Templo Mayor of Tenochtitlan and Its Role in Regard to Warfare," in Andrew K. Scherer and John W. Verano, eds., *Embattled Bodies, Embattled Places: War in Pre-Columbian Mesoamerica and the Andes,*" (Washington, DC: Dumbarton-Oaks, 2014), pp.171-197, and *Sacrificio humano y tratamientos postsacrificiales en el Templo Mayor de Tenochtitlan,* (Mexico City: INAH, 2017); and Alfredo López Austin and Leonardo López Lujan, "El sacrificio humano entre los mexicas," *Arqueología Mexicana* 17 (2010), pp.24-33. An especially comprehensive discussion of the motivations behind ritual killings can be found in Michel Graulich, "Aztec Human Sacrifice as Expiation," *History of Religions* 39 (2000), pp.352-371. Catherine R. DiCesare discusses the ritual killings associated with the Ochpaniztli festivals

Bibliographic Essay

in *Sweeping the Way: Divine Transformation in the Aztec Festival of Ochpaniztli* (Boulder: University Press of Colorado, 2009). For the month of Panquetzaliztli, John F. Schwaller's book, *The Fifteenth Month: Aztec History in the Rituals of Panquezaliztli* (Norman: University of Oklahoma Press, 2019) is a methodological *tour de force* that sheds much light on the history, geography, sacrificial practices, and symbolism of this important ceremony. Guilhem Olivier discusses representations of the attitudes of a variety of those sacrificed in "'No estimavan en nada la muerte ...' El destino sacrificial en Mesoámerica: aceptación, rechazo y otras actitudes de las futuras víctimas," *Estudios de Cultura Náhuatl* 65 (2023): 75–114.

Elizabeth Graham makes the argument that ritual killings occurred in relation to war and empire, not religion, asserting that it was Spaniards who created the idea of "human sacrifice" in her book *Maya Christians and Their Churches in Sixteenth-Century Belize* (Gainesville: University Press of Florida, 2011). Others who profess that Aztecs did not engage in such practices and that Spaniards invented them include Peter Hassler, "*Human Sacrifice among the Aztecs?*," www.eccser.org/readings/readhassler.pdf (1992); and Kurly Tlapoyawa, "*Did 'Mexika Human Sacrifice' Exist?*" (n.d.). http://eaglefeather.org/series/Mexican%20Series/Did%20Mexica %20Human%20Sacrifice%20Exist.pdf. Bernard R. Ortiz de Montellano thoroughly evaluates and discredits the protein argument in "Aztec Cannibalism: An Ecological Necessity?" *Science* 299 (1978), pp.611–617. Lizzie Wade describes the tzompantli and skulls found by a team of archaeologists led by Raúl Barrera Rodríguez and Lorena Vázquez Vallín at the Templo Mayor site in "Feeding the Gods: Hundreds of Skulls Reveal Massive Scale of Human Sacrifice in Aztec Capital," *Science* 360 (2018), pp.1288–1292.

Extracted quotations come from Burkhart, "Mexica Women on the Home Front," p.41; The René Girard quote comes from *Violence and the Sacred*, transl. Patrick Gregory (Baltimore: The Johns Hopkins University Press, 1977), p.31, cited in D. Carrasco, *City of Sacrifice*, p.3; Durán, *History of the Indies*, p.173; D. Carrasco, *City of Sacrifice*, p.162.

3 Communities, Kingdoms, Empires

A number of primary sources discussed earlier in this essay contain evidence about the rulers of basin altepeme, not just on their roles but on their lives, successes and failures, their methods of gaining prestige, the costs of losing it, their marriages and families, and the wars they fought. These sources describe the conduct of warfare and the tribute paid when wars were lost, the internal structure of altepeme and their governance, the construction of confederations and development and shifting power structures within empires. Durán's historical volume and Alvarado Tezozomoc's *Historia mexicana* contribute much to the study of Mexica wars. Other sources such as Chimalpahin's annals as well as histories by Alva Ixtlilxochitl and Muñoz Camargo speak to the political histories of Chalco, Tetzcoco, and Tlaxcallan respectively but also provide some perspective on how these altepeme, especially their rulers, viewed Tenochtitlan and its leaders. Books 6 and 8 of the FC tell us a lot about rulership, especially for the Mexica. On tribute, the CM is essential; other sources that shed light on specific topics relating to politics are mentioned in the text of this chapter.

A recent comprehensive overview of the rise and structure of Aztec polities can be found in Lane F. Fargher, Richard E. Blanton, and Verenice Y. Heredia Espinoza, "Aztec State-Making, Politics, and Empires: The Triple Alliance," in *The Oxford Handbook of the Aztecs*, pp.143–159. Other important essays that treat political topics in that volume include Frances F. Berdan, "Structure of the Triple Alliance Empire," pp.439–450; and Marco Antonio Cervera Obregón, "Mexica War: New Research Perspectives," pp.451–462. Van Zantwijk reconstructs, to the extent possible, the early history of Tenochtitlan's political organization in *The Aztec Arrangement*. The role of founding couples is discussed by Stephanie Wood in "Power Differentials in Early Mesoamerican Gender Ideology: The Founding Couple," in Guilhem Olivier, ed., *Símbolos de poder in Mesoamérica* (Mexico City: UNAM, 2005), pp.517–531.

Bibliographic Essay

The "mother-father" as a way to conceptualize leadership is described by Susan Kellogg, "From Parallel and Equivalent to Separate but Unequal: Tenochca Mexica Women, 1500–1700," in *Indian Women of Early Mexico*, pp.123–143; and Julia Madajczak, in "Life-Giver: The Pre-Hispanic Nahua Concept of 'Father' through Colonial Written Sources," *Ancient Mesoamerica* 28 (2017), pp.371–381.

For the development of city-state political structures and the rise of and organization of confederations and empires, see J. Rounds, "Lineage, Class, and Power in the Aztec State," *American Ethnologist* 6 (1979), pp.73–86; Edward E. Calnek, "Patterns of Empire Formation in the Valley of Mexico, Late Postclassic Period, 1200–1521," in George A. Collier, Renato I. Rosaldo, and John D. Wirth, eds., *The Inca and Aztec States 1400–1800: Anthropology and History*, (New York: Academic Press, 1982), pp.43–62; and Elizabeth M. Brumfiel, "Aztec State Making: Ecology, Structure, and the Origin of the State," *American Anthropologist* 85 (1983), pp.261–284. The politics of units within altepeme is given in-depth treatment in Benjamin D. Johnson, *Pueblos within Pueblos: Tlaxilacalli Communities in Acolhuacan, Mexico, ca. 1272–1692* (Boulder: University Press of Colorado, 2017). Mary Hodge, *Aztec City-States* (Ann Arbor: Museum of Anthropology, University of Michigan, 1984); and James Lockhart, *The Nahuas after the Conquest: A Social and Cultural History of the Indians of Central Mexico, Sixteenth through Eighteenth Centuries* (Stanford: Stanford University Press, 1992) provide extensive ethnohistorical information on altepeme, their political organization, functionaries within them, and the role of these units in political, economic, social, and cultural life. For the tlayacatl in particular, see Susan Schroeder, *Chimalpahin and the Kingdoms of Chalco* (Tucson: University of Arizona Press). The nature of altepeme from an archaeological perspective is covered by Smith, *Aztec City-State Capitals*. Variations in political structures are discussed in Lane F. Fargher, Verenice Y. Heredia Espinoza, and Richard E. Blanton in "Alternative Pathways to Power in Late Postclassic Highland Mesoamerica," *Journal of*

Bibliographic Essay

Anthropological Archaeology 30 (2011), pp.306–326. Blanton and Fargher's book *Collective Action in the Formation of Pre-Modern States* (New York: Springer, 2008) examines forms of governance through the lens of collective action across multiple societies, including the Aztecs. The possibility of commoners holding high positions in military governance is covered in Virve Piho, "Tlacatecutli, Tlacochtecutli, Tlacateccatl y Tlacochcalcatl," *Estudios de Cultura Náhuatl* 10 (1972), pp.315–328. On law in Aztec societies, especially the altepetl of Tetzcoco, see Jerome A. Offner, *Law and Politics in Aztec Texcoco* (Cambridge: Cambridge University Press, 1983).

A detailed description of the role of the cihuacoatl and life of Tlacaelel can be found in Susan Schroeder, *Tlacaelel Remembered: Mastermind of the Aztec Empire* (Norman: University of Oklahoma Press, 2016). For the political roles of "women of discord," see Susan D. Gillespie, *The Aztec Kings: The Construction of Rulership in Mexica History* (Tucson: University of Arizona Press, 1989). This book also relates the many and often contradictory accounts of the founding of and succession patterns within the Tenochca Mexica ruling dynasty.

The structure of the Excan tlatoloyan empire is discussed in detail by Pedro Carrasco, *The Tenochca Empire of Ancient Mexico: The Triple Alliance of Tenochtitlan, Tetzcoco, and Tlacopan* (Norman: University of Oklahoma, 1999), which builds on the pioneering efforts to map and analyze this empire in Robert H. Barlow, *The Extent of the Empire of the Culhua Mexica* (Ibero-Americana, 28, 1949). For the term "Excan tlatoloyan" and its variations, see María del Carmen Herrera Meza, Alfredo López Austin, and Rodrigo Martínez Baracs, "El nombre náhuatl de la Triple Alianza," *Estudios de Cultura Náhuatl* 46 (2013), pp.7–35. Many topics related to the functioning of Triple Alliance imperial practices are covered in Frances F. Berdan, Richard E. Blanton, Elizabeth Hill Boone, Mary G. Hodge, Michael E. Smith, and Emily Umberger in *Aztec Imperial Strategies* (Washington, DC: Dumbarton Oaks, 1996). Aztec warfare, empire building, and the role of tlatoque in wars are analyzed by Ross Hassig, *Aztec Warfare: Imperial Expansion and Political Control* (Norman:

University of Oklahoma Press, 1988). Susan D. Gillespie questions whether there was a Triple Alliance empire in "The Aztec Triple Alliance – A Postconquest Tradition," in Elizabeth Hill Boone and Tom Cummins, *Native Traditions in the Postconquest World* (Washington DC: Dumbarton Oaks, 1998), pp.233–263; Ross Hassig covers Mesoamerican warfare in longer term perspective in *War and Society in Ancient Mesoamerica* (Berkeley: University of California Press, 1992). On weaponry, in particular, Jesús Monjarás-Ruiz discusses that topic in detail, "Panorama general de la guerra entre los Aztecas," *Estudios de Cultura Náhuatl* 12 (1976), pp.241–266. The way the Aztec accoutrements of war could inspire fear in opponents is explored in Justyna Olko, *Insignia of Rank in the Nahua World: From the Fifteenth to the Seventeenth Century* (Boulder: University Press of Colorado, 2014).

The characteristics of and motivations behind xochiyaoyotl are discussed in Frederic Hicks, "'Flowery War' in Aztec History," *American Ethnologist* 6 (1979), pp.87–92; Barry L. Isaac, "The Aztec 'Flowery War': A Geopolitical Explanation," *Journal of Anthropological Research* 39 (1983), pp.415–432; and Laura Alicino, "El concepto de xochiyaoyotl en el mundo prehispánico según las Relaciones de Chimalpahin Cuauhtlehuanitzin," *Ancient Mesoamerica* 30 (2019), pp.235–244.

Examples of women's fighting come from the primary sources discussed above as well the *Anales de Cuauhtitlan* and the *Anales de Tlatelolco*, an important section of which is translated into English by James Lockhart in *We People Here: Nahuatl Accounts of the Conquest of Mexico* (Berkeley: University of California Press, 1993). Women, gendered symbolism, and war among the Aztecs are discussed by Klein, "Fighting with Femininity." June Nash discusses gender inequality in "The Aztecs and the Ideology of Male Dominance," *Signs* 4 (1978), pp.349–362 as does María Rodríguez Shadow, *La mujer azteca*, 3rd ed. (Toluca, Mexico: Universidad Autónoma del Estado de México, 1991). Gender complementarity and parallelism is discussed by Louise Burkhart in "Mexica Women on the Home Front" and Kellogg, "From Parallel and Equivalent to Separate but Unequal."

Pedro Carrasco analyzed the role of marriage in structuring inter-dynastic relations in "Royal Marriages in Ancient Mexico," in H. R. Harvey and Hanns J. Prem, eds., *Explorations in Ethnohistory: Indians of Central Mexico in the Sixteenth Century* (Albuquerque: University of New Mexico Press, 1984), pp.41–81. The place of marriages in Aztec politics, uniting or disrupting dynasties and their alliances, is further discussed in Lori Boornazian Diel, "Till Death Do Us Part: Unconventional Marriages as Aztec Political Strategy," *Ancient Mesoamerica* 18 (2007), pp.259–272; and Camilla Townsend, "Polygyny and the Divided Altepetl: The Tetzcocan Key to Pre-conquest Nahua Politics," in Jongsoo Lee and Galen Brokaw, eds., *Texcoco: Prehispanic and Colonial Perspectives* (Boulder: University Press of Colorado, 2014), pp.93–116.

The FC (Books 1 and 3) provide narratives about the creation of the sun and the struggle between Huitzilopochtli and Coyolxauhqui. Durán's *Historia*, Alvarado Tezozomoc's *Crónica mexicana*, and the *Leyenda de los Soles* provide related narratives. Elizabeth Brumfiel explains the importance of agriculture-related rites in communities that did not emphasize warfare to the degree the Mexica and Tlaxcalteca did in "Aztec Hearts and Minds: Religion and the State in the Aztec Empire," in Susan Alcock, Terence D'Altroy, Kathleen Morrison, and Carla Sinopoli, eds., *Empires: Perspectives from Archaeology and History* (New York: Cambridge University Press, 2001), pp.283–310.

Extracted quotations come Johnson, *Pueblos within Pueblos*, p.41 and Ann Laura Stoler, *Duress: Imperial Durabilities in Our Times* (Durham: Duke University Press, 2016), p.56.

4 Creating Value: Producing, Exchanging, Consuming

The most important primary sources for this chapter are Books 9 and 10 of the FC, which offer much information on merchants, artisans, and the organization of production, buying, and selling in markets. On tribute, of course the CM is fundamental. Other primary sources are mentioned in the text, but the second letter of Hernan Cortés to the king of Spain, *Five Letters of Cortés to the Emperor*, transl., J. Bayard Morris (New York: W.W. Norton, 1969) gives a vivd, if oft-quoted, description of the main marketplace in Tlatelolco, the largest and most important in the Basin of Mexico. Another source referred to in this chapter are early colonial last wills and testaments that give insights into property – land, houses, and smaller items – especially relevant for understanding land categories for this chapter and the familial relationships discussed in Chapter 5. Important collections of wills include S. L. Cline and Miguel León-Portilla, eds., *The Testaments of Culhuacan* (Los Angeles: UCLA Latin American Center, 1984); Susan Kellogg and Matthew Restall, *Dead Giveaways: Indigenous Testaments of Colonial Mesoamerica and the Andes* (Salt Lake City: University of Utah Press, 1998); Teresa Rojas Rabiela, et al., eds., *Vidas y bienes olvidadas*, 5 vols., (Mexico City: CIESAS, 1999–2004); Caterina Pizzigoni, ed., *Testaments of Toluca* (Stanford: Stanford University Press and UCLA Latin American Studies Center, 2007); and Mark Christensen and Jonathan Truitt, eds., *Native Wills from the Colonial Americas: Dead Giveaways in a New World* (Salt Lake City: University of Utah Press, 2016).

On environments and agricultural productivity in the Basin of Mexico, see William T. Sanders, Jeffrey R. Parsons, and Robert S. Santley, *The Basin of Mexico: Ecological Processes in the Evolution of a Civilization* (New York: Academic Press, 1979), and Jeffrey R. Parsons, "Environment and Rural Economy," in Elizabeth M. Brumfiel and Gary M. Feinman, eds., *The Aztec World* (New York: Abrams, 2008), 23–52. "El metepantle (milpa entre magueyes) antiguo sistema con futuro sostenible" by Gustavo Viniegra González, https://invdes.com.mx/politica-cyt-i/el-metepantle-milpa-entre-magueyes-antiguo-sistema-con-futuro-sostenible/ (August 2019), describes an ancient agricultural practice still in use today that dates back at least to the Aztecs. Land tenure, classifications, and patterns of land transmission, are discussed in Paul Kirchhoff, "Land Tenure in Ancient Mexico, A Preliminary

Sketch," *Revista Mexicana de Estudios Antropológicos* 14 (1st part, 1954–1955), pp.351–361; H. R. Harvey, "Aspects of Land Tenure in Ancient Mexico," in *Explorations in Ethnohistory*, pp.83–102; S. L. Cline, *Colonial Culhuacan, 1580–1600: A Social History of an Aztec Town* (Albuquerque: University of New Mexico Press, 1986); Charles Gibson, *The Aztecs under Spanish Rule* (Stanford: Stanford University Press, 1964); and Lockhart, *The Nahuas after the Conquest.*

Aztec agriculture is discussed in detail by Teresa Rojas Rabiela in *Las siembras de ayer: la agricultura indígena del siglo XVI* (Mexico City: SEP and CIESAS, 1988). Recent review essays that describe Aztec agricultural techniques and impact on the basin landscape include Emily McClung de Tapia and Diana Martínez Yrizar, "Aztec Agricultural Production in a Historical Ecological Perspective," pp.175–188; and Christopher T. Morehart, "Aztec Agricultural Strategies: Intensification, Landesque Capital, and the Sociopolitics of Production," pp.263–279, both found in *The Oxford Handbook of the Aztecs*. An important aspect of Aztec agricultural productivity was the use of chinampa agriculture for which there is an extensive literature. Works to start with include Pedro Armillas, "Gardens in Swamps," *Science* 174 (1971), pp.653–671; William E. Doolittle, *Canal Irrigation in Prehistoric Mexico* (Austin: University of Texas Press, 1990); Teresa Rojas Rabiela, ed., *Presente, pasado y future de las chinampas* (Mexico City: CIESAS, 1995). A recent discussion of chinampas from an ecological perspective in the altepetl of Xochimilco, where these plots still remain in use, is to be found in Richard M. Conway, *Islands in the Lake: Environment and Ethnohistory in Xochimilco, New Spain* (Cambridge: Cambridge University Press, 2021). For the rituals for water and plant fertility, see Johanna Broda, "Las fiestas aztecas de los dioses de la lluvia," *Revista Española de Antropología Americana* 6 (1971), pp.245–327 and "The Sacred Landscape of Aztec Calendar Festivals: Myth, Nature, and Society," in *Aztec Ceremonial Landscapes*, pp.74–120.

Bibliographic Essay

Elizabeth M. Brumfiel discusses households and crafts production in "Elite and Utilitarian Crafts in the Aztec State," in Elizabeth M. Brumfiel and Timothy Earle, eds. *Specialization, Exchange, and Complex Societies* (Cambridge: Cambridge University Press, 1987), pp.102–118 as does Kenneth G. Hirth, "Craft Production, Household Diversification, and Domestic Economy in Prehispanic Mesoamerica," in Kenneth G. Hirth, ed., *Housework: Craft Production and Domestic Economy in Ancient Mesoamerica*, Washington, DC: Archaeological Publications No. 19, American Anthropological Association (2009), pp.13–32. On cotton and textile production, see Frances F. Berdan, "Cotton in Aztec Mexico: Production, Distribution, and Use," *Mexican Studies/Estudios Mexicanos* 3 (1987), pp.235–262. Essays describing other forms of craft production such as of pottery, obsidian blades, as well as metallurgy to name several can be found in *The Oxford History of the Aztecs*. On the meanings and production of Aztec feather works, see Alessandra Russo, "Plumes of Sacrifice: Transformations in Sixteenth-Century Mexican Feather Art," *RES: Anthropology and Aesthetics* 42 (2002), pp.225–250. On women as weavers, see Elizabeth M. Brumfiel, "Weaving and Cooking: Women's Production in Aztec Mexico," in Joan M. Gero and Margaret W. Conkey, eds., *Engendering Archaeology: Women and Prehistory* (Oxford: Blackwell, 1991), pp.224–251; and Sharisse D. McCafferty and Geoffrey G. McCafferty, "Spinning and Weaving as Female Gender Identity in Post-Classic Central Mexico," in Margot Blum Schevill, Janet C. Berlo, and Edward B. Dwyer, eds., *Textile Traditions of Mesoamerica and the Andes: An Anthology* (New York: Garland, 1991), pp.19–44. Patricia Rieff Anawalt discusses Aztec clothing, its uses, production, and trade in *Indian Clothing before Cortés: Mesoamerican Costumes from the Codices* (Norman: University of Oklahoma Press, 1981). Cecelia F. Klein and Thelma Sullivan discuss cotton, spinning and weaving, female deities, and the place of spinning and weaving in Aztec cosmological thinking in (respectively) "Woven Heaven, Tangled Earth: A Weaver's Paradigm of the Mesoamerican Cosmos," in Anthony F. Aveni and Gary Urton, eds., *Ethnoastronomy and Archaeoastronomy in the American Tropics*, Annals of the New York Academy of Sciences 385 (New York: NY Academy of Sciences, 1982), pp.1–35 and "Tlazolteotl-Ixcuina: The Great Spinner and Weaver," in Elizabeth Hill Boone, ed., *The Art and Iconography of Late Post-Classic Central Mexico* (Washington, DC: Dumbarton Oaks, 1982), pp.7–36. For obsidian production, see Cynthia Otis Charlton, Thomas H. Charlton, and Deborah L. Nichols, "Aztec Household-Based Craft Production: Archaeological Evidence from the City-State of Otumba, Mexico," in Robert S. Santley and Kenneth G. Hirth, eds., *Prehispanic Domestic Units in Western Mesoamerica: Studies of the Household, Compound, and Residence* (Boca Raton; CRC Press, 1993), pp.147–171; Cynthia Otis Charlton, "Obsidian as Jewelry: Lapidary Production in Aztec Otumba, Mexico," *Ancient Mesoamerica* 4 (1993), pp. 231–243; and Alejandro Pastrana, *La explotación azteca de la obsidiana de la Sierra de las Navajas* (Mexico City: INAH, 1998); *La distribución de obsidiana de la Triple Alianza en la Cuenca de México* (Mexico City: INAH, 2007).

For Aztec trade and commerce (and an excellent bibliography on the large literature on those subjects), see Hirth, *The Aztec Economic World*. For the tlamemeque and other aspects of the distribution of goods, see Ross Hassig, *Trade, Tribute, and Transportation: The Sixteenth-Century Political Economy of the Valley of Mexico* (Norman: University of Oklahoma Press, 1987). Essays on economic topics in Michael E. Smith and Frances F. Berdan, eds., *The Postclassic Mesoamerican World* (Salt Lake City: University of Utah Press, 2003) put the Aztec economy in a broader and very dynamic Mesoamerican context, including Michael E. Smith's essay on "Key Commodities," pp.117–125 about the major items made or traded for by Aztecs.

For Aztec class structure, see Frederic Hicks, "The Middle Class in Ancient Central Mexico," *Journal of Anthropological Research* 55 (1999), pp.409–427; and Michael E. Smith and Frederic Hicks, "Inequality and Social Class in Aztec Society," in *The Oxford Handbook of the Aztecs*, pp.423–436.

On laborers, especially the mayeque and tlacotin, see Ursula Dyckerhoff and Hanns S. Prem, "La estratificación social en Huexotzinco," in Pedro Carrasco et al., *Estratificación social en la Mesoamérica prehispánica* (Mexico City: SEP-INAH, 1976), pp.157–180. Carlos Bosch García, *La esclavitud entre los Aztecas* (Mexico City: El Colegio de México, 1944) and Yolotl González Torres, "La esclavitud entre los Mexica," in *Estratificación social en la Mesoamérica prehispánica* discuss the history of slavery in detail.

On long-distance trade and traders, in addition to Hirth, *The Aztec Economic World*, see Miguel Acosta Saignes, "Los pochteca: ubicación de los mercaderes en la estructura social tenochca," *Acta Antropológica* (1, 1945); Frances F. Berdan, "Principles of Regional and Long-Distance Trade in the Aztec Empire," in J. Kathryn Josserand and Karen Dakin, eds., *Smoke and Mist: Mesoamerican Studies in Memory of Thelma D. Sullivan* (Oxford: BAR International Series 402, 1988), Vol. II, pp.539–656; and Janine Gasco and Frances Berdan, "International Trade Centers," in *The Postclassic Mesoamerican World*, pp.109–116. On Aztec currencies and exchange values, see Jacqueline de Durand-Forest, "Cambios económicos y moneda entre los Aztecas," *Estudios de Cultura Náhuatl* 9 (1971), pp.105–124 and Hirth, *The Aztec Economic World*.

Extracted quotations come from the *FC 6*, p.168; *FC 10*, p.46; Motolinia, *El libro perdido*, p.406; Durán, *History of the Indies of New Spain*, p.209; Hassig, *Aztec Warfare*, p.41; Durán, *History of the Indies of New Spain*, p.336, 366; Cortés, *Five Letters*, p.87.

5 Sex and the Altepetl: Gender, Sexuality, and Aztec Family Values

The primary sources used in this chapter have, for the most part, been described in preceding chapters and will be mentioned in the text when relevant. But one type of source upon which analysis of household size and structure rests – an important theme – has not previously been discussed. This source is the early census material, ca. 1540s, from communities near Tetzcoco, Cuauhnahuac, Tepoztlan, and the Morelos region. All these areas were east and somewhat south of Tenochtitlan. They include house-to-house population counts undertaken, most likely, to calculate numbers of tributaries. They describe kin relationships within households and sometimes include information on who was or was not baptized, lands that household members farmed, and the tribute payments made by household heads. For Tepoztlan, see data and analysis in Jerome Offner, "Household Organization in the Texcocan Heartland," in *Explorations in Ethnohistory*, pp.127–146; H. R. Harvey, "Household and Family Structure in Early Colonial Tepetlaoztoc: An Analysis of the Códice de Santa María Asunción," *Estudios de Cultura Náhuatl* 18 (1986), pp.275–294; and the *Codex Vergara*, Barbara J. Williams and Frederic Hicks, eds., *El códice Vergara: edición facsimilar con comentario: pintura indígena de casas, campos y organización social de Tepetlaoztoc a mediados del siglo XVI* (Mexico City: UNAM and Apoyo al Desarollo de Archivos y Bibliotecas de México, 2011). For Cuauhnahuac, see Eike Hinz, Claudine Hartau, and Marie Luise Heimann-Koenen, eds. and transls., *Aztekischer Zensus. Zur indianischen Wirtschaft und Gesellschaft im Marquesado um 1540: Aus dem "Libro de Tributos" (Col. Ant. Ms. 551) im Archivo Histórico, México*, 2 vols., (Hanover: Verlag für Ethnologie, 1983); and Brígida von Mentz, *Cuauhnáhuac 1450–1675, su historia indígena y documentos en "mexicano," cambio y continuidad de una cultura nahua* (Mexico City: Miguel Ángel Porrúa, 2008). On Tepoztlan, see Julia Madajczak, ed., *Fragments of the Sixteenth-Century Nahuatl Census from the Jagiellonian Library: A Lost Manuscript* (Leiden and Boston: Brill, 2021), and for Morelos, see Pedro Carrasco, "Family Structure of 16th-Century Tepoztlan," in Robert A. Manners, ed., *Process and Pattern in Culture* (Chicago, Aldine, 1964), pp.185–210; and "The Joint Family in Ancient Mexico: The Case of Molotla," in Hugo Nutini, Pedro Carrasco, and

James M. Taggart, eds., *Essays on Mexican Kinship* (Pittsburgh: University of Pittsburgh Press, 1976), pp.45–64; S. L. Cline, ed. and transl., *The Book of Tributes: Early Sixteenth-Century Nahuatl Censuses* (Los Angeles: UCLA Latin American Center Publications, 1993) presents an English translation of one volume of the Morelos material. Another source that adds information on the inheritance of property (land, houses, items owned by household members) are wills. Patterns of property transmission provide information about household composition and relationships among household members, other family members, and a variety of other individuals. Information on collections of early colonial Nahuatl-language wills translated into English or Spanish can be found in the section of this essay on Chapter 4.

The literature relating to topics covered in this chapter is vast. Several works provide information on gender, family, households, socialization and education, and the life cycle relevant to many of the chapter's topics. These include Susan Kellogg, *Weaving the Past: A History of Latin America's Indigenous Women from the Prehispanic Period to the Present* (Oxford and New York: Oxford University Press, 2005); Pennock, *Bonds of Blood*; and Sousa, *The Woman Who Turned into a Jaguar*. While some interpretations in Alfredo López Austin, *El cuerpo humano: las concepciones de los antiguous nahuas*, 2 vols. (Mexico City: UNAM, 1980) have come into question, the book remains essential for examining Aztec thought on the body, sexuality, and the life cycle. Although I consulted the Spanish-language publication, it has been translated into English as *The Human Body and Ideology: Concepts of the Ancient Nahuas*, Thelma Ortiz de Montellano and Bernard Ortiz de Montellano, transls., 2 vols., (Salt Lake City: University of Utah Press, 1988).

In addition to López Austin's discussion of how fetuses were formed in *El cuerpo humano*, the father's contribution is analyzed by Madajczak, in "Life-Giver: The Pre-Hispanic Nahua Concept of 'Father'." The relationship between words for bone and semen is discussed in Richard Haly, "Bare Bones:

Rethinking Mesoamerican Divinity," *History of Religions* 31 (1992), pp.269–304. The literature on Aztec sexuality includes Guilhem Olivier, "Homosexualidad y prostitución entre los nahuas y otros pueblos del posclásico," in Pablo Escalante Gonzalbo, ed., *Mesoamérica y los ambitos indígenas de la Nueva España* (Mexico City: El Colegio de México, 2004), Vol. I, pp.301–338; Pete Sigal, "The *Cuiloni*, the *Patlache*, and the Abominable Sin: Homosexualities in Early Colonial Nahua Society," *Hispanic American Historical Review* 85 (2005), pp.555–594 and *The Flower and the Scorpion: Sexuality and Ritual in Early Nahua Culture* (Durham: Duke University Press, 2011); and Lisa Sousa, "Flowers and Speech in Discourses on Deviance in Book 10," in *The Florentine Codex: An Encyclopedia*, pp.184–199. Rosemary A. Joyce discusses the development of gender identity in "Girling the Girl and Boying the Boy: The Production of Adulthood in Ancient Mesoamerica," *World Archaeology* 31 (2000), pp.473–483. The plasticity of Aztec gender roles, created and performed, is described in Joyce's book *Gender and Power in Prehispanic Mesoamerica* (Austin: University of Texas Press, 2000). These discussions of the development of gender identities can be compared to earlier works that argued for more fixity and the low status of women such as June Nash, "The Aztecs and the Ideology of Male Dominance," *Signs* 4 (1978), pp.349–362; and Rodríguez-Shadow, *La mujer azteca*. Cecilia F. Klein discusses gender plasticity and flexibility in "None of the Above: Gender Ambiguity in Nahua Ideology," in Cecelia F. Klein, ed., *Gender in Pre-Hispanic America* (Washington, DC: Dumbarton Oaks, 2001), pp.183–253.

Alberti Manzanares discusses the education of priestesses in "Mujeres sacerdotisas aztecas." Miguel León-Portilla provides the example of a woman song writer in *Fifteen Poets of the Aztec World* (Norman: University of Oklahoma Press, 1992), and Dominique Raby elaborates on themes in songs relating to love and sexuality and considers the possibilities of women composers in "Xochiquetzal en el cuicacalli. Cantos de amor y voces femeninas entre los antiguos nahuas," *Estudios de Cultura*

Bibliographic Essay

Náhuatl 30 (1999), pp.203–229. Beyond the tonalamatl marriage prognostications found in the *Codex Borgia*, see Boone, *Cycles of Time and Meaning* for a discussion of prognostication sections in a variety of codices. On the circumstances, complications, and implications of polygynous marriages, in addition to Camilla Townsend's "Polygyny and the Divided Altepetl," see "'What in the World Have You Done to Me, My Lover?' Sex, Servitude, and Politics among the Pre-Conquest Nahuas as Seen in the *Cantares Mexicanos*," *The Americas* 62 (2006), pp.349–389; Kay A. Read and Jane Rosenthal, "The Chalcan Woman's Song: Sex as a Political Metaphor in Fifteenth-Century Mexico," *The Americas* 62 (2006), pp.313–348; Ross Hassig, *Polygamy and the Rise and Demise of the Aztec Empire* (Albuquerque: University of New Mexico Press, 2016); and Katarzyna Granicka, "Marital Practices of the Nahuas and Imposed Sociocultural Change in Sixteenth-Century Mexico," *Ethnohistory* 69 (2022), pp.81–100.

Aztec housing is discussed in Edward Calnek, "Conjunto urbano y modelo residencial"; Susan Kellogg, "The Social Organization of Households among the Tenochca Mexica before and after Conquest," in Robert S. Santley and Kenneth G. Hirth, eds., *Prehispanic Domestic Units in Western Mesoamerica: Studies of the Household, Compound, and Residence* (Boca Raton: CRC Press, 1993), pp.207–224; and Michael E. Smith, "Houses and the Settlement Hierarchy in Late Postclassic Morelos: A Comparison of Archaeology and Ethnohistory," in Santley and Hirth, *Prehispanic Domestic Units in Western Mesoamerica*, 191–206. Susan Toby Evans summarizes and updates her extensive research on rulers' palaces in "Aztec Palaces and Gardens, Intertwined Evolution," in *The Oxford Handbook of the Aztecs*, pp.229–245. For the dimensions of palaces, see Smith, *Aztec City-State Capitals*. On the changing housing patterns of Xaltocan see Elizabeth M. Brumfiel, *Production and Power at Postclassic Xaltocan* (Mexico City and Pittsburgh: INAH and University of Pittsburgh Press, 2005); and Kristin DeLucia and Lisa Overholtzer, "Everyday Action and the Rise and Decline of

Bibliographic Essay

Ancient Polities: Household Strategy and Political Change in Postclassic Xaltocan, Mexico," *Ancient Mesoamerica* 25 (2014), pp.441–458. David M. Carballo discusses the diversity of household organization in Aztec and other Mesoamerican societies of the late Postclassic in "Advances in the Household Archaeology of Highland Mesoamerica," *Journal of Archaeological Research* 19 (2011), pp.133–189.

On Aztec concepts of kinship and how these relate to household organization, see Offner, *Law and Politics in Aztec Texcoco*, and Susan Kellogg, "Kinship and Social Organization in Early Colonial Tenochtitlan," in *Supplement to the Handbook of Middle American Indians*, Ethnohistory (ed., Ronald Spores, with the assistance of Patricia A. Andrews., Austin: University of Texas Press, Vol. IV, pp.103–121). Lockhart's *Nahuas after the Conquest* also contains an extensive discussion of kinship terminology and how it changed after colonial rule became established. Residence after marriage, especially for young women, is discussed by Cline in *The Book of Tributes* and by Sousa in *The Woman Who Turned into a Jaguar*. House societies are discussed in Rosemary A. Joyce and Susan D. Gillespie, eds., in *Beyond Kinship: Social and Material Reproduction in House Societies* (Philadelphia: University of Pennsylvania Press, 2000). P. Carrasco discusses the unity of household groups in "Social Organization of Ancient Mexico."

In addition to Pennock's excellent discussion of old age and death in *Bonds of Blood*, see Ximena Chávez Balderas, *Rituales funerarios en el Templo Mayor de Tenochtitlan* (Mexico City: INAH, 2007); and Kay A. Read, "Death and the Tlatoani: The Land of Death, Rulership, and Ritual," in *Representing Aztec Ritual* pp.143–174. Archaeologists' findings on Aztec burials are summarized by Lisa Overholtzer, "Aztec Domestic Ritual," *The Oxford Handbook of the Aztecs*, pp.623–639. For the discussion of souls, see López Austin, *Cuerpo humano*; Jill McKeever Furst, *The Natural History of the Soul in Ancient Mexico* (New Haven: Yale University Press, 1995); and Justyna Olko's and Julia Madajczak's important revisionist work, "An Animating Principle in Confrontation with

Christianity: De(re)constructing the Nahua 'Soul'," *Ancient Mesoamerica* 30 (2019), 75–88. For ceremonies honoring the dead, see Hugo G. Nutini, "Pre-Hispanic Components of the Syncretic Cult of the Dead in Mesoamerica," *Ethnology* 27 (1988), pp.57–78.

The role of elder sister deities in migration and group and altepeme formation is discussed by Schroeder in "Chimalpahin and Why Women Matter in History." Diel considers the role of Moquihuix's wife in the Tenochca war with Tlatelolco in detail in "Till Death Do Us Part." Pennock identifies many women of discord in Aztec narratives and argues that conflict associated with women reflected their power in "Women of Discord: Female Power in Aztec Thought," *The Historical Journal* 61 (2018), pp.275–299.

Extracted quotations come from the *FC 6*, p.216; Joyce, "Girling the Girl and Boying the Boy"; *FC 6*, p.214; Fray Juan Bautista, ed., Miguel León-Portilla, transl., Librado Silva Galeana, *Huehuetlatolli. Que contiene las pláticas que los padres y madres hicieron a sus hijos, y los señores a sus uasallos, todas llenas de doctrina moral y política* (México City: Comisión Nacional Conmemorativa del V Centenario del Encuentro de Dos Mundos, 1988 [1600]), cited in Arthur J. O. Anderson, "Aztec Wives," in *Indian Women of Early Mexico*, pp.61–62; *FC 3*, p.157; Durán, *Book of the Gods and Rites*, p.149; *FC 4*, p.114; Zorita, *Life and Labor in Ancient Mexico*, p.125; *Anales de Cauhtitlan*, pp.48–49; *Codex Chimalpahin*, Vol.I, p.138.

6 Resilience: Part One, Aztec Intellectual Life

Some primary sources used in this chapter such as the CM have already been described in earlier chapters. In addition to many art pieces analyzed by art historians to discuss Aztec art, I also rely on texts relating to Indigenous medical practices and writing, especially songs. Sahagún investigated Aztec medicine in some detail in Tepepolco as shown in the PM and then enlarged upon his discussions of disease and herbal cures in

Books 10 and 11 of the FC. Durán also commented on Aztec curing practices. While Sahagún censored some of the medical material to remove discussion of the spiritual causes of disease, the descriptions of disease in the FC are somewhat less influenced by European concepts of disease than those in three other major sources, the *Libellus*, Hernández's *Historia natural*, and Ruiz de Alarcón's *Tratado de las Idolatrías*. The *Libellus de Medicinalibus Indorum Herbis, An Aztec Herbal: The Classic Codex of 1552*, transl. and ed., William Gates (Mineola, NY: Dover Publications, 2000) was written in 1552 at the behest of a viceroy's son, Francisco de Mendoza, for presentation to the Spanish monarch Charles V to support Indigenous religious education being provided by the Colegio de la Santa Cruz in Tlatelolco. Written by Martín de la Cruz, an Aztec physician, then translated into Latin by an Aztec teacher at the colegio, Juan Badiano, the text, despite Indigenous authorship and translation, shows heavy influence by European medical ideas. Between 1572 and 1577, Francisco Hernández, *Historia natural de Nueva España*, 2 vols. (Mexico City: UNAM, 1959 [1577]), traveled around central Mexico collecting information about medicinal plants as directed by the next Spanish monarch Philip II in order to investigate the effectiveness of Indigenous medicine. His training in European medicine colored the manuscript he produced. However, his is the longest listing of plants used to cure and includes some information on Aztec concepts about disease, even though these are filtered through European ideas about humoral flow and the European classification of plants as hot, cold, wet, or dry which is very different from Aztec ideas about disease causation, hot and cold properties, and herbal effects. Ruiz de Alarcón's 1629 *Treatise on Superstitions*, as it is known in English, was the product of his efforts as an ecclesiastical judge to find and stamp out native idolatry in central Mexico. His hatred for both native beliefs and the medical syncretism that the continuing use of native medicines and clandestine supernaturally based practices represented while ignoring Nahua empirically based curing give his text a very unbalanced quality. Yet he provides insights into some of the medicines used as well as how the Aztecs made medical use of divination. For this text, see Hernando Ruiz de Alarcón, *Treatise on the Heathen Superstitions That Today Live among the Indians Native to This New Spain, 1629*, transls. and eds., J. Richard Andrews and Ross Hassig (Norman: University of Oklahoma Press, 1984). On these sources and many aspects of the practice of medicine, including the health implications of dirt, see Bernard R. Ortiz de Montellano, *Aztec Medicine, Health, and Nutrition* (New Brunswick: Rutgers University Press, 1990). López Austin's *El cuerpo humano* is also a foundational reading on Aztec beliefs about the body and illness, and Burkhart discusses the spiritually harmful consequences of contact with dirt or filth in *The Slippery Earth*. For songs, in addition to those in Book 2 of the FC, see Bierhorst, transl., *Cantares Mexicanos*; and John Bierhorst, transl., *Ballads of the Lords of New Spain: The Codex Romances de los Señores de la Nueva España* (Austin: University of Texas Press, 2009).

For Aztec astronomy, see Anthony Aveni, *Skywatchers: A Revised and Updated Version of Skywatchers of Ancient Mexico* (Austin: University of Texas Press, 2001). Also on Aztec ways of keeping time and the many uses of chronology, see Hassig, *Time, History, and Belief*. On systems of water control, see Angel Palerm, *Obras hidráulicas prehispánicas en el sistema lacustre del Valle de México* (Mexico City: INAH, 1973); Mundy, *The Death of Tenochtitlan, The Life of Mexico City*; and Conway, *Islands in the Lake*.

In addition to López Austin and Ortiz de Montellano, for more on the causes of disease, medical practitioners and their methods, and the uses of medicinal plants, see Luis Angel Rodríguez, *La ciencia médica de los Aztecas* (Mexico City: Editorial Hispano Mexicano, 1944); Carlos Viesca Treviño, *Medicina prehispánica de México* (Mexico City: Panorama Editorial, 1986); Gonzalo Aguirre Beltran, *Medicina y mágia: el proceso de aculturación en la estructura colonial* (Mexico City: SEP-INI, 1963); Robert Bye and Edelmira Linares, "Plantas medicinales de México prehispanico," *Arqueología Mexicana* 7 (1999), pp.4–13; Erika Rivera Arce, "Investigación reciente sobre plantas medicinales mexicanas," *Arqueología Mexicana* 7 (1999), pp.54–59; Carlos Viesca Treviño, "Usos de las plantas medicinales mexicanas," *Arqueología Mexicana* 7 (1999), pp.30–35; Juan Alberto Román Berrelleza, "Health and Disease among the Aztecs," in Elizabeth M. Brumfiel and Gary M. Feinman, eds., *The Aztec World* (New York: Abrams, 2008), pp.53–65. For a discussion of ideas, Indigenous and European, on the hot/cold dichotomy, see Jacques M. Chevalier and Andrés Sánchez Bain, *The Hot and the Cold: Ills of Humans and Maize in Native Mexico* (Toronto: University of Toronto Press, 2003). On sweat baths, see José Alcina Franch, Andrés Ciudad Ruiz, and Josefa Iglesias Ponce de Léon, "El 'temazcal' en Mesoamérica: evolución, forma y función," *Revista Española de Antropología* 10 (1980), pp.93–132.

Gordon Whittaker, *Deciphering Aztec Hieroglyphs: A Guide to Nahuatl Writing* (Oakland, CA: University of California Press, 2021) provides a comprehensive overview of the Aztec writing system. Karl Taube discusses Mesoamerican writing systems and how writing differs from images in conveying information in "The Writing System of Ancient Teotihuacan," *Ancient America* 1 (2000), pp.1–56. For the history of efforts to decipher Aztec writing, see Marc Zender, "One Hundred and Fifty Years of Nahuatl Decipherment," *The Pari Journal* 8 (2008), pp.24–37. Alfonso Lacadena also discusses the characteristics of Aztec writing and describes varying scribal traditions in "Regional Scribal Traditions: Methodological Implications for the Decipherment of Nahuatl Writing, *The Pari Journal* 8 (2008), pp.1–22. Whether the Aztecs had a true writing system has been debated as some scholars believe, because many signs could be used across languages and stood for things and ideas as well as sounds. For them, it is better considered "writing without words" or a "graphic communication system." See Elizabeth Hill Boone and Walter D. Mignolo, eds., *Writing without Words: Alternative Literacies in Mesoamerica and the Andes* (Durham: Duke University Press, 1994); as well as Elizabeth Hill Boone and Gary Urton, eds., *Their Way of Writing: Scripts, Signs, and Pictographies in*

Bibliographic Essay

Pre-Columbian America (Washington, DC: Dumbarton Oaks, 2011). For discussions of the Aztec graphic communication system, see Katarzyna Mikulska and Jerome A. Offner, eds., *Indigenous Graphic Communication Systems: A Theoretical Approach* (Louisville, CO: University Press of Colorado, 2018). For the *Codex Borgia* as well as the Borgia Group of codices, excellent essays on both can be found in *The Oxford Encyclopedia of Mesoamerican Cultures*. Boone discusses these codices at length in *Cycles of Time and Meaning*. For the history of Aztec/Nahua papermaking, see Alan R. Sandstrom and Pamela Effrein Sandstrom, *Traditional Papermaking and Paper Cult Figures of Mexico* (Norman: University of Oklahoma Press, 1986).

On Aztec literature and translations of a wide variety of songs and poems; sacred narratives, sacred hymns, prayers, and ceremonies; moral discourses; proverbs, conundrums, and metaphors; and historical narratives, see Miguel León-Portilla and Earl Shorris, eds., *In the Language of Kings: An Anthology of Mesoamerican Literature, Pre-Columbian to the Present* (New York: Norton, 2001). On Aztec dance and music, see Samuel Martí and Gertrude Prokosch-Kurath, *Dances of Anáhuac: The Choreography and Music of Precortesian Dances* (Chicago: Wenner-Gren Foundation for Anthropological Research, 1964); Paul Scolieri, *Dancing the New World: Aztecs, Spaniards, and the Choreography of Conquest* (Austin: University of Texas Press, 2013); and Arnd Adje Both, "Aztec Music Culture," *The World of Music* 49 (2007), pp. 91–104.

Camilla Townsend discusses the connection between the painted and written texts of codices and orality in *Annals of Native America* as does Katarzyna Szoblik in "Traces of Orality in the Codex Xolotl," *Indigenous Graphic Communication Systems*, pp. 204–230. León-Portilla provides important background on collections of Aztec songs, their writers, and their themes in *Fifteen Poets of the Aztec World*. The Bierhorst introductions to the *Cantares* and *Romances* also are very useful despite criticism of Bierhorst's interpretation of the colonial meanings of many songs. A number of translations exist of the Chalca Woman's

Song including Bierhorst's in the *Cantares* and Townsend's excellent one in "'What in the World Have You Done to Me, My Lover?'."

The places to start on Aztec art are H. B. Nicholson, "Major Sculpture in Pre-Hispanic Central Mexico," *Handbook of Middle American Indians*, Vol. X, pp.92–134 on sculpture and Esther Pasztory's magisterial *Aztec Art* (Norman: University of Oklahoma Press, 1983). For Olmecs and their art, see the discussion of Olmec civilization in Coe, Urcid, and Koontz, *Mexico: From the Olmecs to the Aztecs*. Umberger's work on Aztecs referencing earlier artistic styles and uses of history (their own and others) in their art is essential. See "Antiquities, Revivals, and References to the Past in Aztec Art," *RES: Anthropology and Aesthetics* 13 (1987), pp.62–105; "Notions of Aztec History: The Case of the Great Temple Dedication," *RES: Anthropology and Aesthetics* 42 (2002), pp.86–108; and "The Metaphorical Underpinnings of Aztec History: The Case of the 1473 Civil War," *Ancient Mesoamerica* 18 (2007), pp.11–29. On the meaning and uses of history in Aztec monuments, also see Richard F. Townsend, *State and Cosmos in the Art of Tenochtitlan, Studies in Pre-Columbian Art and Archaeology*, Vol. XX (Washington, DC: Dumbarton Oaks, 1979).

There is a voluminous literature on the Mixteca-Puebla style and iconographic system. The most important publications which cover how to define it, how widespread it was, and its overall significance include H. B. Nicholson, "The Mixteca-Puebla Concept in Mesoamerican Archaeology: A Re-examination," in Anthony F.C. Wallace, ed., *Men and Cultures: Selected Papers from the 5th International Congress of Anthropological and Ethnological Sciences* (Philadelphia: University of Pennsylvania Press, 1960), pp.612–617; Michael E. Smith and M. Cynthia Heath-Smith, "Waves of Influence in Postclassic Mesoamerica? A Critique of the Mixteca-Puebla Concept," *Anthropology* 4 (1980), pp.15–50; H. B. Nicholson and Eloise Quiñones Keber, eds., *Mixteca-Puebla: Discoveries and Research in Mesoamerican Art and Archaeology* (Culver City, CA:

Labyrinthos, 1994); Pablo Escalante Gonzalbo, "The Mixteca-Puebla Tradition and H. B. Nicholson," in Matthew A. Boxt and Brian D. Dillon, eds., *Fanning the Sacred Flame: Mesoamerican Studies in Honor of H.B. Nicholson* (Boulder: University Press of Colorado, 2020), pp.293–307; and Elizabeth H. Boone and Michael E. Smith, "Postclassic International Styles and Symbol Sets," in *The Postclassic Mesoamerican World*, pp.186–193. Boone describes the Aztec version of the Postclassic International Style in painted images in "A Web of Understanding: Pictorial Codices and the Shared Intellectual Culture of Late Postclassic Mesoamerica," in *The Postclassic Mesoamerican World*, pp.207–221.

For interpretations of the Coatlicue piece, see Cecilia F. Klein, "Rethinking Cihuacoatl: Aztec Political Imagery of the Conquered Woman," in *Smoke and Mist*, Vol. II, pp.237–277; and "A New Interpretation of the Aztec Statue Called Coatlicue, 'Snakes-Her-Skirt,'" *Ethnohistory* 55 (2008), pp.229–250. Eduardo Matos Moctezuma and Felipe Solís discuss the Calendar Stone and many of the controversies relating to its interpretation in *The Aztec Calendar and Other Solar Monuments* (Mexico City: CONACULTA, INAH, and Grupo Azabache, 2004). A recent book by David Stuart proposes that the stone has specific historical meanings relating to the rulership of Moteuczoma Xocoyotl, see *King and Cosmos: An Interpretation of the Aztec Calendar Stone* (San Francisco: Precolumbia Mesoweb Press, 2021). At least four other depictions of Coyolxauhqui exist besides those discussed in Chapter 6; see Eduardo Matos Moctezuma, "Las seis Coyolxauhqui: variaciones sobre un mismo tema," *Estudios de Cultura Náhuatl* 21 (1991): 15–46.

For Mexica art and empire, see Emily Umberger, "Art and Imperial Strategy in Tenochtitlan," in *Aztec Imperial Strategies*, pp.85–106; "Aztec Presence and Material Remains in the Outer Provinces," *Aztec Imperial Strategies*, pp.151–180; and "Material Remains in the Central Provinces," *Aztec Imperial Strategies*, App.3, pp.247–264. Felipe Solís Olguín considers the Venus of Texcoco a unique piece in "The Art of the Aztec Era," in

Brumfiel and Feinman, *The Aztec World*, pp.153–178. For the imagery of female figurines, see Brumfiel, "Weaving and Cooking." The use of female-related iconography on spindle whorls is analyzed by Geoffrey McCafferty and Sharisse McCafferty in "Pregnant in the Dancing Place: Myths and Methods of Textile Production and Use," *The Oxford Handbook of the Aztecs*, pp.375–384 as well as in Geoffrey G. McCafferty and Sharisse D. McCafferty, "Weapons of Resistance: The Material Symbolics of Postclassic Mexican Spinning and Weaving," *Latin American Antiquity* 30 (2019), pp.707–723.

Continuity between Postclassic and early colonial Aztec pottery making is discussed in Thomas H. Charlton, Cynthia L. Otis Charlton, and Patricia Fournier G. in "The Basin of Mexico A.D. 1450–1620," in Susan Kepecs and Rani T. Alexander, eds., *The Postclassic to Spanish-Era Transition in Mesoamerica: Archaeological Perspectives* (Albuquerque: University of New Mexico Press, 2005), pp.49–63. Ray Hernández-Durán describes continuities and changes in Aztec art in "Aztec Art after the Conquest and in Museums Abroad," in *The Oxford Handbook of the Aztecs*, pp.689–705.

Using alphabetic writing for Nahua purposes is discussed by Stephanie Wood, *Transcending Conquest: Nahua Views of Spanish Colonial Mexico* (Norman: University of Oklahoma Press, 2003); Davíd Tavárez, *The Invisible War: Indigenous Devotions, Discipline, and Dissent in Colonial Mexico* (Stanford: Stanford University Press, 2011); and Mark Christensen, *Nahua and Maya Catholicisms: Texts and Religion in Colonial Central Mexico and Yucatan* (Stanford: Stanford University Press, 2013). Nahua writers would continue the Aztec tradition of literacy by creating literary and historical works to the present day. Nahua intellectuals who created literature and wrote about history and anthropology are discussed by Kelly McDonough in *The Learned Ones: Nahua Intellectuals in Postconquest Mexico* (Tucson: University of Arizona Press, 2014). On Nahua scribes and others – often women – as culture makers, creators and sustainers, and record keepers of governance, ceremonies, and continuities in property ownership, see Miriam Melton-Villanueva,

The Aztecs at Independence: Nahua Culture Makers in Central Mexico, 1799–1832 (Tucson: University of Arizona Press, 2016).

Extracted quotations include Taube, "The Writing System of Ancient Teotihuacan," p.4; from Durán, *Book of the Gods and Rites*, p.396; on songs, Durán, *Book of the Gods and Rites*, p.295, 297; *FC* 2, p.221. For the funerary song, see *FC 10*, p.192. For the song referring to Nezahualcoyotl as a writer, see Bierhorst, *Romances*, pp.118–119 (fols.18v–19r). For the song about grief, see Bierhorst, *Cantares*, pp.214–215 (fol.25r). The song by Macuilxochitl can be found in Bierhorst, *Cantares*, pp.214–215 (fol.53v). León-Portilla uses the phrase "erotic siege" in *Fifteen Poets of the Aztec World*, p.256. For the excerpt from the Chalca Woman's Song, see Bierhorst, *Cantares*, p.391 (fol.73v). Chimalpahin, *Las ocho relaciones*, Vol. II, pp.112; Pasztory, *Aztec Art*, p.71; FC 10, p.191; Pasztory, Aztec Art, p.158.

7 Resilience: Part 2, Trauma, Transformation, Tenacity

The first part of this chapter relies on a number of primary sources, Indigenous, hybrid, and Spanish. The Spanish accounts, although sometimes critical of the actions of Hernan Cortés, tend to treat him as the main actor, justify Spanish actions even when cruel and murderous, and depict Aztecs as weak, superstitious, and cruel. Among early writings about this war, three stand out – by Cortés himself, Bernal Díaz, a fighter who participated, and Francisco López de Gómara, a close associate of Cortés's. These depictions did much to create the "mythistory" that historian Matthew Restall describes as "one of human history's great lies" in *When Montezuma Met Cortés: The True Story of the Meeting that Changed History* (New York: Ecco, 2018), p.xxxii. For Cortés, see *Five Letters*; for Bernal Díaz del Castillo, see *The Discovery and Conquest of Mexico*, transl., A. P. Maudslay (New York: Da Capo Press, 1996 [1555–1584]); and Francisco López de

Gómara, *Conquista de México* (Madrid: Historia 16, 1987 [1552]). Written in the 1520s (Cortés), the early 1550s (López de Gómara), and between the 1550s and about 1584 (Díaz del Castillo), these have been the most influential writings. They remain widely read and convey the triumphal narrative that research with Nahuatl-language sources as well as careful readings of texts by descendants of Aztecs about the war era have had difficulty dislodging, despite repeated scholarly attempts to refocus attention on Aztec thinking and actions. Other accounts by eyewitnesses to these events can be found in Patricia de Fuentes, ed. and transl., *The Conquistadors: First-person Accounts of the Conquest of Mexico* (Norman: University of Oklahoma Press, 1993). An important book that undermined traditional portraits of the conquest as a great Spanish achievement was Miguel León-Portilla's *Visión de los vencidos: relaciones indígenas de la conquista* (Mexico City: UNAM, 1959), published in English as *The Broken Spears*, which gave voice to Indigenous responses to the Spanish invasion. A recent compilation brings together Nahuatl-language and Spanish-language sources: Stuart B. Schwartz and Tatiana Seijas, eds., 2nd ed., *Victors and Vanquished: Spanish and Nahua Views of the Conquest of Mexico* (Boston: Bedford/St. Martin's, 2017). Two books, published nearly simultaneously, deepened scholarly discussion about how and why the "conquest" proceeded as it did: James Lockhart, ed. and transl., *We People Here: Nahuatl Accounts of the Conquest of Mexico* (Berkeley: University of California Press, 1993) which brought additional attention to Indigenous accounts of the Spanish-Mexica War. Another book, using anthropological tools to reconstruct Aztec actions and treat Aztecs as rational actors, leading to a deeper analysis of why Spaniards were successful against the Mexica, is Ross Hassig's *Mexico and the Spanish Conquest* (London and New York: Longman, 1994). I made use of the second, revised edition of this book, (Norman: University of Oklahoma Press, 2006) for this chapter. While relying heavily on Spanish-authored texts, Hassig also draws upon a number of Indigenous-language and Indigenous- or mestizo-authored accounts, as do I. However, I try to rebalance how I read and interpret the FC and the writings of Chimalpahin, Alvarado Tezozomoc, Alva Ixtlilxochitl, Muñoz Camargo as well as the Indigenous-influenced historical chronicle of Diego Durán (these works already mentioned in this bibliographic essay) to emphasize that these texts show Aztec agency within very challenging circumstances. Alvarado Tezozomoc's account of the Spanish-Mexica War ends as Cortés makes first contact with the Tlaxcalteca; Durán's extends beyond that to describe the war and Cortés's conquest efforts after the defeat of the Mexica. A source important to the study of colonial policies impact on Nahuas is the *Códice Osuna*, made up of a number of separate documents from the 1560s that document complaints about the payment of tribute in both goods and services, land loss, and excessive labor demands in several basin communities including Tenochtitlan, Tlatelolco, and Tlacopan. See Luis Chávez Orozco, ed., *Códice Osuna: reproducción facsimilar de la obra del mismo título* (Mexico City: Inter-American Indian Institute, 1947).

Additional works that discuss Indigenous contributions and perspectives on war with Spaniards include Wood, *Transcending Conquest*; Matthew Restall, *Seven Myths of the Spanish Conquest* (New York: Oxford University Press, 2003) and his "The New Conquest History," *History Compass* 10 (2012): pp.151–160; Laura E. Matthew and Michel R. Oudijk, eds., *Indian Conquistadors: Indigenous Allies in the Conquest of Mesoamerica* (Norman: University of Oklahoma Press, 2007); and Susan Schroeder, ed., *The Conquest All Over Again: Nahuas and Zapotecs Thinking, Writing, and Painting Spanish Colonialism* (Eastborne, UK: Sussex Academic Press, 2010). Michel R. Oudijk and María Castañeda de la Paz comment specifically on Mexica deliberations in "Nahua Thought and the Conquest," in *The Oxford Handbook of the Aztecs*, pp.161–171.

Probably the single most important Indigenous account, though not an eyewitness account, is Book 12 of the FC. While the process of composing this book began early, around 1555 during the Tlatelolco period of the FC's production, it was probably edited in the 1570s to create the version today available as Book 12. But Sahagún re-wrote it in 1585 to shift the focus from the Mexica to the Spanish; see *Conquest of New Spain: 1585 Revision*. Book 12 clearly portrays a Tlatelolca-centered perspective on the Spanish-Mexica war, especially about what I describe as the third stage, although Spanish influence can be detected in the style of narration and illustrations. An account of the Spanish-Mexica war, hybrid in a different and fascinating way, is Chimalpahin's annotated version of López de Gómara's *La conquista de México*. Somehow, one of the earliest published versions of that text came into Chimalpahin's hands. He copied it and added commentary with numerous corrections and additions, including titles, honorifics, and genealogical information. He also emphasizes information about women's experiences as hostages, servants, and victims of violence during the Spanish-Mexica War; Susan Schroeder, Anne J. Cruz, Cristián Roa-de-la-Carrera, and Davíd E. Tavárez, eds. and transls., *Chimalpahin's Conquest: A Nahua Historian's Rewriting of Francisco López de Gómara's La Conquista de México* (Stanford: Stanford University Press, 2010).

The issue of whether Moteuczoma and other Mexica believed the Spaniards to be gods, an idea that once was simply assumed to be true, has been given a lot of attention. Hassig in his important revisionist history of the conquest was inclined to believe that they did. Susan Gillespie argues the opposite in "Blaming Moteuczoma: Anthropomorphizing the Aztec Conquest," in Rebecca P. Brienen and Margaret A. Jackson, eds., *Invasion and Transformation: Interdisciplinary Perspectives on the Conquest of Mexico* (Boulder: University Press of Colorado, 2007), pp.25–55, as does Restall in *When Montezuma Met Cortés*. Lockhart pointed out, as mentioned above, that the word "teotl" has meanings beyond that of "deity" and encompasses strange, even frightening, things that called for explanation in Aztec terms. Kevin Terraciano carefully analyzes the Nahuatl-language discourse in Book 12 of the FC around how Moteuczoma and other Mexica leaders addressed Cortés and his fellow Spaniards and concludes that that they likely did consider them deities, at least for a time in "Reading between the Lines of Book 12," in *The Florentine Codex: An Encyclopedia*, pp.45–62. It remains important, however, to remember the Christian influences on Sahagún's co-authors.

For an authoritative biography of Malintzin, see Camilla Townsend, *Malintzin's Choices: An Indian Woman in the Conquest of Mexico* (Albuquerque: University of New Mexico Press, 2006). A number of important works examine her life, the literature about her, and the many different interpretations of her actions and meaning as a cultural figure including Sandra Messinger Cypess, *La Malinche in Mexican Literature: From History to Myth* (Austin: University of Texas Press, 1991); Fernanda Núñez Becerra, *La Malinche: de la historia al mito* (Mexico City: INAH, 1996); and Frances Karttunen, "Rethinking Malinche," In *Indian Women of Early Mexico*, pp.291–312.

Important discussions of the many factors that have been considered as causes of the Mexica defeat include Hassig's in *Mexico and the Spanish Conquest*; Serge Gruzinski, *The Conquest of Mexico: The Incorporation of Indian Societies into the Western World* (London: Polity, 1993); Camilla Townsend, "Burying the White Gods: New Perspectives on the Conquest of Mexico," *American Historical Review* 108 (2003), pp.659–687; and Michel R. Oudijk, "The Conquest of Mexico," in *The Oxford Handbook of Mesoamerican Archaeology*, 459–468. For the incompleteness of conquest and difficulties of Spanish rule, see Restall, *Seven Myths of the Spanish Conquest*. Robert Ricard introduced the phrase "spiritual conquest," in *The Spiritual Conquest of Mexico: An Essay on the Apostolate and the Evangelizing Methods of the Mendicant Orders in New Spain, 1523–1572* (Lesley Byrd Simpson, transl., Berkeley: University of California Press, 1966). Burkhart answered him, showing the notion of "spiritual conquest" to be overly simplistic and inaccurate in *The Slippery Earth*. Two recent books explore how the concept of the "conquest of Mexico" shaped both the history and historiography of Mexico. See Hipólito Rodríguez Guerrero, ed., *La conquista de México y su uso en la historia* (Xalapa: Universidad Veracruzana, Ayuntamiento de Xalapa, 2021) and Peter B. Villella and Pablo García Loaeza, eds., *The Conquest of Mexico: 500 Years of Reinventions* (Norman: University of Oklahoma Press, 2022).

On the traumas induced by war and colonial-imposed rule, see Justyna Olko and Agnieszka Brylak, "Defending Local Autonomy and Facing Cultural Trauma: A Nahua Order against Idolatry, Tlaxcala, 1543," *Hispanic American Historical Review* 98 (2018), pp.573–604. The impact of introduced diseases is discussed in Noble David Cook and W. George Lovell, eds., *Secret Judgments of God: Old World Disease in Colonial Spanish America* (Norman: University of Oklahoma Press, 1991); Noble David Cook. *Born to Die: Disease and New World Conquest, 1492–1650* (New York: Cambridge University Press, 1998); and Suzanne Austin Alchon, *A Pest in the Land: New World Epidemics in a Global Perspective* (Albuquerque: University of New Mexico Press, 2003). Rodolfo Acuña-Soto, David W. Stahle, Malcom K. Cleaveland, and Matthew D. Therrell explain the role of extreme drought and indigenous disease in the extreme population losses of the sixteenth century in "Megadrought and Megadeath in Sixteenth-Century Mexico," *Emerging Infectious Diseases* 8 (2002), pp.360–362. For the larger context of colonial rule's impact on central Mexico, see Gibson, *Aztecs under Spanish Rule*; and Lockhart, *The Nahuas after the Conquest*. Both deal with governance, land, religion, population and households, though in different ways. Gibson relied largely on Spanish-language sources, Lockhart almost solely on Nahuatl-language sources, and he added extensive discussion of linguistic issues as well as forms of cultural expression. The defense by Mexica priests of Aztec religious beliefs can be found in Bernardino de Sahagún, *Coloquois y doctrina cristiana* (Miguel León-Portilla, ed., Mexico City: UNAM, 1986).

On colonial governance in Nahua communities and its continuities with late Postclassic governance, see Robert Haskett, *Indigenous Rulers: An Ethnohistory of Town Government in Colonial Cuernavaca* (Albuquerque: University of New Mexico Press, 1991). William F. Connell examines the conflicts and factionalism that developed in Mexico City's Indigenous government in *After Moctezuma: Indigenous Politics and*

Self-Government in Mexico City, 1524–1730 (Norman: University of Oklahoma Press, 2011), and Conway's discussion of the impact of ecological and economic change on the governance of the altepetl of Xochimilco in *Islands in the Lake* clarifies areas of continuity and change amid ecological shifts, growing exploitation of native labor, and increasing impoverishment. For continuities in Nahuatl land terminologies and Nahua ownership into the eighteenth and nineteenth centuries, see Miriam Melton-Villanueva and Caterina Pizzigoni, "Late Nahuatl Testaments from the Toluca Valley: Indigenous-Language Ethnohistory in the Mexican Independence Period," *Ethnohistory* 55 (2008), pp.361–391; Caterina Pizzigoni, *The Life Within: Local Indigenous Society in Mexico's Toluca Valley, 1650–1800* (Stanford: Stanford University Press, 2012); and Miriam Melton-Villanueva, "Cacicas, Escribanos, and Landholders: Indigenous Women's Colonial Mexican Texts, 1703–1832," *Ethnohistory* 65 (2018), pp. 297–322.

On the development and practices of a Nahua Christianity, in addition to Burkhart's pioneering work in *The Slippery Earth* as well as Lockhart's more institutionally focused discussion, also see (and this is merely a selection from an immense literature) Jorge Klor de Alva, "Spiritual Conflict and Accommodation in New Spain: Toward a Typology of Aztec Responses to Christianity," in *The Inca and Aztec States*; Gruzinski, *The Conquest of Mexico*; Francisco Morales, "The Native Encounter with Christianity: Franciscans and Nahuas in Sixteenth-Century Mexico," *The Americas* 65 (2008), pp.137–159; Patricia Don, *Bonfires of Culture: Franciscans, Indigenous Leaders, and Inquisition in Early Mexico, 1524–1540* (Norman: University of Oklahoma Press, 2010); Tavárez, *The Invisible War*; and Ryan Dominic Crewe, *The Mexican Mission: Indigenous Reconstruction and Mendicant Enterprise in New Spain, 1521–1600* (Cambridge and New York: Cambridge University Press, 2019). Disease's role in influencing Nahua Christianity is explored in Jennifer Scheper Hughes, *The Church of the Dead: The Epidemic of 1576 and the Birth of Christianity in the Americas* (New York: New York University Press, 2021). On Nahuas and the everyday running of churches in Indigenous communities, see Jonathan Truitt, *Sustaining the Divine in Mexico Tenochtitlan: Nahuas and Catholicism, 1523–1700* (Norman: University of Oklahoma Press and The Academy of American Franciscan History, 2018). Church construction and the performance of religious plays proved important vehicles of both change and continuity as shown by Jaime Lara, *City, Temple, Stage: Eschatological Architecture and Liturgical Theatrics in New Spain* (Notre Dame, IN: Notre Dame University Press, 2004); Eleanor Wake, *Framing the Sacred: The Indian Churches of Early Colonial Mexico* (Norman: University of Oklahoma Press, 2010); and Louise Burkhart, *Aztecs on Stage: Religious Theater in Colonial Mexico* (Norman: University of Oklahoma Press, 2011). On saints in colonial Nahua communities, Antonio Rubial García, "Icons of Devotion: The Appropriation and Use of Saints in New Spain," in Martin Austin Nesvig, ed., *Local Religion in Colonial Mexico* (Albuquerque: University of New Mexico Press, 2006), pp. 37–61; Pizzigoni, *The Life Within*; and Truitt, *Sustaining the Divine* all provide important evidence for rural and urban areas.

Primary sources for the study of law and its impact on and uses by Nahuas are discussed in Offner, *Law and Politics in Aztec Texcoco*; Frances F. Berdan, "Crime and Control in Aztec Society," in Keith Hopwood, ed., *Organized Crime in Antiquity* (London: Classical Press of Wales, 1999), pp. 255–269; Berdan, "Living on the Edge in an Ancient Imperial World: Aztec Crime and Deviance," in Mark Galeotti, ed., *Organized Crime in History* (London: Routledge, 2009), pp. 20–34; and Kellogg, *Law and the Transformation of Aztec Culture*. Woodrow Borah discusses the early creation and institutionalization of colonial courts dealing with Indigenous litigants and the kinds of cases they brought in *Justice by Insurance: The General Indian Court of Colonial Mexico and the Legal Aides of the Half-Real* (Berkeley: University of California Press, 1983). The longer-term impact of the Nahua engagement with the colonial legal system is discussed by Brian P. Owensby in *Empire of Law and Indian Justice in Colonial Mexico* (Stanford: Stanford University Press, 2008) and Ethelia Ruiz Medrano, *Mexico's Indigenous Communities: Their Lands and Histories, 1500–2010* (Russ Davidson, transl., Boulder: University Press of Colorado, 2010).

Bibliographic Essay

For Nahua (and other) Indigenous women during the colonial period, see Kellogg, *Weaving the Past* and Sousa, *The Woman Who Turned into a Jaguar*. On Indigenous women in leadership roles during that period, see Margarita R. Ochoa and Sara Vicuña Guengerich, eds., *Cacicas: The Indigenous Women Leaders of Spanish America, 1492–1825* (Norman: University of Oklahoma Press, 2021). Studies on gender ambiguity by Klein, "None of the Above," and Sigal, *The Flower and the Scorpion*, have already been mentioned.

The complex ethnic roots of altepeme, especially Tenochtitlan's, are examined in Van Zantwijk, *The Aztec Arrangement*; Frances Berdan provides an excellent overview of Aztec ideas about ethnicity in "Concepts of Ethnicity and Class in Aztec-Period Mexico," in Frances F. Berdan et al., *Ethnic Identity in Nahua Mesoamerica: The View from Archaeology, Art History, Ethnohistory, and Contemporary Ethnography* (Salt Lake City: University of Utah Press, 2008), pp.105–132. P. Carrasco discusses ethnic identities such as Acolhua that cut across multiple altepeme in *The Tenochca Empire of Ancient Mexico*. For a summary of the labyrinthine anthropological literature on ethnicity placed within the long-term history of Indigenous Mesoamerica, see Barbara Stark and John K. Chance, "Diachronic and Multidisciplinary Perspectives on Mesoamerican Ethnicity," in *Ethnic Identity in Nahua Mesoamerica*, pp.38–63. Both Alan Sandstrom and James Taggart discuss the strength of community-based identities among contemporary Nahuas respectively in "Blood Sacrifice, Curing, and Ethnic Identity among Contemporary Nahua of Northern Veracruz, Mexico," in *Ethnic Identity in Nahua Mesoamerica*, pp.150–182; and "Nahuat Ethnicity in a Time of Agrarian Conflict," in *Ethnic Identity in Nahua Mesoamerica*, pp.183–203. The fragmentation of altepeme is discussed in Lockhart, *The Nahuas after the Conquest* and John Chance, "Indigenous Ethnicity in Colonial Central Mexico," in *Ethnic Identity in Nahua Mesoamerica*, pp.133–149. The uses of pan-Indigenous terminology in Nahuatl is described by Lockhart in his introduction to *We People Here* as well as by Camilla Townsend in *Annals of Native America*.

Census figures for speakers of Indigenous languages in Mexico can be found at www.inegi.org.mx/temas/lengua/. Useful overviews of Nahua populations of the late twentieth and twenty-first centuries include Frans Schryer, "Native Peoples of Central Mexico since Independence," in Richard E. W. Adams and Murdo J. MacLeod, eds., *The Cambridge History of the Native Peoples of the Americas*, Vol. II, Part 2 (Cambridge and New York: Cambridge University Press, 2000), pp.223–273; James Taggart, "Nahua," *The Oxford Encyclopedia of Mesoamerican Cultures*, Vol. II, pp.359–363; and Alan Sandstrom, "The Aztecs and Their Descendants in the Contemporary World," *The Oxford Handbook of the Aztecs*, pp.707–720. Judith Friedlander discusses the persistent influence of Aztec household technologies in *Being Indian in Hueyapan: A Study of Forced Identity in Contemporary Mexico*, 2nd ed. (New York: St. Martin's Press, 2006). On Nahua religious beliefs, including early discussion of the influence of evangelical Protestantism, see William Madsen, *The Virgin's Children: Life in an Aztec Village Today* (Austin: University of Texas Press, 1960); José de Jesús Montoya Briones, *Atla: etnografía de un pueblo nahuatl* (Mexico City: INAH, 1964); Konrad T. Preuss, *Mitos y cuentos nahuas de la sierra madre oriental* (transl., Marian Frenk-Westheim, Mexico City: INI, 1982); Alan R. Sandstrom, *Corn Is Our Blood*; Alan R. Sandstrom and Pamela Effrein Sandstrom, "Sorcery and Counter-Sorcery among the Nahua of Northern Veracruz, Mexico," in Coltman and Pohl, *Sorcery in Mesoamerica*, pp.69–113; Felix Baéz-Jorge and Arturo Gómez Martínez, *Tlacatecolotl y el diablo. La cosmovisión de los nahuas de Chicontepec* (Mexico City: Secretaría de Educación y Cultura, 1998); Timothy J. Knab, *The Dialogue of Earth and Sky: Dreams, Souls, Curing, and the Modern Aztec Underworld* (Tucson: University of Arizona Press, 2004); and Guy Stresser-Péan, *The Sun God and the Savior: The Christianization of the Nahua and Totonac in the Sierra de Puebla, Mexico* (Boulder: University Press of Colorado, 2009). On healing, see Chevalier and Sánchez Bain, *The Hot and the Cold*; and Laura Elena Romero

López, *Cosmovisión, cuerpo y enfermedad: el espanto entre los nahuas de Tlacotepec de Díaz, Puebla* (Mexico City: INAH, 2006). On contemporary uses of ancient plants, see Rivera Arce, "Investigación reciente sobre plantas medicinales mexicanas" and Carlos Zolla, "La medicina tradicional indígena en el México actual," *Arqueología Mexicana* 13 (2005), pp.62–65.

On Nahuas and emotion, see Pablo Escalante Gonzalbo, "El llanto de los antiguos nahuas," *Nexos* 186 (1993), pp.88–91; "La casa, el cuerpo y las emociones," in *Historia de la vida cotidiana en México*, Vol. I, pp.231–259; Jacqueline Holler, "Of Sadness and Joy in Colonial Mexico," in Javier Villa-Flores and Sonya Lipsett-River, eds., *Emotion and Daily Life in Colonial Mexico* (Albuquerque: University of New Mexico Press, 2014), pp.17–43; Catharine Good Eshelman, "Ejes conceptuales entre los nahuas de Guerrero: expresión de un modelo fenomenológico mesoamericano," *Estudios de Cultura Náhuatl* 36 (2005), pp.87–113; "'Trabajando juntos como uno': conceptos nahuas del grupo doméstico y de la persona," in David Robichaux, ed., *Familia y parentesco en México y Mesoamérica. Unas miradas antropológicas* (Mexico City: Universidad Iberoamericana, 2005), pp.275–294; James Taggart, *Remembering Victoria: A Tragic Nahuat Love Story* (Austin: University of Texas Press, 2007); "Narratives of Emotional Experience and Long-Term Fieldwork among the Nahuat of Mexico," *Anthropology and Humanism* 36 (2011), pp.47–54; and Heather J. Allen, "'Llorar amargamente': Economies of Weeping in the Spanish Empire," *Colonial Latin American Review* 24 (2015), pp.479–504. The Robichaux volume, *Familia y parentesco en México* contains a number of important essays on contemporary Nahua family and kinship relations as does the older, but still valuable volume, Hugo G. Nutini, Pedro Carrasco, and James M. Taggart, eds., *Essays on Mexican Kinship* (Pittsburgh, University of Pittsburgh Press, 1976).

Holly Barnet-Sanchez provides brief overview of the treatment of the Indigenous populace and their histories by artists, intellectuals, and government officials in "Indigenismo and Pre-hispanic Revivals," *The Oxford Encyclopedia of Mesoamerican Cultures*, Vol. II, pp.42–44. Both Benjamin Keen and Matthew Restall delve

Bibliographic Essay

deeply into how the Aztecs have been portrayed in and beyond Mexico in, respectively, *The Aztec Image in Western Thought* (New Brunswick: Rutgers University Press, 1971) and *When Montezuma Met Cortés*. Enrique Florescano has examined a series of national myths of Mexico including about the Aztecs in *Memory, Myth, and Time in Mexico: From the Aztecs to Independence* (Albert G. Bork, transl., Austin: University of Texas Press, 1994) and *National Narratives in Mexico: A History* (Nancy T. Hancock, transl., Norman: University of Oklahoma Press, 2006). A discussion of the way bilingual schools promote Spanish at the expense of Nahuatl, can be found in "Modern-day Conquistadors: The Decline of Nahuatl, and the Status of Mexican Bilingual Education," *Harvard International Review* (July 27, 2022; https://hir.harvard.edu/decline-of-nahuatl/). For the history and findings of the Templo Mayor archaeological project, see Eduardo Matos Moctezuma, ed., *El Templo Mayor: excavaciones y estudios* (Mexico City: INAH, 1982); Eduardo Matos Moctzuma, *The Great Temple of the Aztecs: Treasures of Tenochtitlan*, Doris Heyden, transl. (London: Thames and Hudson, 1988); and *Life and Death in the Templo Mayor*, Bernard R. Ortiz de Montellano and Thelma Ortiz de Montellano, transls., (Boulder: University Press of Colorado, 1995). For the site's museum, see https://templomayor.inah.gob.mx.

The Mexican Day of the Dead and its possible Aztec or Indigenous roots has been much studied. Important publications on that topic include Eduardo Matos Moctezuma, et al., "Miccaihuitl: el culto a la muerte," Special issue: *Artes de México* 145 (1971); Hugo G. Nutini, *Todos Santos in Rural Tlaxcala: A Syncretic, Expressive, and Symbolic Analysis of the Cult of the Dead* (Princeton: University of Princeton Press, 1988); Elizabeth Carmichael and Chloë Sayer, *The Skeleton at the Feast: The Day of the Dead in Mexico* (Austin: University of Texas Press, 1992); and Stanley H. Brandes, *Skulls to the Living, Bread to the Dead: The Day of the Dead in Mexico and Beyond* (Malden, MA: Wiley-Blackwell, 2004).

On Aztlan and Chicano identities, see Jack Forbes, *Aztecas del norte: The Chicanos of Aztlan* (Greenwich, CN: Fawcett

Publications, 1973); Gloria Anzaldua, *Borderlands/La Frontera: The New Mestiza* (San Francisco: Spinsters/Aunt Lute, 1987); and Rudolfo Anaya, Francisco A. Lomelí, and Enrique Lamadrid, eds., *Aztlan: Essays on the Chicano Homeland*, revised and expanded ed., (Albuquerque: University of New Mexico Press, 2017). For analysis of the danzas aztecas, see Max Harris, *Aztecs, Moors, and Christians: Festivals of Reconquest in Mexico and Spain* (Austin: University of Texas Press, 2000); Yolotl González Torres, *Danza tu palabra: La Danza de los Concheros* (Mexico City: Plaza y Valdés, 2005); Sandra Garner, "Aztec Dance, Transnational Movements: Conquest of a Different Sort," *Journal of American Folklore* 122 (2009), pp.414–437; and Ruben A. Arellano, "El Es Dios! A Historical Interpretation of Danza Azteca as a Revitalization Movement," *Journal of Festive Studies* 3 (2021), pp.121–147.

The wonderful podcast "Tales from Aztlantis" is another way to learn about Aztecs and how their history relates to the contemporary world; the related website https://mexika.org provides a window onto Aztec history and its relevance to current cultural and political issues in Mexico and the United States. "Mexica: A History Podcast" depicts the Spanish-Mexica War using Indigenous and Spanish sources. Transnational films tend to use Aztec, Maya, or a fanciful sort of Mesoamerican history and symbols in a kind of pastiche, but Aztec-related content appears. Mel Gibson's "Apocalypto" demonstrates this as does Mesoamerican aspects of "Black Panther: Wakanda Forever," though the latter film features Indigenous actors, Indigenous rappers, and aims to provide a respectful picture of Mesoamerican Indigenous people. See Oscar López, "Mexico's Indigenous Rappers Find Rare Spotlight on Wakanda Soundtrack," *The Guardian*, www.theguardian.com/world/2023/jan/27/mexico-indigenous-rappers-pat-boy-black-panther-wakanda-forever-soundtrack. Mexican-made films deal with the history in more serious ways. Three to consider watching are "Retorno a Aztlán," "La otra conquista," and "Erendira Ikikunari." For some examples of contemporary versions of Aztec-style designs, see https://aztecsandtenochtitlan.com/aztec-art/aztec-designs/; for a place name example, see www.aztecnm.gov; for a company name, https://aztecs.net; for a sports team, see https://goaztecs.com (San Diego State University); for a rock group, see https://en.wikipedia.org/wiki/Billy_Thorpe_and_the_Aztecs; and for a variety of games, see www.thegamer.com/best-games-inspired-by-aztec-mythology/?newsletter_popup=1.

In addition to courses and workshops at such universities as UCLA, University of Texas at Austin, and Harvard University, in Mexico, the Zacatecas Institute for Teaching and Research in Ethnology (www.idiezmacehualli.org) offers courses taught by native speakers. There are a number of publications (this is not an exhaustive list) that would be useful for learning the Nahuatl language as spoken by the Aztecs, including: Arthur J. O. Anderson, ed. and transl., *Rules of the Aztec Language: Classical Nahuatl Grammar* (Salt Lake City: University of Utah Press, 1973); Thelma D. Sullivan and Neville Stiles, transls., Wick R. Miller and Karen Dakin, eds., *Thelma D. Sullivan's Compendium of Nahuatl Grammar* (Salt Lake City: University of Utah Press, 1988); and J. Richard Andrews, *Introduction to Classical Nahuatl* (Norman: University of Oklahoma Press, 2003 [rev. ed.]). James Lockhart's translation of Horacio Carochi's classic grammar, like Anderson's, provides essential information, *Grammar of the Mexican Language, with an Explanation of Its Adverbs (1645)* (Stanford: Stanford University Press and UCLA Latin American Center Publications, 2001). The website Lexilogos (www.lexilogos.com/english/nahuatl_dictionary.htm) offers many online resources including dictionaries, grammars, and links to online courses. Two excellent web-based scholarly resources for learning about the Aztecs are Mesolore (www.mesolore.org), a teaching and learning site that offers primary sources texts, debates about major issues relating to gender and Indigenous rights among others, as well as syllabi, lesson plans, and brief biographies of major scholars. Another is Mexicolore (www.mexicolore.co.uk), a British-based site providing teaching and learning resources on Mexico, especially the Aztecs, with articles by experts on a huge range of topics, written for general audiences, including students at the college-level and below.

Extracted quotations include Wood, *Transcending Conquest*, p.145; Taggart, "Narratives of Emotional Experience," p.50; D. Carrasco, *The Aztecs: A Very Short Introduction* (Oxford and New York: Oxford University Press, 2012), p.120.

INDEX

Acamapichtli, 85, 176
Achitometl, 33
Acolhua, 27, 30, 82, 84, 108–109, 272
agriculture
  callalli, 128–129, 130
  calmilli, 128–129
  chinampas, 90, 129
  crops, 125–126, 129
  gender roles in, 126
  hydraulic architecture, 128
  metepantle, 128
  microenvironments, 126
  physical geography, 126–127
  population supported, 122, 125
  ritual, 131–132
  slash-and-burn, 127–128
  urban agriculture, 128–129
  See also land tenure.
Aguilar, Francisco, 14
Aguilar, Gerónimo de, 247, 250
ahuiani, 160, 177, 221–222
Ahuitzotl
  aqueduct construction, 145–146
  cocoltic yaoyotl (angry war), 102, 109
  sumptuary laws, 144
  Templo Mayor dedication, 72, 112–113, 116–117, 234
  tribute, 147
alahua, 5
altepetl (altepeme)
  Alvarado Tezozomoc, Hernando, 14

Amaquemecan, 221–222
Azcapotzalco, 17, 34, 85, 103, 108, 153, 155
Chalco, 96, 100–101, 153, 218, 221–222
characteristics of, 81
Cholollan (Cholula), 65, 96, 101, 241–242, 253
Coatlichan, 106, 153
Codex Borbonicus, 11
Colhuacan, 32–33, 85, 89, 106
Cuauhnahuac, 196–197
Cuauhtitlan, 17, 103, 106, 153
Cuexcomate, 182
fragmentation, 273
Huexotla, 23
Huexotzinco, 96, 101, 103, 170–171, 218
land tenure, 131
merchant barrios, 152–153
Mixcoac, 153
monumental architecture, 35
as organizational mechanism, 19–36
origins of, 83
Otompan (Otumba), 23
physical geography, 94
rulership, 13
Tepeaca, 140
Tepepolco, 17
Tetzcoco, 16, 23, 149
Tlatelolco, 17, 149
Tlaxcallan (Tlaxcala), 16, 149
Tliliuhquitepec, 101
tribute, 142

Index

Tzaqualtitlan Tenanco, 13
Xaltocan, 182–183
Xochimilco, 89, 153
See also calpolli; Tenochtitlan; tlaxilacalli.
altepetlalli, 129–130, 263
Alva Ixtlilxochitl, Fernando de
  confederation building, 106
  deity worship, 52, 62–63
  dynastic succession, 195
  female rulers, 107
  founding couples, 84
  hybrid accounts, 16
  Mexica writers, 219, 220, 243–244
  religious conversion, 266
  ritual killing, 72
  source texts, 214
  warfare, 103
Alvarado Tezozomoc, Hernando, 14, 19, 62–63, 103, 106, 110, 146
amacuahuitl, 214
Amaquemecan, 221, 222
amatl, 11
amoxtli, 214
Anales de Cuauhtitlan
  creation myths, 40
  dynastic formation, 85
  dynastic marriage, 196, 197–200
  female rulers, 106–107
  religion, 66
  ritual killing, 72
  songs, 218
  warfare, 103
Anawalt, Patricia, 137
art
  artistic traditions, 225, 227–228
  Calendar Stone (Sun Stone), 232–233
  ceramics, 242–243

Coatlicue statue, 230
Coyolxauhqui relief carving, 234
Coyolxauhqui sculpture, 233–234
emblems, 229
female figurines, 241
iconography, 229, 230, 232–233, 234
idiosyncratic expression, 224, 239
imperial art, 114, 223, 234–237
media, 228–229
Mixteca-Puebla style (Postclassic International Style), 209, 226, 228, 236
Olmec artistic tradition, 224–225
resistance, 224, 241–243
sculptors, 236
sculpture, 229–232, 237
Spanish accounts of, 238
symbolic value, 237–238
Teotihuacan style, 225–226
Tolteca style, 226–227
transformations, 238
value, 237–238
Venus of Texcoco, 239–240
Xochicalco style, 226
Atamalcualiztli, 47–48
atlatl, 99
Atlatonan, 68
Austin, Alfredo López, 192
Axayacatl, 34, 53, 197, 198, 221–222
Azcapotzalco
  confederation, 108
  merchant barrio, 153
  slaughter of population, 103
  slave markets, 155
Tepaneca, 27, 32, 34, 85, 97, 103, 183, 197, 199–200
Tepaneca capital, 34, 85

Aztecs
  archaeological study of, 6
  as an idea, 280, 281–283
  astronomy, 203
  civilization, 1
  Danza Azteca, 282
  depictions in literature, 7–9
  economy, 4–5, 36
  empire, 1
  ethnohistorical study of, 6
  hunting, 63
  hydraulic architecture, 23, 128, 203
  macehualtin (macehualli), 38, 86–87, 90, 94, 102, 117, 118–119, 122, 129–130, 142–143, 145, 146, 153, 178, 187, 262–263, 274
  material/spiritual integration, 34–35
  materiality studies, 6–7
  middle class, 143–144
  name, use of, 27
  population estimates, pre-contact, 22–23
  religion, 7–8, 58–60, 63–64
  sacredness, 58–60
  societal inequality, 141
  sumptuary laws, 144
  See also balance; cosmology; Excan tlatoloyan; imperial formation (Triple Alliance empire); Mexica; political organization; sources; transformation; value creation.
Aztecs, The (Clendinnen), 8–9
Aztlan migrations, 26–27, 29, 30, 31, 32, 114, 281

balance
  alahua, 5
  binary pairs, 35, 163, 201
  ceremony, 56–57, 60, 68–69, 74, 76, 79, 157, 209, 238–239
  complementarity, 89, 174, 271
  creation stories, 60
  female creation of, 156
  household, 36
  huetzi, 5
  kinship, 184, 191
  medicine, 203, 205
  nextlahualiztli, 5, 68, 76, 77–78
  as organizing principle, 284
  reciprocity, 36, 72–73, 82, 279, 283
  religious conversion, 266
  sculpture, 229, 230
  seeking of, 5
  songs, 222–223
  value and transformation, 4
  See also transformation; value.
Basin of Mexico
  altepetl, 81
  architectural remains, 21
  art, 241–242
  Chichimeca, 29–30
  chinampas, 129
  commerce, 151, 153
  cosmology, 57
  dispersed settlement pattern, 82, 83
  housing patterns, 182–183
  Huitzilopochtli, 62
  hydraulic architecture, 23, 128
  imperial art, 235
  land tenure, 116
  physical geography, 126–127
  political organization, 94, 95
  population estimates, pre-contact, 22, 125
  tecpan, 179
  Tepaneca, 85
  Tlaloc, 56
  Tollan, 29
  trade, 140

Index

xochiyaoyotl (flower war), 100–101
See also agriculture; Mexica; Tenochtitlan.
Bassett, Molly, 59
Bauer, Arnold, 122
Bautista, Juan, 169–170
Benavente, Toribio de (Motolinia), 14, 39–40, 133–134, 175, 215, 243–244
Berdan, Frances, 139, 145
Bierhorst, John, 14
Bonds of Blood (Pennock), 9
Boone, Elizabeth Hill, 62, 216
Breve y sumaria relación de los señores de la Nueva España (Zorita), 15
Brumfiel, Elizabeth, 241
Burkhart, Louise, 20, 51

cabeceras, 273
cabildos, 261
cacao, 150, 151
cacaxtli, 140
calendrics
  Codex Borbonicus, 10–11
  Codex Borgia, 10
  Codex Telleriano-Remensis, 11–12
  divination, 43
  Izcalli, 47, 69, 164–165, 190
  metztli, 44
  nemontemi, 44
  patron deities, 46–47
  tonalamatl, 10, 43, 59, 173, 205, 243, 278
  tonalpohualli, 10, 43, 66, 70, 205, 209, 232–233
  tonalpouhque, 43, 172–173
  trecenas, 43
  xiuhmolpilli, 48–49
  xiuhpohualli, 44–47, 66, 77

Xochicalco, 226
See also ceremony.
callalli, 128–129, 130
calmecac, 63–64, 65, 70, 134–135, 159–160, 166–170, 172
calmilli, 128–129
calpixque, 87, 146
calpoleque, 86–87
calpollalli, 129–130, 263
calpolli
  courts, 92, 267
  development of, 34, 82–83, 88
  fragmentation, 273
  and imperial formation, 117
  integration with altepetl, 81, 82–83
  land tenure, 112, 116, 129–130, 131
  marriage, 186, 196
  residential areas, 21–22, 94
  spatial variation in, 95
  tribute, 142, 144–145, 146
  warfare, 98
calpolli (Azteca sub-group), 31, 32, 84
Camaxtli, 63, 67, 170–171
campan, 34, 86–87
Cantares mexicanos, 217–218, 221
cardinal directions, 38, 49, 54, 57, 58, 233
Carrasco, Davíd, 8, 57, 282
Carrasco, Pedro, 105–106, 186
Castillo, Bernal Díaz del. *See* Díaz, Bernal
cemithualtin, 186
cencalli, 186
cenyeliztli, 187
ceremony
  agricultural ritual, 131–132
  Atamalcualiztli, 47–48
  Atl Cahualo, 67, 73
  ceremonial cycle, 47, 48, 69–70

355

ceremony (cont.)
  ceremonial landscape, 56–57, 79
  Chalchiuhtlicue ceremony, 56
  civic ritual, 71
  daily ritual, 70–71, 77
  fire, 49, 50–51
  household rituals, 51, 239–241
  Huey Tecuilhuitl ceremonies, 68
  Izcalli ceremonies, 190
  merchant ceremonies, 154–155
  Mount Tlaloc, 55–56
  movable feasts, 48
  Ochpaniztli ceremonies, 77
  Panquetzaliztli, 54
  Pillahuanaliztli, 47
  ritual objects, 69
  sacred places, 50–52, 55–57
  Tecuilhuitontli ceremonies, 54–55, 68
  Tezcatlipoca, ritual killing of, 67–68
  Tlacaxipehualiztli ceremonies, 75–76, 146
  tonalpohualli, 70
  Toxcatl, 67–68
  Toxiuhmolpilia, 48, 49–50, 226
  See also sacrifice.
Chalchiuhnenetzin (daughter/niece of Axayacatl), 198–199
Chalchiuhnenetzin (sister of Axayacatl), 197, 198
Chalchiuhtlicue, 38, 56, 60–61, 65, 67
Chalco, 96, 100–101, 153, 218, 221–222
Chantico, 50–51
Chapultepec, 32, 103
Charles V (King of Spain, 1516-1556), 250

Charlton, Cynthia Otis, 136
Chichihualcuauhco, 189
Chichimeca, 29–30, 53, 63, 106, 238
Chicomecoatl, 67
Chicomoztoc, 30–31
Chimalman, 68
Chimalpahin Quauhtlehuanitzin, Domingo de San Antón Muñón (Chimalpahin)
  biographic description, 13
  cocoltic yaoyotl (angry war), 102
  deity worship, 62–63
  dynastic marriage, 196–197, 198
  female rulers, 107
  histories, 12, 20, 84–85, 106
  origin stories, 26–27
  songs, 221, 222
  tlayacatl altepetl, 96
Chimalxoch, 196
Cholollan (Cholula), 65, 96, 101, 241–242, 253
Chololteca, 250–251, 253
cihuacalli, 179
cihuacalmecac, 64
Cihuacoatl
  cihuacoatl (political office), 89
  craft production, 136
  Huey Tecuilhuitl, 68
  midwives, 65, 90
  Teotihuacan, 225
  Toxcatl ceremonies, 67
  warfare, 104–105, 230
cihuacoatl (political office), 88, 89–91, 106
cihuacuacuiltin, 64
cihuapatli, 206, 277
cihuapipiltin (cihuateteo), 62, 189
cihuateopixque, 63–64
cihuatepixque, 171
cihuatequitque, 103

Index

cihuatlalli, 130–131, 263
cihuatlamacazque, 63, 64
cihuatlanque, 125, 173
Cipactli, 38, 55, 57
Cipactonal, 38, 122, 205
Clavijero, Francisco Javier, 27
Clendinnen, Inga, 8–9
Coatepec, 32
coatequitl, 261
Coatlichan, 106, 153
Coatlicue, 32, 114, 225, 230, 233, 241
Codex Borbonicus, 10–11, 40, 205
Codex Borgia, 10, 40, 43, 173, 209
Codex Mendoza, 11, 110, 166, 170, 191, 195, 208, 209
Codex Telleriano-Remensis, 11–12, 40, 72, 77, 85, 110, 161–162, 210–211
Codex Vaticanus 3738, 189
Codex Xolotl, 84
codices
  Codex Borbonicus, 10–11, 40, 205
  Codex Borgia, 10, 40, 43, 173, 209
  Codex Mendoza, 11, 110, 166, 170, 191, 195, 208, 209
  Codex Telleriano-Remensis, 11–12, 40, 72, 77, 85, 110, 161–162, 210–211
  Codex Vaticanus 3738, 189
  Codex Xolotl, 84 *See also* *Florentine Codex*.
cohua, 150
Colegio de Santa Cruz de Tlatelolco, 17
Colhuacan, 32–33, 85, 89, 106
color, 38, 57
commerce
  administration of, 148, 152
  cacao, 150, 151
  market transactions, 149

material value, 152
oztomeca, 151, 152, 154
pochteca, 73, 134, 144, 153–154
quachtli, 137, 145, 150, 156
trade, gender roles in, 152
traders, 151–154
Conquista de México (López de Gómara), 13
Cortés, Hernán
  alliances, 249–250, 254, 257–258
  Aztec wealth, 238
  biased account, 20
  Chololan (Cholula), 253
  dynastic successions, 256
  land appropriation, 263
  Malintzin, 250
  Mexica view of, 248
  Narváez expedition, 254–255
  puppet government, 254
  retreat from Tenochtitlan, 257
  Spanish conquest, 14
  Tlatelolco marketplace, 149
  tribute, 262
  Yucatán expedition, 247
cosmology
  archaeological evidence, 40
  cardinal directions, 38, 49, 54, 57, 58, 233
  ceremonies, 39
  cosmogonic myths, 40–41
  creation cycles, 29, 41–43, 48–49, 233
  creation myths, 38, 55, 57
  cycles of transformation, 38–39
  Fifth Sun, 29, 41–43, 48, 233
  humans, creation of, 38, 42
  Mictlan, 42, 57, 60, 188, 189
  Omeyocan, 60
  sun and moon, creation of, 41, 113–114, 276

cosmology (cont.)
  temple mountains, 51–52
  textual sources, 39–40
  Tlalocan, 55, 189
  tlalticpac, 57
  Topan, 57
  world view, 39
  See also calendrics; deities;
    sacrifice.
Coyolxauhqui, 32, 53, 90, 114,
  233–235, 241, 280–281
craft production
  amanteca, 134–135
  distribution, 139–140
  feather working, 134–135
  full-time specialists, 135
  gender specific, 124, 132, 136
  household production,
    132–133, 135–136, 139
  markets, 149
  metal working, 133–134
  obsidian, 133, 136
  pottery, 132
  regional specialization, 136
  rituals, 132
  stone implements, 133
  textiles, 132, 136–139
  totocalli, 134
Crónica mexicana (Tezozomoc),
  14
Crónica mexicayotl, 84
Crónica X, 19
cuacuauhtin, 118
cuacuiltin, 64
cuahchique, 118
Cuauhnahuac, 196–197
cuauhpipiltin, 118, 143–144
Cuauhtemoc, 247, 257, 258–259
Cuauhtitlan, 17, 103, 106, 153
cuauhtlalli, 101
cueitl, 137
Cuexcomate, 182
cuicacalli, 125, 216

cuiloni, 161
Cuitlahua, 256

Danza Azteca, 282
day count. *See* calendrics:
  tonalpohualli
death
  burials, 189
  cremation, 189
  as cyclical transformation, 188,
    191–192, 283
  deaths in childbirth, 189
  emotional pain of, 188
  funerals, 188–190
  infant deaths, 189
  Mictlan, 57, 188, 189
  remembrance ceremonies,
    190
  sacrificial death, 188
  Tlalocan, 189
  Tonatiuh Ilhuicatl, 189
  warrior deaths, 189
  watery death, 189
deities
  Atlatonan, 68
  Camaxtli, 63, 67, 170–171
  Chalchiuhtlicue, 38, 56, 60–61,
    65, 67
  Chantico, 50–51
  Chicomecoatl, 67
  Chimalman, 68
  Cihuacoatl, 65, 67, 68, 89, 90,
    104–105, 136, 225, 230
  cihuapipiltin (cihuateteo), 62,
    189
  classification, 60–62
  Coatlicue, 32, 114, 225, 230,
    233, 241
  Coyolxauhqui, 32, 53, 90, 114,
    233–235, 241, 280–281
  Ehecatl, 41
  Huehueteotl, 51, 69
  Huitzilopochtli, 26–27, 31, 33

Index

Huixtocihuatl, 54, 68, 136
Itzpapalotl, 106–107,
  162–163
ixiptla (ixiptlahuan), 59, 66–67,
  68, 73–74, 77, 78, 161, 188,
  255
Malinalxoch, 31–32, 90
Mictlancihuatl, 38
Mictlanteuctli, 38
Mixcoatl, 63, 163
Mixcoatl-
  Tlahuizcalpantecuhtli
  Complex, 63
Nanahuatzin, 41, 113, 276
Painal, 54
patron deities, 46–47
Quetzalcoatl, 38, 42, 67,
  162
Tecuciztecatl, 41, 113, 276
Tezcatlipoca, 38, 63, 66,
  67–68, 162, 255
Tlalteuctli, 155, 232
Tlazolteotl, 136, 161–162
Toci, 77
Tonacacihuatl, 38
Tonacateuctli, 38, 52, 189
Tonatiuh, 62, 232
Xilonen, 67, 68
Xipe Totec, 75–76, 119,
  204
Xiuhteuctli, 69, 155
Xochipilli, 68
Xochiquetzal, 62, 68, 136
Yacateuctli, 155
Díaz, Bernal, 14, 238, 253
Durán, Diego
  aqueduct construction,
    145–146
  biographic description, 18–19
  ceremonies, 39
  cocoltic yaoyotl (angry war),
    102
  founding couples, 85

Historia de las Indias, 18–19
housing, class distinctions,
  142
Indigenous sources, 14, 18–19
movable feasts, 48
ritual killing, 71–72, 75,
  112–113
songs, 216–217
Spanish conquest, 255
telpochcalli, 171
tribute, 147, 156
warfare, 103, 110
writing, 215, 243–244

economy
  differential access to goods,
    142
  entrepreneurship, 148
  female labor, 122, 123, 124,
    125, 138–139, 148–156
  household labor, 122, 123, 124
  labor, gender divisions,
    122–124
  male labor, 123
  service labor, 122, 147
  tequitl, 123, 279
  tribute labor, 122, 145–146
  work ethic, 124, 132
  See also agriculture; commerce;
    craft production; markets.
Ehecatl, 41
encomenderos, 262
encomienda, 261
Evans, Susan, 180
Excan tlatoloyan
  borders, 102–111, 146
  dynastic marriage, 107, 197,
    199
  expansion, 83, 105, 108
  Huitzilopochtli, 62
  imperial art, 235, 236, 237
  Mexica dominance, 109,
    117–119

359

Excan tlatoloyan (cont.)
  ritual, 52–53, 60
  ritual killing, 74, 77, 92–94,
    113, 114
  Spanish-Mexica War, 253,
    256–257, 258, 259
  Tetzcoco, 199
  timespan, 111
  tribute, 110–111, 122, 141,
    146, 209, 241
  warfare, 98, 99, 102, 110, 113,
    133

Florentine Codex
  ceremonies, 76
  Cholollan massacre, 253
  commerce, 152
  craft production, 132, 135
  description of, 17–18
  huehuetlatolli, 14
  hybrid source, 16
  interpersonal relations, 195
  marriage, 175
  Mexica vs. Nahua, 272
  midwives, 123
  movable feasts, 48
  negative day signs, 193
  punishments, 170
  religion, 66
  songs, 217, 218
  Spanish as teotl, 248
  sun and moon, creation of, 41
  Tamoanchan, 226
  Toxcatl, 255
  warfare, 91
  xacalli, 179
Fragment de'l Histoire des Anciens Mexicains, 106

gender
  complementarity, 85, 89, 104,
    120, 174, 178, 187, 201, 271
  female social mobility, 104
  gender divisions in labor,
    122–124
  parallelism, 201, 269, 271
  warfare, 103–105
Gillespie, Susan, 90
gobernadores, 261
Good Eshelman, Catharine, 279
Graham, Elizabeth, 77–78
Grijalva, Juan de, 246
Gross, Daniel, 7
Guerrero, Gonzalo, 247

Hassig, Ross, 107–108, 143
Hernández de Córdoba,
  Francisco, 246
Historia de la nación chichimeca
  (Alva Ixtlilxochitl), 72
*Historia de las Indias de Nueva
  España y islas de tierra firme*
  (Durán), 18–19
*Historia de los mexicanos por sus
  pinturas*, 40, 106, 122
*Historia general de las cosas de
  Nueva España* (Sahagún), 18
Historia Tolteca-Chichimeca, 218
*Historia universal de las cosas de la
  Nueva España* (Sahagún), 17
Histoyre du Mechique, 40
Hodge, Mary, 94
Huehueteotl, 51, 69
huehuetlalli, 130
huehuetlatolli, 14, 17, 193,
  194–195, 278
hueltiuhtli, 90
huetzi, 5
Huexotla, 23, 153
Huexotzinco, 96, 101, 103,
  170–171, 218
huey tlatoani (huey tlatoque), 88,
  92, 98, 141, 180–181
huipilli, 137
Huitzilihuitl, 196–197
Huitzilopochco, 151–152

Index

Huitzilopochtli
  ceremonies, 54
  Coatlicue, 230
  Coyolxauhqui, 233–234
  creation myth, 38
  devotional labor, 65
  dynastic marriage, 196–197
  Malinalxoch, 90
  Mexica worship of, 62–63
  origin stories, 26–27, 31, 33
  ritual killing, 55, 100, 113
  Tealtiliztli, 155
  Templo Mayor, 52, 53–54
  Tenochtitlan, origin of, 33
  Tetzcoca, 52
  Toxcatl, 67, 255
  Toxiuhmolpilia, 49
  warfare, 62, 63, 113, 114–115
Huixtocihuatl, 54, 68, 136

ichcahuipilli, 137–138
ihiyotl, 192
Ilancueitl, 85, 106, 176, 210–211
imperial formation (Triple Alliance empire)
  borders, 102–111, 146
  confederations, 108
  dynastic marriage, 105, 107, 197, 199
  economic appropriation, 116
  empire as hegemony, 107–108
  expansion, 105, 108, 110
  female political power, 105–106
  fragility, 111
  governance, 88–89, 91–92, 117–119, 121
  Huitzilopochtli, 62
  imperial architecture, 52–53, 182
  imperial art, 114, 223, 234–237
  imperial origins, 97, 109
  imperial propaganda, 25–26

  legitimization of rule, 116–117
  ritual killing, 74, 76–77
  tribute, 97, 100, 109–110, 114–116, 140–141, 144–147, 178
Indian Clothing before Cortés (Anawalt), 137
indigenismo, 280, 281–282
indio, 273–274
inmecahua, 160
Itzcoatl
  book burning, 215
  Calendar Stone (Sun Stone), 233
  imperial growth, 52, 97, 110
  Tepaneca, overthrow of, 85–86
  warfare, 91, 104–105
Itzpapalotl, 106–107, 162–163
ixiptla (ixiptlahuan)
  deity impersonators, 59, 161
  flaying, 77
  Huey Tecuihuitl, 68
  ritual killing, 66–67, 73–74, 188
  skull decoration, 78
  Tezcatlipoca, 68, 255
ixiuhtli, 191
Ixtlilxochitl (first), 199–200
Ixtlilxochitl (second), 195

Jacobita, Martín, 17
Johnson, Benjamin, 82–83
Joyce, Rosemary, 163, 164

labor
  devotional labor, 65
  female, 122, 123, 124, 125, 138–139, 148–156
  gender divisions, 122–124
  household, 122, 123, 124
  male, 123
  service labor, 122, 147
  tribute labor, 122, 145–146
Lacadena, Alfonso, 212, 215–216

Lady of Tula, 220
land tenure
  altepetlalli, 129–130, 263
  calpollalli, 129–130, 263
  cihuatlalli, 130–131, 263
  corporate administration, 129–131
  huehuetlalli, 130
  mayeque, 130, 142
  milchimalli, 130, 263
  pillalli, 130
  -tech pouhque, 142
  tecpantlalli, 130
  teotlalli, 64, 130
  teuctlalli, 130
  tlalmaitin, 142
  tlatocatlalli, 130
  tlaxilacallalli, 263
Leeming, Ben, 20
León-Portilla, Miguel, 14, 217, 222
Leyenda de los soles, 40, 122
Lockhart, James, 86, 94, 223, 271–272
López de Gómara, Francisco, 13

macehualtin (macehualli)
  Cihuacoatl, 90
  creation myth, 38, 122
  imperial formation, 118–119
  land tenure, 129–130
  marriage, 178
  merchants, 153
  socialization, 187
  state service, 145
  timacehualtin, 274
  tribute, 94, 142–143, 146
  tribute exemptions, 262–263
  warfare, 102, 117, 118
macuahuitl, 99
Macuilxochitzin, 220–221
Malinalxoch, 31–32, 90
Malintzin, 250–252, 254

Mapa Quinatzin, 84
Mapa Tlotzin, 84
markets
  administration of, 150
  craft production, 149
  development of, 147–149
  exchange, 150–151
  goods offered, 149
  market days, 149
  raw materials, 147
  specialization, 150
marriage
  adultery, 175–176
  arranged marriage, 172
  ceremony, 173–174
  class variation in, 175
  dynastic marriage, 105, 107, 197, 199, 200
  monogamy, 178
  polygamy, 176–178
  ritual selection of partner, 172–173
masehuali, 27
Matlalcihuatzin, 175
Matlatzinca, 30, 221
Matlatzincayotl Icuic (Matlatzinca Song), 221–222
Matrícula de Tributos, 11, 139, 209
maxtlatl, 137–138
Maya
  art, 227
  Classic period, 28–29
  confederations, 108
  Malintzin, 250
  pochteca, 154
  ritual killing, 77–78
  Spanish invasion, 247
  writing, 208
  Xochicalco, 226
mayeque, 130, 142
medicine
  disease, causes of, 203–204

Index

disease, treatment of, 204–205
illness and injury, 205–206
medical divination, 205
medicinal plants, 206–208
midwives, 65, 90, 123, 168, 169–170, 206
pregnancy and childbirth, 206
ticitl, 65, 204–205, 242
Mendieta, Gerónimo de, 14, 39
Mesoamerica
  Classic, 28–29, 108
  cross-cultural similarities, 28
  Epiclassic, 226–227, 228
  Olmec, 28, 29, 97, 224
  Postclassic, 29, 48, 83, 105, 108, 112, 156–157, 228, 237, 241
  Preclassic, 28, 29, 97, 224
  See also Aztecs; Maya; Tolteca.
metepantle, 128
Mexica
  artistic tradition, 11
  Axayacatl, 34, 53, 197, 198, 221–222
  Aztlan, 31
  Culhua Mexica, 33
  Fifth Sun, 29
  Huitzilihuitl, 32
  imperial power, 74, 76–77
  name, origin of, 26–27, 31
  origin story, 29–34
  political power, 52–53, 200
  political transformation, 32
  religion, 7
  rewriting of history, 27–28
  sculpture, 53
  Tepaneca, overthrow of, 85–86
  Tlacaelel, 19
  tributary to Tepaneca, 34
  See also Excan tlatoloyan; imperial formation (Triple Alliance empire); political organization; Spanish-Mexica War; Tenochtitlan.
Mictlancihuatl, 38
Mictlanteuctli, 38
midwives, 65, 90, 123, 168, 169–170, 206
milchimalli, 130, 263
mintontli, 191
Mixcoac, 153
Mixcoatl, 63, 163
Miyahuaxihuitl, 196–197
Molina, Alonso de, 4, 58, 186–187, 192
Moquihuix, 34, 53, 197–198, 234
Moteuczoma Ilhuicamina, 52, 90, 97, 109, 119, 144, 196–197, 221
Moteuczoma Xocoyotl, 109, 117, 133, 144, 146, 182, 199, 233
Motolinia. *See* Benavente, Toribio de (Motolinia)
Mount Colhuacan, 31
Muñoz Camargo, Diego, 16

Nahua tenacity
  cooking tools and terminology, 276
  cultural endurance, 279
  emotional expression, 278
  family life, 277–278
  illness and healing, 276–277
  Nahuatl speakers, 275
  ritual practices, 276
  transformation, 283–284
namaca, 150
nanahualtin, 249
Nanahuatzin, 41, 113, 276
Narváez, Pánfilo de, 254–255
nemontemi, 44
New Fire ceremony, 48, 49–50, 226
nextlahualiztli, 5, 68, 76, 77–78

Index

Nezahualcoyotl, 52, 175, 182, 195, 219–220
Nezahualpilli, 117, 194, 198–199, 220, 256–257
nican titlaca, 274
Nicholson, H. B., 40–41, 60, 63, 230
Nonoalca, 30

ocelome, 118
Oçomatzin teuctli, 196–197
Olmec, 28, 29, 97, 224
Olmeca Xicallanca, 30
ololiuhqui, 207
omicetl, 158
omitl, 158
Otomi, 30, 183, 221, 272
Otompan (Otumba), 23, 136, 153
otontin, 118
Oxomoco, 38, 122, 205
oztomeca, 151, 152, 154

Painal, 54
Pastrana, Alejandro, 136
Pasztory, Esther, 223, 229–230, 242–243
patiuhtli, 4
patla, 150
patlache, 161
Pennock, Caroline Dodds, 9
personal conflicts
  adultery, 195–196, 198–199
  divorce, 195–196
  husband-wife relations, 195, 196–197, 199–200
  parent-child relations, 194–195
  prenuptial agreements, 196
  prognostication from day signs, 193
  sibling relations, 193–194
Pillahuanaliztli, 47
pillalli, 130

pipiltin, 87, 141, 143–144
pochteca, 73, 134, 144, 153–154
pochtecatlatoque, 150
political organization
  advisory councils, 91–92
  dispersed settlement, 82–83
  dynastic rule, 85
  female political power, 84, 85
  founding couples, 84–85
  governance, 84, 85, 86, 88–89, 91, 92–94, 187
  judicial system, 92
  nobility, 87–88, 91
  pipiltin, 87, 141, 144
  teccalco, 92
  teteuctin, 87–88, 141
  tlacxitlan, 92
  variations in, 95–97
  See also altepetl; calpolli; tlaxilacalli.
Pomar, Juan Bautista, 16, 218
Prescott, William, 27
Primeros memoriales (Sahagún), 17, 48, 217

quachtli, 137, 145, 150, 156
quechquemitl, 137
Quetzalcoatl, 38, 42, 67, 162
Quinatzin, 196

Relaciones geográficas, 15
repartimiento, 261
residence patterns
  cihuacalli, 179
  class variability, 179, 181–182
  climate and geographic variability, 182–183, 185
  family structure, 183–184
  house compounds, 178–179
  house society, 186–187
  kinship, 184–185
  marriage, 185–186
  pleasure palaces, 180–181

Index

tecpan, 95, 176, 179, 181–182
xacalli, 179
Romances de los señores de Nueva España (Pomar), 218
Ruiz de Alarcón, Hernando, 207

sacred guardians
  calmecac, 63–64, 65, 70, 134–135, 159–160, 166–170
  cihuacalmecac, 64
  cihuacuacuiltin, 64
  cihuateopixque, 63–64
  cihuatlamacazque, 63, 64
  cuacuiltin, 64
  lay devotional labor, 65
  lay practitioners, 65–66
  resource allocation, 64–65
  teocalli, 63
  teopixque, 63–64
  ticitl, 65, 204–205, 242
  tlamacazque, 63
sacred places, 50–52
sacrifice
  animal sacrifice, 55, 71
  blood sacrifice, 49, 63, 65, 67, 70, 73–74
  flaying, 33, 75–76, 77
  human obligation for, 41, 72, 74, 77, 113–114, 155, 188
  nextlahualiztli, 5, 68, 76, 77–78
  ritual cannibalism, 100
  ritual killing, 8, 49, 53–54, 55, 66, 67–68, 71, 73–76, 77, 78–79, 90, 92–94, 100, 101, 112–113, 117, 155, 162, 188
  ritual objects, 55, 67
Sahagún, Bernardino de, 17–18, 39, 215, 217, 248
San Buenaventura, Pedro de, 17
Secret History of Emotion, The (Gross), 7
Seventh Relation (Chimalpahin), 221

sexuality
  ahuiani, 160, 177, 221–222
  conception, 158–159
  creation mythology, 158
  female chastity, 160
  gender identity, 163–164
  gender instability, 161–163
  inmecahua, 160
  same-sex relations, 160–161
  sexual relations, 159–160, 176
Sigal, Pete, 163
slaves. *See* tlacotin
Smith, Michael E., 94, 182
socialization
  calmecac, 63–64, 65, 70, 134–135, 159–160, 166–170, 172
  corporal punishment, 166
  education, 166–171, 187
  elders, 191
  gender differentiated names, 164
  gender differentiated work, 132, 136, 165–166
  huehuetlatolli, 14, 17, 193, 194–195, 278
  infants as raw material, 164, 191
  kinship terms, 191
  life cycle ceremonies, 164, 187
  See also telpochcalli.
sources
  archaeological, 10
  biases, 20
  Breve y sumaria relación de los señores de la Nueva España (Zorita), 15
  civil accounts, 15
  Codex Borbonicus, 10–11, 205
  Codex Borgia, 10, 43, 173, 209
  Codex Telleriano-Remensis, 11–12, 72, 77, 85, 110, 161–162, 210–211

Index

sources (cont.)
  codices, 10–12
  Crónica mexicana (Alvarado Tezozomoc), 14
  ethnography, 26
  eyewitness accounts, 14–15
  Historia de las Indias de Nueva España y islas de tierra firme (Durán), 18–19
  huehuetlatolli, 14
  hybrid accounts, 16–20, 106
  interpretation of, 20–21
  judicial records, 14, 15
  material remains, 21–26
  Nahuatl, 10–16
  Relaciones geográficas, 15
  songs, 14, 216–223
  Spanish, 14–15
  tlacuiloque, 12
  written, 9–10
  See also Codex Mendoza; Florentine Codex.
Sousa, Lisa, 65
Spanish imperial rule
  congregación, 263–264
  disease, 260–261
  female authority, 269–271
  forced religious conversion, 264–265
  gender based violence, 269
  Indigenous governance, 261–262
  Indigenous identity, 271–275
  judicial system, 267–268
  labor organization, 261–262
  land ownership, 263–264
  Nahua influence on Christianity, 266–267
  private apostasy, 264–265, 266
  public conversion, 265–266
  tribute, 262–263
Spanish-Mexica War
  causes of defeat, 259–260

Cholollan massacre, 253
Cortés, Yucatán expedition, 247
disease, 256, 258
Excan tlatoloyan political chaos, 256–257
gifts as Mexica imperial diplomacy, 249
initial explorations, 246–247
Malintzin, 250–252, 254
Mexica intelligence gathering, 247–248
Mexica wealth, 247, 249
Moteuczoma Xocoyotl, compromised rule, 254
Moteuczoma Xocoyotl, death of, 256
Moteuczoma Xocoyotl, imprisonment of, 254
ships, 257–258
Spanish alliances, 249–250, 252–253, 254, 258
Spanish as teotl, 248–249
Spanish entry into Tenochtitlan (first), 253–254
Spanish entry into Tenochtitlan (second), 258
Spanish retreat from Tenochtitlan, 256, 257
Spanish tactical disadvantages, 257
Templo Mayor massacre and uprising, 255–256
Tenochtitlan, fall of, 258–259
Tetzcoca, 258
Tlatelolco, 34
Tlaxcalteca, 63, 228, 250, 252–253, 254, 255–256, 257, 259
Stoler, Ann Laura, 111–112

Taggart, James, 278
Tamoanchan, 226

Tapia, Andres de, 14
Taube, Karl, 208
teaanque, 171
teahui, 69
tealtianime, 155
teccalco, 92
teccalli, 95, 96, 142, 144–145, 157, 267
-tech pouhque, 142
techan tlaca, 186
tecpan
  art, 238
  cuicacalli, 171
  personnel, 176, 179–181
  political integration, 95, 117–118, 142, 179, 187
  singers, 219–220
  size of, 181–182
  slaves, 143
  totocalli, 134
tecpantlalli, 130
Tecuciztecatl, 41, 113, 276
telpochcalli
  fictive kinship, 193
  marriage, 172
  schooling, 70, 166
  sexual companions, 160
  sexual relations, 159–160, 176
  telpochtlato, 92
  warfare, 91, 98, 160, 170
telpochtlato, 92
temalacatl, 146
temazcalli, 206
Tenoch, 88
Tenochca, 34, 85, 104, 197–198, 216
Tenochtitlan
  architectural remains, 21
  calpoleque, 86–87
  cihuacoatl (title), 88, 89–91, 106
  governance, 87, 88–89
  house compounds, 178–179
  hydraulic architecture, 23

imperial art, 223
literature, 7
markets, 148–149
material remains, 25–26
origins of, 33–34
population estimates, pre-contact, 1, 22–23
Sahagún, Bernardino de, 17
songs, 218
subdivisions, 34
Templo Mayor, 23–25, 49, 52, 53–55, 72, 78, 114, 280–281
Tenochca, 34, 85, 104, 197–198, 216
tlatoani, 68–69
tribute, 146
urban layout, 21
tensions. See personal conflicts
teocalli, 63
teopixque, 63–64
Teotihuacan
  artistic tradition, 225–226
  confederations, 108
  deities, 60
  Late Formative period, 28–29
  Mexica creation stories, 113–114
  settlement structure, 82
  sociopolitical units, 83
  songs, 218–219
  Templo Mayor, 227
  warfare, 97–98
  writing, 208
teotlalli, 64, 130
teoxihuitl, 59
Tepaneca
  Azcapotzalco, 34
  confederation, 32
  dynastic marriage, 197, 199–200
  Excan tlatoloyan, 27, 183
  Mexica tributary status, 34
  Tepaneca War, 85, 97, 103
  warfare, 103

Tepeaca, 140
Tepepolco, 17, 217
tepezcohuite, 277
tequitl, 123, 279
tequitlato, 87, 146
Terraciano, Kevin, 248
teteuctin, 87–88, 141
tetla, 69
Tetzcoca
  architecture, 228
  art, 239
  dynastic marriage, 196, 197–200
  female rulers, 107
  political alignment, 52
  religious conversion, 266
  songs, 218
  Spanish invasion, 258, 259
  writing, 213, 216
Tetzcoco
  dispersed settlement, 82
  dynastic marriage, 198–200
  dynastic succession, 195, 256–257
  histories, 16, 84
  imperial expansion, 108–109
  markets, 149
  merchant barrio, 153
  Nezahualpilli, 117, 194, 198–199, 220, 256–257
  political organization, 92
  political power, 117
  population estimates, pre-contact, 23
  songs, 218
  Spanish invasion, 258
  tecpan, 181–182
  tribute, 110
  writing, 212
teuctlalli, 130
teuctli, 96
teyolloquani, 203
Tezcatlipoca, 38, 63, 66, 67–68, 162, 255

Tezozomoc, 199–200
tiachcahuan, 171
tianquizpan tlayacanque, 150
ticitl, 65, 204–205, 242
tierra caliente, 126
tierra fría, 126
tierra templada, 126
timacehualtin, 274
Tizaapan, 32
Tlacaelel, 19, 86, 90–94, 97, 101, 103, 220–221
tlacamecayotl, 184
tlacateccatl, 91
tlachiuhqui, 151
tlacochcalcatl, 91
tlacochtli, 99
tlacotin, 54, 74, 75, 142–143, 150, 153, 155
tlacuiloque, 12, 168, 210, 212, 217, 244, 248
tlacxitlan, 92
tlahuitolli, 99
tlalcohualli, 263
tlalmaitin, 142
Tlaloc, 38, 52, 54, 59–66, 67, 204, 207, 230
Tlalocan, 55, 189
Tlalteuctli, 155, 232
tlalticpacayotl, 159
tlamacazque, 63
tlamanacac, 151–152
tlamemeque, 140, 149
tlanecuilo, 152, 153
tlaquimilolli, 138, 156
Tlatelolco
  amanteca, 134–135
  dynastic marriage, 197–198
  hybrid sources, 17
  market, 148, 149–150
  merchant barrio, 153
  merchant deities, 155
  pochteca, 153–154
  political organization, 84, 85

Index

residence patterns, 179
settlement of, 34
Spanish invasion, 258–259
warfare, 53, 103–104, 234
tlatoani (tlatoque), 13, 19
  Acamapichtli, 85, 87, 176
  Ahuitzotl, 72, 87, 102, 109,
    112–113, 116–117, 144,
    145–146, 147, 234
  authority, 119–120
  Axayacatl, 87
  Chimalpopoca, 87
  cosmic order, preservation of,
    68–69
  Cuauhtemoc, 247, 257,
    258–259
  Cuitlahua, 87, 256
  deity propitiation, 119
  Huitzilihuitl, 87, 196–197
  Itzcoatl, 52, 85–86, 87, 91, 97,
    104–105, 110, 215, 233
  Ixtlilxochitl (first), 199–200
  Ixtlilxochitl (second), 195
  Moteuczoma Ilhuicamina, 52,
    87, 90, 97, 109, 119, 144,
    196–197, 221
  Moteuczoma Xocoyotl, 87, 109,
    117, 133, 144, 146, 199, 233
  Oçomatzin teuctli, 196–197
  political order, 74
  symbolic value, 119
  Tezozomoc, 199–200
  Tizoc, 87
  warfare, 98
tlatocacihuatl, 125
tlatocan, 92
tlatocatlalli, 130
tlatocayotl, 96
Tlaxcallan (Tlaxcala)
  artistic style, 216
  Camaxtli, 67
  commerce, 150
  governance structure, 96–97

markets, 149
sexual relations, 171
Spanish invasion, 252–253,
  256, 257
tutelary deity, 63
warfare, 114
Tlaxcalteca, 63, 228, 250, 254,
  256, 257, 259
tlaxilacallalli, 263
tlaxilacalli
  administration of, 87
  courts, 267
  development of, 82–83
  fragmentation, 273
  and imperial formation, 117
  integration with altepetl, 81
  judicial system, 92
  land tenure, 112, 116,
    129–130, 131
  marriage, 186, 196
  political organization, 86–87,
    95
  political power, 91, 119
  residential areas, 21–22, 32, 94
  spatial variation in, 95
  tribute, 142, 144–145, 146
  warfare, 98
tlayacatl, 34, 86, 96, 98, 273
tlayacatl altepetl, 96
Tlazolteotl, 136, 161–162
Tliliuhquitepec, 101
Toci, 77
Tollan
  artistic tradition, 225
  Mexica dynastic descent from,
    85
  rise of, 29
  ritual killing, 66
  sculpture, 226–227
  Templo Mayor, 227
  warfare, 97–98
Tolteca
  artistic style, 226–227, 228

Tolteca (cont.)
  Chapultepec, 32
  feathered garments, 238
  Mexica dynastic descent from, 85, 176
  Nahuas, 272
  nucleated settlement pattern, 82
  as stereotype, 29–30
  Templo Mayor, 53
  warfare, 103
  See also Tollan.
tolteca (luxury goods workers), 134
Tomiyauh, 107
Tonacacihuatl, 38
Tonacateuctli, 38, 52, 189
tonalamatl, 10, 43, 59, 173, 205, 243, 278
tonalli, 158–159, 192
tonalpohualli, 10, 43, 66, 70, 205, 209, 232–233
tonalpouhque, 43, 172–173
Tonatiuh, 62, 232
Torquemada, Juan de, 14
totocalli, 134
Totonaca, 247, 249–250, 252–253
Townsend, Camilla, 107
Toxiuhmolpilia, 48, 49–50, 226
Transcending Conquest (Wood), 274
transformation
  art, 229, 235, 238, 242–243
  bodily instability, 161, 163
  celestial monsters, 62
  ceremony, 51, 56–57, 79–80, 209
  childbirth, 159
  complementarity, 271
  creation stories, 38–39, 225
  of female power, 268–270
  goal of, 4
  medicine, 283–284
  natural cycles of, 42–43, 188, 191–192, 283
  patterns of, 5
  political, 81–82, 119
  religious conversion, 265–267
  ritual deification, 67–68, 76, 82
  shape-shifting, 65–66, 161
  songs, 222–223
  value creation, 4, 35, 121, 157, 283
tribute
  Ahuitzotl, 147
  altepetl (altepeme), 142
  calpolli, 142, 144–145, 146
  Cortés, Hernán, 262
  Excan tlatoloyan, 110–111, 122, 141, 146, 209, 241
  imperial formation, 97, 100, 109–110, 114–116, 140–141, 144–147, 178
  macehualtin (macehualli), 94, 142–143, 146
  Spanish imperial rule, 262–263
  Tenochtitlan, 146
  Tetzcoco, 110
  tlaxilacalli, 142, 146
Tzaqualtitlan Tenanco, 13
tzompantli, 23, 78, 100

Valeriano, Antonio, 17
value
  art, 223–224, 238
  by transformation, 4, 283
  commerce, 148, 157
  craft production, 134, 139, 215
  female creation of, 82, 122, 139, 156
  female identity, 104
  goal of, 4
  household creation of, 174–175
  material value, 4–5
  patiuhtli, 4
  political relationships, 82

Index

ritual offerings, 72–73, 155
songs, 222–223
symbolic value, 5, 42
tlatoani, 119
tribute, 146
Vegerano, Alonso, 17
Velásquez, Diego (governor, Cuba), 250, 254–255
Vocabulario en lengua castellana y mexicana y mexicana y castellana (Molina), 4

warfare
  armor, 99, 110
  army organization, 98–99
  atlatl, 99
  Aztec development of, 97–98
  captives, 100, 112–113
  cocoltic yaoyotl (angry war), 98, 99–100, 102–103
  cuauhpipiltin, 118, 143–144
  cuauhtlalli, 101
  female participation in, 103–104
  goals of, 101–102, 114–116
  ideology of, 113, 114
  leadership, 91
  macuahuitl, 99
  military orders, 118
  motivations for, 112
  social benefits of, 116–117, 118
  telpochcalli, 70, 91, 92, 98, 159–160, 166, 170, 172, 176, 193
  tlacateccatl, 91
  tlacochcalcatl, 91
  tlacochtli, 99
  tlahuitolli, 99
  violence against women, 103
  weaponry, 99
  xochiyaoyotl (flower war), 100–101
  yaomitl, 99

yaotlalli, 101
Wood, Stephanie, 274
writing and literature
  Aztec writing system, 208
  books, forms of, 214
  books, types of, 215
  female writers, 220–221
  Nahuatl syntax, 210–211
  paper, 214–215
  post-conquest traditional writings, 212–214
  songs, 216–223
  Spanish influence on writing, 212, 244
  spoken literature, 216
  uses of writing, 208–210
  writing, regional variation in, 211–212, 213, 215–216
  See also codices.

xacalli, 179
Xaltocan, 182–183
Xicalanco, 154
xicolli, 137–138
Xilonen, 67, 68
Xipe Totec, 75–76, 119, 204
xiuhpohualli, 44–47, 66, 77
Xiuhteuctli, 69, 155
Xochicalco, 226, 236
Xochimilco, 89, 153
Xochipilli, 68
Xochiquetzal, 62, 68, 136
Xoconochco, 154
Xolotl, 107

Yacateuctli, 154, 155
yaomitl, 99
yaotlalli, 101
yoli, 192
yolia, 192
yolloxochitl, 207

Zorita, Alonso de, 15

371